The Economist as Public Intellectual

The Economist as Public Intellectual

Annual Supplement to Volume 45
History of Political Economy

Edited by Tiago Mata
and Steven G. Medema

Duke University Press
Durham and London 2013

Copyright 2013 by Duke University Press.
Printed in the United States of America
on acid-free paper. ISBN 978-0-8223-6795-6.
This is the 2013 supplement to
History of Political Economy, ISSN 0018-2702.

Contents

Cultures of Expertise and the Public Interventions of Economists   1
TIAGO MATA AND STEVEN G. MEDEMA

"Perhaps I'm a Don Quixote but I'm Trying to Be a Paul Revere":
Irving Fisher as a Public Intellectual   20
ROBERT W. DIMAND

Observers, Commentators, and Persuaders:
British Interwar Economists as Public Intellectuals   38
CHRIS GODDEN

Inside Out: Keynes's Use of the Public Sphere   68
ROGER E. BACKHOUSE AND BRADLEY W. BATEMAN

Walter Lippmann: The Making of a Public Economist   92
CRAUFURD GOODWIN

Lionel Robbins: Political Economist   114
SUSAN HOWSON

Henry Hazlitt as an Intellectual Middleman
of "Orthodox Economics"   137
PETER BOETTKE AND LIYA PALAGASHVILI

Federal Reserve Bank Presidents as Public Intellectuals   166
ROB ROY MCGREGOR AND WARREN YOUNG

Age of Certainty: Galbraith, Friedman,
and the Public Life of Economic Ideas 191
ANGUS BURGIN

Economic Indicators as Public Interventions 220
GIL EYAL AND MORAN LEVY

Becker and Posner: Freedom of Speech
and Public Intellectualship 254
JEAN-BAPTISTE FLEURY AND ALAIN MARCIANO

Private Intellectuals and Public Perplexity:
The Economics Profession and the Economic Crisis 279
PHILIP MIROWSKI AND EDWARD NIK-KHAH

Contributors 312

Index 317

Cultures of Expertise and the Public Interventions of Economists

Tiago Mata and Steven G. Medema

The inaugural winner of the Pulitzer Prize for nonfiction in 1964 was Richard Hofstadter's *Anti-intellectualism in American Life*. In a year mourning the assassination of a vibrant and eloquent president, the book spoke to a shared sense of loss and revolt. However, the popular acclaim it received was not matched by academic applause. The DeWitt Clinton Professor of American History at Columbia University collected only timid approval from his peers, who discounted the work as personal and polemic (Brown 2006, 139–40). Hofstadter would not have been surprised by this judgment, since he understood the difficulty of his task. Anti-intellectualism was a troublesome subject to historicize, brought into view by assembling disjoint bodies: the evangelical priesthood rejecting contemporary culture, democratic politics celebrating innate popular wisdom, a business interest applying a narrow pecuniary metric to value social worth, and the theorists of mass education favoring vocation and pragmatism over the

---

Correspondence may be addressed to Tiago Mata, Department of History and Philosophy of Science, University of Cambridge, Free School Lane, Cambridge CB2 3RH, UK (e-mail: tiago.mata@gmail.com); and to Steven G. Medema, Department of Economics, University of Colorado Denver, Campus Box 181, Denver, CO 80217-3364 (e-mail: steven.medema@ucdenver.edu). The present volume collects essays prepared for a conference held at Duke University on April 13 and 14, 2012. The meeting was made possible by support from Duke University Press and the European Research Council grant "Economics in the Public Sphere" awarded to Tiago Mata. We thank Scott Anthony, Roger E. Backhouse, Angus Burgin, Harro Maas, Edward Nik-Khah, Malcolm Rutherford, Thomas Stapleford, Tomas Undurraga, and E. Roy Weintraub for comments and suggestions.

life of the mind. Anti-intellectualism had not only corrupted the religion, politics, economy, and education of the 1950s but was also for Hofstadter (1963, 19) a chronic ailment of American culture, with recurring bouts of bashing intellectuals as "pretentious, conceited, effeminate, and snobbish; and very likely immoral, dangerous and subversive." The book has remained in print for half a century, a longevity that testifies to the force of its message succinctly carried by the title.

Through the pens of a multitude of writers, the examination of the status of the intellectual in culture has gained the uses of a trope (Townsley 2006) where alarm is sounded even if there is no agreement on the threat. One can read that "real intellectuals are only found elsewhere, in other countries, in the past, or in the mind; intellectuals aren't speaking out when they should be; once upon a time intellectuals were important; only intellectuals have ever thought intellectuals were important; happy is the land which has no intellectuals; . . . some variant on what one may call 'the 3-D version'—the decline, disappearance or death of the intellectual" (Collini 2002, 207). In this tangle of writings, intellectuals are either too many, too few, or too bad, and they have died many deaths, although remaining vital enough to die again.

The noun *intellectual* is a capacious term.[1] In its vast semantic field one finds definitions that may or may not include the professoriat, writers, artists, bohemians, the avant-garde, and the professional classes. Commentators and analysts typically work around some combative duality, such as clerks against laymen (Julien Benda), traditional against organic intellectuals (Antonio Gramsci), universal against specific intellectuals (Michel Foucault), legislators against interpreters (Zygmunt Bauman), or public intellectuals against academics (Russell Jacoby), to name the most prominent formulas.[2] The distinctions are not merely markers of some historical development; they are charged with moral purpose. They intend to describe the natural kinds of the life of the mind but also to adjudicate on the proper conduct for intellectuals: a commitment to the universal values

---

1. For a genealogy of the term and its traffic, notably in Britain, see Collini 2006, 45–65. Collini argues that the term is not as foreign to the English language as generally assumed. Most other writers suggest the term originates either as the label for nineteenth-century Russian men of letters (*intelligentsia*) who challenged the autocracy of the czar (Seton-Watson 1960) or as a label for both individual and class that owes its significance to the Dreyfus affair at the turn of the century, when a group of writers campaigned for the exoneration of a French Jewish army officer from fabricated charges of treason (Charle 1990).

2. Some recent binaries seek to describe changes to the identity of intellectuals and their media of communication, such as print-versus-screen intellectuals (Frank 2005) or curtly old-versus-new intellectuals (Davis 2009).

of justice and peace (Benda), to social change (Gramsci), to community (Foucault), to communicating across communities (Bauman), to universality and discourse to the public (Jacoby). To write about intellectuals is in the above sense to elaborate identities and to cast intellectuals as either champions or usurpers of civic life.

Anti-intellectualism was infused with the moralizing vigor so characteristic of its subject. But its sights were trained less on the standing of knowledge in the polity than on the exceptional character of the American polity. At the book's conception lay Hofstadter's disappointment and puzzlement at Adlai Stevenson's failed bid for the presidency and the rise of Joseph McCarthy. Hofstadter could not agree with his friends at the *Partisan Review* who in a 1952 symposium—"Our Country, Our Culture"— proclaimed the end of a struggle between America and its men of letters and the arts. Beyond the West Village, America did not value ideas. To interrogate the place of intellectuals in culture has been to examine national character, inviting (un)complimentary glances across borders. France gets the most admiring attention. The iconic Jean-Paul Sartre competes with the Dreyfusards as exemplars for intellectual engagement for both American and British commentators, and American authors have directed similar admiration for the British gentility of the interwar period (Collini 2006, 221–44).

The essays contained in this volume stay at a safe distance from Manichaean narratives of progress or regress and their national scorekeeping. We do not set out to resolve the conflicting definitions of the public intellectual or to assess the volume and quality of literate culture across borders. Instead we approach the "intellectual" less as a "social type [than as] the capacity to make a public intervention" (Eyal and Buchholz 2010), a capacity many actors may claim and that is constructed in time and place.[3] Our strategy is to privilege action over actor and to contextualize interventions and their range of diversity.

The title of our volume—*The Economist as Public Intellectual*— signifies our desire to study the encounters between economists and their publics. From the vantage point of the history of twentieth-century economics, our selection of cases will appear peculiar for its inclusion of journalists and other nonacademics. As we shall see, many of the participants in popular discourse have lacked doctoral credentials and university offices. The identity of the economist is, not unlike that of the intellectual, also subject to contestation and conflicting definitions across our period of

---

3. For a review of the sociological canon on intellectuals, see Kurzman and Owens 2002.

study. The full reach of economics is realized by the circulation of its discourse and practices and by their influence on an expanded set of actors that include media and knowledge brokers. From the vantage point of intellectual history, our focus on the economist may appear quaint. The twentieth-century economist has been the epitome of the expert, with access to the corridors of power and relying on a discourse that is inscrutable to the wider public.[4] The economist appears as the negation of the humanist, who is the preferred stand-in for the men and women of ideas. Not all economists fit this representation of gray insider, and some of the exceptions, Irving Fisher, John Maynard Keynes, John Kenneth Galbraith, and Milton Friedman, are subjects of essays in the volume. More importantly, our studies of the public interventions of economists offer an expanded, and we hope provocative, view of intellectual life. Our vantage point enables us to observe how publicity has served different purposes in evolving configurations of academe, business, government, and media in the course of the twentieth century, at times meeting democratic ends, at others epistemic, on occasion ludic.

The unifying claim of our collection is that economists' public interventions have been of profound consequence for both the structure and the content of the public sphere. In the volume we constrain ourselves to a long twentieth century in the United States and the United Kingdom, fenced at one end by the Progressive Era and Fabianism and the ongoing economic crisis at the other.[5] In this introductory essay we rehearse a tentative chronology that connects the volume's essays with the outlying literatures of intellectual history and the sociology of knowledge, while exploring the evolving relationships between economists and their publics.

Social Intelligence

At the turn of the century, the site for the meeting of knowledge and civic action was the city. In the 1880s one looked to Paris, London, Frankfurt,

---

4. The twentieth-century economist stands in stark contrast with the political economist of the eighteenth and nineteenth centuries inhabiting coffeehouses and filling pages of magazines. To examine that difference would add fascinating layers to the story we sketch here, but we could not do justice to it in this volume (see, e.g., Collini 1993).

5. A criticism that can be laid upon our conference and this volume is that they reflect a narrow geographic focus. The narrative(s) one can devise looking at public life in the United States and in Great Britain would surely be enriched by considering developments in other nations. The sociology of economics offers us a glimpse of what there is to gain (Fourcade 2009). We consider the present volume as a starting point, and it is our hope that this effort will stimulate scholarship on this vast topic.

Berlin, New York, Chicago, and Cleveland to find experimentation in social policy and its principal actors: the Fabians, left liberals, and progressives. The best illustration of the period's combination of knowledge, action, and place is the social survey movement in the work of Charles Booth's *The Life and Labour of the People of London* (1889–1903) and in Jane Addams's and Florence Kelley's remarkable careers, as both social workers and social thinkers, that culminated with their *Hull House Maps and Papers* of 1896. While modernity crossed oceans, politics, philanthropy, and publishing shared tight quarters in the urban setting (Rodgers 1998).

London had perhaps the longest exposure to the emerging force of the partnership between social science, reform, and social policy. London had given refuge to the revolutionary thinkers of the 1840s and volunteered printers and pulpits for their ideas. Yet the British were the least likely to recognize transnational debts. American social scientists returning from study in Continental Europe were the most vocal about novel visions for science and society that they freighted with their doctoral degrees. Upon their return, the urban-based world of learning was being dismantled and reconfigured around the college campus. They participated in affirming the secular university as a privileged site for knowledge.

The story of the emergence of American social science has been well researched and told. A. W. Coats, Mary Furner, Thomas Haskell, and Dorothy Ross have collectively shown how in the early decades of social science, controversy ensued when the radical energy of the professors met the conservative priors of legislators, trustees, and university presidents. One available response was to draw on the city to counter academicization. Hence, when protesting social scientists left Columbia University to found the New School for Social Research, they relied on the staff and offices of the magazine the *New Republic* and on New Yorkers as mature students who cared not for a degree but valued intellectual engagement (Bender 1993). In Britain, the Fabians' London School of Economics and Political Science (LSE) was conceived in 1895 at a time when Sidney Webb's attention was focused on the reform of public education in London. The school began with virtually no dedicated staff. Classes were in the evenings and conferred no degrees. Like the New School decades later, the LSE drew on city resources, even the "enemy," with funding from the London Chamber of Commerce. Integration into the University of London in 1900 aligned the LSE with emerging academic standards (Dahrendorf 1995).

A different response to the threat of patrons was the creation of professional institutions. The examples most significant for the story of economics are, in the first generation, the various learned societies, and later the American Association of University Professors, the Brookings Institution, the National Bureau of Economic Research, and the Social Science Research Council. These organizations both competed and collaborated with universities to establish the social science professions as the primary constituencies to deliberate on knowledge disputes. Economists seem to have held a preference for this professional response. Wesley Mitchell, who famously founded the National Bureau of Economic Research (in 1920), was also among the dissidents converging on the New School (in 1919), but he soon abandoned that venture. With the judgment that upon a more conventional platform he could effect change in economics, he returned to Columbia (Bender 1987).

The pre-twentieth-century generation of American social scientists saw themselves providing leadership to the mass citizenry, be it through the Knights of Labor and the People's Party in the United States or the Labour Party in Britain. At Wisconsin, Richard T. Ely, John R. Commons, and Selig Perlman lectured to the labor movement as an integral part of the act of knowledge production and of the necessary development of that movement (Fink 1997). Social science prided itself on providing understanding and blueprints for "social control" that would fortify the polity against the disruptive forces of private interest (Rutherford 2011). Irving Fisher's biography is animated by the moral and civic zeal that moved this generation of scholars. Facing the prospect of his mortality, this inventive academic, with unfailing confidence in his intelligence and intelligibility, launched himself into educating the public and reforming society. Robert W. Dimand (this volume) reviews Fisher's efforts to guide public opinion on subjects, notably public health and international relations, that lay beyond his academic expertise. Neither politics nor economics brings Fisher and the Wisconsin trio together, but their enthusiasm for public education and engagement are strikingly similar.

In the United States, World War I and labor unrest in the 1910s shattered social scientists' and political philosophers' confidence in the efficacy of mass politics. Walter Lippmann was both witness to and theorist of the nascent disappointment with popular deliberation. The youthful Lippmann, true to his teachers William James, George Santayana, and Graham Wallas, held high hopes for democratic engagement in *A Preface to Politics* (1913) and *Drift and Mastery* (1914). As Craufurd Goodwin (this volume) shows, Lippmann's war experience with propaganda and as handler of government advisers led him to favor increasing discretion for experts in such later writings as *Liberty and the News* (1920), *Public*

Opinion (1922), and *The Phantom Public* (1925). John Dewey's response to Lippmann occasioned one of the most important set pieces of political philosophy of the 1920s and the interwar period (Fink 1997). Goodwin shows that Lippmann's stance as commentator on the economy, and as proto-Keynesian, stood between his pre- and postwar proclamations. Lippmann never tired of educating his readers, carrying them to the cloistered conversations of experts and political decision makers, but he also never invited his public to arbitrate in the crucial deliberations. He would take them to the threshold but no farther.

In Britain, the contrast between economists' pre- and postwar expectations of the public was less stark. The professionalization of economics was imbued with the elitism of Oxbridge and the imperial civil service, leaving little room for a populist imagination (Maloney 1985). Chris Godden (this volume) examines how economic writers in the interwar period worried that the public might not comprehend the challenges facing the British economy and would be likely to resist and delay a necessary transition. While part of their campaigning was the defense of free trade, which had the longest and most distinguished of pedigrees, these economists also addressed the managerial class to persuade it to embark on new investments and the necessary adjustment to a new world economy. The most compelling voices of the letters and of broadcasting, and certainly the most remembered, were from those with apartments at Bloomsbury, and prominent among them was the economist John Maynard Keynes.[6] Roger E. Backhouse and Bradley W. Bateman (this volume) reveal an unfamiliar Keynes, more journalist than academic, mindful of the copyright and syndication of his words and attentive to all aspects of the printed medium. Using the *Manchester Guardian* and the *Nation and Athenaeum* to carry his policy prescriptions to a liberal and sympathetic elite, Keynes's goal was not to educate the public. He sought to create, for the benefit of the policy maker and the educated readers, venues beyond the Houses of Parliament and the international summits for reflection and consensus deliberation. Publicity served as a trial of ideas, with urgency and the strain of persuasion clarifying the issues and parsing right from wrong. To

---

6. Although the answer falls beyond the remit of our studies, it would be interesting to know whether and how the roles played by different media (electronic, both radio and television; print, both newspapers and magazines) may have varied between the UK and the United States and how the roles and influence of different media within each country evolved over the century. One hypothesis worth exploring is whether through the influence of the BBC, radio and television were privileged media for public intellectual expression in the UK.

move public sentiment was thus not the only, nor was it the dominant, purpose achieved by activating public controversy in interwar Britain.

The unraveling of the Progressive Era and social scientists' depressed expectations about public education and engagement were shadowed by the development of social science metrics. Changes to epistemic standards and enthusiasm for mathematics and statistics aligned with new uses for social science in the public sphere. If the mass public could be manipulated and was unlikely to show the capacity for reason and judgment, as wartime propaganda had so clearly demonstrated, perhaps social scientists could mediate the communication between state and citizenry. Sarah Igo (2007) has traced the career of several projects describing the United States, its "Middletown" (Muncie, Indiana), its sexuality, its political opinion, and has shown what filters and slants obtained from applying the social science lenses. It is in this period that polling takes hold of the political imagination and of mass campaigning and marketing (Herbst 2003). Thomas Stapleford's (2009) history of price indexes reveals how economics stood in for the voice of the consumer public and the substance of their grievances. Irving Fisher ran an Index Number Institute from his home with numbers as the necessary complement to his weekly syndicated newspaper column (Dimand, this volume). To the above, one should add the multiple business barometers that spawned from economics faculties and were soon taking over the covers of magazines such as *Business Week* or Keynes's *Manchester Guardian* supplements. As Gil Eyal and Moran Levy (this volume) argue, these attempts at measurement are interventions in the public sphere, with the capacity to frame discourse, agendas, and the cast of authoritative actors. Tools for social and economic observation construct images of the public, their lives, feelings, opinions, and finances, and feed these images into the media space and the deliberations of the state. With greater prominence in the United States and in international organizations, indicators of various kinds have gained in prominence, reinforcing a culture of trust in numbers (Porter 1996).

Popularization

Economists' access to policy making in Britain deepened in the interwar period with a series of institutional innovations. The Economic Advisory Council was created in 1930 with the purpose of installing economists as the prime minister's "eyes and ears on economic questions." Initially economists were asked to compete for the PM's attention alongside businessmen and trade unionists, but soon the chambers of economic advice were cleared of any "representative" undertones to rely solely on the technocratic ideal and on economists' deliberations (Howson and Winch 1977).[7] Unlike the model of expert consultation then being adopted in the United States, the brief of British advisers included secrecy and exclusivity, and the record of their role is notoriously hard to evaluate. The war did not enhance the influence or public prominence of economists in Britain. Their service was focused on financing and on controlling inflation, and the Treasury itself was diminished by the creation of new ministries and a novel impetus in developing science and technology. War and militarization at midcentury were of profound consequence for the governance of British science and technology (Edgerton 2005), but, unlike the United States, celebrations of the expert were tinged by ambivalence. In addition, associations between social science and natural science were made only hesitantly or not at all.[8] The social sciences featured nowhere in C. P. Snow's famous Rede Lecture of 1959 on the "two cultures." They were neither "the sciences" nor "the humanities" and offered no distinctive political or cultural project for Britain (Ortolano 2009).[9] After Keynes's ubiquity, economists installed as government aides risked seeming invisible and mute.

One man connects all these important developments. Lionel Robbins was at the Economic Advisory Council and at the Economic Division, and in the aftermath of Snow's lecture, he was head of the committee that advised on the reform of higher education. As Susan Howson (this volume) shows, Robbins was a master persuader, and his talents worked best when applied to sway the Treasury and the government. While he would write to the public about the affairs of state, he was just as often addressing the state on behalf of the public in inquiry commissions on the arts and higher education, to name the most significant. Robbins's language was never moral or political: he spoke in the words of the Treasury and of state rationality

---

7. The successor to the Economic Advisory Council was the 1939 Central Economic Information Service within the Cabinet Office that led to the Economic Section of the War Cabinet, which after the war transitioned to the Treasury. In 1947 the Economic Planning Board was set up, staffed by economists.

8. So much so that the 1930s and 1940s project of enlisting science in the service of socialism, spearheaded by John Desmond Bernal, J. B. S. Haldane, Lancelot Hogben, Hyman Levy, and Joseph Needham, found no echoes in economics or in economic journalism (Werskey 1978).

9. In a "Second Look," Snow did recognize the "human sciences" as a possible third culture, but one subordinate to the primary pair, with the potential to soften the "difficulties of communication" between the two principals.

with sober calculations of cost and benefit or supply-demand analysis. Although Robbins is in many ways exceptional, his public posture was not unique. Like him, Alec Cairncross was a man of government who joined a grasp of the policy arena, its terms and players, with a sober public voice.

Technocracy was lived differently in America. On the eve of the publication of Hofstadter's *Anti-intellectualism*, President John F. Kennedy gave a much-remembered commencement address at Yale University. To the assembled youth the president lamented how his generation "enjoy[ed] the comfort of opinion without the discomfort of thought" and recruited the graduates to the task of "more basic discussion of the sophisticated and technical questions involved in keeping a great economic machinery moving ahead." The postideological polity proclaimed by Kennedy was one that Daniel Bell (1960) and others had tagged a few years earlier and that was in the making well before the Democratic Party's victory at the ballot box.[10] In tandem with their British peers, American economists had penetrated government; with Franklin D. Roosevelt's "brain trust" the professor had been called away from the opinion pages to become a thinking organ of the state (Barber 1996). Ostensibly, which is to say with publicity, economists would convene to imagine the policy alternatives of the state, as in the postwar Council of Economic Advisors or the Joint Economic Committee (Bernstein 2001).

Paul Samuelson had been an unofficial but influential economic adviser to the Kennedy campaign and to the president-elect. In 1961 he too was a president, of the American Economic Association, and at Christmas of that year, he had the privilege of addressing its members. Samuelson's address was a leisurely tour through the canon of economics, grading the originality and legacy of his forebears. He closed with the famous lines: "Not for us is the limelight and the applause. . . . In the long run, the economic scholar works for the only coin worth having—our own applause." The applause Samuelson certainly received on cue. One should be surprised by this statement's deflation of celebrity and civic engagement. Samuelson was regularly tapped for comment by the White House and Congress. He was often on the phone with the specialist press and in a couple of years would join *Newsweek* as a columnist alongside Henry Wallich and Milton Friedman. When the three professors joined *News-*

---

10. In the Kennedy administration, the personification of efficiency's dominion over political passion was a Berkeley economics graduate and former Ford executive, Secretary of Defense Robert Strange McNamara, who held court over a staff of RAND-trained "whiz kids" (Shapley 1993).

week they replaced Henry Hazlitt. A New York reporter with no formal training in economics, Hazlitt represented the economic journalism that flourished after World War II in business and newsmagazines. As Peter Boettke and Liya Palagashvili (this volume) review, Hazlitt offered a defense of orthodox economics enlivened by philosophical argument, appeal to tradition, and political intuition. Hazlitt was a crucial broker for many members of the profession in the anxious years of the early Cold War, who famously shepherded publication of Friedrich Hayek's *Road to Serfdom* in *Reader's Digest*. By 1960 the assertive technocrat seemed to dispense with such intermediation.

Yet the self-presentation of insulation from the callings of celebrity and public office was an important cultural value for Samuelson and his generation.[11] Science was a key to social mobility for those coming of age circa World War II (Hollinger 1995). The American model of science governance conceived during the war and fortified during the early Cold War conscripted scientists to the service of the state, generously funded by both federal and military agencies and finding through the state their privileged route to civic engagement (Mirowski 2002; Amadae 2003; Robin 2003). Service to the state came to mean the same as service to the public.[12] The preeminent status afforded the expert's opinion gave economists increased discretion in setting the policy agenda and the terms of knowledge brokerage and made them sought-after sources for the news media. As Rob Roy McGregor and Warren Young (this volume) show, Federal Reserve presidents, often economists in background or disposition, associated themselves with academic trends and attempted to make these intelligible and important to their constituencies. The public voices developed in this period in the United States were no longer tuned to move public sentiment but to expose the complexity and sophistication of economic science and to solicit public appreciation for it (Mata 2011). Popularization in the

---

11. The cultural and bohemian life of New York City has long held a grip on the historiography of the intellectual in the United States. Its popular appeal is enhanced by the fascinating lives of its inhabitants that in uncompromising and surprising ways challenged the mores of conservative society (Wetzsteon 2002). One central theme of the literature surrounding this group is their self-proclaimed status as independent from academe, business, and politics, another kind of insulation. Yet the New York intellectuals were never out of time or society, and they relied on family patronage and the readers of the complex of magazines to where their energies converged, such as the *Nation, New Masses, New Republic, Partisan Review, Politics*, and *Commentary*.

12. There were dissenters on the matter of conflating the state with the polity, and no case was more dramatic than that of Robert Oppenheimer (Thorpe 2008).

United States meant to make a case for continued public support for science and for trust in scientists, a discourse that bridged the social and natural sciences divide (Lewenstein 1992).[13]

Intellectual Life as Market

The prestige of economics (and social science more broadly) as a policy science began to unravel in the late 1960s.[14] Social scientists were unable to deliver what they had promised, not least consensus and value neutrality. This became apparent when the civil rights, antiwar, environmental, and feminist movements began asking the difficult questions. A series of scandals implicated social scientists with the choices and blunders of the state, and the privacy of their advice seemed to serve only moral obfuscation, as the scandal over Project Camelot put in the starkest relief (Nisbet 1966; Mata 2010). The immediate response to this crisis was a surge of moral argument and of ideology, which in its full, left-wing force proved ephemeral (Horowitz 2004; Ollman and Vernoff 1982). The longer-term legacy was very nearly the opposite. Among policy and corporate elites developed a metaphor of a market of ideas that deterred discussions of moral responsibility.

In the year of the publication of Hofstadter's jeremiad, George Stigler inaugurated the Occasional Papers series of London's Institute of Economic Affairs, with an essay titled "The Intellectual and the Market Place." Stigler's essay was at odds with the conservative representation of intellectuals. Joseph Schumpeter in *Capitalism, Socialism, and Democracy* (1940) had explained the revolt of intellectuals against capitalism as an outcome of deflated expectations. Although they were groomed for a position of influence, the reality of the capitalist economy made little room for intellectuals. The argument of disaffection was championed in the writings of Edward Shils and in his interpretation of Karl Mannheim's sociology of class. Shils (1972, 18–21, xii) wrote that although intellectuals were diverse in their traditions—scientism, romantic, apocalyptic, populist, and anti-intellectual—the critics all arose from "the alienated

---

13. One can identify efforts at popularization in Britain from the late 1960s, and closely associated with the careers of Peter Jay and Samuel Brittain, but their content was more directed to doctrinal disputes, that is, endorsement of monetarism, than the American counterpart of the 1950s and 1960s (Parsons 1989).

14. At the time Britain was expanding the number of economist advisers with the creation of the Department of Economic Affairs and the National Plan.

sector of the intellectual stratum." In other, later versions, the alienation theme led to representing intellectuals as a class with no "instrumental" role for commercial and civic life, and that hence resorted to justifying their claims to power with humanist critiques of capitalism. The historical precedent that spiked the dread of these writings was the Russian experience and contemporary readings of the rise of Bolshevism (Feuer 1975).

For Stigler in 1963, intellectuals were not alienated. They inhabited an ideal polity. Despite the evil looks exchanged between the worlds of business and of intellect, the two were surprisingly the same. He wrote that "both fields pay a fair amount of attention to packaging and advertising, and both fields place an absurdly high value on originality" (Stigler 1963, 5), and more fundamentally, both were voluntary systems. Rehearsing themes that appeared regularly in his scholarly and advocacy work, Stigler asserted the market system as a model polity, where "neither fraud nor coercion is within [its] ethics." It was not in punishing intellectuals for their ungratefulness that Stigler deserves our attention, since that populist vein was not so different from critiques leveled from the 1950s to the present day (Kahan 2010). What was novel was to conceive intellectuals inhabiting a polity where power and coercion were sterilized by the operations of a marketplace of ideas.[15]

It is significant that Stigler's essay was carried by the Institute of Economic Affairs (IEA), an institution that revolutionized Britain's public sphere. The institute drew from a stock of local and international scholars and journalists to aggressively court the attention of politicians. Richard Cockett has chronicled how the IEA privileged academic contacts and notably university students to proselytize market solutions to Britain's troubled 1970s economy (Cockett 1994). Margaret Thatcher's victory in the polls and her budgets that rejected the sanction of accredited economists (and led to their sanctioned rejection) repositioned the economist in the polity. In selecting voices of influence, criteria of career or institutional prestige were trumped by ideology, the public relations machine, and the think tank apparatus. What was true of the Conservative Party would become true of Labour when the think tank Demos played a crucial role in developing New Labour doctrine.

From the 1903 Anti-Protectionism letter signed by sixteen economists to the letter signed by 364 economists in 1981 against Geoffrey Howe's budget, economists had joined together to amplify their authority in public.

---

15. See also the essays contained in Stigler 1982.

The collectivization of economists' public interventions is therefore not new, and it is its opposite that we should find exceptional. Economists in the twentieth century have relied on institutions of their own making, partnerships with journalists and editors, and partnerships with the state to make their voices and their knowledge effective in the polity. Only a few economists appear to owe their prominence single-handedly to talent and perseverance: Keynes, and perhaps Galbraith and Friedman. While Samuelson was eliding his own record as a media personality to construct the image of the economists' economist, Friedman and Galbraith, presidents-to-be of the American Economic Association, were writing successful mass-market paperbacks, and Samuelson's textbook was counting millions of copies sold. In the late 1970s and early 1980s both men tried the medium of television. An examination of their duel reveals that they were not battling alone. Angus Burgin (this volume) shows how the BBC conceived of Galbraith's *Age of Uncertainty* as science popularization, an ambitious, expensive, long-form essay on the history of social knowledge. To the eyes of conservatives and neoliberals, who promptly filled pages of reviews of the program, Galbraith's *Age* was propaganda. Friedman's *Free to Choose* was to counter Galbraith's elitism with lower production values but mass distribution. Significantly, *Free to Choose* in its message and visual language atomized social experience, placing personal testimony and direct observation on par with social scientific claims to knowledge (Rodgers 2011).

In the last third of the twentieth century, the values of "humanistic" or "scientific" culture were in many quarters replaced by material and market consciousness.[16] Expertise was unbound from occupational judgment and calls for representing social or public interests articulated through the state, to be sold skill-based and tool-based in the marketplace (Brint 1994). Changes to economists' values and self-images can be paired with a changing demography of the profession. Although in the twentieth century the number of yearly economics majors in the United States rose only modestly, and steadily, doctoral degrees nearly quadrupled between 1960 and 1970 and have remained at a high plateau.

---

16. Samuelson's "coin" was the symbolic acclaim of scientific equals; although Stigler was on the threshold of something else, he could endorse a similar disciplinary worldview. When Stigler asked himself the question "Do economists matter?" and set out on a canonical tour of his own, he found that economists had never steered history and so should not try. Their calling was to labor in disciplinary obscurity (Stigler 1976) and to expect their work to "inevitably and irresistibly enter into the subject of public policy" (Stigler 1965). Like Samuelson, Stigler did not follow his own advice.

So while the place of social scientists within the state was under challenge in the 1970s, their numbers were multiplying, fortifying an industry of economic consultancy (Fourcade 2009).

On matters of public import, economists are hired by the state and by private interests, and all sides in dispute, to participate in communicative practices in which economists might have limited discretion, as public relations experts orchestrate campaigns and their materials. It would be too extreme to say that the neoliberal moment has erased autonomy from the voices of economists; rather, its most striking feature is the increasing value attached to publicity and celebrity, as economists compete among themselves for contracts and attention. An example of a career poised between celebrity and the state is offered by Lawrence Summers. Early on a star faculty member at Harvard, tenured at a young age, Summers dedicated most of his career to advising government and the financial industry, a profile furthered by a string of appointments at the White House, a catastrophic tenure as president of Harvard, regular lecture tours, and a column at the *Financial Times*. Summers has courted controversy, and it has only enhanced his profile as an expert. The embrace of controversy is also apparent in the case of Gary Becker and Richard Posner (Fleury and Marciano, this volume): two accomplished scholars with resources to effect change on higher education, law practice, and academic research devoted themselves to writing a blog to an unidentified public. Although neither Becker nor Posner is dour in his scholarship, the riskiness and experimentalism exhibited in the blogging show them courting novelty and scandal. This late-century genre of economic discourse is predicated on capturing attention, more hits on websites, more copies of books and magazines sold, and it is epitomized by *Freakonomics*, the blog, the book, the movie, the consultancy company. Posner's *Public Intellectuals: A Study of Decline* (2003) can be read as a reflective exercise whereby one public intellectual visits the secondary literature to project his generation's conception of the polity and intellectual life as idealized markets. Not shying away from the usual tropes, Posner castigates the present state of culture for the low quality of opinion and punditry, but he does not seek the reference of enlightenment or humanistic values to edify his ideal polity. Instead, he breaks down the problem into supply and demand components to diagnose an absence of quality controls and to call for a better market of ideas.

The politics of attention shapes the kinds of questions asked in the public sphere, the questions one might ask about the economic crisis that began in 2007. Philip Mirowski and Edward Nik-Khah (this volume) offer a demonstration of how the echo chambers of networked think tanks can shut down discussion, divert, and distract. They review how public ignorance about the causes of the crisis is constructed, with alternative accounts of government failure crowding out any examination of the rule of markets. Like Posner's review of intellectual life, the proposed solution by these contemporary actors is more and better markets. Mirowski and Nik-Khah reveal economists' new identity: in a polity conceived as a market, they are market designers.

Our introduction offers one itinerary of the insights contained in this volume. There is more in the pages that follow than we could do justice to in this space. The essays draw from the biographies of actors to ask how they perceived their location in culture, politics, and knowledge. The essays examine the individual talents and energies and the institutional resources deployed to achieve public influence. They interrogate the consequences of public engagement for the careers of actors. Our partial exercise was to sketch a chronology that begins a discussion of what might be the deeper factors animating changes to economists' public interventions. We have paid special attention to how cultures of expertise inflect the modes of public intervention. The two world wars and the crisis of authority of the 1960s emerge as watershed moments in revising standards of trust in experts and optimism over popular deliberation. We have drawn on a robust body of literature that traces the institutional inroads of economists into the state. We have also drawn on a growing literature on the role of para-academic institutions that amplify the voices of economists and distribute the economic logic across culture. In contrast, we still do not know enough about the history of economic media. Print, broadcast, and digital media all make an appearance in our volume, but we were unable to analyze in depth the role of economists and economics in their evolution. Similarly, although we know much about the history of professional organizations, learned societies, advisory functions in government, and think tanks, we still do not know enough about the role of economists in corporate circles and the public relations industry. Our assessment is that the historiography has reached a stage of maturity that beckons these new and exciting challenges.

All the essays in this volume testify, with some selection bias, that economists then and now have been occupants of the public sphere. But as we hope to show, the search for publicity is never unconditional. To understand economists' encounters with the public, we must appreciate the expectations they bring to the meeting and the institutional contexts that enable the encounters and that constitute the public sphere. We must admit that Paul Krugman's blog posts for the *New York Times* today are nothing like Keynes's *How to Pay for the War* of 1940, and that luncheon seminars at the Brookings Institution in the 1950s bear no reasonable resemblance to the BBC series *Masters of Money* of 2012. Yet histories that connect the public utterances and interventions of economists are possible. They are fundamental to unlock a deeper understanding of the place of economic knowledge in culture.

References

Amadae, S. M. 2003. *Rationalizing Capitalist Democracy: The Cold War Origins of Rational Choice Liberalism*. Chicago: University of Chicago Press.

Barber, W. J. 1996. *Designs within Disorder: Franklin D. Roosevelt, the Economists, and the Shaping of American Economic Policy, 1933–1945*. Cambridge: Cambridge University Press.

Bell, Daniel. 1960. *The End of Ideology: On the Exhaustion of Political Ideas in the Fifties*. New York: Free Press.

Bender, Thomas. 1987. *New York Intellect*. Baltimore, Md.: Johns Hopkins University Press.

———. 1993. "ERA Seligman and the Vocation of Social Science." In *Intellect and Public Life*, 49–77. Baltimore, Md.: Johns Hopkins University Press.

Bernstein, M. A. 2001. *A Perilous Progress: Economists and Public Purpose in Twentieth-Century America*. Princeton: Princeton University Press.

Brint, Steven. 1994. *In an Age of Experts: The Changing Role of Professionals in Politics and Public Life*. Princeton: Princeton University Press.

Brown, David S. 2006. *Richard Hofstadter: An Intellectual Biography*. Chicago: University of Chicago Press.

Charle, Christophe. 1990. *Naissance des "intellectuels": 1880–1900*. Paris: Editions du Minuit.

Cockett, R. 1994. *Thinking the Unthinkable: Think-Tanks and the Economic Counter-revolution, 1931–1983*. London: HarperCollins.

Collini, Stefan. 1993. *Public Moralists: Political Thought and Intellectual Life in Britain, 1850–1930*. Oxford: Oxford University Press.

———. 2002. "Intellectuals as Other People." In *The Public Intellectual*, edited by Helen Small, 203–23. Oxford: Blackwell.

———. 2006. *Absent Minds: Intellectuals in Britain*. Oxford: Oxford University Press.

Dahrendorf, Ralf. 1995. *LSE: A History of the London School of Economics and Political Science, 1895–1995*. Oxford: Oxford University Press.

Davis, Howard. 2009. "Revisiting the Concept of the Public Intellectual." In *Intellectuals and Their Publics*, edited by Christian Fleck, Andreas Hess, and E. Stina Lyon, 261–70. Aldershot, UK: Ashgate.

Edgerton, David. 2005. *Warfare State: Britain, 1920–1970*. Cambridge: Cambridge University Press.

Eyal, G., and L. Buchholz. 2010. "From the Sociology of Intellectuals to the Sociology of Interventions." *Annual Review of Sociology* 36:117–37.
Feuer, Lewis S. 1975. *Ideology and the Ideologists*. Oxford: Blackwell.
Fink, Leon. 1997. *Progressive Intellectuals and the Dilemmas of Democratic Commitment*. Cambridge: Harvard University Press.
Fourcade, M. 2009. *Economists and Societies: Discipline and Profession in the United States, Britain, and France, 1890s to 1990s*. Princeton: Princeton University Press.
Frank, Marcie. 2005. *How to Be an Intellectual in the Age of TV: The Lessons of Gore Vidal*. Durham, N.C.: Duke University Press.
Herbst, Susan. 2003. "Polling in Politics and Industry." In *The Cambridge History of Science: The Modern Social Sciences*, edited by Theodore M. Porter and Dorothy Ross, 577–90. Cambridge: Cambridge University Press.
Hofstadter, Richard. 1963. *Anti-intellectualism in American Life*. New York: Knopf.
Hollinger, D. A. 1995. "Science as a Weapon in Kulturkampf in the United States during and after World War II." *Isis* 86 (3): 440–54.
Horowitz, Daniel. 2004. *The Anxieties of Affluence: Critiques of American Consumer Culture, 1939–1979*. Amherst: University of Massachusetts Press.
Howson, Susan, and Donald Winch. 1977. *The Economic Advisory Council, 1930–1939: A Study in Economic Advice during Depression and Recovery*. Cambridge: Cambridge University Press.
Igo, Sarah Elizabeth. 2007. *The Averaged American: Surveys, Citizens, and the Making of a Mass Public*. Cambridge: Harvard University Press.
Kahan, Alan S. 2010. *Mind vs. Money: The War between Intellectuals and Capitalism*. New Brunswick, N.J.: Transaction.
Kurzman, C., and L. Owens. 2002. "The Sociology of Intellectuals." *Annual Review of Sociology* 28:63–91.
Lewenstein, B. V. 1992. "The Meaning of 'Public Understanding of Science' in the United States after World War II." *Public Understanding of Science* 1 (1): 45.
Maloney, John. 1985. *Marshall, Orthodoxy, and the Professionalisation of Economics*. Cambridge: Cambridge University Press.
Mata, T. 2010. "The Enemy Within: Academic Freedom in 1960s and 1970s American Social Sciences." In *The Unsocial Social Science? Economics and Neighboring Disciplines since 1945*, edited by Roger E. Backhouse and Philippe Fontaine. *HOPE* 42 (supplement): 77–104.
———. 2011. "Trust in Independence—the Identities of Economists in Business Magazines, 1945–1970." *Journal of the History of Behavioral Sciences* 47 (4): 359–79.
Mirowski, P. 2002. *Machine Dreams: Economics Becomes a Cyborg Science*. Cambridge: Cambridge University Press.
Nisbet, Robert A. 1966. "Project Camelot: An Autopsy." *Public Interest* 5:45–69.
Ollman, B., and E. Vernoff. 1982. *The Left Academy: Marxist Scholarship on American Campuses*. New York: McGraw-Hill.
Ortolano, Guy. 2009. *The Two Cultures Controversy*. Cambridge: Cambridge University Press.

Parsons, Wayne. 1989. *The Power of the Financial Press: Journalism and Economic Opinion in Britain and America*. Aldershot, UK: Edward Elgar.
Porter, T. M. 1996. *Trust in Numbers: The Pursuit of Objectivity in Science and Public Life*. Princeton: Princeton University Press.
Posner, R. A. 2003. *Public Intellectuals: A Study of Decline*. Cambridge: Harvard University Press.
Robin, Ron. 2003. *The Making of the Cold War Enemy: Culture and Politics in the Military-Intellectual Complex*. Princeton: Princeton University Press.
Rodgers, Daniel T. 1998. *Atlantic Crossings: Social Politics in a Progressive Age*. Cambridge: Harvard University Press.
———. 2011. *Age of Fracture*. Cambridge: Harvard University Press.
Rutherford, M. 2011. *The Institutionalist Movement in American Economics, 1918–1947: Science and Social Control*. Cambridge: Cambridge University Press.
Schumpeter, Joseph Alois. 1940. *Capitalism, Socialism, and Democracy*. 4th ed. London: Allen and Unwin.
Seton-Watson, Hugh. 1960. "The Russian Intellectuals." In *The Intellectuals: A Controversial Portrait*, edited by George Bernard de Huszar, 41–50. Glencoe, Ill.: Free Press.
Shapley, Deborah. 1993. *Promise and Power: The Life and Times of Robert McNamara*. London: Little, Brown.
Shils, Edward. 1972. *Intellectuals and the Powers and Other Essays*. Chicago: University of Chicago Press.
Stapleford, Thomas A. 2009. *The Cost of Living in America: A Political History of Economic Statistics, 1880–2000*. Cambridge: Cambridge University Press.
Stigler, G. J. 1963. "The Intellectual and the Market Place." Occasional paper 1, the Institute of Economic Affairs, London.
———. 1965. "The Economist and the State." *American Economic Review* 55 (1–2): 1–18.
———. 1976. "Do Economists Matter?" *Southern Economic Journal* 42 (3): 347–54.
———. 1982. *The Economist as Preacher*. Oxford: Blackwell.
Thorpe, Charles. 2008. *Oppenheimer: The Tragic Intellect*. Chicago: University of Chicago Press.
Townsley, Eleanor. 2006. "The Public Intellectual Trope in the USA." *American Sociologist* 37 (3): 39–66.
Werskey, Gary. 1978. *Visible College*. London: Allen Lane.
Wetzsteon, Ross. 2002. *Republic of Dreams: Greenwich Village, the American Bohemia, 1910–1960*. New York: Simon and Schuster.

"Perhaps I'm a Don Quixote but I'm Trying to Be a Paul Revere": Irving Fisher as a Public Intellectual

Robert W. Dimand

An Economist and a Public Intellectual

Irving Fisher (1867–1947) was not merely a scientific economist. He was a fully engaged public intellectual, seeking to influence public opinion and policymakers not just on economic issues such as his "compensated dollar" plan for monetary policy (varying the dollar price of gold to hold a price index steady) or the definition of taxable income (excluding saving) but also a national Department of Health, compulsory health insurance, diet reform (in collaboration with Dr. Kellogg of Battle Creek, of cornflakes fame), eugenics, limitation of immigration, prohibition of alcohol, revision of the calendar (so that each month would have the same number of days), and the League of Nations (which he believed himself to have invented—not entirely without reason), debates in which he drew on his reputation as an authoritative economic expert. In addition to hundreds of articles in the popular press and scholarly journals, Fisher wrote three books opposing repeal of Prohibition and two advocating US entry into the League of Nations, as well as a leaflet endorsing the Equal Rights Amendment (which he may not have entirely understood, since he based his support on respect for motherhood). His greatest best seller, *How to Live* (written with Eugene Lyman Fisk, a physician), appeared in twenty-

Correspondence may be addressed to Robert W. Dimand, Department of Economics, Brock University, St. Catharines, ON L2S 3A1, Canada; e-mail: dimand@brocku.ca.

one editions from 1915 to 1945 and eventually sold more than 400,000 copies, not counting 12 to 15 million copies of a condensation distributed by Metropolitan Life (Allen 1993, 139–40). His last book proposed an icosahedral world map projection that would avoid Mercator's exaggeration of areas far from the equator. Fisher took part in political campaigns (e.g., leading the Pro-League Independents in 1920) and gave advice to presidents and central bankers, much of it unsolicited. He had private meetings with every president from Theodore Roosevelt to Franklin D. Roosevelt (except Calvin Coolidge), including seven with FDR from August 1933 to January 1936, and wrote one hundred letters to FDR, receiving twenty-five letters from him (much of the correspondence between Fisher and FDR is reprinted in Fisher 1997, vol. 14: *Economic Policy, 1930–47*, chapters 2, 4, and 5; see also Allen 1993, 252, 256; and Fisher 1956, 278).

Fitting Steve Fuller's (2005, 1, 3) criteria for an intellectual, Fisher "spoke truth to power, when power was not accustomed to being addressed in that fashion," and "was willing and able to convey any thought in any medium," from a weekly newspaper column (circulated by Fisher's Index Number Institute to accompany its weekly price index) to Fox Movietone News, from congressional testimony to presidential addresses to scholarly associations to exchanges of open letters with outsiders to the economics discipline such as Professor Frederick Soddy (monetary heretic and Nobel laureate in chemistry) or William Trufant Foster (see Dimand 1991). Fisher reported in 1934 that on just one of his subjects, price-level stabilization, "My secretary counts up . . . 99 addresses, besides 37 letters to the press, and 161 special articles, as well as 9 testimonies at hearings held by government bodies and 12 privately printed circulars, together with 13 books bearing on the subject" (autobiographical appendix to Fisher 1934, quoted in Fisher 1956, 188; for details, see Fisher 1961). He made his first radio broadcast in March 1922, just a few months after the first regularly scheduled radio station began broadcasting (Allen 1993, 169). Fisher used every available medium to propagate his views except one: his university courses, except for his course on national efficiency, were based on his opinions about personal and public health. Indeed, he largely gave up teaching to have time for his careers as a public intellectual and an entrepreneur. His Yale colleague Ray Westerfield reported in his *American Economic Review* obituary of Fisher that "because of his exceedingly busy life, during the last twenty-five years of his professorship he was unable to give much time to teaching: he gave few courses and was on leave a great deal. His practice was to offer a course on the subject on which he was at the time writing a book or which he was investigating and to employ his pupils" (reprinted in Dimand 2007, 3:384). The books on which Fisher based his courses were his academic books on general equilibrium (the subject of his course The Mathematical Theory of Prices in the 1890s), monetary economics, index numbers, or capital and interest, not his popular books on Prohibition or the League of Nations. His half-time teaching at Yale (finally made permanent in 1926), returning his entire salary to the university in most years in the 1920s, meant that typically Fisher taught only one semester a year, giving one course to a handful of graduate students (Allen 1993, 192). He followed the advice of Stanley Fish (2008) to professors to "save the world on your own time."

Fish (1995, 1) contrasts "an organic intellectual in the Gramscian sense" with "a specialist, defined and limited by the traditions of his craft.... it is a condition of his labours, at least as they are exerted in the United States, that he remain distanced from any effort to work changes in the structure of society." Fisher's specialist writings on the quantity theory of money (marshaling statistical evidence on the long-run neutrality and short-run nonneutrality of money), on the monetary theory of economic fluctuations, and on index number theory provided the basis for his vociferous efforts to reform the economic system by mandating the monetary authority to vary the dollar price of gold so as to peg the Fisher ideal price index (the geometric mean of the Paasche and Laspeyres indexes), to abandon the gold standard in the early 1930s, or to separate the medium of exchange from risky financial intermediation by imposing 100 percent reserve requirements on demand deposits. But, just as Max Weber declared "I am not a donkey and I do not have a field," Fisher was no specialist restricted to a single field. Of eighty-six publications by Fisher in the single year 1917 (the year before he became president of the American Economic Association, and two years before the Prohibition Amendment was ratified), nineteen were in economics, eighteen on healthy living, seventeen on Prohibition, thirteen on health insurance, four on a league of nations, two in statistics, and one each on topics from the causes of war to relative enlistment in states (Allen 1993, 154; Fisher 1961). On Prohibition, the League of Nations, *How to Live*, and revision of the calendar and the world map projection,[1] Fisher moved as a public intellectual entirely

---

1. See Fisher 1997, vol. 13: *Crusader for Social Causes*, 284–99, 236–49, for his 1943 *Geographical Review* article on the icosahedral world map projection and his 1930 paper from the *Proceedings of the International Conference of Accountants* advocating a thirteen-month year with twenty-eight-day months (statistical analysis would be easier if all months were the same length).

beyond any connection with his academic specialty, although, as John Kenneth Galbraith (1977, 192) remarks, Fisher's case for Prohibition included an economic aspect: Fisher "argued, no doubt correctly, that men were more productive when off the sauce" (see Fisher 1926).

Economists who move beyond academic circles to participate as public intellectuals sometimes inspire strong reactions. Raj Patel of the University of California, Berkeley, has been unable to persuade a fringe religious group, Share International, that he is not the Messiah (Grant 2011). In contrast, the factory reformer Lord Shaftesbury confided to his diary in 1868 that John Stuart Mill was the Antichrist (Best [1964] 1975, 69). Murray Rothbard (1972, 159) declared that "Ralph Hawtrey proved to be one of the evil geniuses of the 1920's" because he favored central bank cooperation to stabilize the price level,[2] rather than a declining price level. But Fisher, an earnest, exceptionally industrious man devoted to what he saw as the public good, and also a brilliant and productive scientific economist, ended his career as a public intellectual by becoming a comic figure because of his statements about stock prices having reached a permanently high plateau in October 1929, the only academic economist featured in *The Experts Speak: The Definitive Compendium of Authoritative Misinformation* (Cerf and Navasky 1984, 47, 49, 50). Galbraith (1977, 192) remarked that in the stock market crash, Fisher "lost between eight and ten million dollars. This was a sizeable sum, even for an economics professor."[3] Galbraith went on to recognize that "what is now called the Keynesian Revolution began with Irving Fisher. This Keynes himself affirmed" (195), but the irresistible wisecrack came first. Robert Loring Allen's (1993) biography of Fisher includes a chapter title, "Theorist, Reformer, Loser (1930–2)," and indeed he was all three on a grand scale.

But Fisher was not always an object of ridicule, and even in the 1930s he was active in economic policy debates, though by then his indirect influence through James Harvey Rogers and George F. Warren exceeded his direct influence (Barber 1996, 14–18, 46–48, 81–82; Dorfman 1946–59, 5:685–88). For decades Fisher was the most widely known, influential, and outspoken figure among American economists. He was by no means always victorious: for example, Fisher and his close ally Senator Robert L. Owen

---

2. Along with Fisher, see Rothbard 1972, 157, 159, 160, 163, 272, 274, 276, 277.

3. Fisher amassed a fortune of $10 million in the 1920s exercising stock options with borrowed money (notably options to buy stock in Rand Kardex, which took over his Index Visible, which became the Rolodex), and then lost $11 million, leaving him a million dollars in debt to his sister-in-law (an Allied Chemical heiress and retired president of Wellesley College), who forgave the debt in her will when she died in 1945 (see Allen 1993).

failed to get a mandate for price-level stability included in the Federal Reserve Act in 1913 (see Owen 1919 and Fisher 1934), and Fisher's Yale classmate (and secretary of war) Henry Stimson did not accept Fisher's advice to prohibit alcohol near army camps during World War II and give the soldiers ice cream instead. He was not nominated for the US Senate as an Independent Republican in 1932 or as a Democrat in 1934, when FDR declined to impose Fisher as a running mate on Connecticut governor Wilbur Cross.[4] Nonetheless, Fisher was a force to be taken into account unlike most professors and, to the consternation of some economists, widely considered the public face of the US economics profession. The press gave him not only frequent attention but sometimes large blocks of space: in 1917, the *Philadelphia Public Ledger* published in full Fisher's six Hitchcock Lectures given at the University of California, Berkeley (later collected in book form as *Stabilizing the Dollar*, 1920), and the McClure Newspaper Syndicate's six-part serialization of Fisher's *League or War?* (1923) was carried in full by such newspapers as the *New York Evening Post*.

Fisher's involvement in economic policy debates both in the public press and in policymaking circles was long sustained. The two economists most often cited in the index to William Barber's *From New Era to New Deal: Herbert Hoover, the Economists, and American Economic Policy, 1921–1933* (1985) are Fisher, with twenty mentions, and Columbia University's business cycle expert Wesley C. Mitchell, founder of the National Bureau of Economic Research (NBER) and, like Fisher, a president of both the American Economic Association and the American Statistical Association, with twelve (followed by Alvin Hansen and Rexford Tugwell with ten each, John Maurice Clark and Paul Douglas with eight each, and Edwin Kemmerer with six). But in Barber's *Designs within Disorder: Franklin D. Roosevelt, the Economists, and the Shaping of American Economic Policy, 1933–1945* (1996), Fisher receives nineteen index entries and Mitchell none (with eight entries for Hansen, four for Clark, one for Douglas, and three for Kemmerer—but seventeen for Tugwell, Brains Trust member and undersecretary of agriculture), even though Mitchell remained a central figure in academic research until his death in 1948. Granted that Barber, the editor of *The Works of Irving Fisher*, is a Fisher expert, this is consistent with Fisher's active participation (at times

---

4. Cross, the longtime dean of Yale's Graduate School and the provost of Yale before his four terms as governor, knew Fisher well, so Fisher did not bother seeking Cross's support directly.

exceeding his influence) in US economic policy debates throughout the interwar period. Conspicuous by their absence from both books, and from all other accounts of interwar economic policy discussion, are Fisher's and James Harvey Rogers's Yale colleagues, whose vehement denunciation of the New Deal attracted little attention (Fairchild et al. 1935).[5]

The Turning Point

In 1898, the year he turned thirty-one, Irving Fisher was promoted to full professor of political economy at Yale and was told that he had six months to live. Fisher's attitude toward life was transformed by his struggle from 1898 to 1904 with tuberculosis, the disease that had killed his father, a Congregational minister. Fisher emerged from his ordeal with a dedication to improving the world, a conviction that he had been spared so that he could do good, and a confidence that he knew which changes to the world would be improvements. In a letter to his wife in July 1924, written in San Francisco while on a speaking tour promoting US entry into the League of Nations (and the doomed presidential campaign of John W. Davis), Fisher reflected,

> Perhaps I'm a Don Quixote but I'm trying to be a Paul Revere. Had it not been for those long years [in sanatoriums] in Saranac Lake, Colorado Springs and Santa Barbara I wouldn't be on these missions but would be the regular college professor interested in my mathematical economics almost exclusively. But that illness and your sweet noble unselfishness aroused the latent altruism which my preacher Father, I suppose, transmitted to me and from that time forth I have felt the urge of the preacher and have wanted to make up for the waste spaces in my own life by preventing some of the needless waste of this wastrel world. First the tuberculosis fight, then hygiene in general and the Life Extension Institute, and now the Eugenics and Peace Movements have appealed to me. . . . I do want before I die to leave behind something more than a book on Index Numbers, much as I love my strictly professional work. I feel that I have found a niche in making application of my scientific training. (Fisher 1956, 213–15)

5. Striving to be comprehensive, Joseph Dorfman (1946–59, 5:734–35) did notice a *Yale Review* article by Fred R. Fairchild in 1932 deploring suggestions that monetary and fiscal expansion could restore prosperity. Fairchild, Furniss, and Buck, all former students of Fisher, wrote the best-selling economic principles textbook of the time. Furniss and Buck each served as provost of Yale University.

Fisher's professional formation as an economist shows in his view of the goal of his proposed reforms as the prevention of "needless waste," the theme of the *Report on National Vitality: Its Wastes and Conservation* (1909) that Fisher wrote for the National Conservation Commission appointed by President Theodore Roosevelt.[6]

There was much to be done, and Fisher had no doubts that he knew what should be done. In his December 1916 presidential address to the American Association for Labor Legislation (AALL), Fisher (1917, 9) lamented that "at present the United States has the unenviable distinction of being the only great industrial nation without compulsory health insurance" but noted that "Germany showed the way in 1883 under the leadership of Bismarck. . . . Her wonderful industrial progress since that time, her comparative freedom from poverty, reduction in the death rate, advancement in hygiene, and the physical preparedness of her soldiery, are presumably due, in considerable measure, to health insurance."[7] That soon became an unfortunate example to cite: one pamphlet opposing state health insurance in the November 1918 California referendum warned, "It is a dangerous device, invented in Germany, announced by the German Emperor from the throne the same year he started plotting and preparing to conquer the world" (quoted in Starr 1982, 253). Although endorsed by the American Medical Association and several state labor federations, the AALL's health insurance proposals were defeated by a coalition of insurance companies, Christian Scientists, some state medical societies, and the American Federation of Labor (Starr 1982, 243–57; Moss 1996, chap. 8).[8]

---

6. "Roosevelt believed that the publications of the findings [the three-volume report of the National Conservation Commission, with Fisher's report in vol. 3] would be a historical landmark of his administration, and a turning point in conservation history (though in truth it never acquired any true cogency)" (Brinkley 2009, 773).

7. Contrast Fisher's presidential address to the American Economic Association two years later: "We now know that German professors in general, from theologian to chemist, have prostituted their professional services to serve Germany's criminal purposes," especially those economists who in "an economics professors' war . . . helped to lay the foundations for the war . . . a predatory economics, the economics of a beast of prey, the economics of loot by war" (Fisher 1997, 13:7). He also spoke of "the red flag of class warfare" and of academic economists who were apologists for "trade unionism, socialism, and even Bolshevism, syndicalism, or I.W.W.ism," yet Allen (1993, 158) insists that in that speech "he measured his words with care, his rhetoric was mild. . . . He did not make rabble-rousing statements."

8. Irving Fisher, a neoclassical economist and the fifth president of AALL, and Yale's Henry Farnam, a paternalistic conservative who was AALL's second president and main financial benefactor, collaborated across methodological and political lines in that research and advocacy group with University of Wisconsin institutionalists and Progressives such as Richard T. Ely (founding president of AALL), John R. Commons (second secretary of AALL), and John B.

Fisher took an interest in public policy before his battle with tuberculosis. At the invitation of *Economic Journal* editor F. Y. Edgeworth, Fisher (1894) applied his hydraulic mechanism illustrating the quantity theory of money to analyzing the mechanics of bimetallism. In his monograph *Appreciation and Interest*, published by the American Economic Association, Fisher (1896) invoked the distinction between "virtual interest" (the real interest rate) and "money interest" (the nominal interest rate) in response to bimetallist arguments advanced by Populists, notably by William Jennings Bryan in his "Cross of Gold" speech accepting the Democratic presidential nomination that year. Populists held that declining prices under the gold standard since 1873 imposed an unjust burden on debtors such as farmers with mortgaged farms, and urged free coinage of silver as well as gold to increase the money supply and raise the price level. Fisher pointed out that declining price levels (appreciation of the purchasing power of money) would have real effects only if the decline was a surprise. Expected changes in the purchasing power of money would be reflected in the money interest rate. "I took part in the 'Sound Money' campaign against Bryan in 1896," recalled Fisher in 1934. "Had that campaign occurred at the present time, I would not have been so strenuous an opponent of Mr. Bryan; for I now know that the evil of which he complained was more real than I then thought. His proposed remedy—bimetallism at 16 to 1—was, I still think, far from good" (quoted in Fisher 1956, 187). These important early scholarly publications were contributions to the intense debate over bimetallism, but they appeared in the *Economic Journal* and in the *Publications of the American Economic Association*, addressed to Fisher's fellow economists, and only indirectly to policymakers and the general public. Only after his recovery from tuberculosis did Fisher begin in earnest his career as a public intellectual, seeking all outlets for his ideas, denouncing tobacco in the magazine *Boy Patriot*, and giving the editor of North Dakota's *Grand Forks Herald* an exclusive interview advocating Prohibition (Allen 1993, 150–51).

A League to Enforce Peace

On August 16, 1914, twelve days after Germany invaded Belgium, the *New York Times* published "After the War, What?" (Fisher 1997, 13:208–

Andrews, Commons's long-serving successor as secretary of AALL (see Moss 1996). Commons also took part in Fisher's various Stable Money organizations: differences in economic methodology did not prevent their cooperation as social reformers.

16), a revised version of a paper that Fisher had given to the Yale Political Science Club in 1890 proposing "a league for peace." The Christian Peace Union reprinted it as a pamphlet, with a preface by Lord Bryce, the former British ambassador to Washington. Two weeks later, the *Times* followed up with another long Fisher article, "Some Probable Economic Effects of the War" (1997, 13:217–25). After four dinner meetings at the Century Club in New York with fifteen or twenty others (including former president and future chief justice William Howard Taft, then a Yale law professor, and Harvard president A. Lawrence Lowell), Fisher and three hundred others met in Independence Hall in Philadelphia in 1915 to start a campaign for a "league to enforce peace," and he was present at the assembly of two thousand league supporters in Washington in May 1916 at which President Woodrow Wilson endorsed the proposal (Fisher 1956, 165). Others, notably John A. Hobson (1915) and Leonard Woolf (1916), English cofounders of the League of Nations Society (Glendinning 2006, 204–6), independently proposed an international body to arbitrate disputes and preserve peace, but Fisher's proposal preceded theirs, being published before theirs at the very start of World War I as a revision of a talk given a quarter of a century before and, most importantly, was the one that came to the attention of Wilson (a founding member of the council of the American Economic Association, hence already familiar with Fisher's standing as an economist). The underlying idea of a federation of free states to preserve peace can be traced back much earlier, to Immanuel Kant's essay *Perpetual Peace* ([1795] 1963) and to the lesser-known Émeric Crucé, whose 1613 proposal for a permanent European council to maintain world peace (to include representatives of the Ottoman Sultan, Morocco, Japan, and the Great Mogul) was followed five years later by the outbreak of the Thirty Years War (Hale 1994, 141–42). Fisher wrote extensively on the need for American entry into the League of Nations, the subject of thirty-three of his eighty-five publications in 1923 (outnumbering the twenty-eight on money and economics), and campaigned for it passionately, with a commitment strengthened by the belief that the league was his idea (see Fisher's letters to his wife from the 1920 and 1924 election campaigns, in Fisher 1956, 203–16). Like David Lloyd George and Georges Clemenceau, Fisher would have been willing to accept ratification of the Versailles Peace Treaty subject to Senator Henry Cabot Lodge's reservations, but Wilson would not and instructed his followers to join with diehard opponents of the treaty to deny ratification with reservations the necessary two-thirds majority in the Senate: "The squelching of Wilson's dream was a bitter personal blow to Father" (Fisher 1956, 202).

The 1923 *New York Times* review of Fisher's first book on the League of Nations expressed a judgment that could be applied to Fisher's reformist writings in general:

> Charles Lamb's plea in defense of a certain warmth or vehemence in dispute should be invoked in behalf of Professor Fisher. His book, despite its controversial aspect, carries the weight of conviction. To him the problem is perfectly simple—he condenses it in his title, "League or War?"—and with the intensity of an ardent advocate proceeds to explain that the choice is between American isolation resulting in a world war ending civilization and American participation in the present League, followed by peace, prosperity and plenty. To less warm partisans than Professor Fisher this conception of the League as the all-powerful, all-embracing, only-begotten healer of the world's troubles will be irritating. So, also, to many persons who are inclined to be internationally minded, Professor Fisher's insistence that America alone is able to save the world, while flattering to American pride, will probably seem too jingoistic. (reprinted in Dimand 2007, 1:203–4)

The reviewer, N. Roosevelt, added, "Here, by way of parentheses, let it be said that in enlisting the late Colonel [Theodore] Roosevelt's support in behalf of Article X he is guilty of precisely the same fault for which he condemns the anti-Leaguers—applying the opinions of a dead man to problems that arose after his death" (205).

Fighting Demon Rum

Fisher wrote extensively and vehemently about prohibiting alcohol, the subject of 26 of his 128 publications in 1927 alone. He did much to lower the tone of the debate. Fisher (1926, 179–80) cited the testimony of the "editor of the official organ of the railroad labor organizations at Washington, D. C. . . . that it was the general opinion of newspaper men from New York to San Francisco that the liquor interests when licensed had never obeyed the law, and had been in combination with all other evil interests in cities and states to secure unjust advantages." Fisher denounced "the brewers' interest in German propaganda during the War" with particular attention to "the effort of pro-German factions to control one of the great metropolitan dailies in order to use its vast resources, local and national, for the promotion of German interests, including a plan for articles agitating 'Personal Liberty'" (200–201). In a section titled "John Koren: Brewers' Writer," Fisher exposed a former president of the American Statistical

Association as having addressed the Brewers' Congress in Atlantic City in 1910, published signed and unsigned articles in the brewers' yearbooks, and accepted a retainer from the United States Brewer's Association, revelations that in Fisher's mind conclusively refuted Koren's arguments about Prohibition without any need to tell Fisher's readers what Koren's arguments were (201–2). In his 1947 *Economic Journal* obituary of Fisher, G. Findlay Shirras recalled, "He abstained from alcohol and tobacco and was a vegetarian.[9] . . . I well remember his strong views on these subjects and his judgment was sometimes a little warped. 'A man who has had one beer is one beer drunk'" (quoted in Dimand 2007, 3:389). Fisher's Yale colleague Ray Westerfield, memorializing Fisher in the *American Economic Review* in 1947, wrote of Fisher's books on Prohibition that "it seemed to many he, unconsciously no doubt, selected his data to prove his position rather than to find the truth" (quoted in Dimand 2007, 3:382).

Fisher's ferocious stance on the arguments, evidence, and motives of those who disagreed with him about the economics of Prohibition may explain his cool treatment by Clark Warburton, who might have been expected to be Fisher's ally in upholding the quantity theory of money against Keynesianism in the 1930s and 1940s (on Warburton as a "pioneer monetarist," see Bordo and Schwartz 1979 and Cargill 1979). The nineteen papers from 1945 to 1953 collected as Warburton 1966 contain only a handful of references to Fisher (for a list, see Dimand 2000, 341), none of them acknowledging that Fisher ever said anything about the role of money in economic fluctuations or about the stability of the velocity of circulation, or mentioning *The Purchasing Power of Money* (1911) (the same holds for Warburton 1981). In January 1947, Warburton declined to join Fisher's Anti-Inflation-and-Deflation Committee (Fisher 1997, 14:247–49).

Warburton had another academic interest besides the quantity theory of money: his book and Columbia PhD thesis *The Economic Results of Prohibition* ([1932] 1968), followed by the entry on Prohibition in the *Encyclopedia of the Social Sciences*, an article whose bibliography omitted Fisher even though Fisher's three books had been cited in Warburton's book, which rejected Fisher's claims of improved industrial efficiency because of Prohibition (Warburton [1932] 1968, 195), of hops having a nonbrewing market in yeast manufacture (30), and of uses of corn sugar

---

9. But I. N. Fisher (1956, 114) reports, "Contrary to the usual impression, Father never adopted vegetarianism *in toto* . . . at home we always had roast chicken on Sunday and red meat was not entirely absent from our table."

other than in making alcoholic beverages (50). Warburton's Columbia professor, E. R. A. Seligman, editor of the *Encyclopedia*, wrote to Fisher on December 23, 1932, to firmly recommend Warburton's book as "the only impartial effort that has yet been made to discuss the economic aspects of prohibition. . . . If you read that, you will get a better idea of what the economics students think of prohibition" (Fisher 1997, 13:148). That letter would not have pleased Fisher better if he read it in conjunction with the statement by Warburton ([1932] 1968, 5) that "this study of the economic results of prohibition was initiated early in 1929 at the request of the Association Against the Prohibition Amendment, and I am indebted to the Association for financial support in the first few months of the investigation." Sharp disagreement about the economics of Prohibition would not have facilitated cooperation between Fisher and Warburton in monetary economics.

Stabilizing the Dollar

Fisher invoked his credentials as an economist and statistician when insisting on the economic benefits of Prohibition, world peace, and immigration restriction or the statistical convenience of a thirteen-month year in which each month had the same number of days, or when giving the press ten reasons to vote for Wilson in 1912 or ten reasons to vote for Herbert Hoover in 1928. The situation with monetary policy reform was different: there Fisher actually had impressive, relevant credentials, and his policy proposals stemmed from his central scientific interests. From *Appreciation and Interest* through *The Purchasing Power of Money* and his debt-deflation theory of Great Depressions to his very last researches (see Dimand 2000), Irving Fisher believed that misperceived and incorrectly expected monetary shocks caused costly economic fluctuations and destabilized the economy. He correlated money interest, the volume of economic activity, and unemployment with distributed lags of past price-level changes to show that real variables fluctuated because of slow and incomplete adjustments of inflationary expectations. He proposed a formula for an "ideal index" of prices (the geometric mean of the Paasche and Laspeyres indexes) both to educate the public out of "money illusion" and to provide the basis for a "compensated dollar" monetary policy rule to stabilize the purchasing power of money by varying the dollar price of gold (replaced in Fisher's *100% Money* in 1935 by advocacy of open market operations to hold the price level stable with a flexible exchange rate).

Following University of Chicago economists such as Henry Simons (and also the monetary heretic Frederick Soddy), Fisher (1935) proposed to insulate the medium of exchange from the risks of financial intermediation by a 100 percent reserve requirement on bank deposits. Since governments did not then produce price indexes, Fisher created the Index Number Institute, located in his home at 460 Prospect Street, New Haven, and every Monday announced the weekly price index, accompanied by Fisher's weekly explanatory article, offered free to newspapers. His policy agenda sometimes impeded his scientific efforts, as in 1912 when his simultaneous efforts for an international society for the encouragement of mathematics in economics and an international conference on the high cost of living both failed: economists who were wary of the proposed conference on the cost of living as an obvious scheme to promote Fisher's compensated dollar plan extended their suspicions to his planned society to reform economic method. As Don Patinkin (1993) stressed, Fisher's attempt to make his price-level stabilization plan acceptable to defenders of the gold standard, by fixing the dollar price of gold and altering it at regular intervals instead of letting it float, undermined the scheme by making it vulnerable to speculative attack (Humphrey 1992).

Surprisingly, this aspect of Fisher's career as a public intellectual, the part based on his genuine expertise as a monetary theorist, has been often misunderstood in the literature (see Dimand 2003). Richard Timberlake (1978, 1993), Perry Mehrling (2002), and Alan Meltzer (2003) all hold that Fisher first proposed his plan for stabilizing the dollar value of a price index in *Stabilizing the Dollar*, much too late to be relevant to the debates leading to the passage of the Federal Reserve Act in 1913. In the words of Timberlake (1993, 407), "The first comprehensive proposal for a stable price level policy was made by Irving Fisher in his book *Stabilizing the Dollar*, published in 1920." But that was only the first time he published an entire book on the plan (and even that book was given as public lectures in 1917, which were published in newspapers at the time). Fisher devoted the concluding chapter of *The Purchasing Power of Money* to his compensated dollar plan, followed in 1912 by a much-publicized speech to the International Congress of Chambers of Commerce, meeting in Boston, and articles by Fisher on the compensated dollar in the *Economic Journal* in 1912, the *Quarterly Journal of Economics* in 1913, the conference supplement to the *American Economic Review* in 1913 (reprinted in the second edition of *The Purchasing Power of Money* in 1913 and in Fisher 1997, vol. 4), the *Revue d'économie politique* in 1913, and "Objections to a Compensated Dollar Answered" in the *American Economic Review* in 1914 (reprinted in Fisher 1997, vol. 4). Apart from many journal articles in English (e.g., articles by David Kinley, Frank Taussig, John Maurice Clark, and E. M. Patterson, all reprinted in Dimand 2007, vol. 2) and extensive newspaper coverage, by 1914 Fisher's plan had been the subject of journal articles in Swedish (by Knut Wicksell and David Davidson), Danish (by Frederick Zeuthen), German, French, Italian (including one by Corrado Gini), Dutch, and Japanese. Senator Robert Latham Owen (D-OK), previously Fisher's ally in an attempt to create a Department of Health, persuaded the Senate to include a price-level stabilization mandate in the Owen-Glass Bill that became the Federal Reserve Act, but it was removed by the House of Representatives at the urging of Representative Carter Glass (see Owen 1919 and Fisher 1934). Yet the modern secondary literature (including Mehrling, Meltzer, and Timberlake) insists that Fisher first proposed price-level stabilization in 1920, so it cannot have figured in the debates leading to the creation of the Federal Reserve System. Fisher's longtime associate Senator Owen has also disappeared from the literature on the origins of the Fed, so thoroughly that he was omitted from the *Dictionary of American Biography* and *American National Biography*, perhaps partly because of his later enthusiasm for conspiracy theories of the origins of World War I (Owen 1927) and of the control of money creation by sinister international bankers (Owen [1934] 1971, v–xii). Fisher was an active and important figure in US monetary policy debates not only in the 1920s and 1930s (see Barber 1985, 1996) but also before World War I, in the period from the crisis of 1907 to the formation of the Fed.

Conclusion: The Economist as Man of La Mancha

Irving Fisher, the outstanding scientific economist in the United States before 1940, was also a fully engaged public intellectual, determined after his struggle with tuberculosis to prevent "some of the needless waste of this wastrel world," wishing to "leave behind something more than a book on Index Numbers . . . What is everybody's business is nobody's business and so I'm making it my business!" (letter to his wife, July 12, 1924, quoted in Fisher 1956, 214). Perhaps often wrong but never in doubt, Fisher plunged into public controversies on subjects to which he brought a depth of expert knowledge—and on many other subjects, too, for Fisher displayed little recognition of the limitations of his authority. Fisher's successful battle with tuberculosis left him with a quasi-religious fervor to improve the world by giving it the benefit of his presumed superior knowledge and understanding as a social scientist.[10] His involvement in eugenic arguments for selective immigration (1997, 13:160–207) had a distinctly racist aspect[11]—but his belief that smoking is unhealthy was prescient. His warnings about the possibility of another world war were overwrought—but not unfounded. Fisher helped shape public opinion about monetary policy and bombarded policymakers with advice, often with little sense of how the advice would be received.[12] Some causes, such as the thirteen-month calendar and, most importantly, the expansive plans for government intervention sketched in his American Economic Association presidential address, were abandoned by Fisher when they failed to resonate with their audience. Fisher's public reputation and private fortune were devastated by the stock market crash of 1929, and after 1930 professional citations of Fisher gave way to citations of Keynes. Some of Fisher's causes attracted ridicule, such as his conviction that mathematics has a role in economics: his colleague and former student Ray Westerfield, in his 1947 *American Economic Review* memorial to Fisher, regretted that "his liberal use of mathematics and physics not only delimited his audience but also led to many misunderstandings, for it minimized the psychological factor and his similes did not fit the facts too well" (quoted in

---

10. An alternative suggested at the *HOPE* conference is that Fisher's public persona was "orchestrated to reflect the expectations of the public and its tinkering inventor (Edison) expectations about what was authoritative knowledge." Although Fisher clearly gave much thought to how to achieve maximum dissemination of his various messages, he does not seem to have ever experienced doubt about his standing to pronounce authoritatively on the proper monetary policy rule, world map projection, calendar reform, diet and healthy living, prohibition of alcohol, a league to enforce world peace, immigration laws, the ideal index number for prices, or whether "Yes, we have no bananas" is grammatically correct. Fisher claimed, in his presidential address to a presumably startled American Statistical Association, that he had predicted the 1929 stock crash (but admitted to underestimating its extent), and apparently went to his grave believing that his "formulary for anticipating short-time changes in market action" actually worked (Sasuly 1948, 268). The picture that emerges from Fisher 1997, vols. 13 and 14, Fisher 1956, and Allen 1993 is of a man fervently driven to improve the world by giving it the benefit of his superior knowledge, not thoughtful about his own claims to authority, and only thoughtful about the space of public discourse to the extent of considering how to find maximum exposure for his own views.

11. On Fisher's involvement in eugenics and views about racial differences in time preference, see Aldrich 1975, Cot 2005, and Dimand 2005.

12. See Fisher's letter to William Trufant Foster on January 20, 1936, congratulating Foster on his appointment to the Federal Reserve Board, which Fisher had recommended to FDR (Fisher 1997, 14:105). Foster was not appointed.

Dimand 2007, 3:380). In fact, Fisher reached an audience far beyond those interested in his mathematical economics. As he jested, he was partly a Don Quixote while trying to be a Paul Revere, but, more than almost any other American academic economist of his time,[13] Irving Fisher was a force as a public intellectual.

References

Aldrich, M. 1975. "Capital Theory and Racism: From Laissez-Faire to the Eugenics Movement in the Career of Irving Fisher." *Review of Radical Political Economics* 7 (3): 33–42.

Allen, R. L. 1993. *Irving Fisher: A Biography*. Malden, Mass.: Blackwell.

Barber, W. J. 1985. *From New Era to New Deal: Herbert Hoover, the Economists, and American Economic Policy, 1921–1933*. Cambridge: Cambridge University Press.

———. 1996. *Designs within Disorder: Franklin D. Roosevelt, the Economists, and the Shaping of American Economic Policy, 1933–1945*. Cambridge: Cambridge University Press.

Best, G. F. A. (1964) 1975. *Shaftesbury*. Reprint, London: Mentor Books.

Bordo, M. D., and A. J. Schwartz. 1979. "Clark Warburton: Pioneer Monetarist." *Journal of Monetary Economics* 5 (1): 43–65.

Brinkley, D. 2009. *The Wilderness Warrior: Theodore Roosevelt and the Crusade for America*. New York: Harper.

Cargill, T. F. 1979. "Clark Warburton and the Development of Monetarism since the Great Depression." *HOPE* 11 (3): 425–49.

Cerf, C., and V. Navasky. 1984. *The Experts Speak: The Definitive Compendium of Authoritative Misinformation*. New York: Pantheon.

Cot, A. L. 2005. "'Breed Out the Unfit and Breed In the Fit': Irving Fisher, Economics, and the Science of Heredity." *American Journal of Economics and Sociology* 64 (3): 793–826.

Crunden, R. M. 1984. *Ministers of Reform: The Progressives' Achievement in American Civilization, 1889–1920*. Urbana: University of Illinois Press.

Dimand, R. W. 1991. "Cranks, Heretics, and Macroeconomics in the 1930s." *History of Economics Review* 16:11–30.

———. 2000. "Irving Fisher and the Quantity Theory of Money: The Last Phase." *Journal of the History of Economic Thought* 22 (3): 329–48.

---

13. The University of Wisconsin Progressives, most notably Ely and Commons, were influential as public intellectuals through the Chautauqua and Social Gospel movements, the Progressive Party, and the AALL (see Rader 1966, Crunden 1984, and Moss 1996). Ely's greatest influence was in the late nineteenth century, before Fisher's emergence as a public intellectual. Despite differences in methodology between the institutionalist Commons and the neoclassicist Fisher, they collaborated in trying to influence public opinion through the AALL (see Moss 1996) and the Stable Money Association.

———. 2003. "Competing Visions for the US Monetary System, 1907–1913: The Quest for an Elastic Currency and the Rejection of Fisher's Compensated Dollar Rule for Price Stability." *Cahiers d'Economie Politique* 45:101–22.

———. 2005. "Economists and the Shadow of 'The Other' before 1914." *American Journal of Economics and Sociology* 64 (3): 827–50.

———, ed. 2007. *Irving Fisher: Critical Responses*. 3 vols. London: Routledge.

Dorfman, J. 1946–59. *The Economic Mind in American Civilization*. 5 vols. New York: Viking.

Fairchild, F. R., E. S. Furniss, N. S. Buck, and C. H. Whelden Jr. 1935. *A Description of the "New Deal."* Rev. ed. New York: Macmillan.

Fish, S. 1995. *Professional Correctness: Literary Studies and Political Change*. Oxford: Clarendon.

———. 2008. *Save the World on Your Own Time*. New York: Oxford University Press.

Fisher, I. 1894. "The Mechanics of Bimetallism." *Economic Journal* 4:527–37.

———. 1896. *Appreciation and Interest*. New York: Macmillan.

———. 1909. *Report on National Vitality: Its Wastes and Conservation*. In vol. 3 of *Report of the National Conservation Commission*. Washington, D.C.: Government Printing Office.

———. 1911. *The Purchasing Power of Money*. With H. G. Brown. New York: Macmillan.

———. 1917. "The Need for Health Insurance." *American Labor Legislation Review* 7 (1): 9–23.

———. 1920. *Stabilizing the Dollar*. New York: Macmillan.

———. 1923. *League or War?* New York: Harper and Brothers.

———. 1926. *Prohibition at Its Worst*. New York: Macmillan.

———. 1934. *Stable Money: A History of the Movement*. With H. R. L. Cohrssen. New York: Adelphi.

———. 1935. *100% Money*. New York: Adelphi.

———. 1997. *The Works of Irving Fisher*. Edited by W. J. Barber; assisted by R. W. Dimand and K. Foster; consulting editor J. Tobin. London: Pickering and Chatto.

Fisher, I. N. 1956. *My Father Irving Fisher*. New York: Comet.

———. 1961. *A Bibliography of the Writings of Irving Fisher*. New Haven, Conn.: Yale University Library.

Fuller, S. 2005. *The Intellectual*. Cambridge: Icon Books.

Galbraith, J. K. 1977. *The Age of Uncertainty*. Boston: Houghton Mifflin.

Glendinning, V. 2006. *Leonard Woolf: A Life*. London: Simon and Schuster.

Grant, T. 2011. "'No Desire for Deification': Economist and Activist Raj Patel Says He Would Prefer to Talk about Abolishing Economic Injustices in the World Rather Than the Fact That Some People Think He's the Messiah." *Globe and Mail* (Toronto), February 12.

Hale, J. R. 1994. *The Civilization of Europe in the Renaissance*. New York: Athenaeum.

Hobson, J. A. 1915. *Towards International Government*. London.

Humphrey, T. M. 1992. "A Simple Model of Irving Fisher's Price-Level Stabilization Rule." *Federal Reserve Bank of Richmond Economic Review* 78 (6): 12–18.
Kant, I. (1795) 1963. *Perpetual Peace.* In I. Kant, *On History*, translated by L. W. Beck, 85–135. Indianapolis, Ind.: Bobbs-Merrill, Library of Liberal Arts.
Mehrling, P. 2002. "Economists and the Fed: Beginnings." *Journal of Economic Perspectives* 16:207–18.
Meltzer, A. H. 2003. *A History of the Federal Reserve.* Vol. 1, *1913–1951.* Chicago: University of Chicago Press.
Moss, D. 1996. *Socializing Security: Progressive-Era Economists and the Origins of American Social Policy.* Cambridge: Harvard University Press.
Owen, R. L. 1919. *The Federal Reserve Act.* New York: Century Company.
———. 1927. *The Russian Imperial Conspiracy, 1892–1914: The Most Gigantic Intrigue of All Time.* New York: A. and C. Boni.
———. (1934) 1971. Foreword to G. M. Coogan, *Money Creators: Who Creates Money? Who Should Create It?* Hawthorne, Calif.: Omni.
Patinkin, D. 1993. "Irving Fisher and His Compensated Dollar Plan." *Federal Reserve Bank of Richmond Economic Quarterly* 79 (3): 1–33.
Rader, B. 1966. *The Academic Mind and Reform: The Influence of Richard T. Ely in American Life.* Lexington: University of Kentucky Press.
Rothbard, M. 1972. *America's Great Depression.* Los Angeles: Nash.
Sasuly, M. 1948. "Irving Fisher and Social Science." *Econometrica* 16:255–78.
Starr, P. 1982. *The Social Transformation of American Medicine.* New York: Basic Books.
Timberlake, R. H. 1978. *The Origins of Central Banking in the United States.* Cambridge: Harvard University Press.
———. 1993. *Monetary Policy in the United States: An Intellectual and Institutional History.* Chicago: University of Chicago Press.
Warburton, C. (1932) 1968. *The Economic Results of Prohibition.* New York: AMS.
———. 1966. *Depression, Inflation, and Monetary Policy: Selected Papers, 1945–53.* Baltimore: Johns Hopkins University Press.
———. 1981. "Monetary Disequilibrium Theory in the First Half of the Twentieth Century." *HOPE* 13 (2): 285–99.
Woolf, L. 1916. *International Government.* London: Fabian Society.

Observers, Commentators, and Persuaders: British Interwar Economists as Public Intellectuals

Chris Godden

Britain's Interwar Economy and Popular Economic Literature

The public discussion of economic topics is a long-standing feature of British public culture (Fourcade 2009, 129) and one related to the increased demand for economic analysis that developed from the mid-nineteenth century (Fetter 1962, 1965; Kadish and Tribe 1993). The unprecedented instability of Britain's economy during the 1920s and 1930s certainly served as a fertile ground for economic debate. This period of economic confusion, reflected in, among other things, the loss of once-secure export markets and prolonged unemployment, saw many British economists move beyond the confines of academic texts to utilize a range of media sources—newspapers, magazines, and later radio broadcasts—to actively engage in public economic discourse. In doing so, they offered their opin-

Correspondence may be addressed to Chris Godden, Samuel Alexander Building-N.2.6, School of Arts, Languages and Cultures, University of Manchester, Manchester M13 9PL, UK; e-mail: Christopher.Godden@manchester.ac.uk. The research on which this work is based was made possible with support from the Economic and Social Research Council. My gratitude is expressed to Theo Balderston, Robert Milward, Stuart Jones, Jim Tomlinson, Till Geiger, and Tom Dixon for their comments and suggestions on previous drafts. A previous version of this article was presented at the annual Conference of the European Society for the History of Economic Thought held in Porto in April 2006. I would like to thank all participants for their helpful comments and advice. I am also grateful to the referees and editors of this journal for their suggestions and generous work in revising the submitted article.

History of Political Economy 45 (annual suppl.)   DOI 10.1215/00182702-2310944
Copyright 2013 by Duke University Press

ions and insights on a variety of contemporary economic, social, and policy matters to an audience largely determined by class, background, and profession.

What did these economists see their public role as being? What functions did they see themselves as performing? How does an investigation into their popular writings assist us in defining their status as "public intellectuals"? By concentrating on the popular economic material published during the interwar period, this essay seeks to draw nearer to an understanding of the public role and responsibilities that interwar British economists saw *themselves* as having within contemporary society. The argument presented below therefore concentrates on the evolving public role of British economists during the interwar period. As I demonstrate, this public economic discourse was heavily focused on identifying factors that, in these authors' opinions, were undermining the rhythmic influence of the postwar cycle. Recognition of permanent changes in the international economic environment saw this idea vanish, and in its place emerged arguments concentrating on the unalterable and inevitable process of economic development. The resulting interpretations offered by economists in their popular writings raised public awareness of important, and unavoidable, changes taking place within Britain's postwar economy. As a consequence of this, the social purpose that underpinned the public pronouncements of this body of public (economic) intellectuals came to embody two, interconnected themes: a desire to influence the economic behavior of society while defending established economic doctrine against the attacks of spurious, ill-advised, pseudo-economic myths that festered within the public consciousness.

This essay is intended to contribute to the broad study of "economic talk" (Ruccio 2008) and the growing recognition of a need to explore beyond the traditional confines associated with the history of economic thought (Daunton and Trentmann 2004). It is also intended as a call for a great investigation into the little-explored archive of popular economic writings published during the interwar period. The main work in this area is Gary Dean Best's (2007) study of popular economists in the United States during the Great Depression and the New Deal. While it takes little effort to identify a body of British public (economic) intellectuals who were actively engaged in applying both economic theory and economic history to the sphere of public life during the interwar period, the historiography is largely ignorant of many of these writers, and there is certainly no systematic study of this popular (nonacademic) economic material.

Ultimately, of course, it is the ephemeral quality of such material, coupled with the sheer volume produced, that explains why it has come to suffer the ignominy of neglect. The desire to impart an immediate view on some issue, associated with events at a particular moment in time, inevitably meant that economists were reliant on the most transitory of media.

Several of the writers whose ideas are outlined below—such as Theodore Gregory, George Daniels, and John Harry Jones—have received little attention from historians of economic thought, relegated (if discussed at all) to the role of bit-players in an established narrative concerned with the activities of an academic elite during the "years of high theory." Some attention has been given to Henry Clay (Backhouse 2008), although more should be done to fully assess the activities of this neglected writer. Given that a number of the British economists referred to in this essay may not be immediately recognizable to readers, a brief dramatis personae has been provided in an appendix to assist in understanding their careers, status, and responsibilities. Some names do not immediately come to mind as being "economists" at all, but to address the issue of economists as "public intellectuals," it is necessary to appreciate how particular individuals, together with their work and activities, were identified by the society in which they lived. It is perfectly possible to judge an "economist" against some particular standard connected with the modern standing of economics, for example, identifying an economist in terms of a position within academe, and hence teaching and/or research responsibilities. Yet this judgment becomes meaningless once it is appreciated that there were many writers in the 1920s and 1930s who, although not holding academic positions, were widely recognized as economists by their readership. Arthur Pigou and Dennis Robertson were clearly identifiable to an interwar audience as economists because of their academic positions and are identifiable to modern historians for precisely the same reason. But there are some who are discussed in this essay—such as Harold Cox and John Atkinson Hobson—who, on first inspection, appear to fall into a different category. Can we legitimately identify these two men as "economists"? To a modern audience, their careers do not correspond to the conventional schema against which an "economist" is to be judged. Yet to their readers in the 1920s and 1930s, these men were certainly identified as having legitimate claim to the title of "economist." This fact can easily be established from an inspection of their obituaries. For example, Cox was described as an "economist and journalist" (*Times*, May 2, 1936), while Hobson's obituaries identified him as both an "economist and author" (*Times*, April 2, 1940) and, more interestingly, as an "economist and humanist" (*Manchester Guardian*, April 2, 1940; see also Backhouse 2008). An economist during this period may therefore be seen as an individual who presented himself to the public and who was accepted by the public in that role. The selection of the economists discussed below has therefore been based on how interwar society identified them as public producers and disseminators of economic knowledge and opinion.

This essay is structured as follows. The first section briefly explores wartime and early postwar views on the trajectory of the British economy, focusing on the approaches that economists took in identifying impediments to the movement of the postwar trade cycle. The second section looks at shifting explanations of Britain's postwar economic difficulties and explores how earlier views that concentrated on a cyclical downturn eventually gave way to ideas that emphasized the unavoidability of structural changes within Britain's economic system. Connected with this is a reconstruction of contemporary arguments about these structural changes, as well as the image or vision of the "new" economy, presented by economists, that was being forced into existence. The third section (divided into four parts) concentrates on economists' pronouncements of issues or problems that they identified as impeding the necessary process of change. This discussion includes their views on the public's attitudes toward economic change, the issues surrounding the erroneous use of unemployment statistics, criticisms of rationalization policies, and the need to neutralize public demands for protectionism. The fourth section discusses the key features of the popular economic writings of the interwar period and the role of publicly engaged economists. This includes an evaluation of the shifting nature of their interpretations, the necessary issues that they believed needed to be tackled (and hence the social benefits they believed would result), and their defense of formal economic theory against popular opinions and desires. The fifth section offers some conclusions, together with a brief discussion of the contribution of the study of popular economic literature to the history of economics.

Wartime and Early Postwar Views

I begin with a brief reference to Britain's wartime popular economic literature and the views and opinions presented by different authors about the likely direction of postwar conditions and problems—the so-called after-war literature. Elements within this literature clearly focused on forces that, it was feared, could weaken postwar reconstruction. Such interpretations concentrated on the probable postwar disintegration of national unity (Cole 1915a, 1915b; Hobson 1916b), expected problematic postwar relations between Britain and the Empire (Cannan [1915] 1997), and the long-term impact of punitive taxation required to tackle a parasitic national debt (Hobson 1916a; Marshall 1916; Pigou 1916a, 1916b, 1916c, 1917, 1918). From a more positive perspective, some economists argued that postwar prosperity could be secured through a physically and morally revitalized labor force, improved industrial relations, and an enhanced technical and administrative structure (Marshall 1917; Scott 1915). It was also believed that Britain's postwar trade would benefit from international approval of Britain's judicial conduct of the war, as well as the opportunities for increased international trade that a defeated Germany would provide. Potential threats to Britain's economic power were downplayed, although Hobson (1916a, 8) did consider the extent to which Japan had seized a trading advantage and encroached on Britain's Chinese markets.

Predictions about postwar reconstruction and prosperity were largely associated with the established ebb and flow of economic activity. For the sake of ease, Sydney Chapman's (1918) stylized presentation of the cycle is a useful contemporary representation of this automatic, four-stage sequence: first, an interim break associated with demobilization and the transition of industry to civil conditions; second, the tremendous release of war-restrained effective demand associated with the backlog of capital investment and the replenishing of stocks; third, the inescapable problem of reaction; and, fourth, the return to normal conditions.

Britain's immediate postwar economic history followed closely the first two stages of this predicted cycle. Yet it was with phase 3—the inescapable problem of reaction—that severe problems developed. Indeed, the severity of this period of reaction meant that by early 1921, mass unemployment had inflicted its suffering in many branches of British industry. By examining the popular writings of economists from the early postwar years, it becomes apparent that the severity of this reaction was widely interpreted in terms of a normal movement of the cycle that had been dramatically exacerbated by postwar complications and impediments (Henderson [1923] 1955; Hobson 1924; Pigou 1924). In 1921, for example, John Maynard Keynes (1921a, 259) presented Britain's postwar problems in terms of "an exceptionally severe cyclical fluctuation," while in 1924 we find William H. Beveridge (1924, 8) outlining the case of a "cyclical depression of trade with post-war complications."

How did economists interpret such postwar complications in their popular writings? Given that the available space does not permit a full examination of the contemporary popular economic literature, the following list provides a flavor of the opinions and interpretations that found their way into the economic discourse of the early 1920s. These included an examination of postwar economic and political factors that were seen to be generating rapid wage fluctuations (Cannan 1920; Keynes 1921b; Stamp 1923); institutional failings in the operation of the Labour Exchanges (Cox 1921b, 206); issues over Britain's postwar national debt and the question of whether increased taxation was exerting a discouraging effect on enterprise (Cole 1924a; Dalton 1923; Jones 1924, 198–200; Pigou 1919, 1922, 1923); fears of the corrosive influence of excessive postwar government bureaucracy (Cox 1921a, 400–401; Hirst 1924); and the unnecessary handicaps imposed on business through an inefficient transport and communication system (Acworth 1919a, 1919b, 1920, 1921, 1922; Cole 1921). The common theme running through these various popular pronouncements was that Britain's postwar economic problems were purely *temporary* and that, in the long run, Britain's economy possessed sufficient flexibility to reestablish its prewar position. This refers to stage 4 of Chapman's stylized cycle: the return to prewar conditions.

By the mid-1920s the interpretations offered in the popular economic literature underwent radical change. While the sheer breadth of the contemporary literature precludes a precise delineation between various intellectual positions, it is nonetheless apparent that the unremitting presence of unemployment in Britain had forced a reevaluation of interpretations that emphasized the existence of temporary impediments. Indeed, even in the early 1920s, Edwin Cannan (1922) raised the possibility that faith in the inherently rhythmic quality of economic activity was distorting a complete appreciation of the postwar situation and so serving as a possibly dangerous stimulus to erroneous economic analysis. By the late 1920s it is possible to identify a complete change of emphasis within the interpretations offered by economists in their popular writings. Whereas, in the early 1920s, Keynes and Beveridge had supported a cyclical interpretation to explain postwar difficulties, by the late 1920s we find Clay (1929, 23) writing that "no conceivable exaggeration of ordinary trade fluctuations" could explain Britain's postwar economic difficulties. A discernible shift is apparent in the assumptions that underpinned economists' popular pronouncements on Britain's postwar economic malaise. Given the clear differences between the prewar and postwar economic situations, and between the expected trajectory of the postwar economy and the reality that emerged, it became impossible to sustain a view centered on temporary impediments undermining the cycle's curative properties. The shift that can be identified within the popular economic literature from the mid-1920s onward was one of interpretation—away from discussions of *temporary* problems and impediments and toward discussions of issues and events that signaled *significant and permanent* changes in Britain's economic structure.

Industrial Development and the Emergence of a New Economy

The possibility of permanent changes to Britain's economy had been identified some years before by Robert Giffen (1900), only to be quickly dismissed by him on the grounds that there was an inherent stability to the conditions underpinning Britain's prosperity. It was therefore argued that developments of a chronic nature were unlikely to be traceable for many years, possibly generations, to come. By the mid-1920s, however, economists in Britain were increasingly coming to recognize that such "chronic" changes had emerged significantly sooner than earlier writers (such as Giffen) had anticipated. It is important to appreciate the extent to which this new interpretation formed a key feature of the popular economic literature from the mid-1920s onward. At the heart of these new ideas was an engagement with the study of economic history and the development of interpretations that centered on the impact of global economic trends, starting in the late nineteenth century, on Britain's established economic structure. Examples of nineteenth- and early twentieth-century literature relating to these ideas include, among others, William Cunningham's *Growth of English Industry and Commerce in Modern Times* (1892), Hobson's *Evolution of Modern Capitalism* (1894), Richard T. Ely's *Studies in the Evolution of Industrial Society* (1903), and David Macgregor's *Evolution of Industry* (1911). Within these texts and the popular economic literature of much of the interwar period, long-term economic development was visualized as a chronological sequence in which structures were transformed through technical innovations, the expansion of overseas markets, and the international division of labor. Indeed, in this generalized form, the basic interwar presentation of the complexities of Britain's long-run economic development was not dissimilar from the Rostovian "take-off" model of the 1960s.

By increasingly drawing such development ideas into their popular economic writings, economists began to attribute Britain's postwar economic difficulties to several key factors—the lasting consequences of nineteenth-century capitalist imperialism, the obvious impact of a devastating and protracted international war, and the explosion of a desire within poorer, developing countries to expand their industrial base behind protectionist barriers. The resulting ability of developing nations to compete with, and ultimately undercut, British producers therefore signaled permanent changes to Britain's long-held position within international markets. From the mid-1920s, economists repeatedly used their popular economic writings to argue that such changes *had* to be recognized because of the importance they held for the global position of British manufacturers and established export markets. It was now recognized, and widely presented to readers, that wartime and early postwar expectations about the direction of postwar demand (i.e., an expectation centered on the continued expansion of international markets) had been significantly exaggerated. This expectation had led to the early postwar misdirection of British capital and labor into heavily localized and specialized industries that had now come to yield (and would, in the new international environment, continue to yield) low economic returns. The story presented in the popular economic literature from the mid-1920s onward was clear: the economic confusion of the postwar period (large-scale unemployment, collapse in demand for exports, etc.) did not represent temporary impediments, or "confusion" compared with prewar "normality," or even the general crisis of capitalism—it was simply evidence of an inevitable process of economic development and maturity, and a process to which the British economy had to respond (Bowley 1929; Clay 1929, 17–23; Cole 1927, 1928c; Cox 1926a; Daniels 1931a; Henderson [1926] 1955a, [1926] 1955b; Hobson 1931; Jones 1930, 1935a; Robertson 1931b).

Yet it was not sufficient to simply argue that the securities of the "old" economic order were rapidly fading; there was also the important issue (an issue that a public-engaged economist had to face) of offering some predictions as to the eventual form that Britain's evolving economic structure would take. This question became another trend within the popular economic literature of the interwar period. By drawing together various strands from this literature, it is possible to construct a stylized impression of how this new, emerging economic structure was visualized. For example, in the same way that agriculture had been surpassed by industry, it was accepted that Britain's altered position in international markets necessitated the development of economic activity beyond the narrow confines of industry. Diversification, in other words, lay at the heart of Britain's future prosperity. Henderson ([1926] 1955a, [1926] 1955b) noted that the necessary transformation of Britain's economic structure was leading to industries localized in the old centers yielding pride of place to industries of a new form. Yet it was also recognized that, even with the continuing presence of increased competition in international markets, Britain would be unable to disengage completely from international trade. As low-grade production passed to other countries, expanding opportunities would emerge, as efficient British firms developed new export trades concentrating on specialized, high-quality goods, thereby leading to growth and the profitable reemployment of displaced labor. In addition, the growth of the distributive and service industries would increase consumer expenditure; secure changes in social habits, fashions, and leisure times; and open demand for commodities previously beyond the reach of the masses (Cole 1928a, 1929c, 1931; Daniels 1931a, 1931b; Henderson [1930] 1955a; Hilton 1934d; Jones 1926, 1927b, 1937a).

The popular economic literature of the period also demonstrates that, while it was accepted as essential that Britain undertake this adjustment to its economic structure, some commentators did not believe that the process would necessarily lead to an economic or social utopia. Jones (1930, 1936, 1938a), for example, feared that the increased importance attached to tourism would, by the very nature of this particular activity, generate increases in seasonal and casual employment, while the capriciousness of fashion meant an almost unstable demand for many of the products of the distributive and service industries. It was also feared that the increasing mechanization and standardization of the production process would stifle humanity's insatiable desire for independence and self-expression (Cole 1925; Jones 1937c; Sargant Florence 1930b).

Resolving Psychological Reactions

The shock to Britain's existing economic system would be expected to set in motion dynamic changes associated with the redistribution between capital and labor and the restructuring of economic activity (Cole 1926a; Jones 1935b; Robertson 1931a). Yet economists discussing these issues were not simply prepared to map the changing contours of the economic landscape. The social purpose of these popular economic writings rested in the role that economists saw for themselves. This involved (1) emphasizing the narrative of economic development and (2) identifying and discussing impediments that were seen to exert—or were seen to have the potential to exert—a negative effect on this process of development. I discuss the issues associated with the second point in more detail in the following section.

Large sections of the period's popular economic literature focused on identifying the causes of what, for want of a better description, may be termed "psychological reactions." One example, offered by Clay (1931), presented Britain's response to her postwar difficulties as being identical to that exhibited by primitive societies. It was well recognized, Clay argued, that primitive man had attributed unpleasant, extraordinary, or inexplicable events (such as bad harvests or solar eclipses) to the malevolent power of supernatural forces. It was Clay's belief that this sense of fear and amazement still existed within twentieth-century British society. The extent of postwar distress and confusion had therefore led different sections of society to endow human agencies, be it "socialism" and "capitalism" (or, more personally, "the capitalist"), with diabolical powers. It was, in other words, a situation of unenlightened fear: people simply reacted against what they did not understand. It was this fear, Clay argued, that was undermining the established principles of the market, thus preventing the economy from responding quickly enough to changing postwar conditions. Put another way, the widespread belief that malevolent forces were governing Britain's destiny was seen to prevent society from appreciating, and hence facilitating, the necessary, and inevitable, process of change.

For other writers, including George Cole (1926b, 1928b), John Hilton (1934b), and Jones (1927b, 1930, 1937a), "psychological reactions" stemmed from the wider issue of a nation reacting against the reality of Britain's postwar economic reality. Throughout the eighteenth and nineteenth centuries, Britain had established its industrial, commercial, and financial prestige by exporting a few, comparatively simple commodities produced by the great staple industries (e.g., coal and cotton textiles). By the mid-1920s, it was becoming increasingly apparent that Britain would not be able to retain this impressive position. Britain's apparent inability to respond to the new conditions was therefore attributed by these writers to a combined sense of national anger, disillusionment, and despair at the thought of Britain having to relinquish its long-held position as the world's most powerful economic nation. There was seen to be a general tendency in the postwar population to reflect on, and react toward, the glorious days of mid-Victorian prosperity. Yet this was only one side of the problem. While it was clear that the economy had enjoyed some postwar success in motor manufacturing, electrical engineering, and the production of artificial silks, it was felt that there was a lingering hostility within the nation to the prospect of miscellaneous domestic trades replacing industrial manufacturing. Although postwar society had increased the proportion of national income devoted to the consumption of goods and services beyond the subsistence needs of food and clothing, the development of many of the distributive and service industries—such as the sale of motorcycles, gramophones, cigarettes, or newspapers, and even extending to decorating chocolates or enameling golf balls (Hilton 1934b, 323)—was interpreted as signifying the loss of those standards that had represented Britain's industrial power. Any economic success associated with expanding domestic production appeared insufficient to counteract the loss of Britain's prewar position among manufacturing nations. What was lost on the swings could not be made up on the roundabouts!

This line of argument was presented in several areas of the period's popular economic literature and settled around the view that Britain was caught between two forces: on the one hand, a psychological reaction appeared to inhibit the necessary transformation of Britain's economic structure; on the other, any events that suggested that labor and capital could be profitably employed within the established export industries discouraged diversification and disrupted the necessary momentum toward readjustment. The temporary closure of the Ruhr pits during the French and Belgian occupation, and the granting of coal subsidies in 1925 and 1926, had insulated Britain from postwar economic reality and so delayed the inevitable process of adjustment. Similarly, a bumper crop in the United States had led to a catastrophic fall in the price of raw cotton. With such a fall in prices expected to stimulate consumption, it was logical that Lancashire cotton producers would expect a recovery in the demand for cotton goods. The dangerous feature was that unless Lancashire appreciated the temporary nature of the revival of cotton, it would interpret it as a return to normal conditions. It was only through such high-profile failures as the Cotton Yarn Association, and the realization that excess productive capacity could no longer be justified in relation to likely future conditions, that the necessity for Britain's economy to undergo widespread change was fully exposed (Cole 1928c; Clay 1932b; Jones 1927b; Keynes 1926).

Comparisons of Prewar and Postwar Unemployment Statistics

Another element of these "psychological reactions" interpretations concerned the view that problems stemmed from the public's naive use of postwar statistical data, and what was seen as a general tendency among the public to make inaccurate comparisons between prewar and postwar unemployment statistics. The most obvious reason for this was connected with the mighty outpouring of facts and figures generated by government departments. In many instances, statistics arising as a by-product of government activities served an important social purpose. The Health Insurance Acts, for example, had brought to light social conditions and incipient illnesses that could be easily treated, while the land tax survey had enabled better valuation of death duties. Yet it was feared that through an exaggerated degree of confidence in the published unemployment statistics, postwar society had fallen into a vicious circle whereby the presentation and perception of postwar unemployment undermined society's ability to speedily respond to changing postwar economic conditions.

At the beginning of the nineteenth century, the state had attached few, if any, restrictions on employment and private enterprise; by the beginning of the twentieth century, public opinion had forced the introduction of legislation relating to the safety, hygiene, and remuneration of labor. Fueled by the proposals of the Poor Law Commission (1905–9), this general extension of state activities demonstrated that, by the outbreak of the Great War, Britain had discarded the cloak of nineteenth-century morality. The development of a national unemployment insurance scheme therefore was a remarkable experiment in economic and social organization. Provided at reasonable cost, administered through the Unemployment Exchanges, and with apparent safeguards against abuse, the intention of the scheme was to ease the needless suffering of people who, through no fault of their own, were relegated to the ranks of the unemployed. When first introduced in 1911, the insurance scheme applied to a select group of occupations. Proposals for the gradual extension of the scheme were eroded by the war, but by August 1920 it was rapidly applied to the majority of all trades (with agricultural workers and domestic servants being the noticeable exceptions).

As a brief aside, it is worth noting the highly critical reaction that emerged in some quarters to what was seen as the damaging social and economic consequences of unproductive social expenditure associated with such social welfare measures. It was argued by Cox (1927, 195–96; 1931b, 15; 1931c, 291), for example, that social expenditure impeded the functioning of the economy by both expanding the corrosive effects of bureaucracy and creating an emotionally stunted and mulish workforce. One key element of this criticism concerned the role of benefit payments for the unemployed. Cox (1921b, 192–94; 1927, 197; 1931b, 9) displayed little faith in the character of labor, arguing that the universality of an unprotected benefit system had distorted the hardworking characteristics of the labor force by serving as a powerful disincentive to work. Henderson ([1930] 1955a) further suggested that the incentive of unemployment benefit had altered the economic significance of temporary stoppages, so leading dishonest workers to deliberately engineer the temporary breakdown of machinery, or the nondelivery of materials, in order to claim state relief. For the vast majority of interwar commentators—including Beveridge (1931c), Cannan (1930), Cole (1924a), and Jones (1925)—any suggestion that there existed a large body of idle, thriftless individuals, prepared to abuse the state relief scheme, and so accept money benefit over standard rates, was dismissed as nothing short of insanity.

Returning to the main point, the key feature of the unemployment scheme was that it generated regular statistics highlighting the extent of postwar unemployment. Thus, from 1922 to 1929, the level of recorded unemployment in Britain, according to contemporary statistics, had averaged 11.5 percent; this compared with prewar estimates of just 4.5 percent. Estimates of prewar unemployment, however, had been constructed from limited trade union returns (some figures dating as far back as 1854), which tended to ignore unemployment among unskilled workers. It was nonetheless widely accepted that, even in good times, the actual level of prewar unemployment was higher than that recorded in the union figures (Beveridge 1931a). At the same time, postwar unemployment statistics also failed to constitute an official census in that they were influenced by the administrative requirements of the insurance scheme, and only included those who, for a variety of incentives, had "lodged" their insurance cards at the Exchange in order to draw benefit. There was a tendency to ignore some proportion of the unemployed from these statistics, such as the "black coat" (nonmanual or professional) workers who refused to endure the ignominy of registering for benefit, and the unemployed laborers who constantly moved from one ward to another (Hilton 1934a).

Yet the composition and comparison of these prewar and postwar unemployment statistics were widely discussed in the popular economic literature from the late 1920s and early 1930s. The central argument presented here was simple: while economists were prepared to question a government statistic of so many million unemployed, they felt that the general public's belief in the work of highly trained officials, coupled with faith in the British spirit of democracy, had led them to slavishly accept government unemployment figures as a definitive economic pronouncement! With unquestioning faith in the veracity of government statistics (transmitted through the press), and comparisons with equally erroneous prewar statistics seen to exaggerate Britain's postwar position, the resulting negative psychological feedback effects contributed to a perception of diminishing economic power, and hence a widespread and prolonged climate of fear and insecurity (Beveridge 1931b; Cole 1924b; Jones 1927c, 1937b).

Rationalization: Nasty Medicine or Slow Poisoning?

Impediments to postwar economic development were also identified in the character of Britain's industrial leadership, most noticeably dynastic and semifeudal attitudes through which industrial authority was handed to an individual—the heir apparent—who, having received no training in business, found himself unprepared for the role he was required to fulfill (Clay 1932a; Cox 1930; Jones 1938a; Sargant Florence 1930a, 1930c; Stamp 1930). Such criticisms naturally lead to the suggestion that actions to promote the reconditioning of Britain's industrial structure would have found favor with economists.

Ideas of industrial reconditioning were represented in the interwar political and economic debates by the principles of "rationalization." At its most basic, this represented a system of organization aimed at securing the greatest possible mechanization and standardization of the production process to reduce excess capacity, lower costs, and secure profits from a smaller margin on the sale of an increased quantity of goods. This policy, hailed by many politicians and business leaders as the path to economic salvation, was both praised and criticized by economists. The fact that rationalization was identified by economists such as Cole (1926b, 1929a) and Philip Sargant Florence (1930b) as signifying a "second industrial revolution" demonstrates the perceived contemporary appreciation of the need to reinvigorate industry through the wider social and cultural spirit of dynamism and modernity. An interesting feature of the contemporary literature, however, is that there was a reaction among many economists to the ideas underpinning the principles of "rationalization." Was it not a fact, argued Robertson (1931a), that profit-conscious producers were always striving to secure improvements in industrial efficiency? What was so novel about the idea of systematic industrial exploitation associated with rationalization? Similarly, Sargant Florence (1930a) doubted whether the policy of rationalization differed from the "trustification" that had exercised socialist and university circles in prewar days; Gregory (1930b) believed that it merely echoed old debates between Ricardo, McCulloch, Babbage, and Senior; Hobson (1932) dismissed the whole project as pedestrian; while Macgregor (1934, 33–34) saw the term as nothing more than an affectation equivalent to saying terra firma instead of firm earth. Such ideas were echoed by both Shadwell (1929, 292) and Hilton (1934c), who believed that the widespread adoption of the term had arisen from its general vagueness while still providing expression and encouragement to postwar attitudes. The drive toward decisive action—the essential dynamism of capitalism that was seen to be lacking in the postwar economy—had therefore found expression in a word that, although seen by many to be devoid of theoretical originality, captured the postwar spirit of modernity.

Such criticisms of the concept of rationalization in the popular economic literature of the period led economists to consider other questions: would rationalization be successful in alleviating Britain's difficulties? Was rationalization to be seen as "a nasty medicine" capable of securing the necessary process of adjustment or "a process of slow poisoning" (Sargant Florence 1930c, 706)? Although the policy clearly had the *potential* to overcome impediments to change, it was identified by some economists as bringing other possible problems in its wake. Put simply, rationalization was not identified as a process that would necessarily serve as a catalyst to sustainable economic recovery. There were, for example, questions about the technical changes associated with rationalization, and the necessary reduction in labor inputs required to produce each unit of output. Could rationalization actually bring about greater employment? Although theoretically possible, there were some who urged their readers to question whether the policy of rationalization would bring about the expected positive outcomes. Writers including Clay (1932b), Cole (1929b, 1929c), and Hobson (1930) questioned the sufficiency of demand for the output of the rationalized industries (and hence the ability of industry to spread the costs of standardization across an expanded market) while also fearing that the elimination of loss-making firms would lead to a desperate struggle among the survivors. A further concern that they urged their readers to consider related to the moral problems associated with rationalization. By concentrating production in particular factories, and increasing the scale of economic activity, was there not a possibility that rationalization would actually impose a governmental structure on large sections of the British economy? No matter how modern or dynamic rationalization appeared, organization and control always remained the responsibility of fallible human beings. The postwar potential for technical and administrative error was as great under rationalization as, say, during Britain's economic development in the nineteenth century, yet the sheer scale of the rationalized system meant that the effects of all managerial decisions were magnified. Under such circumstances, any managerial miscalculation had the potential to affect the destiny of a great many people.

Romanticized Public Impressions of Protectionism

Finally, we should note that economists' views about impediments to Britain's necessary transformation were also located in their discussions of public demands for protectionism and economic autarky. Such discussions inevitably found their way into the popular economic literature of the period. As the wave of protectionism swept across interwar Europe, Britain economists were unfaltering in their commitment to an economic doctrine that had dominated British commercial policy since the mid-nineteenth century. The period's economic literature certainly shows economists engaging with the debate over international free trade and protectionism (Beveridge 1931d; Gregory 1923a, 1923b; Keynes 1923a, 1923b). The only firm economic support for a tariff (in this instance a "revenue tariff") emerged when, in the spring of 1931, a quarrel within the Economic Advisory Council overflowed into the national press (Daniels and Gregory 1931; Keynes 1931; Robbins 1931).

Elements of the popular economic debate attacking protectionism focused on several issues, including the more obvious technical and administrative issues, the complexities surrounding the politically sensitive policy of "dumping," and probable dangers arising from disruptions to resource supplies and the increased cost of essential raw materials (Beveridge 1932; Cox 1931a; Jones 1927a). Another aspect concerned criticisms of press support for the political and economic consolidation of the Empire (such as Lord Rothermere and Lord Beaverbrook's Empire Crusade Campaign), and the dismissal of such ideas as nothing more than an overromanticized interpretation of Britain's imperial history that ignored established commitments and, more importantly, administrative difficulties (Beveridge and Hicks 1931; Cox 1931a; Gregory 1930a; Hirst 1926, 1931; Hobson 1929). For many economists, the romanticized impression of economic prosperity secured under cover of the British flag, or by the return to some kind of Garden of Eden, was seen as a dangerous absurdity that either promoted unrealistic expectations of the future direction of the economy or impeded the important process of economic adjustment. A reinvigorated spirit of enterprise, it was argued, did not reside with proposals whose basic impact would be to (1) call into question the moral and material aspects of Britain's allegiance to internationalism, and (2) distract attention and resources from the necessary redevelopment of Britain's industrial and commercial structure (Beveridge and Hicks 1931; Cole 1930; Cox 1926b; Gregory 1931; Hobson 1931; Shadwell 1930). It was deemed essential that Britain did nothing to promote forces that would prevent producers and manufacturers from enjoying the advantages of international trade.

The Public Role of Economists

This essay has focused on the role that popular economic literature played in defining British interwar economists as public intellectuals, and the objectives that these economists sought to achieve within the public sphere. As David Macgregor (1934) observed, economists present their ideas in "un-rationalized competition" with one another. Yet a discernible feature of the popular economic literature of the interwar period is the strength of the collective attitude and responsibilities that these writers adopted toward the "public." These public writings do not show writers seeking to popularize economic ideas for their own sake; rather, such writings illustrate the existence of a commitment to observing economic activity, commenting on policy decisions, and, where necessary, trying to influence public sentiment. As I discuss below, the issue of observing and influencing public sentiment related to understanding problems within the postwar economy and, where necessary, defending the reputation of formal economic discourse from assault by a confused and misguided public. Through their popular writings, we see economists acting as observers, commentators, and persuaders.

It is important to appreciate that the production of such popular economic material occurred within a different environment, and proceeded through different stages of scrutiny and refinement, than pieces intended for an academic audience. The necessity of remaining intelligible to a nonacademic audience required economists to simplify problems, condense topics, and express ideas in as lucid a style as possible. Even a brief survey of this popular material demonstrates that British economists adopted a patient tone and sought to express their views and critiques through unashamedly bold, clear literary strokes. Humor was one element of this presentation, and the substance of ideas was occasionally hidden behind sparkling, whimsical passages. Yet this method was employed with caution: humorous asides were intended to explain events, advance an idea, and possibly sweeten a bitter pill.

One element of the activities of the publicly engaged economist involved identifying economic dynamics and trends. These reflected the themes of postwar economic life, whether associated with the ebb and flow of the cycle or, as later realized, dramatic structural transformation. While there are clear differences in the interpretations offered by individual writers, it is nonetheless possible to identify a coherent approach within the popular economic literature of both the early postwar period and from the mid-1920s onward. This involved the issue of forces—whether they were impediments to the trade cycle or impediments to a necessary process of industrial change—that were preventing the smooth functioning of economic activity. In both sets of material, we see a collective sense of purpose based around the efforts of economists to use their public writings to identify problems and, where necessary, enlighten and educate their readership in hopes of facilitating socially beneficial results. A significant change in emphasis is discernible between the early postwar and later postwar literature. As already mentioned, in the early postwar writings, the collective focus was on identifying, and trying to deal with, temporary impediments to the cycle; from the mid-1920s onward, the focus became one of eradicating physical and psychological factors that were identified as undermining, or having the potential to undermine, the necessary and speedy restructuring of Britain's postwar economy. One identifiable feature of this shift in interpretation was the greater attention that economists paid in their popular writings to engaging with public understanding of economic processes. It need hardly be said that economists do not hold a monopoly on the production of economic knowledge: economic issues are part of a perpetual human conversation ("economic talk") that is discussed throughout society (Ruccio and Amariglio 2003, 252). This general attention given to economic phenomena in everyday discourse was famously recognized by Joseph Schumpeter (1954, 38) and the distinction he drew between "economic thought" and "economic analysis":

> Economic Thought . . . is the sum total of all the opinions and desires concerning economic subjects, especially concerning public policy bearing upon these subjects that, at any given time and place, float in the public mind.

Faced with the economic uncertainty of the interwar period, British economists from the mid-1920s onward brought the public to the fore of their public discussions. They came to regard the "opinions and desires" of the public as worthy of both investigation and engagement. Their responses, conducted through the public economic literature of the period, were an attempt to make the public appreciate and accept the necessary economic developments taking place. This focus on seeking to understand the public mind led economists to identify fears and concerns that, they believed, had emerged within the postwar nation. For example, they identified a public eager to cling to the hope that Britain's future prosperity could still reside with the established (prewar) economic order (and hence unable to appreciate the necessity for postwar change); a public that required guidance in order that it did not fall prey to overly pessimistic sentiments; and an uncritical public that seized on the ideas of rationalization without appreciating its potential limitations and consequences. Clear differences within these interpretations can, of course, be identified. For example, we see economists occasionally critical of their readership (as in the case of Clay, who viewed large sections of the public as guilty of superstitious thinking), while others viewed the public as simply refusing to come to terms with necessary structural changes that were taking place or suffering from some an irresistible urge to draw erroneous conclusions from prewar and postwar statistical comparisons. Nonetheless, the public engagement of economists from the mid-1920s clearly centered on an attempt to publicize the superiority of economic discourse as a way to combat what were seen as the spurious ideas and potentially ill-advised proposals that festered within the public consciousness.

It was also noted above that many British economists identified a public prepared to offer uncritical acceptance of overromanticized impressions of imperial unity or protectionism. On first inspection, this argument leads directly to the points raised above, that is, economists saw their role as providing an intellectual barrier against political and economic flummery that could impede the necessary transformation of Britain's economic structure. Yet it may also be argued that, within their public pronouncements about the long-term, malevolent effects of protectionism, economists were seeking to address another issue. The issue here was the intellectual prestige and reputation of economic thought.

The doctrine of free trade held primacy over the public pronouncements of economists because of its position as the pillar of modern economic thought (such issues relate back to the triumph of the abstract-deductive approach over the historical school in the late nineteenth and early twentieth centuries). By refining Adam Smith's principles, and establishing the relationship between production, distribution, and free trade, David Ricardo had successfully placed the theory of international trade at the pinnacle of Anglo-Saxon economic theory. All proposals for long-term protectionism during the late nineteenth and early twentieth centuries had repeatedly been destroyed by the force of comparative advantage. Yet repeated calls within interwar "economic talk" to revoke the policy of free international trade, thereby facilitating a descent into the murky pool of protectionism, raised the possibility of weakening the intellectual power of modern economics and, by extension, the authority of economists. This concern was openly expressed by Daniels (1936), who feared that the advent, and potential dominance, of protectionism would undermine the lasting reputation of economics as an academic discipline by leading the public to simply dismiss the practical application of much of economic theory on the grounds that the subject possessed validity only as long as particular economic conditions prevailed.

From the perspective of the publicly engaged economist during the interwar period, the support for protectionism that existed as part of the perpetual "economic talk" within society raised two important issues. The first of these, as already mentioned, was the dangerous potential of the policy to obstruct Britain's economic regeneration. The second was the potential that protectionism had for undermining the intellectual standing of the established body of economic theory. While economists were prepared to use economic history to understand the dramatic changes taking place within postwar society, they were not prepared to allow these changes to undermine a central tenet of economic theory. Free international trade was therefore a clear intellectual principle that economists had to cling to, and which they promoted in their popular economic writings, in an effort to survive the intellectual storm that engulfed them.

Conclusion

This essay has been intended as an initial step toward filling a gap within the historiography, and reasons of space have necessitated the adoption of a somewhat limited and selective approach. Indeed, any investigation into the popular writings of interwar British economists forces the historian to appreciate the frailty, novelty, and, most importantly, sheer extent of such material.

The opening questions of this essay centered on understanding the public role that British interwar economists saw themselves as performing and the use of their popular economic writings in assisting our understanding of their status as "public intellectuals." Set against a backdrop of persistent unemployment, the popular economic material of the interwar period clearly captures much of the energy and immediacy of contemporary economic forces. The public role that economists adopted through this material was neither intellectually nor emotionally vacuous, and an affinity with the events, problems, and injustices of the period is often palpable. The public activities of these writers possessed a powerful purpose built around their combined roles of observers, commentators, and persuaders. Put simply, the engagement of these economists as public intellectuals revolved around the complex, social psychological process of persuasion. Although outwardly reflecting a simple transfer of information from the economist (the "orator") to the "public" (the "hearer") (Harré 1985, 127), an examination of the popular economic literature of the period illustrates the deeper assumptions that motivated such activity. These assumptions involved the belief of economists in regard to their ability to influence the thoughts and actions of their readers, with such changes intended to secure definite, and necessary, social benefits. This collective purpose acquired a greater sense of urgency as the problems of the period continued, with popular writings coming to also embody a need to defend the central principles of economic theory from attack.

It is appropriate at this stage to offer some brief comments on the relationship between the study of both popular economic literature and popular economic opinion ("economic talk") and the history of economics. Let me begin with the obvious issues: popular economic literature does not provide any significant contributions to economic theory, and "economic talk" can be regarded as nothing more than half-baked, pseudo-economic ideas constructed without proper theoretical foundations. In both of these cases, clear deficiencies immediately suggest that there is little reason for further investigation as part of any serious research program built around exploring the internal consistency and logical construction of economic theories. Yet, as discussed above, it is impossible to ignore the fact that "economic talk" is a constant element of human existence taking place outside the official discipline of economics. It was this fact that many interwar economists appreciated, and sought to engage with, in their popular writings. The popular writings of economists are therefore important social documents, presented in non-technical language, that reflected the thoughts and observations of their authors on contemporary issues. Put simply, the publicly engaged economist during the interwar period—the economist operating as a public intellectual—recognized, and responded to, the fact that economics was not the preserve of economists. An appreciation of the relationship between "economic talk" and the role of publicly engaged economists suggests clear possibilities for new avenues of investigation into the history of economic thought.

Appendix 1
Dramatis Personae

The following list has been constructed from the *Times* obituary index, the *Manchester Guardian* obituary index, and the biographical appendixes to Middleton 1998, Moggridge 1992, and Skidelsky 1992.

Acworth, William Mitchell (later Sir William) (1850–1925): Leading authority on railway economics; member, Board of Trade Committee on Railway Accounts and Statistics (1906); chairman, Committee on Indian Railway Policy and Administration (1920–21).

Beveridge, William Henry (later Lord Beveridge) (1897–1963): Economist, social reformer, and administrator; director of Labour Exchanges (1909–16); minister of Munitions and Food (1915–18); director, LSE (1919–37); Liberal member of Parliament (1944–45).

Bowley, Arthur Lyon (later Sir Arthur) (1869–1957): Economist and statistician; professor of economics and mathematics, University College, Reading (1907–13); professor of statistics, London University (1919–36); director, Oxford University Institute of Statistics (1940–44).

Cannan, Edwin (1861–1935): Economist; lecturer in economics, LSE (1897–1907); professor of political economy, LSE (1907–26).

Chapman, Sydney John (later Sir Sydney) (1871–1951): Economist and civil servant; Stanley Jevons Professor of Political Economy, Manchester University (1901–18); permanent secretary, Board of Trade (1919–27); chief economic adviser, H.M. Government (1927–32); vice chairman, Central Price Regulation Committee (1940).

Clay, Henry (later Sir Henry) (1883–1954): Economist; lecturer in economics to the Workers' Educational Tutorial Classes (1909–17); Jevons Professor of Political Economy, Manchester University (1922–27); professor of social economics, Manchester University (1927–30); economic adviser to the Governors of the Bank of England (1930–44); economic adviser, Board of Trade (1941–44).

Cole, George Douglas Howard (1889–1959): Socialist political theorist, writer on economic and social questions; reader in economics, Oxford University (1925–44); Chichele Professor of Social and Political Theory, Oxford University (1944–57); coauthor of detective novels and short stories with his wife, Margaret Isabel Cole.

Cox, Harold (1859–1936): Economist and journalist; Cobdenite free trader, staunch adherent of the orthodox school of economics, and energetic denouncer of the evils of bureaucracy; secretary of the Cobden Club (1899–1904); Liberal member of Parliament (1906–9); editor, *Edinburgh Review* (1912–29).

Dalton, (Edward) Hugh John Neale (later Lord Dalton) (1887–1962): Economist and Labour politician; lecturer in economics, LSE (1919–25); Cassel Reader in Commerce, LSE (1925–36); chancellor of the exchequer (1945–47).

Daniels, George William (1878–1937): Economist; reader in administration, Manchester University (1920–21); professor of commerce, Manchester University (1921–27); Stanley Jevons Professor of Political Economy, Manchester University (1927–37).

Gregory, Theodor Emanuel Gugenheim (later Sir Theodore) (1890–1970): Economist; assistant lecturer in economics, LSE (1913–19); Cassel Professor of Economics, LSE (1927–37); professor of social economics, Manchester University (1930–32); member, Irish Free State Banking Commission (1934–37); economic adviser, government of India (1938–46).

Henderson, Hubert Douglas (later Sir Hubert) (1890–1952): Economist and journalist; lecturer in economics, Cambridge (1919–23); editor, *Nation and Athenaeum* (1923–30); joint secretary, Economics Advisory Council (1930–34); economic adviser, H.M. Treasury (1939–44); Drummond Professor of Political Economy, Oxford (1945–51).

Hilton, John (1880–1943): Civil servant and industry commentator; journalist, *Yorkshire Post* (1911–21); assistant secretary (later director of statistics), Ministry of Labour (1919–31); Montague Burton Professor of Industrial Relations, Cambridge University (1931–43); director of home publicity, Ministry of Information (1939–40).

Hirst, Francis Wrigley (1873–1953): Writer on economic and political affairs, and disciple of the school of Mill, Cobden, and Gladstone; lecturer in political science, LSE (1897–1900); editor of the *Economist* (1907–16); editor of *Common Sense* (1916–21); married Helena Cobden, grand-niece of Richard Cobden.

Hobson, John Atkinson (1858–1940): Economic heretic, sociologist, journalist, and imperial critic.

Jones, John Harry (1881–1973): Economist; assistant lecturer in economics, Liverpool University (1907–9); lecturer in economics, Glasgow University (1909–13); professor of economics, Leeds University (1919–46); chairman, Nova Scotia Royal Commission of Economic Enquiry (1934).

Keynes, John Maynard (later Lord Keynes) (1883–1946): Economist, civil servant, and journalist; civil servant, India Office (1906–8); editor, *Economic Journal* (1912–45); economic adviser, H.M. Treasury (1915–19); chairman, *Nation and Athenaeum* (1923–31); chairman, *New Statesman and Nation* (1931–46); economic adviser, H.M. Treasury (1940–46).

Kirkaldy, Adam (1867–1931): Economist; professor of finance, Birmingham University (1906–18); subcommissioner for trade exemption (West Midlands), Ministry of National Service (1918–19); professor of economics and commerce, University College, Nottingham (1919–31).

Macgregor, David Hutchinson (1877–1953): Economist; professor of political economy, Leeds University (1908–19); Stanley Jevons Professor of Political Economy, Manchester University (1919–22); Drummond Professor of Political Economy, Oxford University (1922–45); assistant editor, *Economic Journal* (1925–37).

Robertson, Dennis Holme (later Sir Dennis) (1890–1963): Economist; lecturer in economics, Cambridge University (1924–28); Girdlers' Lecturer, Cambridge University (1928–30); reader in economics, Cambridge University (1930–38); Cassel Professor of Money and Banking, LSE (1938–44); professor of political economy, Cambridge University (1944–57).

Sargant Florence, Philip (1890–1982): Economist; lecturer in economics, Cambridge University (1921–29); professor of commerce, Birmingham University (1929–55).

Scott, William Robert (1868–1940): Economist and economic historian; lecturer in political economy, St Andrews University (1899–1915); Adam Smith Professor of Political Economy, Glasgow University (1915–40).

Shadwell, Arthur (1854–1936): Commentator on socioeconomic, industrial, and public health issues; special correspondent on Russian and German cholera epidemic, the *Times* (1892); labor correspondent, the *Times* (1908–28); editor, the *Democrat* (1922–23).

Stamp, Josiah Charles (later Lord Stamp) (1880–1941): Statistician, business administrator, public servant, and recognized expert on British taxation system; assistant secretary, Board of Inland Revenue (1916–19); director, Bank of England (1928–41); chairman, Survey of Financial and Economic Plans (1939–41).

References

Acworth, W. M. 1919a. "The Position and Prospects of the Railways." *Contemporary Review* 116:504–10.
———. 1919b. "Transport Reconstruction." *Edinburgh Review* 229:19–38.
———. 1920. Letter—Railway Congestion. *Times*, January 2.
———. 1921. Letter—Cheaper Postage. *Times*, November 8.
———. 1922. Letter—Road Transport. *Times*, February 10.
Backhouse, Roger E. 2008. "Faith, Morality, and Welfare: The English School of Welfare Economics, 1901–29." In *Keeping Faith, Losing Faith: Religious Belief*

and Political Economy, edited by Bradley Bateman and H. Spencer Banzhaf. *HOPE* 40 (supplement): 212–36.
Best, Gary Dean. 2007. *Peddling Panaceas: Popular Economists in the New Deal Era*. New Brunswick, N.J.: Transaction.
Beveridge, W. H. 1924. "International Trade and Unemployment." In *Unemployment in Its National and International Aspect*, 7–11. Geneva: International Labour Office.
———. 1931a. "Diagnosing the Disease of Unemployment." *Listener* 5:835–36.
———. 1931b. "Is Dear Labour a Cause of Unemployment?" *Listener* 5:931–32.
———. 1931c. "Social Malingering." *Listener* 5:1014–16.
———, ed. 1931d. *Tariffs: The Case Examined*. London: Longmans, Green.
———. 1932. Letter—Tariff Revenues. *Times*, March 26.
Beveridge, W., and J. R. Hicks. 1931. "The Possibilities of Imperial Preference." In *Tariffs: The Case Examined*, edited by W. H. Beveridge, 135–47. London: Longmans, Green.
Bowley, A. L. 1929. "The Numerical Importance of Foreign Trade." *Economist*, February 9, 277–78.
Cannan, E. (1915) 1997. "Strategic Jealousies Masked as Commercial." In *An Economist's Protest*, 26–28. London: Routledge/Theommes.
———. 1920. Letter—The Regulation of Wages. *Times*, October 20.
———. 1922. Review—"The Trade Cycle," by F. Lavington. *Economic Journal* 32:355–59.
———. 1930. "The Post-War Unemployment Problem." *Economic Journal* 40:45–55.
Chapman, S. J. 1918. "The State and Labour." In *After-War Problems*, edited by W. H. Dawson, 123–36. London: Allen and Unwin.
Clay, H. 1929. *The Post-War Unemployment Problem*. London: Macmillan.
———. 1931. "Irresponsibility in Economic Life." *Political Quarterly* 2:64–81.
———. 1932a. "The New Industrial Organisation." *Listener* 7:459–60.
———. 1932b. "What Is Rationalisation?" *Listener* 7:147–48.
Cole, G. D. H. 1915a. "The Meaning of the Trade Union Congress." *Nation and Athenaeum* 17:767–68.
———. 1915b. "Through Terror to Triumph?" *Nation and Athenaeum* 18:288–89.
———. 1921. "The Development of the Post Office." *New Statesman* 17:124–25.
———. 1924a. "The Future of Social Insurance." *New Statesman* 23:7–8.
———. 1924b. "The Need for Publicity." *New Statesman* 24:259–60.
———. 1925. "Bad Temper in Modern Industry." *New Statesman* 24:709–10.
———. 1926a. "A Challenge to British Capitalism." *New Statesman* 26:771–72.
———. 1926b. "Fordism." *New Statesman* 27:729–30.
———. 1927. "Economic Nationalism versus Common Sense." *New Statesman* 29:302–3.
———. 1928a. "The Mobility of Labour." *New Statesman* 31:319–20.
———. 1928b. "Need We Export More?" *New Statesman* 30:616.
———. 1928c. "Over-Capitalisation." *New Statesman* 31:281–82.
———. 1929a. "Rationalisation." *New Statesman* 34:152.
———. 1929b. "Where Stands the Industrial North?" *Listener* 1:106.

———. 1929c. "Work or Doles?" *New Statesman* 33:768–70.
———. 1930. "The Trades Union Congress on Empire Trade." *New Statesman* 35:401–2.
———. 1931. "Britain's Economic Future." *New Statesman and Nation* 2:216–17.
Cox, H. 1921a. "The New Protection." *Edinburgh Review* 233:387–408.
———. 1921b. "The Public Purse." *Edinburgh Review* 234:192–208.
———. 1926a. "England's Treasure by Trade." *Edinburgh Review* 243:385–401.
———. 1926b. "The Imperial Conference." *Edinburgh Review* 244:385–402.
———. 1927. "Franchise Reform." *Edinburgh Review* 246:194–202.
———. 1930. "Some Real Causes of the Slump." *Contemporary Review* 138:554–61.
———. 1931a. "The Drift towards Protection." *Contemporary Review* 139:416–23.
———. 1931b. "Our Financial Position and Prospects." *Contemporary Review* 140:9–15.
———. 1931c. "The Economy Report." *Contemporary Review* 140:284–92.
Cunningham, William. 1892. *Growth of English Industry and Commerce in Modern Times*. Cambridge: Cambridge University Press.
Dalton, H. 1923. "The Financial Situation." *Contemporary Review* 123:554–61.
Daniels, G. W. 1931a. "Overseas Trade of the United Kingdom in Recent Years as Compared with 1913." *Manchester School* 2:1–9.
———. 1931b. "The Present Economic Situation." *Manchester School* 2:65–76.
———. 1936. "Economic Theory and National Policy." *Manchester School* 7:91–104.
Daniels, G. W., and T. E. Gregory. 1931. Letter—a Revenue Tariff. *New Statesman and Nation* 1:103.
Daunton, M., and F. Trentmann. 2004. *Worlds of Political Economy: Knowledge and Power in the Nineteenth and Twentieth Centuries*. Basingstoke: Palgrave.
Ely, R. T. 1903. *Studies in the Evolution of Industrial Society*. London: Macmillan.
Fetter, F. W. 1962. "Economic Articles in the Westminster Review and Their Authors, 1824–51." *Journal of Political Economy* 70:570–96.
———. 1965. "Economic Controversy in the British Reviews, 1802–1850." *Economica* 32:424–37.
Fourcade, M. 2009. *Economists and Societies: Discipline and Profession in the United States, Britain, and France, 1890s to 1990s*. Princeton: Princeton University Press.
Giffen, R. 1900. "Our Trade Prosperity and the Outlook." *Economic Journal* 10:295–307.
Gregory, T. E. 1923a. "Free Trade: Facts and Figures—I." *Nation and Athenaeum* 34:307–8.
———. 1923b. "Free Trade: Facts and Figures—II." *Nation and Athenaeum* 34:339–40.
———. 1930a. "Empire Free Trade." *Political Quarterly* 1:231–47.
———. 1930b. "Rationalisation and Technological Unemployment." *Economic Journal* 40:551–67.
———. 1931. "Economic Nationalism." *International Affairs* 10:289–306.
Harré, R. 1985. "Persuasion and Manipulation." In *Discourse and Communication: New Approaches to the Analysis of Mass Media Discourse and Communication*, edited by T. A. van Dijk, 126–42. Berlin: Walter de Gruyter.

Henderson, H. D. (1923) 1955. "Monetary Policy." In *The Inter-War Years and Other Papers*, edited by H. Clay, 5–8. Oxford: Clarendon.
———. (1926) 1955a. "The Economic Trend." In *The Inter-War Years and Other Papers*, edited by H. Clay, 23–27. Oxford: Clarendon.
———. (1926) 1955b. "The New Industrial Revolution." In *The Inter-War Years and Other Papers*, edited by H. Clay, 28–32. Oxford: Clarendon.
———. (1930) 1955a. "The Development of New Industries." In *The Inter-War Years and Other Papers*, edited by H. Clay, 61–65. Oxford: Clarendon.
———. (1930) 1955b. "The Present Unemployment." In *The Inter-War Years and Other Papers*, edited by H. Clay, 56–60. Oxford: Clarendon.
Hilton, J. 1934a. "Are the Unemployment Figures Accurate?" *Listener* 12:823.
———. 1934b. "Hands and Machines." *Listener* 11:323–26.
———. 1934c. "Putting Industry's House in Order." *Listener* 11:449–51.
———. 1934d. "What Is the Future of British Industry?" *Listener* 11:622–23.
Hirst, F. W. 1924. Letter—Official Expenditure. *Times*, February 16.
———. 1926. "Mr. Churchill's Second Budget." *Contemporary Review* 129:693–704.
———. 1931. "An Emergency Budget." *Contemporary Review* 139:681–87.
Hobson, J. A. 1894. *The Evolution of Modern Capitalism: A Study of Machine Production*. London: Walter Scott.
———. 1916a. *Labour and the Costs of War*. London: Union of Democratic Control.
———. 1916b. "The War and British Liberties—IV: Liberty as a True War Economy." *Nation and Athenaeum* 19:524–25.
———. 1924. *The Economics of Unemployment*. London: Allen and Unwin.
———. 1929. "The United States of Europe." *Contemporary Review* 136:545–52.
———. 1930. Review—"The Post-War Unemployment Problem," by Henry Clay. *Political Quarterly* 1:135–38.
———. 1931. "A World Economy." *New Statesman and Nation* 1:274–75.
———. 1932. Review—"The Social Aspects of Rationalisation," by I. L. O. *Political Quarterly* 3:457–60.
Jones, J. H. 1924. "The Future of British Industry." In *Is Unemployment Inevitable? An Analysis and Forecast,* edited by J. J. Astor et al., 186–204. London: Macmillan.
———. 1925. "Remedies for Unemployment." *Accountant* 73:84–85.
———. 1926. "What of the Future?" *Accountant* 75:855–57.
———. 1927a. "Dumping—I." *Accountant* 77:220–22.
———. 1927b. "The Future of Industry." *Accountant* 76:835–36.
———. 1927c. "Unemployment." *Accountant* 77:189–91.
———. 1930. "Changes in World Demand." *Accountant* 83:731–33.
———. 1935a. "Geographic Trends in Industry." *Accountant* 92:218–20.
———. 1935b. "Some Aspects of Industrial Change." *Accountant* 92:75–77.
———. 1936. "Industry and the Seasons." *Accountant* 95:182–85.
———. 1937a. "Expanding Industries." *Accountant* 96:115–16.
———. 1937b. "Government Statistics." *Accountant* 97:580–82.
———. 1937c. "Speed in Industry." *Accountant* 96:574–76.
———. 1938a. "Leadership and Industrial Development." *Accountant* 99:69–70.
———. 1938b. "Luxury and Leisure." *Accountant* 98:31–33.

Kadish, A., and Tribe, K. 1993. *The Market for Political Economy: The Advent of Economics in British University Culture, 1850–1905.* London: Routledge.

Keynes, J. M. 1921a. "The Depression in Trade." In *Treaty Revision and Reconstruction*, vol. 27 of *The Collected Writings of John Maynard Keynes*, 259–65. London: Macmillan.

———. 1921b. "The Earnings of Labour." In *Treaty Revision and Reconstruction*, vol. 27 of *The Collected Writings of John Maynard Keynes*, 265–72. London: Macmillan.

———. 1923a. "Free Trade—I." *Nation and Athenaeum* 34:302–3.

———. 1923b. "Free Trade—II." *Nation and Athenaeum* 34:335–37.

———. 1926. "The Position of the Lancashire Cotton Trade." *Nation and Athenaeum* 40:209–10.

———. 1931. "Proposals for a Revenue Tariff." *New Statesman and Nation* 1:53–54.

Macgregor, D. H. 1911. *Evolution of Industry.* London: William & Norgate.

———. 1934. *Enterprise, Purpose, and Profit.* Oxford: Clarendon.

Marshall, A. 1916. Letter—The Need for More Taxation. *Economist*, December 30, 1228.

———. 1917. "National Taxation after the War." In *After-War Problems*, edited by W. H. Dawson, 313–45. London: Allen and Unwin.

Middleton, R. 1998. *Charlatans or Saviours? Economists and the British Economy from Marshall to Meade.* Cheltenham, UK: Edward Elgar.

Moggridge, D. E. 1992. *Maynard Keynes: An Economist's Biography.* London: Routledge.

Pigou, A. C. 1916a. Letter—The Need for More Taxation. *Economist*, November 25, 1003–4.

———. 1916b. Letter—The Need for More Taxation. *Economist*, December 9, 1087.

———. 1916c. Letter—The Need for More Taxation. *Economist*, December 23, 1180–81.

———. 1917. Letter—The Income Tax. *Times*, April 23.

———. 1918. "A Plea for Higher Income-Tax." *Contemporary Review* 113:35–39.

———. 1919. Letter—War Fortunes. *Times*, October 27.

———. 1922. Letter—The Burden of Income Tax. *Times*, January 11.

———. 1923. Letter—Capital Levy. *Times*, May 1.

———. 1924. "Correctives of the Trade Cycle." In *Is Unemployment Inevitable? An Analysis and Forecast*, edited by J. J. Astor et al., 91–131. London: Macmillan.

Robbins, L. 1931. "A Reply to Mr Keynes." *New Statesman and Nation* 1:98–100.

Robertson, D. H. 1931a. "The Backwash of Progress." *Listener* 6:870–71.

———. 1931b. "Our Unstable Economic Progress." *Listener* 6:908–9.

Ruccio, D. F. 2008. *Economic Representations: Academic and Everyday.* London: Routledge.

Ruccio, D. F., and J. Amariglio. 2003. *Postmodern Moments in Modern Economics.* Princeton: Princeton University Press.

Sargant Florence, P. 1930a. Review—"The Next Ten Years," by G. D. H. Cole. *Political Quarterly* 1:297–302.

———. 1930b. "The Science of Industrial Relations." *Listener* 5:555.
———. 1930c. "Rationalisation and the Public." *Listener* 4:706.
Schumpeter, J. 1954. *History of Economic Analysis*. New York: Oxford University Press.
Scott, W. R. 1915. "Economics of Peace in Time of War." In *Credit, Industry, and the War*, edited by A. W. Kirkaldy, 1–16. London: Isaac Pitman.
Shadwell, A. 1929. "Rationalisation." *Edinburgh Review* 250:290–307.
———. 1930. Letter—Unemployment. *Times*, August 27.
Skidelsky, R. 1992. *John Maynard Keynes: The Economist as Saviour, 1920–1937*. London: Macmillan.
Stamp, J. C. 1923. Letter—Adjusting Wages by Prices. *Times*, January 18.
———. 1930. "The Management of Industry." *Listener* 4:789–90.

Inside Out: Keynes's Use of the Public Sphere

Roger E. Backhouse and Bradley W. Bateman

It is well known that John Maynard Keynes, perhaps the most closely studied economist of the twentieth century, was a prominent public figure who wrote not only books that sold in large numbers but also numerous articles for newspapers, political and intellectual magazines, government reports, and radio and newsreel broadcasts. The familiarity of his face to the general public probably makes him the most prominent economist in British public life since John Stuart Mill. His activities have been documented in the *Collected Writings of John Maynard Keynes* (1971–89) and analyzed meticulously in three major biographies (Harrod 1951; Moggridge 1992; Skidelsky 1983, 1992, 2000, 2003) and innumerable other works. Given this, our aim is to reexamine certain episodes in his journalistic career, arguing that they establish an involvement in the public sphere that was very different from that of virtually any other economist in the twentieth century.

Historians have routinely explained the immense influence of the *General Theory* by pointing out that Keynes was an insider who could not be ignored. A member of King's College, Cambridge, taught and given his first teaching position by Alfred Marshall, and a high-ranking official in the Treasury, he was at the heart of the establishment. Yet Keynes pre-

---

Correspondence may be addressed to Roger E. Backhouse, University of Birmingham, Edgbaston, Birmingham B15 2TT, UK (e-mail: reb@bhouse.org.uk); and to Bradley W. Bateman, President's Office, Randolph College, 2500 Rivermont Avenue, Lynchburg, VA 24503.

History of Political Economy 45 (annual suppl.)   DOI 10.1215/00182702-2310953
Copyright 2013 by Duke University Press

sented himself as an outsider, as a Cassandra whose voice was unwelcome, attacking the citadel of economic orthodoxy. This fitted with his position as a member of the Bloomsbury Group, whose members saw themselves as unconventional critics of the establishment. Virginia Woolf is perhaps most well known among the members of the group for having explored the boundaries of being an outsider to conventional British society, despite her social position.[1]

Our contention is that although Keynes, as we explain in the next section, also used the inside-outside distinction, he used it in a different way. Moreover, the standard formulation of the distinction does not take us very far in understanding the relationship between his roles in the public sphere, in academe, and in government. The complexity of his position, which differentiates him from virtually all other twentieth-century economists, is that he was not merely a contributor to public debate looking for media through which his voice might be heard; he instead went a step further and sought to *control* the media through which he presented his ideas to the public and his fellow economists.[2] His authority stemmed as much from his activities in the public sphere as from his position in academe, if not more so, raising the question of how his different activities interacted with each other.[3]

The starting point is, as virtually all historians and biographers recognize, his *Economic Consequences of the Peace* (1919; JMK 2).[4] Keynes

---

1. See, for instance, her essay "Am I a Snob?," originally read to the Memoir Club on December 1, 1936, and now reprinted in Woolf 1985.

2. As Chris Godden has pointed out to us, Keynes's appearances on the radio may present a somewhat different picture, since these occurred almost exclusively on the BBC where Keynes had virtually *no* control over the medium and would have needed an invitation to make a presentation. Keynes gave twenty-one radio broadcasts, of which fifteen were published at the time in the BBC's house magazine, the *Listener*, and two were published in the *Nation and Athenaeum*. The transcripts of all twenty-one broadcasts were published in the relevant volumes of Keynes's *Collected Works* and have recently been published together in Keynes 2010.

3. Craufurd Goodwin has pointed out to us that Keynes's work as a public intellectual very much reflected his membership in the Bloomsbury Group, where there was some discomfort with traditional academic roles linked to a desire to change the world.

4. Many of our citations are to volumes in Keynes's *Collected Writings* (Keynes 1971–89), a thirty-volume collection edited by D. E. Moggridge. We cite items from the *Collected Writings* as JMK, followed by the volume and page numbers. The volumes we cite from are as follows: vol. 1, *Indian Currency and Finance*; vol. 2, *Economic Consequences of the Peace*; vol. 3, *A Revision of the Treaty*; vol. 4, *A Tract on Monetary Reform*; vol. 5, *A Treatise on Money*: vol. 1, *The Pure Theory of Money*; vol. 6, *A Treatise on Money*: vol. 2, *The Applied Theory of Money*; vol. 7, *The General Theory of Employment, Interest, and Money*; vol. 9, *Essays in Persuasion*; vol. 17, *Activities, 1920–1922: Treaty Revision and Reconstruction*; vol. 18, *Activities, 1922–1932: The End of Reparations*; and vol. 30, *Bibliography and Index*.

wrote this book because he had an important message. This message was based on economic reasoning, but it was as much political as economic. His authority was that of an insider to the Versailles negotiations—an insider to the extent that the propriety of his publishing an account of the negotiations and the personalities involved could be questioned. He was so confident of the audience for his ideas that he was not satisfied with the production run proposed by his publisher, Macmillan. This prompted him to negotiate an arrangement whereby Macmillan would act as his agent and he would bear the risk himself, thereby giving him control over the price of the book and the size of the print run that authors rarely possess. The arrangement was an immense success, and his subsequent books were published on the same basis. It laid the foundation for a career in which his journalism provided his main source of income, his commitments to Cambridge being kept to a minimum (acting as bursar for King's and giving a single series of eight lectures each year). His reliance on income from writing is part of the story, told by D. E. Moggridge (2006), of Keynes's attitude to his own intellectual property, which can be linked to his attitude to the revolution he sought to foment (Backhouse and Bateman 2010). Moggridge also makes the important point that Keynes was highly attuned to the scope for selling foreign rights, both raising his income and establishing himself as an international figure. However, it is also part of another story about his engagements in the public sphere, for it not only established him as a celebrity, whose views were widely sought, but also laid the foundation for a career in which he bore editorial as well as authorial responsibility for many of his publications, achieving a possibly unique position in relation to the various spheres in which he operated.

We establish this point by bringing together, alongside the story of *The Economic Consequences of the Peace*, two episodes: his work on the reconstruction supplements published by the *Manchester Guardian Commercial* in 1922–23 and his role in the weekly magazine *Nation and Athenaeum*.[5] It is well known that articles published in these outlets formed the basis for several books and pamphlets, including *A Tract on Monetary Reform* (1923; JMK 4), *A Short View of Russia* (1925; JMK 9:253–71), and *Réflections sur le franc* (1928), but the point we want to make is that his position in the public sphere extended beyond this to his role as an editor and a manager. These episodes relate to the early 1920s, but, as we

---

5. The *Manchester Guardian Commercial* was a weekly commercial newspaper started by C. P. Scott and his sons in 1920.

hope to demonstrate, they establish a pattern for his public engagements that marked his work for the rest of his life.[6] There is a parallel here with his academic work, in that he was editor of the *Economic Journal* for over three decades, from 1911 to 1945. Without wishing to suggest that he abused his position as editor by favoring his own work and discussions of it, this gave him a degree of influence over the agenda for debate that those who merely contributed to these publications would not have had. This pattern also sheds a different light on how he presented his *General Theory of Employment, Interest, and Money* (1936; JMK 7). Thus we conclude the essay by reflecting on how his background as a journalist and the public style he developed in that work helped shape the trajectory of his three great works in monetary theory: *A Tract on Monetary Reform*, *A Treatise on Money*, and the *General Theory*.[7]

1. Reconstruction in Europe: The *Manchester Guardian Commercial* Supplements

By the autumn of 1921, Keynes had become a public figure, well known outside the smaller worlds of Cambridge, the India Office, and the Treasury, in which he had navigated during the second decade of the century.

---

6. One of our anonymous referees made the excellent suggestion that we point out that *The Economic Consequences of the Peace* marked an effort by Keynes to reproduce Lytton Strachey's success the previous year with *Eminent Victorians* (1918). The referee's point is, in part, that until the publication of Strachey's book, the members of Bloomsbury had not been able to find a way to successfully support themselves; thus, the success of *Eminent Victorians* showed them that pointed commentary that debunked "the great and the good" could provide commercial success. We have no doubt that the referee is correct that Keynes was deliberately working the same terrain that Strachey had worked in hopes of commercial success. But there are also differences between their situations. On the one hand, Keynes had already found some financial stability in his work for the government and his teaching at Cambridge, something that none of the other Bloomsburies had yet achieved. And while it is undoubtedly true that Keynes's writing for the rest of his life would be characterized by the kind of sharp character sketches and biting commentary in *The Economic Consequences of the Peace*, it is also true that, as we have already begun to explain, he was also able to achieve a degree of control over the publication of his work that other Bloomsburies would attain only much later in their careers, as, for instance, when Leonard and Virginia Woolf set up Hogarth Press.

7. A contrast can be drawn with one of Keynes's friends from Cambridge, Ralph Hawtrey. He served much of the interwar period as the Treasury's resident economist, influencing policy from the inside and influencing academic economists through his writing. He was an important figure at the Genoa conference, helping draft its resolutions and, despite common features in their thinking, was behind some of the policies against which Keynes fought. David Laidler (1999) places the ideas of both Hawtrey and Keynes in the context of interwar developments in monetary theory. We are grateful to Bob Dimand for reminding us of this point.

By this time he was, of course, already highly regarded within these circles, having served with distinction during the First World War, helping secure the regular flow of external funding needed to finance Britain's participation in the war. Likewise, he was already highly regarded within academic economics; he had started lecturing at Cambridge over a decade earlier; and he was the editor of the Royal Economic Society's journal, the *Economic Journal*. But it was *The Economic Consequences of the Peace* that had propelled him into the public eye. Neither his government work nor his distinction within economics had been enough to make him a public figure.

The Economic Consequences of the Peace was a best seller on both sides of the Atlantic. The British edition was reprinted six times in 1920 alone (despite Keynes having arranged for a larger print run than Macmillan thought appropriate), and editions were published in seventeen other countries. In 1920–21, the French edition was reprinted three times, and the German four times (JMK 30:31–32). It gave him a very high public profile not only as an economist but also as a commentator on international relations (see Markwell 2006). He can thus be seen as an insider—a member of the intellectual and ruling elites—who was gaining an audience with the public (the outside). But Keynes was developing his own version of the insider-outsider distinction with which he sought to explain not simply bridging the distance between the elites and the broader public but how the distance was bridged between circles within the elite—between the *most elite* inner circles and the more public, but nonetheless elite, discourse of politicians and journalists.[8] In other words, he was interested in how information such as he had acquired as an insider with access to the highest level of European leaders at Versailles could be made a part of political debate and middlebrow journalism.

This more subtle version of the insider-outsider distinction, thus, almost certainly reflected his own sense of what had happened with his publication of *The Economic Consequences of the Peace*. At Versailles, as a part of the negotiations, he had had access to one kind of insider information; what he had done with the publication of his book was to push that information out into the broader political debate in Britain, in the press and in Parliament. Of course, the book was available to anyone to read, especially to the mass public, but Keynes appears not to have been so con-

---

8. According to the editorial material in JMK 17, the first appearance of Keynes's version of the insider-outsider distinction was in *A Revision of the Treaty* (1922; JMK 3).

cerned with that part of his audience. In his reconstruction of the insider-outsider distinction, he was much more focused on the question of raising the level of elite debate and discussion by seeing that it was informed by what those privileged to the most inner circles were discussing.

The distinction that Keynes was making was not antithetical to the more broadly used distinction between insiders and outsiders, in which the outsiders were taken to be the broader public, but it did show where his own concerns lay and what he took to be the most important link in the dissemination of information: the middlebrow media, policymakers, and politicians.

His work on the *Manchester Guardian Commercial* reconstruction supplements placed Keynes in a new position along the spectrum of insiders and outsiders. He was no longer sitting at the epicenter of the elite world as he had at Versailles trying to send out information into the press and Parliament; now he was working from within the middlebrow media, hoping to influence those at the highest levels while better informing the broader public and political debate about what might be possible and desirable in reconstructing Europe. From the beginning, the negotiations for publishing the supplements reflected Keynes's own status as a figure with authority in other spheres. The idea of the reconstruction supplements came from *Manchester Guardian*'s legendary editor, C. P. Scott, then aged seventy-five and in his fiftieth year as the paper's editor.[9] Scott first approached Keynes about the supplements project in October 1921, traveling to Cambridge to persuade him to take on the task. At that time, Keynes was already involved in negotiations to travel to India to be vice chair of a royal commission that the government of India had asked be formed to examine tariffs, an assignment that drew on both his expertise on government work and his academic stature.[10] Initially, his obligations to be in India for several months for this assignment made it seem unlikely that he could take on the work that Scott proposed. He wrote back that he might be able to contribute to the project, but not in the central way that

9. For example, Woodrow Wilson considered Scott "one of Europe's great men" (Hargreaves 2002, 245).

10. Before approaching Keynes about editing the supplements, Scott had asked Keynes to travel to the United States as the special correspondent for the *Manchester Guardian* for a disarmament conference that was to take place in Washington, DC. Keynes declined the offer, telling Scott that several American newspapers had already offered the assignment (JMK 17:318–19). It is worth noting that the government of India was interested in Keynes's participation in the Royal Commission in order to help ensure that a strong voice for free trade was included in writing the final report (JMK 17:320).

Scott was proposing, as general editor. "In fact, I am not prepared for my name to appear in a way that implies responsibility unless I can really exercise pretty detailed supervision over the writers" (JMK 17:320, 332). Ultimately, Keynes withdrew from the royal commission on tariffs in India, and this ended any possibility for conflict with his work on the supplements.

From the beginning he was intimately involved in almost every aspect of the planning of the supplements, from questions of budgets and the decorative art to be used on the cover page to the efforts to get contributions from European heads of state. One of the most important questions to be faced, of course, was how to organize the supplements: what topics should be covered in the various issues? When the paper was first working to raise advertising revenue, before the contents of the various issues were known, Keynes wrote a rough prospectus for salesmen to carry with them on their visits to potential advertisers. The prospectus nicely captures the range of topics that Keynes was weighing for consideration.

> A difficult age of transition has so broken up our beloved routine that everyone is now inquisitive about the facts and tendencies which are to determine the future. The foreign exchanges, the trade cycle of boom and depression, the demand for labour, the sources of raw material, the rate of interest, the balance of trade between Europe and America are topics of general interest for the first time in history. What is the destiny of Russia? Is Germany bankrupt or is she favourably placed to capture the trade of the world? How will the Allies treat her? Are we to expect great changes in the localization of staple industries? What are the prospects of oil and coal? Will Manchester retain the markets of Asia? Can British iron and steel hold their own against cheap production in Europe? What, in fact, have the purses of the rich and the bellies of the poor to hope or to fear? (JMK 17:323)

Keynes also negotiated with Scott to purchase rights to the "business barometer" produced at the London School of Economics (LSE) as well as the Harvard barometer of business conditions. He wanted to produce authoritative assessments of the situation in Europe at a time before national governments produced statistics on income and unemployment, and the barometers represented what may have been the best available data.

Initially, Keynes planned to make the first number in the series be a survey of shipping in Europe. Soon, however, the logic of international events took over, and he decided to make the focus of the first number be the foreign exchanges. One reason for the topicality of the foreign exchanges was the instability in exchange rates that had resulted from the inflationary spirals into which many European countries had slipped. However, the event that triggered the change of plan was a conference on the reconstruction of Europe arranged at Genoa, scheduled to begin in April 1922. The conference was significant because it represented the first time since the Soviet revolution that Russia had been invited to a European conference and because Germany, marginalized in the peace treaty negotiated at Versailles, was invited to attend.[11] Brokered by the French and English premiers, the conference had been made possible only through a diplomatic agreement among all the European nations that nothing negotiated at the conference could change the terms of existing treaties, thus guaranteeing that the terms of reparations settled at Versailles could not be undone.

In this first issue, Keynes's editorial introduction was sandwiched between endorsements from the British prime minister, David Lloyd George, the prime minister of Czechoslovakia, and Italy's foreign minister. There followed two major articles by Keynes, one on "a plan for Genoa" and the other explaining the theory of exchange rates and purchasing power parity. After an article by a banker, Dudley Ward, on the London foreign exchange market (London was then central to the world financial system) came an even longer article by Keynes, on the forward market for foreign exchange. This was followed by articles on exchange rates and currency markets in the United States and many European countries, many written by experts from the countries concerned, a letter from a member of Parliament with an alternative proposal, the LSE and Harvard barometers, and statistics on economic conditions in other countries. Lighter fare was provided by a lavishly illustrated article, in which Keynes played a significant role, on European banknotes. The supplement justified Lloyd George's description of it as an "expert study of the most urgent question of the day."

Keynes's audience for the supplements, which were also published in French, German, and Italian, is made clear by the action taken when Keynes and Scott realized that the first number of the supplements would not appear until ten days after the conference opened. Because they were so keen to influence the negotiations, Scott agreed to publish Keynes's plan for stabilizing the exchanges as a solo article in the *Manchester*

---

11. The USSR was formed in December 1922.

Guardian a few days before the conference began. Keynes's sense of his own potential role in shaping the negotiations comes through quite clearly when he wrote Scott on March 27, 1922.

> I met the Chancellor of the Exchequer the day before yesterday, who showed a great deal of interest in the Supplements, particularly in the Exchange number. He is anxious to read my scheme for stabilization before he leaves for Genoa, and I have promised to let him see a proof. But I think he would also be glad to see an early copy of the whole number. Would it be possible to make up a copy of for him immediately the page proofs are available? I think it might be good policy for him to have a copy in his possession in plenty of time. (JMK 17:350–51)

Keynes's article on stabilizing the exchanges appeared on April 6 and the conference opened on April 10.

His sense that he might be able to influence the discussions at the highest level proved right. Keynes was in Genoa, reporting on the conference as a special correspondent for the *Manchester Guardian*, with his articles being published around the world under separate contracts that Keynes had worked out in agreement with Scott.[12] Five days after the conference began, Keynes wrote to Scott from Genoa in glowing terms.

> You will be interested to know that my *Manchester Guardian* articles on the exchanges have excited a good deal of interest here among the financial delegations. Soon after my arrival, I was summoned by the Chancellor of the Exchequer for a conference with him and the other official experts to consider whether the proposals of my first article ought to be formally laid before the Conference. In the end they decided adversely because of the weight of conservative opinion against Great Britain coming into any scheme, which is, I think, an intelligible but deplorable attitude. A few days later I was summoned to another conference by the Chancellor to consider whether the proposals in my third article should be adopted. This time the discussion ended favorably and I believe that the British delegation will bring forward a draft embodying my suggestions. (JMK 17:369)

Keynes was thus achieving his aim of bringing inside opinion to the world by sharing it through the middlebrow press and making it available for

---

12. His position as a special correspondent whose byline was being published around the globe just as the supplements were coming out raised both his profile and the profile of the supplements.

debate and discussion in broader political circles. But his articles were actually serving as a kind of two-way conduit: he was sending ideas into the most elite circles at the same time, and by the same media, as he was sending them out into broader circulation. Yet there was no guarantee that his ideas would have the influence that he hoped within the most influential circles.

Keynes never appears to have reflected on this Janus-faced role he played at Genoa. Thus we will perhaps never know exactly in which senses he saw himself as an insider *and* an outsider. But while it is easy to see his ego at play in the correspondence above, it is also possible to see a principled aspect to the way that he worked from the middle ground between the inside and the outside. In particular, as we show, his aim in widely disseminating ideas and making them available for broad discussion and debate reflected a deep commitment to the traditional liberal ideal that all sides of a debate needed to be heard and weighed in making a reasonable decision. In this sense, it was appropriate that he was writing in the *Manchester Guardian*, for it was a leading Liberal newspaper.[13] His liberal position reflected his upbringing and the policy ideas with which he was most widely identified at the time: advocacy of free trade and a return to the gold standard (albeit not at the prewar parity), for instance. His desire to have full and well-informed debate about issues and policies was the liberalism of John Stuart Mill and his own father, John Neville Keynes.

This traditional tolerance to difference of opinion and the desire that all sides be heard in debate was expressed by Scott in an article marking the *Manchester Guardian*'s centenary in 1921: "Comment is free but facts are sacred.... The voice of opponents no less than of friends has a right to be heard" (Ayerst 1971, 435).[14] It was well reflected in Keynes's editing of the supplements. Immediately upon accepting the terms of a contract with Scott, Keynes began to solicit contributions from every country and from people on the left and the right in each country, as well as from different views among academic economists. This proved easier in some cases than in others. In Germany, for instance, he wrote to the man with whom he had made an acquaintance at the Versailles negotiations, Carl Melchior (see JMK 9:389–432). Melchior was so happy to help that he sent Keynes a letter and a telegram indicating his willingness to write something as

---

13. See Ayerst 1971 and Hargreaves 2002 on the history of the paper.
14. For a more critical view of Scott's attitude toward facts, see Hargreaves 2002, 245.

well as to help line up other important government figures and economists to contribute. Melchior even declined payment for the work, saying that he was just happy to be able to help.

Things were considerably more complicated in France. Without much difficulty, Keynes obtained a commitment from his French translator, Paul Franck, to make a contribution. But when Franck, whose "connections veered toward the left," approached Jacques Bardoux, a lieutenant to President Raymond Poincaré, a leader of the political Right, to try to obtain an interview with Poincaré and help in gathering contributions from right-leaning economists, Bardoux became incensed when he learned that a left-leaning politician (who had advocated a policy of compromise with the Germans), Joseph Caillaux, and a left-leaning writer, Anatole France, had already been lined up as contributors. In fact, Bardoux was so upset, he traveled to Manchester to meet with Scott and object. Keynes then wrote directly to Bardoux to try to ameliorate the situation.

> I hope that many opinions, as well as many nationalities, will find in the forthcoming Numbers an opportunity of expression; and that out of this *ensemble* wisdom may emerge. Indeed our criterion is not the opinion of the authors, but their authoritative character, their technical competence, and their representative reputation. For the other European countries I have obtained contributors of the first eminence; and it would be a great misfortune if this was not true of France also. (JMK 17:343)[15]

Keynes's attempt to represent the full range of opinions in the supplements may strike some today as odd given the way that his own name has come to represent a particularly strong pole in ideological debate. But throughout his own career, Keynes advised British governments of all stripes, and while he had strong opinions, he tended to live well within the liberal ethic of allowing and encouraging other voices. His liberal values were clearly stated in the hopes for Europe that he expressed in his reporting from Genoa for the *Manchester Guardian*.

---

15. Keynes also pleaded again with Bardoux for help in getting some kind of statement from Poincaré himself, for there were complicated political problems in selling the supplements in France: because the French translations were being printed in Germany, Poincaré could easily refuse to allow them into the country under the terms of the Versailles treaty.

Many apprehend the issue of the near future as between the forces of Bolshevism and those of the bourgeois states of the nineteenth century type. I do not agree. The real struggle of today, just as in the second quarter of the nineteenth century, is between that view of the world, termed liberalism or radicalism, for which the primary object of government and of foreign policy is peace, freedom of trade and intercourse, and economic wealth, and that other view, militarist or, rather, diplomatic, which thinks in terms of power, prestige, national or personal glory, the imposition of a culture, and hereditary or racial prejudice. To the good English radical the latter is so unreal, so crazy in its combination of futility and evil, that he is often in danger of forgetting, and disbelieving, its actual existence.

If radicalism wins, as by the end of the nineteenth century it had seemed to, then the secondary struggle, internal to radicalism, commences, as to whether the bourgeois state or the socialist state can best promote the economic wealth of the community. But if the diplomatics win, then sooner or later an economic disease spreads which ends in some variant of the *delirium tremens* of revolution.

Bolshevism is such a delirium, bred by besotted idealism and intellectual error out of the sufferings and peculiar temperaments of Slavs and Jews. But we can no more regard this culminating delirium as a lasting fact or influence than the rule of Robespierre or the Jacobins. Soldiers and diplomatists—*they* are the permanent, the immortal foe. (JMK 17:372–73)

Yet despite these strong opinions, with their racist overtones, Keynes worked hard to obtain a full range of opinions about Russia for the fourth supplement, which was devoted to Russia. There were articles from representatives of the Russian government as well from Europeans of all stripes, as well as Americans. At one point he sought to recruit the prominent American intellectual, Walter Lippmann, to write on the Russian problem and the psychological basis of the American attitude toward it:

> The fourth or fifth of these Issues will deal with the subject of Russia. There will be articles from Lenin and other Bolsheviks from their point of view; by Painlevé for France; Orlando for Italy; Lord Robert Cecil for this country and also on the Famine Question by Nansen. (Keynes to Lippmann, April 6, 1922, Walter Lippmann Papers, box 16, folder 240)

As editor, he was committed to representing the full range of opinions on the topic.

In the event, the supplements were a qualified success. The twelve numbers appeared between April 1922 and January 1923 with topics as varied as the foreign exchanges, the state of opinion in Europe, and disarmament and peace.[16] They were "enthusiastically received by the press" across Europe (JMK 17:433). Gustav Cassel, the Swedish economist, wrote Keynes in October 1922 about the quality and importance of the supplements.

> The series of your "Reconstruction Numbers" more and more shows itself to be a most magnificent work for the enlightenment of public opinion.... It seems to me that the *Manchester Guardian*'s Reconstruction Numbers, when complete, will have done more for a solution of this problem than any of the big international conferences, and this mainly by showing us clearly the nature of the real extension [*sic*] of the destruction and thus giving us an adequate conception of the meaning of reconstruction. (JMK 17:447)

Perhaps the sole qualification to the success of the supplements was that they were not profitable. Still, Scott could find a way to see the silver lining in this cloud.

> For our part I think we can look back on the enterprise with some satisfaction. The financial results are a good deal below expectations (owing to Germany). The accounts so far show that we shall almost certainly not make a profit, but if we make a loss it ought not exceed three figures. Even if we made a loss of £1,000 the *Commercial* will have gained more in circulation than it could possibly have gained by the expenditure of the same amount of money in any other way. Also it has gained enormously, of course, in prestige and future developments will be easier. (JMK 17:447)

Keynes had projected that the cost per issue of the supplements, net of actual production costs, would be roughly £650–£750; this would cover the cost of articles, art, the business barometers, and Keynes's salary for editing the issue. Thus the projected loss was in the range of the editorial cost for one issue. As much as Keynes, Scott wanted to influence policymakers, and as Keynes gained in public stature through his activities,

---

16. See the appendix for the topics of the twelve issues.

the *Manchester Guardian* was gaining public stature for the *Commercial* supplements through the reconstruction supplements.

2. Promoting Liberal Internationalism: The *Nation and Athenaeum*

In 1923, Keynes's publishing profile shifted dramatically when he acquired a new platform in the *Nation and Athenaeum*. The background to this was that, starting in 1920, a group of Manchester-based members of the Liberal Party, including C. P. Scott and his son Ted, had begun to meet to discuss the party's future.[17] There was a larger gathering in 1921, at which it was decided to start a series of summer schools at which policy could be worked out. However, promoting the Liberal cause required not just ideas but a platform from which to advertise them. The answer came toward the end of 1922 when the Rowntree family, which had supported a Liberal weekly, the *Nation*, since its establishment in 1907, decided to quit. Keynes, together with three other Liberals,[18] formed a company to take over the paper at a cost of £12,500 and became chairman of the board of directors. However, although the takeover had arisen out of the summer schools, Keynes was adamant that he did not want this group to control editorial policy, which was one reason why he resisted the appointment of Ramsay Muir, one of the organizers of the summer schools and whose *Liberalism and Industry* (1921) had been the main text under discussion at the first summer school, to be its editor. Instead, he offered the position to his Cambridge colleague, Hubert Henderson.

Keynes's replacement of the previous editor, Hugh Massingham, with Henderson rather than Muir was utterly deliberate. Although under an obligation to offer the editorship to Muir, he imposed such strict conditions on his salary and editorial freedom that Muir withdrew. No such restrictions were placed on Henderson, despite his never having edited anything before. Keynes was able to influence the course of the *Nation* because he and Henderson agreed on much and also because Henderson "was highly susceptible to Keynes's intellectual charm" (Skidelsky 1992, 137), exercised in their weekly meetings. For the literary part of the paper, having failed to recruit T. S. Eliot, Keynes turned to his Bloomsbury friend, Leonard Woolf. The Liberalism that the *Nation* was to promote

---

17. This account of the takeover of the *Nation* is based on Skidelsky 1992, 134–39. See also Skidelsky 2003, 318–20; Moggridge 1992, 135–36; and Harrod 1951, 393–97.

18. The others were Arnold Rowntree, Walter Layton, and E. D. Simon (Skidelsky 1992, 136).

paid much attention to finance—this had been the contribution of Keynes, Henderson, and Walter Layton, the Cambridge contingent at the summer schools, distinguishing them from their Oxford counterparts (135). Keynes wanted a less "wishy-washy" Liberalism than that offered by Muir,[19] not in the sense of being more to the left, or more collectivist—given Muir's advocacy of nationalization, more social spending and progressive taxation, and other measures dear to Labour, that would have been difficult— but in the sense of being more practical. There was also a philosophical difference, summarized by Harrod (1951, 395):

> In Keynes's view, they were starting with very little; it was needful to turn a penetrating gaze on contemporary facts and glean from them, by science, by intuition, by political imagination, new types of remedies for new types of evils. It was a voyage of discovery on which they were embarked, to which Liberal principles could contribute little except that underlying spirit and temperament with which one approached the problems. Muir, on the other hand, tended to look inward to discover the truth. . . . Keynes feared that these answers, derived from Muir's inner consciousness, might conflict with new ideas, hitherto unknown to Liberalism, which were derived from a study of the new situation.

This attitude was characteristic of Bloomsbury (see Backhouse and Bateman 2010, 2011).

Having taken over the *Nation*, Keynes used it as his main publication outlet, so much so that he announced that those who wanted to hear his views (at least in Britain) would have to read them there. As with the reconstruction supplements, he contributed several articles to the first issue under the new management, and he was a regular contributor throughout his involvement with the paper but especially in the first two to three years, contributing ninety articles and many features, including at one point a regular series on finance and investment.[20] He had a message he wanted to deliver, and the *Nation* was the vehicle for delivering it. Many articles were republished in papers abroad, and, unusually, some received notices in other British papers.

However, he did more than use the *Nation* as an outlet for his ideas. He may not have been the editor, but Keynes put an immense amount of effort into the paper. He had long discussions with Henderson each week in which, although they did not discuss the editorial line to be taken in

---

19. The adjective is Skidelsky's.
20. Numbers are provided in Skidelsky 1992, 136.

the paper, they discussed issues of the day. Keynes was also involved, as chairman of board of directors, in trying to turn around the *Nation*'s financial position, reducing the price substantially (from 9 pence to 6 pence) and recruiting advertisers. Although he tried to cut other costs, he would not reduce the sums paid to contributors, paying well being the way to attract distinguished writers (including, of course, himself and his Bloomsbury friends). Although the paper came close to breaking even by the end of the 1930s, he failed to make it profitable—circulation fell from eight thousand before the takeover to between six thousand and seven thousand, behind its competitors the *Spectator* and the *New Statesman*, and Keynes put in a further £4,000 to keep it going as well as calling on other backers for support. So when the editorship of both the *Nation* and the *New Statesman* fell vacant toward the end of 1930, a merger was negotiated, with the merged paper being taken over by Kingsley Martin, a friend of Keynes, but someone who was acceptable to both boards. Keynes's connection did not end—the second issue of the *New Statesman and Nation* contained a controversial proposal by Keynes for a tariff to raise revenue—but it was significantly reduced.

The editorial foreword that Keynes wrote for the first issue of the *Nation* under his control made clear his commitment to Liberalism (May 5, 1923, JMK 18:123–26). Arguing in terms of a spectrum of opinion running through Conservative, Liberal, and Labour Parties, Keynes wrote of the confusion that resulted from not knowing where the boundaries between political parties were going to settle. The *Nation*'s preference, Keynes wrote, was "for a Liberal party which has its centre well to the left, a party definitely of change and progress; but with bolder, freer, more disinterested minds than Labour has, and quit of their out-of-date dogmas" (JMK 18:125). Continuing the theme he had addressed in *The Economic Consequences of the Peace*, he contended that the war had completely changed the situation in relation to the two main issues of the day: "peace and disarmament" and "the economic structure" (JMK 18:126). The old policies pursued by the Left, under the Liberal governments of Campbell-Bannerman and Asquith from 1906 to 1914, with support from the fledgling Labour Party, of social reform and redistributive taxation, had been "shattered by the weight of war debt." "Socialism" had therefore become irrelevant to the major problems facing the world. The task was, therefore, to develop new policies that were relevant to the new situation.

In the same first issue, Keynes had one article on the latest German proposals, but he had another on British policy. His intervention was, as in *The Economic Consequences of the Peace*, as much of the political situation as economic analysis. Thus he wrote of Prime Minister Bonar Law being able to defend his actions only by arguing that he was impotent, a series of mistakes having reduced British influence in Europe "to vanishing point." Keynes claimed that, in contrast to this fatalism, Britain did still have influence, for it could offer financial inducements and it could lead and mobilize world public opinion. Idealism should not be abandoned, but it could not be pursued at the expense of the national interest. It was in the national interest that France be offered financial inducements to reach a settlement, that there be no attempt to reach a settlement by deception, and that "the path of legality" was the one to take (JMK 18:130–32). Although the weight of Keynes's statements rested on his reputation as an economist, this was clearly the statement of a public intellectual, appealing both to public opinion and to those in authority, with an amalgam of economic, political, and moral arguments.

In these discussions, Keynes, as a journalist, was an outsider but with strong inside connections. As Moggridge (1992) has made clear, Keynes never lost the ability, when he had a point to make, to ensure that a memorandum was on the desk of the relevant person in government, often with the result that he would be called in to discuss it. There was thus a smooth transition to Keynes's situation in 1931, when negotiations over reparations and international loans were still dragging on. He still wrote on war debts, but now it was as a member of the Economic Advisory Council, of which Henderson was secretary. Thus in June 1931, we find Keynes in the United States, writing to Henderson about the situation in relation to Germany and about American economic conditions. Compared with eight years earlier, his views were expressed not in person, in the offices of the *Nation*, but by mail to the office of the Economic Advisory Council.

3. Monetary Theory: Crossing a New Boundary

When Keynes first entered the civil service, in 1906, it was as a brilliant young graduate with great promise. Despite his limited formal education in economics (eight weeks' private tuition from Marshall), he established his reputation as a monetary economist within the India Office, eventually writing *Indian Currency and Finance* (1913). When, in the same year,[21]

---

21. His invitation to serve on the Royal Commission was based on a reading of the proofs. The book was published on June 9; the commission's deliberations took place between May 5 and the end of the November (Moggridge 1992, 226).

he was appointed to the Royal Commission on Indian Currency and Finance, it was because of his expertise in a field on which the government needed technical advice. He formed the opinion that the witnesses whom the commission was cross-examining failed to defend their positions adequately because they were ignorant "of the facts and opinions on the other side" (Keynes to Foxwell, November 13, 1913, quoted in Moggridge 1992, 226). When he advised the government about how to handle the financial crisis that accompanied the outbreak of war in 1914, the situation was more rushed, but he played the same role—that of a technical expert offering advice that a government minister could use. The lessons from his experience (his proposals were not accepted) were presented to his fellow economists in articles in academic journals, the *Economic Journal* and the *Quarterly Journal of Economics*.

When Keynes was called back into government service on the Economic Advisory Council, which first met in 1929, and on the Macmillan Committee, which began its deliberations in 1930, Keynes was in a very different position. He was, of course, by this stage a well-known economist, whose presence was valued for his expertise on monetary problems. However, his situation was different in two ways that were probably more important. His reputation as an economist rested on his engagements in the public sphere as much as on his academic work. His main work on monetary economics, at that point, was *A Tract on Monetary Reform*, the heart of which was four articles from the reconstruction supplements. He was no longer the academic expert engaging with government, and then reporting on his experiences to the world, but his engagements with policymakers had come through middlebrow publications, put before the public even if their main audience was within the elite. *A Tract on Monetary Reform* may not have had the popular appeal of *The Economic Consequences of the Peace*, but it was clearly framed as more than an academic work. Keynes's interventions in the *Nation* and pamphlets such as *The Economic Consequences of Mr. Churchill* (JMK 9:207–30), or those he wrote in support of Lloyd George's policy of public works to reduce unemployment, were even more clearly aimed at harnessing public opinion to change policy.

Possibly as important as this, his writing, although still involving technical economic arguments, now had a much stronger moral tone—economic and moral arguments were entangled. It was no doubt this characteristic of *The Economic Consequences of the Peace* that appealed to Scott, the reputation of whose paper, in the words of one historian, rested on its editor's "unique sense of moral authority" on account of his willingness to stand up for his convictions and resist popular pressures. Working first with Scott, and then with the *Nation*, Keynes was able to build on the reputation created by *The Economic Consequences of the Peace*. Keynes had become a crusader, harnessing his economic expertise to the causes of peace in Europe (inseparable from the world's financial problems) and the tackling of the problem of unemployment.

His approach is nicely illustrated by *A Tract on Monetary Reform*. Although often treated by historians as an illustration of his early commitment to the "Cambridge" view of the cycle, with their accounts focusing on the technical devices Keynes used, the book was, as its title stated, a tract. He protested against the injustice of deflation—"it is worse, in an impoverished world, to provoke unemployment than to disappoint the *rentier*" (JMK 4:36). He described his purpose as being to tell people the best way "to cure this mortal disease of individualism" (JMK 4:35). Arguably his main argument in the book was not an economic argument but one about social attitudes:

> We must free ourselves from the deep distrust which exists against allowing the regulation of the standard of value to be the subject of *deliberate decision*. We can no longer afford to leave it in the category of which the distinguishing characteristics are possessed in different degrees by the weather, the birth rate, and the Constitution—matters which are settled by natural causes, or are the resultant of the separate action of many individuals acting independently, or require a revolution to change them. (JMK 4:36)

The cartoons that adorned the book (JMK 4:7, 13, 21) were not merely decorative: they supported his argument in a way that noneconomists could immediately understand. It is true that his moral argument was buttressed, in subsequent chapters, by more technical analysis, but that does not blunt the argument that was addressed, through the public sphere, to those in charge of policy. His moral tone helped carry his economic message both inward to the most elite policy circles and outward to the larger public.

However, despite the authority commanded by virtue of his public profile, and the weakness (at least as he perceived it) of his opponents' positions, he failed to get his message through to those who mattered. Whether he thought of it in this way, he can be seen as having, in the 1930s, changed his strategy to focus more on economists. But how should he do this?

Although Keynes had been developing ideas through his interventions in the public sphere, he had not abandoned discussions within academe.

During the 1920s he first worked closely with Dennis Robertson, whose work emerged as *Banking Policy and the Price Level* (1926), a book their fellow economists, let alone the public, found difficult. By the time of the Macmillan Committee, Keynes had produced his own systematic work on monetary economics, *A Treatise on Money* (1930; JMK 5, 6); as with Robertson's book, this was a book to be debated within the community of academic economists. The public might be following Keynes's ideas, but this weighty work, in two volumes, was not addressed to them.

But although Keynes had written the *Treatise* with an eye toward influencing academic debate on monetary policy, he had not been able to completely sever himself from his habits of composing his work publicly and for wider consumption. The seven policy recommendations for dealing with the Slump that were central to the book's argument, for instance, had been worked out carefully in the testimony he gave to the Macmillan Committee. Thus, despite his effort to make the book more scholarly, he rapidly concluded that it was an "artistic failure."[22] He still had not mastered the art of academic composition and had done too much of his work for the book on the fly, as it were, and for public consumption.

During the 1930s, Keynes, as is well known, abandoned the theoretical framework of the *Treatise* and developed the new approach that became *The General Theory of Employment, Interest, and Money*. That story has been told so often that it does not need to be told here. However, at the same time, he adopted a new strategy in relation to the audiences he wanted to address, and this reflected a new style of composition. His ultimate concern remained the policymaking elite. Yet, rather than use his activities in the public sphere to test and craft his arguments, he now turned much more narrowly to influencing the academic economists whose ideas he believed ultimately influenced policymakers, whether consciously or not. After a brief public foray in 1933 with the multiplier arguments that Richard Kahn had developed and which Keynes would fold into the *General Theory*, he stopped composing in public and focused instead on sharing his drafts with a small circle of other academic economists.[23] When the book finally appeared in 1936, its contents had not been widely previewed in journalistic outlets.

---

22. In a letter to his mother on September 14, 1930, three weeks before the *Treatise* was published, Keynes reported of the book: "Artistically, it is a failure" (JMK 13:176).

23. The public foray with the multiplier was a series of newspaper articles eventually published as a pamphlet titled *The Means to Prosperity*. As Don Patinkin (1976, 53, 126) has noted, this pamphlet by Keynes seemed to mark the end of his "magic formula mentality," the idea that a simple formula could give clear and unambiguous policy advice. See also Backhouse and Bateman 2011.

In the oft-quoted conclusion to his book, Keynes wrote, "Practical men, who believe themselves to be quite exempt from any intellectual influences, are usually the slaves of some defunct economist.... I am sure that the power of vested interests is vastly exaggerated compared with the gradual encroachment of ideas" (JMK 7:383). However, although he sought to change the views held by other economists—other insiders— he still did so through the public sphere. The book was marketed widely, the price set at only five shillings, the price of a trade book, not the fifteen shillings at which similar academic works normally sold. The American economist Alvin Hansen (1938, 15) wrote, "The publication of a book with so difficult and complicated an analysis at a popular price is itself indicative of the power and prestige of Mr. Keynes as a social prophet in the current distracted world."

Moreover, although Keynes might make no concessions to those whose economics training was limited (it was, by the standards of the day, uncomfortably mathematical even for some economists), he wrote it as if to a wide audience. "This book is chiefly addressed to my fellow economists. I hope it will be intelligible to others. But its main purpose is to deal with difficult questions of theory, and only in the second place with the applications of this theory to practice" (JMK 7:xxi). His opening chapter could probably hold the general reader, but after that, there was pretty much no relief till chapter 24, on "the social philosophy towards which the general theory might lead," where economic analysis was, as in his public interventions in the 1920s, entwined with moral arguments about a good society. It was no wonder that some reviewers focused almost exclusively on arguments in the final chapter, saying that they would be leaving the rest of the book for the specialists to sort out. The *Times* noted that, although parts of the book were difficult, "the plain reader will both appreciate and enjoy" its "lucid argument, witty and illuminating digression, historical analogy, satire and pointed political judgement" ("Employment and Money" [1936] 1999, 49). In contrast, an LSE economist, Arnold Plant ([1936] 1999, 79), was more critical, writing in the *Fortnightly Review*, "The book is issued at a price destined to give it a circulation far beyond the ranks of economists [but] the ordinary reader will follow little beyond the passages of rhetoric and ridicule."

What Keynes was doing here involved a modification of the strategy he had pursued in the 1920s: of using middlebrow media (in this case a book published at a "trade" price) as a way to reach those in the elite he wanted to reach. The difference was simply that he was addressing outsiders in order to change the views of a different group of insiders—other economists—albeit with a view that he might ultimately influence the insiders he had previously sought to persuade more directly. The book was extremely successful, and his forecast to George Bernard Shaw that it would, within ten years, transform the way the world thought about economic problems turned out to be correct. However, how much was due to his rhetorical strategy, and how much to developments over which he had no control—the Second World War and with it a changed role for government and the rise of mathematical economics—is something that goes beyond the scope of this essay (see Backhouse and Bateman 2011, Backhouse 2013).

Appendix 1
Topics of the Twelve Supplements Keynes Wrote for the *Manchester Guardian Commercial*

Between 1922 and 1923, Keynes wrote twelve supplements for a series on reconstruction in Europe for the *Manchester Guardian Commercial*. Each supplement dealt with at least two subjects. The subjects—which coincided with the titles—of the supplements are listed below. At the head of every supplement was "Manchester Guardian Commercial" (in roman type and in quotation marks), followed by, on the next line, "Reconstruction in Europe" (in large, boldface type). Each supplement was assigned a section number. In the following list, semicolons are used where line breaks appeared in the original.

Section 1 (April 20, 1922): The Stabilization of the Exchanges

Section 2 (May 18, 1922): Principles of Reconstruction; Shipping, Inland Water Transport

Section 3 (June 13, 1922): The Genoa Conference; the Problem of Austria; the Textile Industries of Europe; Financial and Exchange Questions

Section 4 (July 6, 1922): Russia; the Oil Industry

Section 5 (July 17, 1922): National Finances in Europe; Tariff Hindrances; *La vie chère*

Section 6 (August 17, 1922): Population; Agriculture and Food Supply; the Peasant Revolution in Europe

Section 7 (September 7, 1922): Railways; Coal, Iron, Steel; Engineering

Section 8 (September 28, 1922): The Problem of Reparations; the Devastated Areas

Section 9 (October 15, 1922): The Labor Problems of Europe; Oil

Section 10 (November 16, 1922): The United States and Europe; Emigration

Section 11 (December 7, 1922): Stabilization of the Exchanges; the Historic Bank of England; European Banking

Section 12 (January 4, 1923): The State of Opinion in Europe; Disarmament and Peace; the Literature of Reconstruction

References

Ayerst, D. 1971. *Guardian: Biography of a Newspaper.* London: Collins.

Backhouse, R. E., ed. 1999. *Keynes: Contemporary Responses to the General Theory.* Bristol, UK: Thoemmes.

———. 2013. "Responding to Economic Crisis: Macroeconomic Revolutions in the 1930s and 1970s." In *Before and beyond the Global Economic Crisis: Economics, Politics, and Settlement*, edited by M. Benner, 38–54. Cheltenham: Edward Elgar.

Backhouse, R. E., and B. W. Bateman. 2010. "Whose Keynes?" In *Keynes's General Theory: A Reconsideration after Seventy Years*, edited by R. Mundell, A. Vercelli, and R. Dimand, 8–27. London: Palgrave.

———. 2011. *Capitalist Revolutionary: John Maynard Keynes.* Cambridge: Harvard University Press.

"Employment and Money: Mr. Keynes's Views." (1936) 1999. In Backhouse 1999, 49.

Hansen, A. H. 1938. *Full Recovery or Stagnation?* London: Adam and Charles Black.

Hargreaves, R. 2002. *The First Freedom: A History of Free Speech.* Stroud, UK: Sutton.

Harrod, R. F. 1951. *The Life of John Maynard Keynes.* New York: Harcourt, Brace.

Keynes, J. M. 1971–89. *The Collected Writings of John Maynard Keynes.* 30 vols. Edited by D. E. Moggridge. London: Macmillan.

———. 2010. *Keynes on the Wireless.* Edited by D. E. Moggridge. London: Palgrave Macmillan.

Laidler, D. 1999. *Fabricating the Keynesian Revolution: Studies in the Inter-war Literature on Money, the Cycle, and Unemployment.* Cambridge: Cambridge University Press.

Markwell, D. 2006. *John Maynard Keynes and International Relations: Economic Paths to War and Peace.* Oxford: Oxford University Press.

Moggridge, D. 1992. *Maynard Keynes: An Economist's Biography.* London: Routledge.

———. 2006. "Keynes and His Correspondence." In *Cambridge Companion to Keynes*, edited by Roger E. Backhouse and Bradley W. Bateman, 136–59. Cambridge: Cambridge University Press.
Muir, R. 1921. *Liberalism and Industry*. Boston: Houghton Mifflin.
Patinkin, D. 1976. *Keynes's Monetary Thought*. Durham, N.C.: Duke University Press.
Plant, A. (1936) 1999. "A Challenge to Orthodoxy." In Backhouse 1999, 79–83.
Robertson, D. H. 1926. *Banking Policy and the Price Level*. London: P. S. King.
Skidelsky, R. 1983. *John Maynard Keynes: Hopes Betrayed, 1883–1920*. London: Macmillan.
———. 1992. *John Maynard Keynes: The Economist as Saviour, 1920–1937*. London: Macmillan.
———. 2000. *John Maynard Keynes: Fighting for Britain, 1937–1946*. London: Macmillan.
———. 2003. *John Maynard Keynes, 1883–1946: Economist, Philosopher, Statesman*. London: Macmillan.
Strachey, Lytton. 1918. *Eminent Victorians*. London: Chatto and Windus.
Woolf, V. 1985. *Moments of Being: Autobiographical Writings*. 2nd ed. New York: Harcourt.

Walter Lippmann: The Making of a Public Economist

Craufurd Goodwin

In the decade and a half from the onset of the Great Depression to the end of World War II, Americans were faced with a long and agonizing series of economic policy questions. What had caused the economic collapse and what could be done about it? How should the domestic economy be reformed to make it resistant to future crises? How might the distribution of income and wealth be reshaped to become more equitable and humane? Should large concentrations of power in capital and labor be broken up or constrained in some way? How might the dramatic soil erosion in the south and southwest, symbolized by the Dust Bowl, be reduced? Could human liberty be preserved if the economy were reconstructed to meet these problems? With the collapse of the European empires after World War I, how might the global economic system be reconstructed to achieve both efficiency and justice? As more and more countries during the 1930s abandoned the gold standard and free trade, what new institutions could be envisaged to resist the drive toward autarky? As the war clouds gathered toward the end of the decade and war was declared in 1941, new and urgent questions were raised about how to mobilize a free market economy for war and then about how to return to peace.

At this time in America there were few professional economists like Milton Friedman, John Kenneth Galbraith, and later Paul Krugman

Correspondence may be addressed to Craufurd Goodwin, Department of Economics, Duke University, Box 90097, Durham, NC 27708-0097; e-mail: craufurd.goodwin@duke.edu.

History of Political Economy 45 (annual suppl.) DOI 10.1215/00182702-2310962
Copyright 2013 by Duke University Press

skilled at addressing a lay audience. Nor were there many spokesmen in government and the private sector, or members of the media, who could enlighten the public about economic affairs. There were many commentators, of course, but few interpreters. Henry Hazlitt was an exception. The public could not turn to friends and neighbors for informed advice because few had been to college or taken a course in economics. But there *was* Walter Lippmann! From 1931 until 1967 he wrote a column for the *New York Herald Tribune* and then the *Washington Post* titled Today and Tomorrow, initially four days per week and then three. Ultimately the column was syndicated in more than two hundred newspapers across the country. At his peak Lippmann wrote for an educated, elite audience estimated at more than 10 million in a standard format of approximately one thousand words in the middle of the paper. He addressed primarily three areas of concern, with a focus on whichever seemed most urgent at the moment: domestic politics, foreign affairs, and economic policy. Over the fifteen years from 1931 until 1946 he wrote around one thousand columns concerned substantially with economic issues. Toward the end of World War II he became so exercised by what he perceived to be mistakes in US foreign policy that he left economic policy largely to a new generation of commentators who came on the scene after war service and passage of the Employment Act of 1946.

Lippmann's style was distinctive and very effective with his audience. He did not patronize and was resolutely nonpartisan. He could and often did change his mind about people and policies. His approach in most cases was to explain the salience of a problem and then set out the relevant considerations. He used social, economic, and political theory in arriving at conclusions but seldom with citations. Privately he consulted scholars widely about the matters he had under review, but their names did not appear often in the columns. Whether this was because he wished to persuade without the use of authority, hoped to protect the privacy of his sources, presumed his audience did not care about bibliography, or believed ideas should be in the public domain is not clear. His style was to lay out his arguments simply and without jargon, often repeating them in a series of daily columns. There is a large literature about Lippmann's life and achievements, including an excellent biography (Steel 1980), an edition of his letters (Blum 1985), and republished collections of his articles. Usually he is portrayed as a pioneer journalist, social theorist, and political philosopher. It is suggested here that, together with all these things, he was a remarkable public economist.

Early Years

The only child of an upper-middle-class family in New York City, Lippmann led a privileged, even pampered life. His parents decided quite early to devote themselves mainly to pleasure, and so he became accustomed to summers in Europe, starting when he was ten, and regular visits to luxurious spas. He haunted the picture galleries of Europe in cities that his parents visited, and he demonstrated very early on what would be a lifelong magnetism for celebrities. One summer in Paris Mrs. Jack Gardner, the great Boston patroness of the arts, befriended him in a museum and became his guide.

Lippmann's early and continuing attachments to the humanities and the arts help explain his close friendships with artists and humanists over his lifetime, including Bernard Berenson and Kenneth Clark the art historians, Laurence Stallings the novelist and screenwriter, Lee Simonson the set designer, Deems Taylor the composer, Marsden Hartley the painter, and various members of Mabel Dodge's salon in Greenwich Village. Through these connections Lippmann was open to opinions, insights, and values often at odds with those of the politicians, social scientists, and journalists with whom he spent much of his life. His training in the classics and creative literature led him to use metaphors, analogies, and short narratives to illustrate his policy positions and distinguish his style from that of most of his journalistic contemporaries. For example, to illuminate the position of FDR after Pearl Harbor Lippmann wrote about George Washington at Valley Forge (*Herald Tribune*, December 11, 1941). He came increasingly to conclude that a liberal education rather than simply intense specialization was essential for developing effective leadership skills in all walks of life. Especially in the social sciences, he found that too strong a focus on a few variables rather than on a larger context could lead to absurd conclusions. In July 1942 when he was reflecting that poor leadership explained the setbacks of US forces in Libya he told the story of an American professor of geography (unnamed) who had proposed that Switzerland be carved up and delivered to the European powers so as to "meet democratic specifications" (*Herald Tribune*, July 4, 1942). He concluded that this professor "had become so immersed in the abstractions of the science that he had lost all sense of the realities of the world, that Switzerland for him was not actually Switzerland, but a patch of color on a map and some statistics about the languages of the Swiss nation." "Why should this ignorance exist?" he asked. "We must dig deeper, I submit, and ask ourselves then why a man could emerge from the academic study of bloodless and soulless abstractions, come out into the real world and not know that men cannot be dealt with as if they were paper dolls and inanimate objects." Lippmann remarked that John Milton had noted that a liberal education should precede the study of "economics" as well as of other social sciences. "If Western civilization is to survive and renew its vitality, we shall have, therefore, to revive and renew our schools. So when the war is over, we have a rendezvous with ourselves to consider as a matter of high priority, the restoration and reconstruction of American education."

Lippmann attended a good private school in Manhattan, the Sachs Collegiate Institute. He entered Harvard in 1906, described by William Leuchtenburg in 1985 as "by all accounts one of the most gifted undergraduates to attend Harvard in this century" (introduction to Lippmann [1914] 1985). His class included such later luminaries as T. S. Eliot, Stuart Chase, and Heywood Broun (Chase 1930). At first he was determined to continue with the arts and humanities and took courses mainly in literature, history, and philosophy. "I took almost no courses in government or economics." Instead, he was attracted to philosophy. "I very soon converged on the philosophy department and took all of Santayana's courses at Harvard, I think without exception." George Santayana remained an inspiration over Lippmann's lifetime. "I felt a good deal of personal inspiration from Santayana. He had a profound influence on my life. I read all his books again and again, particularly *The Life of Reason*" (Lippmann 1950, 25–26). A critical transformation occurred in Lippmann's attitude to scholarly endeavor as a result of a fire in 1908 in Chelsea, the working-class suburb of Boston, that made him aware for the first time of poverty and destitution. For guidance on how to help change these distressing conditions, he found the humanities lacking. He could not find answers in the works he was reading at the time, Goethe, Dante, Lucretius, or in the fine arts. So he turned to "political writers such as Veblen, Ward, and Beard" and then to the social sciences. In economics he seems to have taken three courses but was not impressed by them, especially because of their behavioral assumption. In Econ. 1, the introductory class taught by F. W. Taussig, the texts were John Stuart Mill's *Principles of Political Economy* and Henry R. Seager's *Introduction to Economics* (1904). The latter remained an object of ridicule with Lippmann for years to come. All the same, he made a strong impression on Taussig, who wrote a formal letter of appreciation of a kind received by few students in an introductory economics course from a leader of the discipline. It said, "I congratulate you upon your work in Economics 1, which has been of the first order and not less so because your point of view is in some ways different from mine. I judge that, from your being a candidate for a degree, you are to leave the university this year. I should have been glad to have the opportunity to see you in a course like Economics 2" (Walter Lippmann Papers [WLP], series 1, F1192). The low point in Lippmann's career in economics at Harvard was a course given by Thomas Nixon Carver, one of the most doctrinaire American classical economists of the time. Lippmann took it, he said, to see how the other side thought.

The approach and soft socialism of the British Fabians appealed most to Lippmann, and Karl Marx figured not at all. "I had been reading people like Shaw and Wells, and therefore I began to pick up that side of them. Then I went on to the Webbs. The book which made me at that time a socialist was a book of Fabian essays. I never read Karl Marx. In fact, I took it for granted from reading essays which despised Marx as an obsolete economic thinker. I never read Karl Marx until twenty years later" (Lippmann 1950, 32). There was a practical quality about the Fabians that appealed to Lippmann; he found some of the American reformers too utopian. "I thought Bellamy's *Looking Backward* was a fascinating book, but I wouldn't say it had any great influence, because I was too non-Utopian in my own feeling about things to believe that that was to be taken seriously as a project of society" (33). He joined the British Fabian Society in 1909, and he attended the Fabian Summer School in 1914 where he met G. D. H. Cole and other leaders of the movement. Lippmann's departure from Harvard in 1910, in his fourth year, without even waiting for his MA degree, signaled his rejection both of the mainstream social sciences as disciplines to which he could devote his life and of the academic world as a place in which to dwell.

Lippmann's first serious job after Harvard gave him an insight into one career choice that lay before him, investigative journalism. The prominent muckraker Lincoln Steffens was planning an exposé of Wall Street similar to those he had conducted of municipal governments. He came to Harvard looking for an assistant and asked who had "the ablest mind that could express itself in writing" (Hartshorn 2011, 184). He was told Walter Lippmann. The subsequent investigation in which Lippmann did most of the legwork yielded an eight-part series called "It" in the popular periodical *Everybody's Magazine* in 1910–11; this documented monopoly in the banking industry and the overwhelming power of J. P. Morgan. The furor it created was fuel for a congressional inquiry (the Pujo Committee) that led up to the Federal Reserve Act of 1913. Lippmann appreciated that muckrakers drew attention to issues of public concern that otherwise might be neglected by government and the scholarly community. But he worried that their methods were not sufficiently thorough and careful to provide a basis for policy formation. Throughout his life he looked for the right balance in writings about public policy between rigor and relevance, and here he thought the weight was much too heavily on relevance.

It was natural for Lippmann to shift his allegiance from socialists to the nonsocialist reformers, as he did in his first book *A Preface to Politics* (1913). But his reform was to be of a particular kind. It is anachronistic to call Lippmann an institutionalist economist because that term and the body of thought that the term connotes were still in the future, but he was responding to the same questions and problems that were inspiring Wesley Mitchell, Walton Hamilton, and others at this time, men who would be at the core of the institutionalist movement and would become his friends in just a few years. Lippmann's argument in this book was that conventional social scientists concerned with reform were, like Thomas Nixon Carver, merely drawing up lists of rules that were based on simple models of human behavior. In essence these reformers were what he called "routineers" when they should be inventors. Eighteenth-century thinking too often embodied a static perspective. A new evolutionary approach had to be introduced. "Our own Federal Constitution is a striking example of this machine conception of government. It is probably the most important instance we have of the deliberate application of a mechanical philosophy to human affairs" (Lippmann [1913] 1962, 16). Lippmann called for a turn away from the knee-jerk public policy positions of classical economists, like the punishment of monopolies and imposition of land value taxation, because the full consequences of such positions were not well understood.

During his last semester at Harvard, Lippmann took part in a seminar led by Graham Wallas, one of the leaders of the Fabian Society visiting from the London School of Economics, and the experience was memorable for both parties. Later Wallas dedicated his book *The Great Society* (1914) that contained the substance of the seminar to his student Lippmann, and Lippmann claimed that he read the book repeatedly for inspiration. Wallas's message was that progress in the social sciences called for much more study and especially application of the evolving discipline of social psychology. This message was repeated prominently by Lippmann in *A Preface to Politics*, and indeed throughout much of his writing thereafter. About economics Lippmann ([1913] 1962, 62) wrote, "The Economic

Man—that lazy abstraction—is still paraded in the lecture room; the study of human nature has not advanced beyond the gossip of old wives tales." And more generally, "We deny truth, falsify facts, and prefer the coddling of our theory to any deeper understanding of the real problem before us" (124). Self-interest should not simply be assumed; it must be examined thoughtfully and critically. Despite these reservations about the current state of economic science, the message of *Preface* was optimistic. If only economists and other scientists would attend to Charles Darwin and Sigmund Freud, they could produce a modern body of thought that would willingly be accepted and used by statesmen faced with the daunting task of reconciling the eighteenth-century emphasis on human freedom with the twentieth-century reality that government was needed for social improvement. The reception of this short book by a little-known recent college graduate was remarkable. Lippmann was pleased that Freud reviewed the book favorably in his journal *Image* (Lippmann to Frederick J. Hoffman, November 18, 1942, WLP, series 2, F1059). It was a stroke of good luck that Teddy Roosevelt took the book with him on vacation in Brazil and was charmed, partly no doubt by the positive references to his own wisdom and accomplishments (Lippmann [1913] 1962, 186, 214, 226; 1950, 5, 67). This led to a meeting with Lippmann in May 1914 and a warm friendship thereafter.

An Institutionalist Fabian

Drift and Mastery, first published in 1914, was infused with new thinking and new personal contacts, but the essential message was unchanged. This second book was written in England, where Lippmann saw much of Wallas, Wells, Shaw, Hobson, the Webbs, and other Fabians. It seems as if, all of a sudden, Lippmann discovered the richness of the wide range of reformist thinking then in the air and was stimulated by what it might provide. This book, like *Preface*, reflects a deep reading of Thorstein Veblen but also anticipates *The Modern Corporation and Private Property* (1932) by Adolf Berle and Gardiner Means. Lippmann had come to conclude that "drift," meaning acceptance of the status quo, must be overcome and "mastered" by the application of science, meaning mainly social science, and psychology in particular, to current problems. Lippmann offered a capsule history of economics in which he claimed that Adam Smith and Marx had the deepest insights into the economies of their own times but were largely irrelevant in the modern world.

In the consideration of public policy, Lippmann ([1914] 1985, 16) proposed leaving aside all inherited verities, "the sanctity of property, the patriarchal family, hereditary caste, the dogma of sin, obedience to authority" and starting from scratch. He conceded that muckraking had revealed many of the real problems of the economy. "Muckraking is full of the voices of the beaten, of the bewildered, and then again it is shot through with some fine anticipation. It has pointed to a revolution in business motives; it has hinted at the emerging power of labor and the consumer—we can take those suggestions, perhaps, and by analyzing them, and following them through, gather for ourselves some sense of what moves beneath the troubled surface of events" (34). But in finding solutions for these troubles, neither the muckrakers nor the orthodox economists had been successful. It was necessary, first of all, to go beyond the conventional notion of the economic man: "The old economists were bad psychologists and superficial observers when they described man as a slot machine set in motion by inserting a coin" (36–37). It must be understood that the business manager no longer truly represented the interests of the owners (what we now think of as the principal agent problem), and their behavior must be examined afresh. "The managers are on salary, divorced from ownership and from bargaining. They represent the revolution in business incentives at its very heart" (43). Similarly the fiction of consumer sovereignty had to be replaced by a sophisticated theory of consumer behavior: "Few consumers feel any of that sense of power which economists say is theirs" (52). It had to be recognized that consumption was not the result so much of innate tastes as of education. "Advertising is in fact the weed that had grown up because the art of consumption is uncultivated" (53). He was especially impressed by Ordway Tead's book *Instincts in Industry* (1918). Attempts to enrich economics from psychology were not yet widely accepted in economics, and Lippmann was on the frontier. He was a frequent advocate for Freud, urging his own publisher Kennerly to publish Freud in English. In 1915 he argued with Wesley Mitchell, who could not see the potential contribution to economics from Freud. One of Lippmann's first articles for the *New Republic* was titled "Freud and the Layman" (April 17, 1915). He kept in close touch with Carleton Parker, the Berkeley economist and fellow disciple of Graham Wallas, who was taking the lead in efforts to incorporate psychology into economics.

Concentration of industry intrigued Lippmann at this point in his career, and he regretted that the Sherman Act had been based simply on emotion rather than on serious analysis. Concentration, he observed, could come from economies of scale, in which case it should be encouraged, or from collusion in restraint of trade, in which case it should be proscribed. The challenge was to tell the difference: "Big business is a business that has survived competition. But when competition is done away with, who is the Solomon wise enough to know whether the result was accomplished by superior efficiency or by agreement among the competitors or by both?" (Lippmann [1914] 1985, 84–85). Simple prohibition of concentration grew out of the traditions of an earlier era of small-scale production and could lead to the loss of the benefits of technological progress. "Those who cling to the village view of life may deflect the drift, may batter the trusts about a bit, but they will never dominate business, never humanize its machinery, and they will continue to be the playthings of industrial change" (87).

At this early date he toyed with the idea of national planning. "You have to make a survey of the natural resources of the country. On the basis of that survey you must draw up a national plan for their development" (98). Then the state must intervene whenever the case was overwhelming to do so. "You have to see to it that technical schools produce men trained for such work; you have to establish institutes of research that shall stimulate the economic world not only with physical inventions, but with administrative proposals" (98). He was sympathetic even to something like the modern regulated economy. "You have to find ways of making the worker an integral part of his industry. That means allowing him to develop his unions, and supplying the unions with every incentive by which they can increase their responsibility." Consumers too should expect some constraints. "You have to devise and try out a great variety of consumers' controls. For some industries you may have to use public ownership, for others the cooperative society may be more effective, for others the regulating commission" (99).

In 1913 Lippmann joined Herbert Croly as a member of the editorial board of the *New Republic* then getting under way as a weekly medium of progressive thought. But this did not last long. Soon, as the nation mobilized for war, he was pressed into government service in a job he had somewhat disingenuously suggested for himself. In a letter of May 5, 1916, he proposed to recently appointed Secretary of War Newton Baker that he needed more staff, perhaps organized in something like an in-house think tank. "I was wondering whether it might not be a good plan to do what I understand the British Treasury Department did at the outbreak of the war. They went to Oxford and Cambridge and got a number of specialists in economics and said to them: 'Now you have no administrative work whatsoever—your job is to think out and report on certain large theoretical problems.' Mightn't it be a good scheme for you to have a voluntary, inconspicuous number of people whose business it would be to analyze and make suggestions about the kind of thing we talked of and digested—reports about conditions of public opinion in this country and elsewhere. To formulate methods not only of censorship but of positive press agenting and to deal in general with all those matters of morale d.c. [District of Columbia?] army men are not so likely to understand, and for which people like you tied to a devastating task cannot have time to think about at length" (Lippmann to Baker, May 5, 1916, WLP, series 1, F97). Baker replied that he had read Lippmann's letter "several times" and needed to reflect on whether he might not get such advice as Lippmann offered from the War College, but he was cautiously positive about the proposal.

Lippmann's original plan was more nearly followed when he was seconded by Colonel E. M. House, President Woodrow Wilson's close adviser, to become executive secretary of what became known as "The Inquiry," a secret research group set up in New York City to prepare advisory material for the president in a manner very much like that proposed by Lippmann in his letter to Baker and in concept somewhere between a Council of Economic Advisers and a RAND Corporation. Initially Lippmann was deeply impressed by the application of the social sciences that went on at the Inquiry. The approximately 150 researchers, some from Columbia University just down the road, were largely given their head, and he even engaged Veblen as consultant (Dorfman 1934, 374). He recalled later that Veblen's memo of advice arrived the week when they were charged to provide explanatory background material for Wilson's Fourteen Points.

In 1918 Lippmann was given a commission in military intelligence and attached to the general staff in Europe, one of six officers in a "psychological warfare unit." His orders from the War Department, dated July 3, 1918, which he may have drafted himself, were quite breathtaking in their generality. They said, "You are authorized and directed to proceed to England, France, and Italy for the purpose of making special studies in economic and political matters for the use of this Department in connection with the work being done at the direction of Colonel E. M. House in conjunction with the Department of State. . . . It is felt that it is best to leave entirely to your discretion, the methods to be pursued by you in prosecuting your studies." Secretary Baker was more specific in a letter to General John J. Pershing: "Captain Walter Lippmann has been commissioned to assist the War Department in the dissemination of propaganda. . . . the vigorous prosecution of his work on behalf of the Inquiry and the State Department will aid us in the preparation of the material to be used as propaganda." Lippmann's studies were well received. Baker wrote him on August 29, 1918, "Your letters of August 9th and 15th have just reached me. They are so full of interest that I am sending them to the President for his information" (WLP, series 1, F1221). Wilson, who had come to know Lippmann during the presidential campaign of 1916, wrote to Baker on August 22. "I am warmly obliged to you for having let me see the enclosed. Lippmann is always not only thoughtful but just and suggestive" (Wilson to Baker, August 22, 1917, WLP, series 1, F97).

Lippmann's final experience in government was as an aide to President Wilson at the Peace Conference in Versailles, and there again he felt acutely the need for a mechanism to provide effective intelligence and policy advice. He was compelled to write a summary memo of interpretation for the president on the Fourteen Points without any files or background materials. Moreover, he was uneasy about the way the Inquiry was moving, and he wrote to Colonel House: "The greatest weakness of the Inquiry is its divorce from responsibility and from intimate knowledge of current affairs. That a certain objectivity has been gained from this is undeniable, but the time has come to ask ourselves whether the Inquiry is not now in danger of becoming too academic and out of touch with European ways of thinking." In contrast to the muckrakers who moved too far toward relevance, these academics were committed too much to rigor. Like John Maynard Keynes in the British delegation, Lippmann grew increasingly frustrated with the peace negotiations and was glad to return home and, despite his heady experience in government and the military, move back into the private sector.

Scholarly Reputation

By the end of World War I Lippmann was known as a brilliant young intellectual who had scaled the heights of government in an amazingly short time and had attracted the attention of powerful patrons. But he did not yet have much of a presence either in the media or in the academic world. That changed in the 1920s. He returned to the *New Republic* in 1919 but left in 1922 to join the editorial staff of the *New York World,* the most prominent progressive newspaper in the country. There he gained a reputation within the scholarly world, and the economics discipline in particular, that served him well. He found respect among leaders of the field and came to be seen not merely as an interpreter of their work but as a contributor in his own right. He wrote three books in particular that attracted wide scholarly attention. He also took on various roles within the discipline that were typically reserved for insiders, such as gatekeeper to publication, and he developed close friendships with prominent economists, most notably Keynes.

The three important works that Lippmann produced during the 1920s while helping edit a major daily newspaper were *Public Opinion* (1922), *The Phantom Public* (1925), and *A Preface to Morals* (1929). Whereas his two prewar books were intellectual calls to arms, these three included attempts to construct new arms. The first arose from Lippmann's brief but intense experience during World War I with propaganda and censorship where he had to face the reality that the "public" was not inclined necessarily to support well-reasoned public policy. Voters could be manipulated even to accept policies that were contrary to their best interests. Lippmann left the army with this concern clearly in mind. He wrote Ellery Sedgwick, editor of the *Atlantic Monthly*, in April 1919: "I have started to write a longish article around the general idea that freedom of thought and speech present themselves in a new light and raise new problems because of the discovery that opinion can be manufactured. The idea has come to me gradually as a result of certain experiences with the official propaganda machines, and my hope is to attempt a restatement of the problem of freedom of thought as it presents itself in modern society under modern conditions of government and also with a modern knowledge of how to manipulate the human mind" (Lippmann to Sedgwick, April 7, 1919, WLP, series 1, F1104). The short book that emerged from the proposed long article was titled *Public Opinion* and looks more like Lippmann's reading notes on the subject than a finished product. He cites writers from a wide range of disciplines to form his ideas: classics, history, political theory, economics, modern fiction, and above all psychology. He emphasized that the "pictures in our head" may be very different from "the world outside," as Plato had observed from the cave. This made public policy formation difficult. Lippmann rejected the Benthamite explanation for human behavior. "Try to explain social life as the pursuit of pleasure and the avoidance of pain. You will soon be saying that the hedonist begs the question, for even supposing that man does pursue these ends, the crucial problem of why he takes one course rather than another likely to produce pleasure, is untouched. Does the guidance of man's conscience explain? How then does he happen to have the particular conscience which he has? The theory of economic self-interest? But how do men come to conceive their self-interest in one way rather than another?" (Lippmann [1922] 2007, 14). In his discussions of psychology Lippmann was responding to current enthusiasms inside as well as outside academe. For example, in 1922, the year in which *Public Opinion* was published, Dorothy Straight, the wealthy patron of the *New Republic*, to address "certain psychological questions," organized a discussion group in her home that included, in addition to Lippmann, William Ogburn, Judge Learned Hand, Croly, Thomas Lamont, Leo Wolman, Alvin Johnson, Eugene O'Neill, Heywood Broun, and Sherwood Anderson. The group set out to examine how the "new" psychology might enlighten humans about themselves, the economy, education, conflict, religion, creativity, and old age (Straight to Lippmann, November 21, 1922, WLP, series 1, F1166).

In *Public Opinion* Lippmann complained of secrecy in government and poor performance by the newspapers in bringing facts to light. He was concerned also by the increasing use of models in the social sciences. He worried that "stereotypes" based on ignorance, including those that went into social-scientific models as assumptions, obscured reality. The resulting myth caused people to put too much trust in theory: "Our attention is called to those facts which support it, and diverted from those which contradict. So perhaps it is because they are attuned to find it, that kindly people discover so much reason for kindness, malicious people so much malice" (Lippmann [1922] 2007, 43). Classical economists as well as socialists used stereotypes, and they were both misled. "Both assume that the unlearned dispositions fatally but intelligently produce a certain type of behavior. The socialist believes that the dispositions pursue the economic interest of a class; the hedonist believes that they pursue pleasure and avoid pain. Both theories rest on a naïve view of instinct" (63).

In most cases, Lippmann argued, the notion that there was a meaningful "public opinion" to be discovered and taken into account was mistaken. Individuals did not think as part of a community. "Leaders often pretend that they have merely uncovered a program which existed in the minds of their public. When they believe it, they are usually deceiving themselves. People do not invent themselves synchronously in a multitude of minds. That is not because a multitude of minds is necessarily inferior to that of the leaders, but because thought is the function of an organism, and a mass is not an organism" (79). The idea of a public consensus rested on a false presumption of "a pre-established harmony, inspired, imposed, or innate, by which the self-opinionated person, class, or community is orchestrated with the rest of mankind" (85).

One way to interpret Lippmann's finding that stable public opinion is a fiction could be that a successful democracy must have rule by a select group of expert philosopher-kings, who can discover what is best for the public and then implement it. But this is not the way Lippmann saw it. Indeed quite the contrary. His plea is for reasoned study by many specialists of all the issues that face a society and for effective distribution of the results of that study to all parts of society by government, the mass media, the educational system, and by well-informed individuals like the British Fabians. To a critic of *Public Opinion* who complained that the book was "an argument for the omnicompetence of the scientific spirit," he replied, "That's just what it isn't. It is the most convincing demonstration I could make of the inadequacy of the scientific spirit. . . . In fact, the chief emphasis of the book is directed against the dry, thin rationalist" (Lippmann to Gerald Johnson, May 18, 1928, WLP, series 1, F618).

The last two major books by Lippmann in the 1920s, *The Phantom Public* and *A Preface to Morals*, do not bear directly on his role as public economist. In the first he restated the message of *Public Opinion* more bluntly for a less-sophisticated audience. He emphasized the importance of public education not only because some members of the public were expert and others not but because some were insiders and others not. Rather than seek to discover the public's views on a complex subject so as to act on them, leaders should explain a problem as clearly and simply as possible to the various segments of the public with the pros and cons of the possible policy options laid out for public choice. There are parallels to this rejection of the myth of citizen sovereignty in 1925 by Lippmann to the rejection of the myth of consumer sovereignty by John Kenneth Galbraith in *The Affluent Society* three decades later. In both cases the questioning of these accepted verities caused some dismay among readers who saw rejection of democracy in the first case and of the market economy in the second. But these are not fair interpretations. Lippmann and Galbraith called for improvement in democratic government and in the free market to make the world a better place.

A Preface to Morals, Lippmann's last big book before starting his life as a columnist, is as much a contribution to theology and cultural history as to social science. He begins with a discussion of "the dissolution of the ancestral order," the structure that had provided moral guidance and values to a society. But now the successors, humanism and formal religion, were both in crisis. The modern state was challenged to discover a new basis for distinguishing good from evil, and for regulating institutions and social practices within itself. This was by far the most popular book by Lippmann to date and was a Book-of-the-Month Club selection.

Lippmann's serious works during the 1920s certainly helped establish his reputation as a scholar as well as a journalist. But more prosaic roles he played with respect to the economics profession during that decade contributed also to his reputation. First, he became an influential gatekeeper to publication. Economists who wished to publish the results of their research in the 1920s had several directions to which they could turn: scholarly journals, publications of professional organizations, university presses, commercial book publishers, popular weekly and monthly magazines, and daily newspapers. In the last three of these, at least, they might easily face Walter Lippmann. His reputation for native brilliance, eclectic interests, wide contacts, and speed reading made him the ideal acquisitions editor and referee. This began with the *New Republic*, where he helped build up a stable of distinguished contributors. His most famous acquisitions coup was Keynes's *Economics Consequences of the Peace* in 1919 for the *New Republic* as a series of articles and then as a book for Harcourt where he had taken on a supplementary editorial position. Harcourt used Lippmann regularly as referee and, for example, insisted that he read Gustav Cassel's *Theory of Social Economy* before publication in the United States. Those who submitted to the magazine and to Harcourt, and those whom Lippmann solicited, could expect from him much more than a perfunctory examination. He usually read the work himself and gave detailed comments. His correspondence files are full of evidence of this function. By the end of the 1920s leaders of the profession had come to see Lippmann as a public spokesman for sound policy views, and he received many letters of thanks and congratulation. After Lippmann was elected a Harvard overseer in 1933, he was appointed to the visiting committee to the economics department. He was routinely consulted on appointments, curriculum changes, and disputes within the department. The high regard for Lippmann at Harvard never flagged. Taussig wrote him in 1924. "Let me say just a word in appreciation of the way in which you are handling the editorial columns of 'The World.' You are doing all that we expected of you, and that is saying a great deal. I do not always agree with you, but what you say always makes me sit up and think; and it always makes me respect the intellectual quality and moral spirit which pervade it" (Taussig to Lippmann, June 2, 1924, WLP, series 1, F1192).

The breadth of Lippmann's friendships during the 1920s is breathtaking, from Harry Houdini to Winston Churchill, from Gene Tunney to Abraham Flexner. Among economists his closest contacts, understandably, were with those in New York, where he lived, and at Harvard, to which he often traveled. He was eclectic in his relations. Lippmann went to E. R. A. Seligman, Richard T. Ely, Herbert Feis, Jacob Hollander, Adolf Berle, Frank Tannenbaum, Harold Moulton, and A. G. Hart for comment on policy issues in their areas of expertise, and they used him in return. Lippmann was especially close to Alvin Johnson at the New School with whom he had worked at the *New Republic*, and he had a warm relationship with Allyn Young of Harvard, with whom he served on the Inquiry. He was comfortable with the growing community of institutionalists in and around New York, and it is symbolic perhaps that when Wesley Mitchell and Walton Hamilton wished to gain membership for a colleague in the Cosmos Club they turned to Lippmann as the third nominator.

It was not only economists who saw Lippmann as an effective spokesman for their ideas and their discipline. He was in great demand more widely, with political scientists often in the lead. Harold Laski and Graham Wallas of the London School of Economics and Charles Merriam of the University of Chicago were leading political scientists who came often to his door. Prominent sociologists included Howard Odum and Lewis Mumford. And his professional friendships were not limited to academics. He carried on a discussion of the supply-side effects of tax reductions with Congressman Ogden Mills, later secretary of the treasury, and he debated the merits of building hydroelectric dams with Senator George Norris. Alfred Zimmern, a young historian trained in Britain but with broad interests and many connections in Europe, was introduced to Lippmann by Wallas in 1911 and remained a close friend and adviser for many years. Among other things, Zimmern introduced Lippmann to Austrian economics in 1916 through an article by Ludwig von Mises that he translated for Lippmann's use.

Lippmann's warm friendship with Maynard Keynes was most important. It began when they served together in 1919 at Versailles and lasted until Keynes's death. To understand the closeness of this relationship, it helps to reflect on the close parallels in their careers and characters. They were born only six years apart into family privilege and moved effortlessly through excellent schools and universities. They struck everyone, even in the earliest years, as child prodigies. Despite their later engagement with economics, neither was attracted to it at first. Their initial interests were in philosophy, literature, and the arts. They took little economics as undergraduates and found the prospect of postgraduate study and a full-time career in academe unappealing. They both wanted to walk on a wider stage and speak to a larger audience. They both went through periods when they edited magazines and newspapers. By their twenties both were recognized by the political leaders of the countries in which they lived as talented and valuable, but they themselves stayed on the edge of political parties. They were shrewd businessmen, amassed substantial wealth, and lived in comfort and style. They were both prolific writers and followed the same strategy of mixing serious academic works (*Treatise on Money*, *General Theory*, *Public Opinion*, *The Good Society*) with publications aimed at a larger audience and richer market (*The Economic Consequences of the Peace*, *A Preface to Morals*). By middle age both gained celebrity status enjoyed by few intellectuals in their time. Much of the thinking of Lippmann and Keynes is remarkably congruent. They were both concerned to save democracy and free market capitalism, not to threaten, profoundly change, or destroy them. Their evolving positions on macroeconomic questions are similar. Their positions on domestic market issues varied because of the different circumstances in which they lived. They were both shrewd and manipulative, and despite the warmth of their friendship it is clear that each used the other: Lippmann for his connections and political influence in America, Keynes for his ideas and contacts in Britain. One of Keynes's distinct contributions was to link up Lippmann and his publishers with Bloomsbury: Lytton Strachey, Virginia Woolf, Leonard Woolf, and Clive Bell were all part of the exchange. Here are some of Lippmann's reminiscences in 1950 of his friendship with Keynes:

> I have a very profound admiration for Keynes. I really believe that he's one of the most influential men of our century and that Keynes will be remembered as Adam Smith is remembered—on the same level of eminence. I think he's changed the thinking and the policies. What he really did from my point of view, and the thing I'll always remember, is that he, to my mind, really knocked out the Marxian analysis of what capitalism had to do—the theory of the inevitability of cycles and the

helplessness of man in dealing with the business cycle, which would have resulted in the overthrow of the whole free society of the world and which did result in the overthrow of the German society and the Weimar Republic. Keynes has broken that, and we know now that with all the faults of these modern states, they have a remedy against unemployment that did not exist before Keynes. Unemployment was an act of God that you couldn't do anything about. Keynes's ideas have now filtered through to the governments, and they've filtered through to the people. (Lippmann 1950, 152–53)

He acknowledged the warmth of this friendship.

I had general discussions with Keynes over a period of twenty years. He always visited me when he came here, and I always visited him when I went to England. We corresponded. He was sort of like a man of the renaissance. His interests were general.

I once said to him, "You know, I've only learned what economics I know since I left college. I never studied economics in college."

He said, "Neither did I. I never took an economics course the whole time I was in college." (153–54)

Lippmann and Keynes often exchanged ideas and manuscripts before they were published, and Lippmann was alert to defend Keynes from critics in America (e.g., Lippmann to W. M. Reedy, May 4, 1920, WLP, F1029, concerning an article critical of Keynes in *Reedy's Mirror*, St. Louis, Mo.).

Depression Columnist

Lippmann approached the economic issues of the 1930s much in the way that economics textbooks did in the 1950s and thereafter, macro theory and policy separate from micro, two realms whose policy dimensions he called "recovery" and "reform." Indeed, he claimed that many of the problems of the decade arose from getting these two categories confused and entangled when addressed together. He thought that as much as possible recovery should be achieved before reform was even contemplated, and the consequence of failing to proceed in sequence could be catastrophic. He attributed the rise of dictators around the world to the human suffering that grew out of protracted depression. As Lippmann began his life as a columnist in 1931, his familiarity with economic theory was elementary. He had taken several undergraduate courses in the orthodox doctrine of the time, and he had been attracted particularly to the institutionalists' creative approach to problem solving, but he remained skeptical of the discipline overall and open to new ideas within it. Interestingly, over the decade he came to reject the orthodoxy of macroeconomics and to gain increasing respect for the orthodoxy of micro.

In his very first few columns he showed that he remained in thrall to respectable macroeconomics, strengthened in his beliefs by informal lectures from his friends in the banking and financial communities. The only responsible way to fight the depression, he insisted in 1931, was to wait for market adjustments to take effect. Deflation sooner or later would restore equilibrium in competitive markets and unemployment would disappear. The adjustment process could be accelerated by strengthening the confidence of the business community in responsible behavior by government, meaning firm adherence to monetary and fiscal respectability: the gold standard, fixed exchange rates, and a balanced fiscal budget. But Lippmann's adherence to these principles was sufficiently tentative that he remained receptive to alternative explanations. One of the first macro policy icons to fall for him was the necessity to respect a hands-off approach in the monetary sphere. After extensive correspondence with successive chairmen of the Federal Reserve Board, Eugene Meyer and Mariner Eccles, as well as with the economist Lauchlin Currie, he became convinced that a managed monetary policy could contribute to a revival of economic activity through more liberal lending by banks made possible by active open market operations. He thought it likely also that the modest inflation called for by President Franklin D. Roosevelt's monetary advisers, the Cornell economists G. F. Warren and F. A. Pearson, would make a positive contribution. By various correspondents he was persuaded that continued adherence to the gold standard made little sense and constrained recovery. He favored some kind of stability of exchange rates to discourage competitive devaluations, perhaps fixed rates subject to occasional readjustments and kept in balance by pools of foreign currency, similar to the model of the International Monetary Fund that came out of Bretton Woods.

In 1933 Lippmann undertook his most thorough rethinking of macroeconomic theory and practice, partly during the summer spent in London covering the ill-fated London Economic Conference and talking with Keynes, and partly tucked away reading in the Maine woods. He ended the year with the conviction that the supposed need to maintain a balanced fiscal budget was wholly unfounded. Instead he proposed a "compensated economy" in a series of Godkin Lectures at Harvard in 1934 and published with the title *Method of Freedom* that brought together Keynesian doctrine, especially the emphasis on aggregate demand, with the social psychology that had intrigued him since college days. The argument was quite simple. Humans were mercurial in their behavior and could not be counted on to deliver enough aggregate demand to sustain full employment. Therefore the government of a successful democracy must be prepared to "compensate" for any shortfall. This conversion to an extension of Keynes's macroeconomic doctrine was permanent for Lippmann and was not reversed as his microeconomic position evolved.

When Lippmann began his *Herald Tribune* columns in 1931 he was far from being a starry-eyed admirer of the free market. He was, in fact, deeply suspicious of many of the supposedly optimum economic outcomes promised by free marketers, and he often pointed to negative market externalities such as environmental degradation, monopolistic concentration, and poverty. But paradoxically his enthusiasm for the free market grew through the painful decade. Partly, it was that he could see no better alternative. He was persuaded by the socialist calculation debates that no planning regime could be as efficient as a competitive market system. He also found compelling the exposition of the close relationship between free markets and personal liberty by Mises and other Austrians, especially Friedrich Hayek, and Lionel Robbins. Lippmann was startled and depressed to discover how much free markets were under attack and in need of defenders, with various forms of public and private monopoly apparently on the ascendant. He noted with dismay the smooth passage of the Hawley-Smoot tariffs to protect industry, the increasing strength of organized labor, and even the farmers' endorsement of a range of schemes to limit competition. None of these components of the American economy, he feared, understood that the destruction of competition would lead inevitably to arbitrary action by government and a suffocating bureaucracy.

Some of Lippmann's earliest worries about the future of democracy concerned the difficulty experienced by the public in distinguishing among policy alternatives and in the evident malleability of public opinion. Now he was startled to observe how ready the public seemed to be to adopt monopolies of all kinds, even when against their own self-interest. This seemed to call for spirited defense of the free market by spokesmen like himself.

Lippmann observed that attacks on the free market and the liberal order increasingly came from a most unsavory collection of characters that needed to be exposed. There were the usual profiteers who had been around since mercantilist times. John L. Lewis, who headed the mine workers, was just like the head of a guild against which Adam Smith had preached. Then there were unorthodox reformers (cranks) like Major Douglas, Frederick Soddy, and the industrial technocrats who muddied the waters and seemed not to appreciate the loss of freedom, as well as efficiency, embodied in their schemes. There were also well-meaning intellectuals, otherwise perfectly respectable, who were able to operate within the policy mainstream and act as pied pipers of collectivization for politicians who did not know any better. Rexford Tugwell and other New Deal advisers embodied this type. Finally, there were some political leaders who were in all respects cynical and corrupt and used market control as a way to maintain political domination. It was especially discouraging that this category seemed to be growing steadily in the 1920s and 1930s with Stalin, Hitler, Mussolini, Franco, and Juan Perón. Lippmann was careful to place FDR not in this last group of dictators but in the prior group of misguided intellectuals.

Lippmann combined his newfound macro-heterodoxy and his resolute micro-orthodoxy in his well-known work, *The Good Society* (1937), in which he explored political philosophy, economic history, and current events in a landmark defense of liberalism. This led to engagements with like-minded intellectuals who went on to mount efforts in support of their principles that included plans for a new journal and a research institute. The only plan that came to pass was for the Mont Pèlerin Society, which emerged from a conference in Lippmann's honor held in Paris.

Conclusion

By the end of the 1930s Walter Lippmann had sampled many possible careers, some at a distance and some up close: investigative journalism, the professoriat, public service at the municipal and high federal levels, and editorship of a major magazine and influential daily newspaper. None of these had the continuing fascination for him equal to that of columnist and public economist. He was regularly importuned with job offers from all over, and his response to one is revealing. After he delivered a commencement address at the University of North Carolina in 1930, Lippmann was approached by a well-connected North Carolinian who said he believed there were enough enthusiastic board members to support Lippmann's election as university president. There was nothing wrong with the university, this man wrote, "except there has been no education done there for many years," and now it was challenged by "an enormous pile of stones, arranged somewhat gothically, by Mr. Duke's money" only twelve miles away (letter to Lippmann, May 27, 1930, WLP, series 1, F774). Lippmann expressed gratitude for the inquiry but explained: "It is more fun to write than it is to be an executive of any kind, however noble, however useful, however honorific. I could not endure being a public character. I have had just enough direct experience of being a public official never to want to have anything remotely resembling it again. That's about all there is to it" (Lippmann, May 29, 1930, WLP, series 1, F774).

References

Berle, Adolf, and Gardiner Means. 1932. *The Modern Corporation and Private Property.* New York: Macmillan.

Blum, John Morton. 1985. *Public Philosopher: Selected Letters of Walter Lippmann.* New York: Ticknor & Fields.

Chase, Stuart. 1930. "The Harvard Class of 1910." Offprint, Walter Lippmann Papers, series 1, F241.

Dorfman, Joseph. 1934. *Thorstein Veblen and His America.* New York: Viking.

Hartshorn, Peter. 2011. *I Have Seen the Future: A Life of Lincoln Steffens.* Berkeley, Calif.: Counterpoint.

Lippmann, Walter. Papers. (MS) 326, Manuscripts and Archives, Yale University Library. Cited herein as WLP, followed by the series and file numbers.

———. (1913) 1962. *A Preface to Politics.* Ann Arbor: University of Michigan Press.

———. (1914) 1985. *Drift and Mastery.* Madison: University of Wisconsin Press.

———. 1915. "Freud and the Layman." *New Republic*, April 17.

———. (1922) 2007. *Public Opinion.* N.p.: BN Publishing.

———. (1925) 2009. *The Phantom Public.* New Brunswick, N.J.: Transaction.

———. (1929) 2009. *A Preface to Morals.* New York: Macmillan.

———. (1937) 1943. *The Good Society.* New York: Grosset and Dunlap.

———. 1950. *Reminiscences of Walter Lippmann.* Columbia University Center for Oral History Collection, New York.

Steel, Ronald. 1980. *Walter Lippmann and the American Century.* Boston: Atlantic Monthly Press.

Tead, Ordway. 1918. *Instincts in Industry.* Boston: Houghton Mifflin.

Wallas, Graham. 1914. *The Great Society: A Psychological Analysis.* London: Macmillan.

Lionel Robbins: Political Economist

Susan Howson

The British economist Lionel Robbins, professor of economics at the London School of Economics from 1929 to 1961, engaged in public debate on economic policy issues for six decades: in public lectures and radio broadcasts, in talks to clubs and discussion groups, and in popular and semipopular contributions to newspapers and magazines, as well as in academic journal articles and books. He had the opportunity to influence UK economic policy directly during the Second World War. After the war he exerted a strong influence on government policy for the arts and higher education, especially since his diplomatic and persuasive skills were recognized by appointment to public committees. He gained an additional forum in the House of Lords in 1959. The apparent irony is that, in his own words, "it has been held that . . . I advocated the abstention of the economist from all interest or activity outside his own interest . . . in spite of activities which I feared had become notorious" (Robbins 1935b, viii).

This essay describes how he fulfilled what he saw as his *duty* to use his expertise to enlighten nonexperts once he had been appointed to his chair in economics at the London School of Economics (LSE) in 1929. His sense of duty was ingrained from his nonconformist (Strict Baptist) childhood. In his youth he lost belief in God but not in good works,

---

Correspondence may be addressed to Susan Howson, University of Toronto, Department of Economics, 150 St. George Street, Toronto, ON M5S 3G7, Canada; e-mail: s.howson@utoronto.ca.

History of Political Economy 45 (annual suppl.) DOI 10.1215/00182702-2310971
Copyright 2013 by Duke University Press

especially the obligation to try to improve the lot of others (Robbins 1924b; 1932b, 136–39). His parents' home was also a Liberal household. Robbins was a free trader like his father—a very successful farmer who resigned from the Council of the National Farmers' Union in protest over agricultural protection in 1932—and his views were reinforced by his early training in economics. His first attempt to influence opinion was a note for his father to use as ammunition against other NFU Council members in 1923, while he was still an undergraduate at LSE.

Robbins entered LSE in October 1920, after seeing active service as an artillery officer on the Western front in 1917–18 and, having become a socialist during the war, working for eighteen months in the Labour movement. At LSE he specialized in the history of political ideas under the left-wing Harold Laski but became increasingly interested in economic theory, impressed by its analytical rigor and by the fair-minded way it was taught at LSE by both the politically active (in the Labour Party) Hugh Dalton and the relatively apolitical Edwin Cannan (a friend of the Fabians who founded LSE in 1895 but not himself a Fabian). Robbins explained in a 1930s talk to students that by the time he had graduated and began working as an economist, he had come to realize that socialists had not grappled with fundamental economic problems and that their favored policies would not work. He emphasized his "final disillusionment": that since these difficulties were not mentioned, intellectuals attaching themselves to a party seemed to be in danger of losing their intellectual independence, of not saying things that did not fit the party line. Hence the "best thing [was] to be outside." After the fall of the first Labour government in 1924, he decided he would vote Liberal, if only by default (Robbins 1924a). By the time he became a peer in 1959, he had voted for all three major parties; in the Lords he sat on the cross benches.

He therefore made a clear distinction between economics, which he regarded as positive and scientific, and political economy, which is admittedly normative. His speaking and writing as a public intellectual—as a "political economist," as he preferred to put it—were firmly in the latter category. He saw no contradiction of logic or morality between his view of economics as a science and his own public activities. Indeed he thought he *ought* to intervene in public discussion to try to influence public opinion against misguided economic policies, such as protectionist policies in the 1930s and unduly expansionary monetary policies in Britain after the Second World War.

In his early academic career (at LSE during 1925–27 and New College Oxford during 1927–29), Robbins published only a short popular book, *Wages* (1926), and a handful of articles. But in 1924 and 1925, while working first as a research assistant to William Beveridge (director of LSE) and then as a temporary lecturer at New College, he gained experience in economic journalism writing for the *Outlook*, "a mildly Liberal weekly" magazine, thanks to an introduction to the financial journalist Oscar Hobson through one of his closest student friends at LSE (Georg Tugendhat) (Howson 2011, 113–14). The invitation to write the *Wages* book also came through friends, this time the great Liberal journalist A. G. Gardiner, who was Robbins's father-in-law.

In the 1930s Robbins produced a dozen academic articles and five books, one of which was a collection of "essays in political economy" (1939a) that he had given as talks or written for publications such as *Lloyds Bank Review*. His papers contain notes for talks and lectures to a wide variety of audiences, including political and economic discussion groups and economic conferences. His writing for magazines and newspapers then and later was directed to what might be called "educated public opinion": readers of the quality newspapers (the *Times*, the *Manchester Guardian*, the *Daily Telegraph*) and of the intellectual magazines such as the *New Statesman* and the *Spectator*, and the subset interested in economics and finance who read the *Economist*, the financial newspapers, and the bank reviews; some of these might also read his more popular books (1934, 1937a, 1939a, 1939b, 1954a, 1963, 1966, 1971b, 1980).

The Young Professor

His first year as professor coincided with the onset of the worldwide slump. In the summer of 1930 he was disturbed about popular demands for protection by tariffs or other barriers to international trade and upset when economists were prepared to abandon the free-trade position. On holiday he wrote to his father and said that he had not yet quite decided to jump into the fray: "Controversy is very fascinating but scientific work is so much more important & respectable" (Howson 2011, 179). While Robbins was on holiday, however, John Maynard Keynes invited him, as the new professor of economics at LSE, to join the Committee of Economists chaired by Keynes and intended to advise the Labour prime minister (James Ramsay MacDonald) on the causes of the slump and possible remedies for it. Keynes's intention of producing "an agreed diagnosis" of and policy recommendations for Britain's economic problems was thwarted by Robbins's refusal to go along with Keynes's suggestions for public works and the introduction of a tariff. The committee's report went to MacDonald on October 24 with a "minority report" by Robbins, which explained why, "as regards those sections of the Report which relate to tariffs and similar measures, I am in complete disagreement with the majority of my colleagues" (Howson and Winch 1977, 229). But he was respected by those colleagues (Hubert Henderson, A. C. Pigou, and Josiah Stamp) and by Keynes once Keynes had got over his anger.

Robbins continued his fight against protection publicly with articles in newspapers and magazines and with his LSE colleagues. The day after the final meeting of Keynes's committee, Robbins and the professor of commerce Arnold Plant dined with Beveridge, Walter Layton (editor of the *Economist* and, like Beveridge, an active Liberal), and Sir Arthur Salter (recently director of the economic and financial section of the League of Nations). Beveridge suggested they form another "committee of economists" to write a popular book expounding the arguments against tariffs. When a larger group, including other LSE economists and Dennis Robertson from Cambridge, met again on October 29 they agreed the introduction "should include a statement of faith in Free Trade and an indication of general agreement with the contents of the book," and the book would be written by Beveridge on the basis of material supplied by the others. It eventually appeared in October 1931, signed by only the LSE economists plus Layton.[1] Like the reports of the Committee of Economists, it had no effect on UK economic policy. MacDonald's Labour government had a staunch free trader as chancellor of the exchequer; his "National" coalition government that succeeded it in August 1931 soon had a Conservative chancellor whose long-held ambition was to introduce a tariff, which he quickly did. Robbins continued his fight for free trade.

When Keynes came out publicly with his tariff proposals in the *New Statesman and Nation* in March 1931 the (left-wing) editor, Kingsley Martin, invited Robbins to reply. Robbins and Beveridge made sure that other economists wrote letters against Keynes to the magazine—prompting Keynes to write further articles and Robbins to respond in further letters. Robbins (1931a) had already challenged Keynes's arguments in a

---

1. Robbins (1971a, 158) thought that apart from chapters signed by individual authors (Frederic Benham, J. R. Hicks, Plant, Robbins, and G. L. Schwartz) the statement of the case for free trade was "mediocre," with "far too much of the vulnerable traditional free-trade argument to satisfy the fastidious."

November 1930 talk to the London Economic Club, which had been founded in 1890 and included City people and financial journalists; he also attacked the Labour Party's proposals for "import boards" in the new journal *Political Quarterly* (Robbins 1931b) and would have done so at a Liberal free trade conference in May had he not had chickenpox.

Britain's departure from the gold standard in September 1931 prompted another burst of letters from Robbins to the "quality" newspapers, pointing out that the argument for a tariff as a way to improve the balance of trade no longer applied. He raised the question "Does the trade balance need treatment?," answering in the negative, to a meeting of the Political Economy Club (the club founded by the friends of David Ricardo in 1821), whose members included senior civil servants and prominent politicians, in December, criticizing recent arguments for tariffs and for control of capital movements. At that time he was also in favor of returning to gold soon at a new lower parity, but friends in the City (Oscar Hobson, Georg Tugendhat, and Jacques Kahane, another student friend from LSE) persuaded him it was impractical given the UK's low gold reserves; when Robbins gave his first radio broadcast in a series on currency problems in January 1932 he confined himself to criticizing the authorities for not defending the pound with higher interest rates before September 1931. He always preferred fixed exchange rates to floating rates, because he feared that without the discipline of fixed rates, governments would be too inclined to allow their currencies to depreciate and thus risk inflation. In 1932 he was also worried that depreciation of sterling would prompt other countries to resort to exchange controls. He described the adverse effects of trade restrictions on international capital movements when he spoke at a world conference of economics organized by the *Berliner Tageblatt* newspaper in Berlin in May (Howson 2011, 209–12, 225). In his first *Lloyds Bank Review* article in October (Robbins 1932c), he argued for the superiority of an international gold standard over (managed) floating exchange rates.

Robbins was also concerned about domestic economic policy. He took every opportunity to try to influence public opinion to distrust any panaceas offering an "easy way" out of the depression.

In February 1932 the prime minister asked Robbins to serve on another committee, this one intended to advise him on the effects of the public expenditure cuts made during the 1931 crisis.[2] The committee, which

---

2. This committee and the Committee of Economists were officially subcommittees of the government's Economic Advisory Council, whose varied membership included industrialists, trade unionists, and economists (including Keynes, Henderson, and Stamp) that had been set up by MacDonald in 1930.

included Stamp and Henderson, agreed the cuts had been necessary to balance the budget and avoid tax increases, but only Robbins argued *further* cuts might be desirable. As in the Committee of Economists, he was not in favor of public works undertaken to provide employment. Robbins (1932a) was in his "Austrian" phase, when, impressed especially by Friedrich Hayek's recent work, he espoused an Austrian monetary overinvestment theory of the cycle. This implied that since the boom was characterized by excessive investment because of unduly low interest rates, recovery from the slump could not be speeded up by expansionary fiscal or monetary policy. As he admitted in his autobiography,

> I realized that these constructions led to conclusions which were highly unpalatable as regards practical action. But I was convinced that they were valid and that therefore it was my duty to base recommendations as regards policy upon them. There was a touch of the Nonconformist conscience here. (Robbins 1971a, 153)

Accordingly, when the *Economist* urged the government to make a declaration of its monetary policy to include the desirability of a 30 percent rise in wholesale prices as well as lower interest rates, Robbins reacted strongly, writing to the editor on May 14 "to question very seriously whether the remedy you propose is not likely to prove worse than the disease. . . . You propose to cure the patient by a small dose of the same poison that has brought him to his present condition." When other readers criticized him strongly he responded equally vigorously in two more letters. In the summer he readily contributed to a debate on "spend or save?" in the *Spectator*, which opened with articles by the underconsumptionist economist and journalist J. A. Hobson and himself. He argued for "save" on Hayekian lines (Howson 2011, 227–30). When the *Times* in October published a letter from D. H. Macgregor (professor of political economy at Oxford), Keynes, Layton, Pigou, Salter, and Stamp arguing the case for increased private and public spending in depressed conditions, Robbins, with his professorial colleagues Theodore Gregory, Hayek, and Plant, responded strongly with their argument for encouraging *saving* and discouraging public investment.

Robbins (1971a, 154) later regretted his noninterventionist attitude to economic depression, characterizing it as "denying blankets and stimulants to a drunk who has fallen into an icy pond on the ground that his original trouble was overheating." The beginning of his changed macroeconomic views can be seen in a February 1937 talk at Toynbee Hall (the universities settlement in the East End of London), which became an article: "How to Mitigate the Next Slump" (Robbins 1937b). He never regretted his opposition to Keynes's tariff proposal.

Robbins made further attempts to influence opinion in favor of the gold standard as an international monetary system and to fight the good fight against the devil of protectionism, using the columns of the *Times* and other newspapers and, especially, *Lloyds Bank Review*, most notably in a series on currency stabilization, for which he provided the opening paper and persuaded the exiled former German chancellor Heinrich Brüning to contribute to an anonymous "dialogue between a foreign statesman and an English student of affairs" (Robbins 1935a, 1935c). Robbins joined a Royal Institute of International Affairs study group on international monetary problems in July 1933 but did not sign the report (RIIA 1935) because of his views on the gold standard. Most importantly, he gave a series of four Saturday afternoon lectures on the depression to the Royal Institution of Great Britain in November–December 1933, which he then turned into a book intended to be both popular and academically respectable (1934). Whether or not it influenced public opinion, it was reviewed worldwide and had to be reprinted within three months. The first three lectures/chapters outlined the course of events since the Great War, "misconceptions," that is, theories that failed to explain the events of 1929–33, and his own preferred explanation in terms of an Austrian-style monetary overinvestment theory. His fourth lecture on the severity of the depression he expanded into three chapters on the *many* contributory factors: political problems, agricultural depression, misguided monetary policies, and the collapse of the international monetary system followed by trade and exchange restrictions. As he put his overall argument succinctly in another radio broadcast, the world slump—"the aftermath of the collapse of a boom like so many slumps in the past . . . [but which] unlike the slumps of the past . . . has been an abnormally long time disappearing"—had been initiated by inflationary policies before 1929 and aggravated by restrictionist government interventions since (Robbins 1935d). A separate chapter of his book was devoted to denouncing restrictionism and planning.

Invited to lecture at the Graduate Institute of International Studies in Geneva in 1935, he spoke on what became *Economic Planning and International Order* (1937a). There he expatiated on the dire effects of national planning on the international economy; the inadequacy of "partial" international planning such as bilateral trade agreements, international cartels and commodity agreements, which benefited only particular groups of producers in one industry or one country; and the impracticality of "complete" international planning. The only solution to the "stupendous problem" of devising a world economic order that would maximize the welfare of the world's citizens *as a whole* and prevent wars between independent nation states was an international political *federation*, in which states would surrender certain powers (especially of making policies inimical to the welfare of citizens of other countries within the federation) to an international authority.

Lecturing in Geneva again in April 1939, he directly addressed the question of economic causes of war. He critically analyzed Marxian theories, but while he did not accept the theories he did believe there were economic causes of war: sectional interests, which were fostered by trade barriers and protected by restrictions on immigration. The way to prevent these leading to conflicts between national governments was to limit national sovereignty, by a federation of at least the European states. As he admitted in his preface to the book (Robbins 1939b), "The earlier argument is a preparation [for the demonstration] of the fundamental inappropriateness to modern conditions of the present political organization of the world and the necessity of replacing the independent sovereign states by larger federal unions."

On reading *Economic Planning and International Order* in the summer of 1939 Lionel Curtis of the RIIA urged Robbins to get in touch with the three young men who were setting up a Federal Union organization in Britain. On the outbreak of war in September Robbins produced a memorandum on a proposal regarding war aims and their realization—the proposal being an immediate federation of Britain and France—which Curtis circulated. In October, when Beveridge helped set up a Federal Union research department, Robbins joined its economists committee, attending conferences and writing memoranda and reports. He lectured in a series of LSE public lectures on federation, contributed an essay to a "symposium" on Federal Union, and planned to write a book on the economics of federation with LSE colleagues including Plant and Hayek. He advocated an Anglo-French federation still more publicly in articles to the *Spectator* in November 1939 and March and April 1940. His last activity was to attend an Anglo-French economists conference in Paris in April, which discussed one of his reports, just as the phony war of 1939–40 came to an end (Howson 2011, 345–52).[3]

---

3. Winston Churchill as prime minister offered a political union to France on June 16, 1940, the day before France fell.

Robbins's writings on the economic causes of war and the economic aspects of federation "are today considered fundamental contributions to federalist theory." In the 1940s they had their greatest (and lasting) impact on Altiero Spinelli and Ernest Rossi, to whom Luigi Einaudi sent them when they were confined as antifascist militants on the island of Ventotene (Ransome 1991, 39–40; Pinder 1998).

Interlude: The Second World War

In September 1939 Robbins feared he would not be offered a wartime government job because he had "offended so many people in high quarters by inconvenient criticisms of policy." But he was not tempted by a chance to move to the United States in January 1940. If he was not offered a government job, he could perhaps influence outside opinion: "While any hope remains of exerting this in a direction favourable to winning the war & making a real peace, it would be almost an act of desertion to escape" (Howson 2011, 329, 348). Soon after the formation of Winston Churchill's coalition government in May 1940, Robbins was, along with several other relatively young economists (from Glasgow, Manchester, and Swansea as well as Oxford and Cambridge), asked to join what became the Economic Section of the Cabinet Offices; in September 1941 he became its director.

In his first year of government service Robbins initiated the discussions, wrote the memoranda, and persuaded ministers and civil servants in the process that led to points rationing for food in 1941—"one of [the] big home front successes of the war" (Hancock and Gowing 1949, 332). He backed Keynes's proposals on how to pay for the war and helped persuade senior Treasury officials to allow the preparation of national income and expenditure estimates by James Meade and Richard Stone needed to implement the proposals.[4] His active support of Meade's work on postwar employment policy was crucial in getting this work out of the Section and into wider circulation and discussion at the highest levels of government in 1943; he defended the Section's proposals against formidable opposition from the most senior civil servants in Whitehall. They rightly credited him with the most significant contribution in furthering the final outcome: the 1944 white paper *Employment Policy* (Cmd 6527). As one Treasury

---

4. I have argued elsewhere (Howson 2011, 417–18, 665–66, 1085) that the creation of these estimates was an important factor in convincing Robbins that macroeconomic management was feasible as well as desirable.

official put it, "We all owe you a lot—more, I suppose, than anyone is ever likely to know. In fact the story of Points Rationing over again writ large" (Howson 2011, 1083).

Robbins was lucky in working for Sir John Anderson as the minister responsible for the Section. Anderson was an outstanding administrator who could be counted on to read his briefs and, if he agreed with the advice, to fight for it. Alec Cairncross and Nita Watts (1989, 54) emphasize that "Robbins hit it off with Anderson and enjoyed his complete trust. It was this more than anything that allowed the Section to play an important and useful part as economic advisers." It also made him one of Keynes's most influential allies. Robbins continued to advise Anderson after Anderson became chancellor of the exchequer in September 1943, especially on international economic policy.

After the fall of France in 1940, Robbins's hopes centered on Anglo-American cooperation to bring about a multilateral postwar international order based on fixed exchange rates and relatively free trade. He was thus "strongly attracted" to Keynes's clearing union plan in October 1941 and fought hard and persistently for it and for Meade's complementary plan for an international commercial union. His talents for economic diplomacy were much needed: it was not just a matter of persuading officials and ministers in London that these schemes offered the best hope of Britain's postwar prosperity but of trying to persuade economists in the US administration that these would fit in with American requirements for the postwar settlement. His personal contributions were vitally important at the first UN conference at Hot Springs and in discussions with US officials in Washington in 1943 and at the 1944 UN Monetary and Financial Conference at Bretton Woods, which created the International Monetary Fund and the World Bank.

Robbins's free-trade position led ultimately to his most important contribution to the postwar settlement. On his last mission to Washington he and Percivale Liesching of the Board of Trade succeeded in October–November 1945 in finally obtaining an agreement with the US administration on postwar commercial policy, in the form of *Proposals for Consideration by an International Conference on Trade and Employment*, whose principles were incorporated in the General Agreement on Tariffs and Trade (or GATT) in 1947. With such an agreement required as the "consideration" for the receipt of wartime lend-lease, it was an essential prerequisite for a postwar loan from the US government: without the commercial policy agreement there would have been no financial agreement.

Furthermore, in the difficult negotiations led by Keynes for the financial agreement, which Robbins joined in November 1945, his diplomacy and tact were often crucial in keeping the negotiations going. Without his interventions in the later stages of these negotiations, there might well have been no American loan.

While Robbins was highly effective as a temporary civil servant and enjoyed economic diplomacy, he was always determined to return to academic life and regain the opportunity to try to influence policy *publicly*. He told his sister (the American historian Caroline Robbins) in October 1941 that

> nothing in the world . . . would tempt me to continue as a government servant once the war is over: the moment I can get away without feeling that I am shirking essential duties you won't see me for dust. I was not born for the twilight of bureaucracy; and the prospect of one day once again being able to call a spade a spade (and a fool a fool) without rocking someone else's boat is for me one of the main hopes of peace. (Howson 2011, 423)

But there is no doubt that the contacts he made in his five and a half years in Whitehall, with civil servants and government ministers, were to increase greatly the influence he could exert as a public intellectual after the war.

After the War

When Keynes died at Easter 1946, one of Robbins's wartime colleagues, Norman Chester, suggested that Robbins would have to take up Keynes's mantle, since he was "now the leading 'political economist' in the best sense of the term" (Howson 2011, 645). After observing the convention that newly retired civil servants do not comment on the issues they were officially concerned with, Robbins entered public debate again in January 1947 with an article on Britain's "economic prospects" in *Lloyds Bank Review*. Just as his article was both encouraging and alarmist—the reconversion of industry and the expansion of exports were well under way, but the recovery of the balance of payments was threatened by a shortage of labor and wage inflation—so his article, and a letter to the *Times* four weeks later, received both criticism and support, especially of his proposal that foreign labor should be recruited to work in the coal mines where the manpower shortage was acute. As he told his son (prophetically) in February (Howson 2011, 658), "I have been so troubled about all this that I have plunged into public controversy. . . . I fancy I shall remain in that state for some months or years to come."

After the coal crisis of February–March 1947 there came the convertibility crisis of July–August 1947, when the postwar Labour government was forced after six weeks to suspend the convertibility of sterling into US dollars, a commitment reluctantly agreed to under the Anglo-American Financial Agreement of December 1945. Robbins's next article for *Lloyds Bank Review* (1947b) is one of his finest and most powerful articles. A cogent analysis of the causes of the crisis, it squarely blamed the government for unduly expansionary macroeconomic policy and for allowing capital outflows not required by the loan agreement. It attracted extensive press comment, invariably complimentary, even from those who had been critical of his earlier pieces. It was soon used by Liberal and Conservative MPs to attack the chancellor of the exchequer (Hugh Dalton) in the House of Commons.[5] Another crisis two years later, which led to a 30 percent devaluation of the pound in September, prompted another *Lloyds Bank Review* article (1949), which attracted considerable attention. (Robbins again tried to alert the public to the adverse balance-of-payments effect of domestic inflationary pressure and argued that while the decision to devalue and by a large amount was right, it did not obviate the need for tighter fiscal and, especially, monetary policy.) Probably most influential in shaping opinion on British postwar economic policy was his Stamp Memorial Lecture, an annual University of London public lecture that attracted an audience of senior civil servants and City people, in November 1951 (Dow 1960, 67–68). He spoke after the general election, which had returned the first postwar Conservative government and just after the first rise in Bank rate since before the war. He argued for the revival of monetary policy and its assignment to the task of maintaining a fixed exchange rate for the pound sterling. This was to remain a theme of many of his public pronouncements during the 1950s and 1960s; thereafter, when exchange rates were floating, he continued to warn year in and year out of the dangers of inflation and the need to keep the money supply under control (e.g., Robbins 1971b, 1974, 1979).

---

5. In 1948, after Dalton had been replaced by Stafford Cripps, Robbins wrote more letters to the *Times* urging a cautious fiscal policy; in 1949 he commended Cripps for the "courage and vision" of his second budget in a radio broadcast (Howson 2011, 672–73, 685–86, 695–96).

Robbins was much exercised by the first moves toward Western European economic and political integration. Since 1940 he had been disillusioned with the idea of a European federation. He also disliked the idea of a customs union, since it was a mixture of free trade and protection. Hence when the French plan for a European coal and steel community was announced in May 1950, he wrote letters to the *Times* in June and a piece for *Lloyds Bank Review* (1950), defending the Labour government's reluctance to become involved and his own preference for a broader arrangement including the United States and the British Commonwealth. The outbreak of the Korean War in June led to another bout of agitation, this time for rearmament and strengthening NATO, with letters to the *Times* and the *Spectator* and participation in an RIIA study group on Atlantic union (McLachlan 1952).

Although Robbins had been remarkably effective as a wartime civil servant, he still strongly preferred *public persuasion* to private advice, to try to influence people publicly, and therefore to say what he really believed, rather than to operate within the civil service, which obliged him to trim his words to suit the preoccupations or prejudices of their political masters (as he had to do on occasion during the war [see, for one instance, Howson and Moggridge 1990, 186]). This was linked with his long-standing distaste for party politics and refusal to be linked with any one political party. Nonetheless, as he admitted in his autobiography, he was consulted twice by the Conservative government in the 1950s (Robbins 1971a, 229). When the new government was trying to cope with its first balance-of-payments crisis in 1952, he was consulted by the permanent secretary of the treasury, Edward Bridges, with whom he had worked closely during the war. Along with economists working in the Economic Section he helped persuade the chancellor (R. A. Butler) not to adopt the controversial ROBOT plan for limited sterling convertibility at a floating exchange rate. In the September 1957 crisis he was consulted by the chancellor of the exchequer, Peter Thorneycroft, a personal friend, who summoned him back from a holiday in Austria, asked for his advice on a draft Cabinet paper, and made him a member of a Treasury working group set up "to consider . . . what steps are required to get effective control of the credit base." One of the specific recommendations for improved monetary control Robbins made to the working group was adopted by the Bank of England in the form of Special Deposits in 1958 (Howson 2011, 738–42, 795–803).

Robbins much preferred to participate in *public* inquiries commissioned by the government such as royal commissions and other ad hoc committees. He was often invited to do so (and turned several invitations down) because of his wartime experience, where his considerable committee skills had become well known to senior officials and government ministers. As he commented, "One thing leads to another" (Robbins 1971a, 249). The most important of the committees on which he agreed to serve concerned—with one major exception—the arts.

The first invitation came from the Labour chancellor of the exchequer Stafford Cripps in August 1950—to join a committee on the export of works of art, which was to be chaired by Robbins's former boss in Whitehall, Sir John Anderson.[6] The problem it addressed had arisen because the export of artworks was still controlled under wartime regulations, and the number of applications for licenses to export artworks had increased sharply since the devaluation of the pound; many applications were rejected and the Treasury's advisers criticized as interested parties. Robbins was very active in this committee, which recommended a permanent Reviewing Committee on the Export of Works of Art that is still in existence (Treasury 1952). He served as its first chairman until he, too, became an "interested party."

The next two requests from the Treasury were to be a member of a committee of the Organization for European Economic Co-operation (now the OECD) charged with reviewing the internal financial situation of member countries in May 1952 and, two years later, to chair a committee on the possible rebuilding of the Queen's Hall, the original home of the Henry Wood Promenade Concerts, which had been destroyed by bombing in March 1941. By 1954 the Proms had moved to the Royal Albert Hall, and the Royal Festival Hall had been built on the South Bank. The Treasury now wanted answers to two questions, "the case on musical and artistic grounds" for another large concert hall and its "economic prospects": could it be run without a subsidy, or "would it in fact be a new Covent Garden [i.e., expensive to sustain]?" Robbins's response was that of an economist: the committee needed to assess the *supply* of concert seats in relation to the likely *demand* for them, to see if there was a case for an additional large hall in London. Even if there was such a case, it was also necessary to compare the possible revenue with the cost of building the hall: if it would require a large subsidy, that would come at the expense of other desirable uses of the money.

---

6. The committee is usually known as the Waverley Committee because Anderson became Lord Waverley in 1952.

Robbins wrote the report himself. On the basis of empirical data on numbers of concerts before and after the war and on ticket prices, he argued that "while the evidence available suggests that there does exist some unsatisfied demand, . . . it would not seem to be of such dimensions as to render the economic prospects of a new Queen's Hall unequivocally favourable"; the size of the estimated subsidy suggested there was no strong ground for giving it a high priority "in the long list of desirable objects of immediate government expenditure"; and there seemed to be more demand for a new *small* hall such as the one on the South Bank to complement the Royal Festival Hall. The Queen's Hall was not rebuilt.

Robbins (1971a, 244–46) suspected that his connection with the Courtauld Institute of Art plus his wartime government experience had led to his appointment to the Waverley Committee and that in turn led to his invitation to become a trustee of the National Gallery in July 1952.[7] In 1956 he joined the board of directors of the Royal Opera House Covent Garden. He served three seven-year terms as a trustee of the National Gallery, and as chairman of the trustees twice (1954–59 and 1962–67); at Covent Garden, having persuaded the chairman of the board to set up a finance committee, he chaired that committee for nearly twenty years, tackling from an economist's point of view the chronic funding problems of mounting opera and ballet,[8] and remained on the ROH board until 1980.

Jonathan Conlin (2006, 184) claimed that "the economist Lionel Robbins was probably the greatest of the Trustees to serve in the [twentieth] century" and "arguably the most effective Trustee the Gallery ever had." His effectiveness was a matter of *persuasion*: of his fellow trustees, civil servants and ministers, and public opinion. The director, Philip Hendy, commented in a radio interview in 1968 that Robbins "had a rather unique relationship with the Civil Service and with governments throughout. It is due more to him than anyone else that the National Gallery Grant was enlarged." Until 1965 the National Gallery (and the Tate) was financed directly by the Treasury. Butler had agreed to the Waverley Committee's recommendation of a 25 percent increase in the grant and to the Reviewing Committee's recommendation of a further 25 percent increase a

---

7. When Robbins was appointed to the senate of the University of London in 1936 he volunteered to join the Courtauld's Committee of Management. He became the committee's chairman in 1948, after the deaths of the institute's founders, Lord Lee of Fareham and Samuel Courtauld, and held this position for nearly thirty years, until 1975.

8. The classic study of these problems (Baumol and Bowen 1966) is dedicated to Iris and Lionel Robbins.

year later, but this left the annual grant at only £10,500. While Robbins was chairman of the trustees, it was raised to £100,000. He also persuaded ministers to provide funds for rebuilding the war-damaged west wing of the Gallery and special grants for acquiring particular paintings whose purchase price could not be found within the annual grants (most notably Paolo Uccello's *St George and the Dragon* in 1959 and Paul Cézanne's *Les Grandes Baigneuses* in 1964). His efforts at persuasion involved a prolonged campaign to mold public opinion: in his forewords to the annual reports (themselves a Robbins innovation), in talks and broadcasts, in meetings with MPs, in letters to the *Times*.[9] By 1957 he thought "the drumfire of propaganda in the last three years has begun to make an impact on the Treasury attitude" (Howson 2005). A financial crisis delayed the Treasury's response, but on January 23, 1959, another chancellor of the exchequer (Derrick Heathcoat Amory) announced the increase in the annual grants to the National Gallery and the Tate to £100,000 and £40,000, respectively. Robbins's life peerage was announced the same day.

Robbins (1963, 53–72) made the general case for government support of the arts in a talk to the Friends of the Birmingham City Museum and Art Gallery in March 1958. He asked: "Is the encouragement of the arts a proper function for political bodies? Is such encouragement compatible with liberal notions of the duties of the state?" His answer was to be expected from the author of *The Theory of Economic Policy in English Classical Political Economy* (1952): "I, personally, would answer unhesitatingly yes. And I would give this answer on the same ground as I would give support to the maintenance of sources of high excellence in learning and pure science, Archaeology, Pure Mathematics, Astronomy, for instance—subjects of no special relevance to practical affairs as such, but which impart quality and meaning to life on this planet by reason of their mere existence." *These good things are public goods*, conferring collective benefits to society as a whole as well as private benefits to individual consumers; hence the market alone cannot be relied on to produce the optimum amount of them. As he emphasized,

> One of the main arguments for the educational function of the state in general and for these forms in particular is just this, that the benefit is

---

9. One of his letters generated the public pressure necessary to induce the government to acquire the bomb site adjacent to the National Gallery on which the Sainsbury Wing was later built (Amery 1991, 40–42).

not merely discriminate, and that the positive effects of the fostering of art and learning and the preservation of culture are not restricted to those immediately prepared to pay cash but diffuse themselves to the benefit of much wider sections of the community in much the same way as the benefits of the apparatus of public hygiene or a well-planned urban landscape. The market mechanism is a splendid thing for ministering to wants and satisfactions which can be discretely formulated. But we oversimplify and run the risk of discrediting a fundamental institution, if we claim that it can formulate demands for all the necessary ingredients of the good society. (Robbins 1963, 58–59)

He repeated his arguments in the *Three Banks Review* in September 1971, when the Conservative "minister for the arts" was threatening to introduce admission charges for publicly funded museums and galleries and refusing to provide a matching grant to help purchase a famous Titian *(Death of Actaeon)*.[10]

Meanwhile Robbins had continued to contribute regularly to newspapers and magazines, sometimes asked to comment on the current economic situation (1954b), other times using *Lloyds Bank Review* to put forward his own policy views (1955, 1958). The *Financial Times* became an important outlet in the later 1950s and again in the 1970s after he had stepped down as chairman of its board, which he had joined in 1960, becoming chairman a year later. In his first speech in the House of Lords in November 1959, he strongly criticized the report of the Radcliffe Committee on the Working of the Monetary System for its downplaying of the importance of the money supply (Robbins 1963, 197–226). But he did not speak at all frequently in the Lords until after the "Robbins Report" on higher education.

Robbins's most famous role in public life was to chair the Committee on Higher Education, which was appointed by the prime minister (Harold Macmillan) and reported in October 1963. Although the 1960s expansion of British universities was already under way, the report influenced the form and the extent of the expansion. Robbins (1971a, 273) took on the task out of a sense of obligation: when asked by a civil servant who knew him well whether the book on economic theory he wanted to write was likely to be as important as trying to sort out the system of higher education, he "could not honestly deny" that the latter had greater "potentiality

---

10. The minister—his former student David Eccles whom he persuaded to allow the rebuilding of the National Gallery when Eccles was minister of works—subsequently backed down on the Titian but not on entrance fees.

of ultimate usefulness."[11] He insisted on a small committee; a committee of twelve, the majority academics or academic administrators with long experience of university teaching and research, and with differing political views, began meeting in March 1961.

Robbins tackled the committee's task in the same way as that of the Queen's Hall Committee. The committee should compile detailed and comprehensive data on higher education in Britain and other countries (the *supply* of education), and it should estimate the likely future *demand* for full-time higher education and compare that with the current supply, in order to work out what extra provision would be needed in the next twenty years. He asked Claus Moser, a lecturer in statistics at LSE, to become the statistical adviser to the committee. Moser in his turn enlisted the help of Richard Layard. As a result, "The figures spread through the Report and its appendices are built into an edifice with a comprehensiveness and consistency that can rarely have been equalled, and support the major recommendations in a way it is impossible to dislodge. The text of Robbins supplies the brass and wind: Moser's figures the strings" (Carswell 1985, 29).

The first research study carried out by Moser and Layard was on the "pool of ability"—the numbers of young people who would be qualified to study at university level in the coming years. According to Moser, the preliminary results "really persuaded Lionel to fight for expansion. Once he was persuaded he persuaded the rest of the committee" (Howson 2011, 876). The report's first guiding principle—the so-called *Robbins principle*—is that "we have assumed as an axiom that courses of higher education should be available for all those who are qualified by ability and attainment to pursue them and who wish to do so."

Robbins did indeed write (most of) the report himself. He wrote the first draft in the summer of 1962; he revised it extensively to meet other members' criticisms over the winter of 1962–63. One of his oldest friends commented when he read the report that he "recognise[d] the structure-of-the-whole as being very much your work—and the same thing struck me as I kept on reading (time and time again)." It has been described (Carswell 1985, 38) as "one of the great state papers of [the twentieth] century. . . . Only the Beveridge Report of 1943 [*sic*] and the Poor Law Report of 1909 can compete with it for copiousness, cogency, coherence and historical influence. It contains memorable passages and is informed by a consistent intellectual attitude."

---

11. The UK National Archives reveal that in ministerial discussion of the composition of the committee only one name was put forward for chairman; the government did not decide on the other members until he had agreed to serve.

Robbins and his colleagues on the committee were united in wishing to preserve the autonomy of academic institutions. They strongly recommended the preservation of the University Grants Committee, in existence since 1919, as a buffer between the universities and the government. But the UGC should not, in their view, come under the Treasury. Neither should arts institutions continue to be financed directly by the Treasury. Robbins thought that for a department that was supposed to be the keeper of the public purse to be directly funding the universities, the National and Tate Galleries, and some other galleries and museums and the Arts Council was more like poaching than gamekeeping. He may have been successful under this system in extracting money for the arts from the Treasury, but he did not think it was the right way to decide the allocation of resources between the arts and competing objectives. A Ministry of Arts and Science, and its minister, would look after all institutions concerned with research, scholarship, and the arts.

The Conservative government—even in the middle of a political crisis that led to Macmillan's resignation as prime minister—immediately accepted most of the committee's recommendations, issuing a white paper to that effect the day after the report was published. It would take the committee's estimates of the number of qualified students for whom places in higher education should be found as its objectives in expanding the universities over the next few years and providing the necessary funds. It would also accept the recommendations that institutions such as the Royal College of Art and the Colleges of Advanced Technology should become universities and would consider the committee's proposals for six new universities including one in Scotland. But neither the Conservative government nor the Labour government that succeeded it in 1964 adopted the proposals that teacher training colleges should become associated with universities and that a new Ministry of Arts and Science should be created to oversee the whole higher education sector. Robbins was particularly upset when Anthony Crosland, the Labour minister of the Department of Education and Science (DES) created by the Conservative government, announced in April 1965 that while the universities would continue to be funded through the UGC, the colleges of education and technical colleges would be funded directly by the DES, and attacked his policy forcefully in the House of Lords in December. The Labour government had already announced that it would not create six new universities. Only one new university was built in response to the Robbins Report: Stirling in Scotland.

In the universities' own response to the report, however, the strongest effect was the expansion of graduate schools, one of the strongest recommendations of Robbins's report. Also, despite the nonaddition of further new universities in England and Wales, the expansion of undergraduate education was greater than Moser and Layard had estimated was needed (Layard, King, and Moser 1969).

Inevitably, for several years Robbins was in the public eye as an expert on higher education, asked to give his views in broadcasts, lectures, and papers in the United States and Germany as well as in Britain (1965, 1966, 1970). But he provided his views on economic policy even more often—in the *Financial Times* and public lectures as well as in the Lords. He contributed to the activities of the Institute of Economic Affairs, often by chairing sessions of their conferences. The IEA also published two of his public lectures (1974, 1977). But it has to be said that he was by now an "elder statesman": one cannot attribute to these talks and papers the influence his earlier public writings—prewar and postwar—had had.

Conclusions

Lionel Robbins (1932b, 132–35) is well known for his insistence in his *Essay on the Nature and Significance of Economic Science* that value judgments have no place in economic science. At the same time he wrote,

> All this is not to say that economists should not deliver themselves on ethical questions. . . . On the contrary, it is greatly to be desired that economists should have speculated long and widely on these matters, since only in this way will they be in a position to appreciate the implications as regards given ends of problems which are put to them for solution. Our methodological axioms involve no prohibition of outside interests! (133–34)

Robbins's own wide-ranging outside interests were reflected in his academic writing—in the subjects he chose to write on and the manner in which he treated them—and in his activities as a public intellectual or political economist. He was happy to serve as an advocate for the arts in Britain—and to contribute directly to their administration at the Courtauld, National Gallery, and Covent Garden—and to participate actively in public debate about politics and economic policy. He believed it was the duty of an intellectual to inform the public of the important theoretical issues (of economics in his case) that lay behind current practical policy problems. He also believed one should be prepared to take unpopular stands and fight for what one believes in—hence his battles over protectionism. He had admired Keynes's stand over Versailles: his resignation of his Treasury position and his writing *The Economic Consequences of the Peace*. Robbins also, of course, admired his father's stand against agricultural protection and his resignation from the NFU Council. But he (usually) enjoyed public debate and controversy and participated frequently and enthusiastically—even to some extent at the expense of his academic reputation.

In his efforts at public persuasion he chose several outlets. He addressed a range of audiences in his talks to conferences and discussion groups, public lectures and radio broadcasts. As already mentioned, his writing for newspapers and magazines was directed to "educated public opinion." Other efforts at persuasion targeted more exclusive audiences, especially in connection with finance for the arts, but some of these were more in the nature of lobbying than public intellectual activity. From 1959 he also had the House of Lords, which he utilized from 1963 with respect to both political-economic issues and higher education.

From time to time he joined committees and study groups, although here, disillusioned with the experience of collaborative work on Beveridge's *Tariffs* book, he tried not to become too involved—*unless he was in the chair*. His skills as a committee chairman were an important factor in his successes at the National Gallery and other bodies connected with the arts. His greatest achievements as a public intellectual came in public inquiries commissioned by the British government after the Second World War: the Waverley Committee (and the Reviewing Committee it created), the Queen's Hall Committee, and the Higher Education Committee. A major reason for his effectiveness in these activities was his utilization of his skills as an economist and his use of empirical data and statistics, a skill he had learned working as an economist in government during the war. This is especially clear with the influential Robbins Report. Another example is the Queen's Hall Committee, a model of the marshaling of factual evidence to tackle a question on which members of the public had strong feelings. As he had pointed out in *Nature and Significance* (1932b, 135–36) when he considered the "unquestionable significance" of economic science: "Surely it consists in just this, that, when we are faced with a choice between ultimates, it enables us to choose with full awareness of the implications of what we are choosing. . . . And it is just here that Economics acquires its practical significance."

References

Amery, Colin. 1991. *A Celebration of Art and Architecture*. London: National Gallery.
Baumol, William, and William Bowen. 1966. *Performing Arts—the Economic Dilemma*. New York: Twentieth Century Fund.
Beveridge, William. 1931. *Tariffs: The Case Examined*. London: Longmans.
Cairncross, Alec, and Nita Watts. 1989. *The Economic Section, 1939–1961*. London: Routledge.
Carswell, John. 1985. *Government and the Universities in Britain*. Cambridge: Cambridge University Press.
Committee on Higher Education. 1963. *Report* (Cmnd 2154). London: HMSO.
Conlin, Jonathan. 2006. *The Nation's Mantelpiece*. London: Pallas Athene.
Dow, J. C. R. 1964. *The Management of the British Economy, 1945–60*. Cambridge: Cambridge University Press.
Hancock, K., and M. M. Gowing. 1949. *British War Economy*. London: HMSO.
Howson, Susan. 2005. "Lionel Robbins's 'Art and the State.'" *HOPE* 37 (3): 619–47.
———. 2011. *Lionel Robbins*. Cambridge: Cambridge University Press.
Howson, Susan, and Donald Moggridge, eds. 1990. *The Wartime Diaries of Lionel Robbins and James Meade, 1943–45*. London: Macmillan.
Howson, Susan, and Donald Winch. 1977. *The Economic Advisory Council, 1930–1939*. Cambridge: Cambridge University Press.
Layard, Richard, John King, and Claus Moser. 1969. *The Impact of Robbins*. Harmondsworth: Penguin.
McLachlan, Donald. 1952. *Atlantic Alliance: NATO's Role in the Free World*. London: RIIA.
Pinder, John, ed. 1998. *Altiero Spinelli and the British Federalists*. London: Federal Trust.
Ransome, Patrick, ed. 1991. *Towards the United States of Europe*. London: Lothian.
Robbins, Lionel. 1924a. "The Case for Liberalism." *Outlook*, October 25, 293.
———. 1924b. "Religion and Economics." *Outlook*, September 27, 217.
———. 1926. *Wages*. London: Jarrolds.
———. 1931a. "Economic Notes on Some Arguments for Protection." *Economica* 11 (February): 45–62.
———. 1931b. "The Economics of Import Boards: A Criticism of Mr. Wise's Proposals." *Political Quarterly* 2 (April): 204–23.
———. 1932a. "Consumption and the Trade Cycle." *Economica* 12 (November): 413–30.
———. 1932b. *An Essay on the Nature and Significance of Economic Science*. London: Macmillan.
———. 1932c. "The Ottawa Resolutions on Finance and the Future of Monetary Policy." *Lloyds Bank Review* 3 (October): 422–38.
———. 1934. *The Great Depression*. London: Macmillan.
———. 1935a. "A Dialogue between a Foreign Statesman and an English Student of Affairs." *Lloyds Bank Review* 6 (May): 266–81.

———. 1935b. *An Essay on the Nature and Significance of Economic Science.* 2nd ed. London: Macmillan.

———. 1935c. "The Problem of Stabilisation." *Lloyds Bank Review* 6 (April): 207–18.

———. 1935d. "The Twofold Roots of the Great Depression: Inflationism and Intervention." In *The Burden of Plenty?*, edited by Graham Hutton, 103–17. London: Allen and Unwin.

———. 1937a. *Economic Planning and International Order.* London: Macmillan.

———. 1937b. "How to Mitigate the Next Slump." *Lloyds Bank Review* 8 (May): 234–44.

———. 1939a. *The Economic Basis of Class Conflict and Other Essays in Political Economy.* London: Macmillan.

———. 1939b. *The Economic Causes of War.* London: Jonathan Cape.

———. 1947a. "Economic Prospects." *Lloyds Bank Review*, n.s., 3 (January): 21–32.

———. 1947b. "Inquest on the Crisis." *Lloyds Bank Review*, n.s., 6 (October): 1–27.

———. 1949. "The Sterling Problem." *Lloyds Bank Review*, n.s., 14 (October): 1–31.

———. 1950. "Towards the Atlantic Community." *Lloyds Bank Review*, n.s., 17 (July) 1–24.

———. 1951. *The Balance of Payments.* London: Athlone.

———. 1952. *The Theory of Economic Policy in English Classical Political Economy.* London: Macmillan.

———. 1954a. *The Economist in the Twentieth Century and Other Lectures in Political Economy.* London: Macmillan.

———. 1954b. "How Firm Is Prosperity?" *Daily Telegraph*, December 9.

———. 1955. "Notes on Public Finance." *Lloyds Bank Review*, n.s., 38 (October): 1–18.

———. 1958. "Thoughts on the Crisis." *Lloyds Bank Review*, n.s., 48 (April): 1–26.

———. 1963. *Politics and Economics: Papers in Political Economy.* London: Macmillan.

———. 1965. "Recent Discussions of the Problems of Higher Education in Great Britain." *Public Policy* 14:203–20.

———. 1966. *The University in the Modern World.* London: Macmillan.

———. 1970. "Present Discontents of the Student Age Group." In *Individuality and the New Society*, edited by Abraham Kaplan. Seattle: University of Washington Press.

———. 1971a. *Autobiography of an Economist.* London: Macmillan.

———. 1971b. *Money, Trade, and International Relations.* London: Macmillan.

———. 1971c. "Unsettled Questions in the Political Economy of the Arts." *Three Banks Review* 91 (September): 3–19.

———. 1974. *Aspects of Post-war Economic Policy.* London: IEA.

———. 1977. *Liberty and Equality.* London: IEA.

———. 1979. *Against Inflation.* London: Macmillan.

———. 1980. *Higher Education Revisited.* London: Macmillan.

Royal Institute of International Affairs (RIIA). 1935. *The Future of Monetary Policy.* London: Royal Institute of International Affairs.

Treasury. 1952. *Report of the Committee on the Export of Works of Art etc.* London: HMSO.

Henry Hazlitt as an Intellectual Middleman of "Orthodox Economics"

Peter Boettke and Liya Palagashvili

> Mr. Henry Hazlitt . . . is the only competent critic of the arts that I have ever heard of who was at the same time a competent economist, of practical as well as theoretical training, and he is one of the few economists in human history who could really write.
> —H. L. Mencken, "Ten Years" (1933)

Henry Hazlitt (1894–1993) began his career as a journalist at the *Wall Street Journal* while still a teenager, and it was there that his interest in economics grew as he embarked on a path of self-study as a matter of practical necessity for job success. He read Philip Wicksteed's *Common Sense of Political Economy*, which he found at the Flatbush, Brooklyn, branch of the New York Public Library, and the book was, as Hazlitt described, "a revelation" to him. Hazlitt, in fact, borrowing liberally from John Keats's "On First Looking into Chapman's Homer," characterized his good fortune in stumbling on *Common Sense* as: "Much have

---

Correspondence may be addressed to Peter Boettke, 324 Enterprise Hall, Economics Department, MSN 3G4, George Mason University, 4400 University Dr., Fairfax, VA 22030-4444 (e-mail: pboettke@gmu.edu); and to Liya Palagashvili at lpalagas@gmu.edu. In writing this essay we benefited greatly from the research assistance of Matthew Boettke and the comments, criticisms, and suggestions of Angus Burgin, Bruce Caldwell, Tyler Cowen, Chris Coyne, David Hebert, Peter Leeson, David Levy, Peter Lipsey, Tiago Mata, Paul Milazzo, Steven G. Medema, and Nick Snow, as well as the participants of the 2012 *HOPE* conference and two anonymous referees.

History of Political Economy 45 (annual suppl.) DOI 10.1215/00182702-2310980
Copyright 2013 by Duke University Press

I traveled in the realms of gold, etc. Yet never did I breathe its pure serene. Till I heard Wicksteed speak out loud and bold."[1] Subsequently, Hazlitt would pursue a lifetime of economic study and economic journalism, and held positions at the *New York Evening Mail*, the *New York Sun*, the *Nation*, the *American Mercury*, the *New York Times*, and *Newsweek*. In addition to his journalistic work, which included writing signed and unsigned economic editorials, Hazlitt was an author of books ranging from literary criticism to social philosophy, with multiple volumes in economics, political economy, and public policy in between. Hazlitt even wrote an economic novel, *Time Will Run Back* (1966), that attempted to illustrate the failures of central planning. *Economics in One Lesson* (1946) is perhaps his best-known work, but his critical work on John Maynard Keynes, as well as his work on social ethics, garnered professional attention with reviews in the *American Economic Review*, the *Journal of Political Economy*, the *Economic Journal*, and *Ethics*. Even when the general thrust of the review was negative, the critic would more often than not begrudgingly acknowledge Hazlitt's unusual strengths in exposition and analysis.

Typically, we think of economists as becoming public intellectuals to complement their scientific careers; here we want to flip that around and consider the case of a public intellectual who through his years of close study of economic problems as a journalist and his own independent study of economic theory and philosophy entered the world of professional economics and utilized his journalistic positions to advance economic understanding both among the public but also within the specialized profession. Hazlitt argued that even if originality is denied to him as an economist, he should be seen as defending the orthodox teachings of economics from Adam Smith onward against the "new economics" that attempted to overturn the classics. "Re-establishing old truths can often be as necessary," Hazlitt insisted, "as discovering new ones."[2] In this way, Hazlitt's central role as a public intellectual was communicating the teachings of classical economics (and early neoclassical economics) and applying the reasoning to the pressing public policy issues of his era.

---

1. Hazlitt, "Eightieth Birthday Talk," November 27, 1974, Henry Hazlitt Archives, Universidad Francisco Marroquin, DOC5603.pdf. The Hazlitt Archives is a digital collection of Hazlitt's documents. Each item in the collection is a pdf file, to which has been assigned a number.

2. See Hazlitt's unpublished autobiography, "My Life and Conclusions," p. 44, Henry Hazlitt Archives, DOC24289.pdf.

As we will see, Hazlitt also maintained an active correspondence with leading economists throughout the twentieth century and developed a close personal relationship with several leading economic thinkers.[3] He actively promoted the ideas of certain economists with timely reviews and behind-the-scenes discussions with publishers. His efforts were not dismissed as the ravings of an outsider, for at the time Hazlitt is writing from the vantage point of being the leading economic journalist of his era, and the author of a publishing phenomenon, *Economics in One Lesson*.[4] Although today Hazlitt's influence on the spread of classical economics is underplayed, we illustrate the intellectual landscape of Hazlitt's time to show that Hazlitt really was the middleman and voice for "orthodox" economics during the Great Depression and post–World War II era, a time before the reemergence of popular free market thinkers. In doing so, Hazlitt also boldly crossed over and attempted to influence the professional discourse in economics. To get a sense of Hazlitt's status at the time among professional economists, consider Jacob Viner's description of him in a letter to Lionel Robbins on November 24, 1934: "I do not know Hazlitt personally, but he is a shrewd and hard-headed commentator on economic events and in my opinion the best American journalist who writes on economic matters."[5]

The essay proceeds as follows: Section 1 discusses Hazlitt's career as an economic journalist, and section 2 focuses on the battle of economic ideas that Hazlitt saw himself as waging throughout the twentieth century. Section 3 discusses how Hazlitt came to see this battle culminate in the Western democracies in the debate over the new economics. Section 4 attempts to explain the connection that Hazlitt saw between his economics and his social philosophy, and section 5 concludes.

1. Economic Journalism

At the age of seventeen, Henry Hazlitt decided to become a professional philosopher. He had already come under the influence of Herbert Spencer

---

3. In his archives there are letters from not only Mises and Hayek, and other representatives of the Austrian School of Economics, but also Lionel Robbins, Frank Knight, Milton Friedman, and even Paul Samuelson.

4. *Economics in One Lesson* rose to number six on the *New York Times* nonfiction best seller list until the publisher ran out of the original print run and had to restock the book. It eventually sold seven hundred thousand copies for the original publisher. With subsequent editions, the estimates are in the multimillions, and there are twelve foreign-language editions as well.

5. Viner to Robbins, November 24, 1934, box 22, folder 14, Viner Papers, Mudd Manuscript Library, Princeton University. Thanks to Angus Burgin for alerting us to this quote.

and read everything he could get his hands on by Spencer. Unfortunately, Hazlitt's family financial situation grew precarious, and rather than head off to Harvard, Hazlitt had to support himself and his mother. He could afford to attend the College of the City of New York full-time only one year, and then half of a second year as a part-time student. He eventually quit attending classes, too exhausted by working full-time to get much benefit from the lectures, but not before taking a class with Morris Cohen, whose *Reason and Nature* Hazlitt would review very favorably for the *Nation* when he was the literary editor for that publication between 1930 and 1933. After a series of jobs working as an office boy, eventually he learned from being on the job and stayed on longer than a few days. These lessons learned at the bottom of the economic ladder were important to Hazlitt, as he attempted to climb out of his and his family's financially precarious situation.[6]

During this time Hazlitt kept reading and engaging serious works in philosophy and psychology. In 1913, he started off with a secretarial job at the *Wall Street Journal*, but soon after transitioned to a reporter. In one of his first assignments, Hazlitt reports, he made an egregious error about the payment of corporate dividends out of ignorance of economic and financial terminology. The discovery of the error and his fear of losing his job gave him the impetus to study the economics and financial literature in more depth.

This quest to learn economics led him to embark on an intense reading of economic works, correspondence with leading economists, and close friendships with economists. As mentioned already, it was during this time that he came to read Wicksteed's *Common Sense of Political Economy*, and he also developed a strong relationship with Benjamin Anderson, author of *Social Value* (1911) and *The Value of Money* (1917), who in 1918 left his teaching position at Harvard to move to the National Bank of Commerce, and eventually to Chase National Bank.[7]

---

6. And later in his work on the economics of unemployment, Hazlitt stressed the importance of the nonrestrictive labor market for unskilled workers to learn from on-the-job training. This is, of course, a point often stressed in the work of Thomas Sowell (e.g., *Markets and Minorities* [1981]) and Walter Williams (e.g., *The State against Blacks* [1982]), but see also the work of William Julius Wilson, especially *When Work Disappears* (1997), for the importance of a vibrant and fluid labor market for the urban poor.

7. Anderson is responsible for alerting Hazlitt to the work of Ludwig von Mises. Anderson's study of the financial history of the United States was published as *Economics and the Public Welfare* in 1949. Anderson worked at Chase from 1920 to 1939, when he returned to academe as a professor of economics at UCLA.

Hazlitt was uniquely equipped to engage in serious self-education as an economist. When he joined the staff at the *Wall Street Journal* at the age of nineteen, he already had written a book manuscript on logic and thinking clearly about arguments and theories, *Thinking as a Science*. Published in 1916, *Thinking as a Science* reflects not only great erudition but also clarity of thought and style that is characteristic of Hazlitt's writing throughout his career. Hazlitt's work contains not only a basic introduction to critical reasoning but careful discussions of arguments in philosophy and social theory that emerge from the works of Spencer, John Stuart Mill, and William Stanley Jevons, as well as William James and Henri Bergson. Given his youth, Hazlitt hesitated at first when he received the acceptance from Dutton to publish the book because he was sure that when they met him they might rescind the offer because of his age. But his teenage peer group in New York City included leading intellectuals such as Lewis Mumford, who were also beginning stellar careers as "men of letters" despite never completing their college degrees.[8]

By 1916, Hazlitt was a published author and building up a reputation as an insightful reporter. He moved from the *Wall Street Journal* to the *New York Evening Post*, where he was responsible for the column Wall Street Paragraphs. Not too long after, Hazlitt left to take a job writing a monthly financial and economic letter for the Mechanics and Metals National Bank of New York. For the next decade Hazlitt moved between various writing and editing jobs with newspapers. In 1921, he moved to the *New York Evening Mail* to write a stock market column.[9] From 1924 to 1929, he worked for the *New York Sun*, where his reputation as a literary critic rose, and eventually the *Nation* hired Hazlitt to work as the literary editor from 1930 to 1933. At the *Nation*, Hazlitt wrote on economics and literary criticism, but his staunch anti–New Deal perspective was a source of contention with the rest of the staff. In 1933, Hazlitt left the *Nation*, but not before he had debated Louis Fischer in print over the meaning of the Great

---

8. Mumford grew ill and was unable to complete his studies at City College and the New School, but he served as the architectural critic and social critic on urban issues for the *New Yorker* for over thirty years.

9. His study of the vagaries of financial markets and the difficulties with offering definitive forecasts produced in Hazlitt a lifetime of disdain for the idea that economists are supposed to be able to predict the economic future. "Of course, some of them sometimes guess right for some specific time; but predicting the business future is not the business of economists. Too many factors must be known, and no one can know them." The business of economists, Hazlitt continued, "is to explain the workings of the market, and the mistakes of the legislators and other politicians. Adam Smith set the pattern in *The Wealth of Nations*, when he pointed out the error of 'protective' tariffs" ("My Life and Conclusions," p. 36, Henry Hazlitt Archives, DOC24289.pdf).

Depression (see Hazlitt 1933b). Rather than the inevitable collapse of the capitalist system as Fischer contended, Hazlitt argued that the Great Depression was a consequence of the necessary adjustment to a postwar economy aggravated by a series of policy mistakes by the government.

Hazlitt was asked by H. L. Mencken to take over as editor of the *American Mercury*, which Hazlitt did until he joined the *New York Times* in 1934 as an editorialist and book reviewer for the *Sunday Book Review* section. Hazlitt stayed at the *New York Times* from 1934 until 1946, when he moved to *Newsweek*, where he wrote the Business Tides column until 1966.[10]

It is his career at the *New York Times* and *Newsweek* that will, for our purposes, be the focal point of explaining Hazlitt's role as the public intellectual as an economist. As Paul Milazzo (2011, xxviii) writes: "Hazlitt matters, because over the course of the twentieth century he became the most important economic and business journalist in the country, the most influential and mainstream purveyor and popularizer of the Austrian School of free market economics, and, prior to the ascendance of monetarists and supply-siders, the most prominent, articulate, and persistent critic of prevailing Keynesian doctrine." From the 1930s through the 1960s, Hazlitt was the main spokesman for the free market to a mass audience. As Murray Rothbard wrote in a 1987 tribute to Hazlitt, "before I had heard of von Mises I knew about Henry Hazlitt. When I was first getting interested in free-market economics, during and just after World War II, Henry was all over the place—in *Newsweek*, on radio and later television—lucid, sound, brilliant, and decisive, carrying the free-market message. And he was the only one."[11] Hazlitt's impact was not just on those like Rothbard who later championed free market ideas, but also a young Paul Samuelson wrote to Hazlitt on September 15, 1966, to explain how as a student at the University of Chicago in the 1930s, he was assigned an article by Hazlitt on the nature of economic argument. Samuelson states: "A writer never knows what his impacts have been. I can say that one of the reasons I decided to go into economics was reading your article."[12]

---

10. Hazlitt's columns for *Newsweek* have been collected into a single volume, *Business Tides* (2011), that runs over eight hundred pages in column format. The introduction to that volume by Paul Charles Milazzo (2011) is highly recommend and is referred to in the present essay.

11. Rothbard's comments were made in the December 1987 issue of the *Free Market*, the newsletter of the Ludwig von Mises Institute. The issue paid tribute to Hazlitt. Rothbard's comments can be found on page 4 of the issue, which is available at mises.org/journals/fm/fm1287.pdf.

12. Samuelson to Hazlitt, September 15, 1966, Henry Hazlitt Archives, DOC 18725_3 .pdf. Hazlitt responded on December 15, 1966: "As you know, I venture to differ with you on

2. The Battle of Economic Ideas

Hazlitt's time at the *Nation* included reviews of philosophical works, literary and artistic criticism, and a series of critical examinations of economic policy and economic doctrine.[13] When he spoke about economic issues, he often focused on questions of monetary policy and inflation, the problems associated with efforts at social control by the government, and the need for new constitutional restrictions on the abuse of the executive branch. The experience prepared him well for the "battle of ideas" that he would be engaged in for the next fifty years of his life.

When he moved to the *New York Times*, his focus was sharpened on economics and political economy in his capacity as the primary economic journalist and editor.[14] But in his capacity as reviewer for the *Sunday Book Review* section, his wide-ranging interests in philosophy, politics, and the arts continued to be reflected.[15] Hazlitt played an important role in introducing the US audience to the writings of the Austrian School of Economics, and in particular Ludwig von Mises and F. A. Hayek. Hazlitt became aware of Mises's writings through his reading and subsequent friendship with Benjamin Anderson. He also understood that Wicksteed was an alternative to works that derived from Alfred Marshall, and also reflected the non-Ricardian branch of British economics. Wicksteed's influence on Hazlitt was immense, and it guided Hazlitt's economic analysis of policies throughout his life. In particular, Hazlitt learned the basics of a consistent and persistent application of marginal utility analysis, which provided Hazlitt with the complete subjectivist and opportunity cost reasoning in contrast to Marshall and provided him with the marginal productivity theory of factor pricing and exhaustion theorem. The continuous use of opportunity cost reasoning is distinctly evident in Hazlitt's work. Hazlitt

---

some propositions in economics, and in my book, The Failure of the New Economics, I may have expressed my differences with less than complete politeness. Nevertheless, I am enormously flattered to learn that something I wrote long ago influenced you and particularly that my article was one of the reasons that you decided to go into economics" (Henry Hazlitt Archives, DOC 18727_3.pdf).

13. Hazlitt's reviews and columns can be accessed in the "From the Archives" section at the *Nation* (www.thenation.com).

14. It is, of course, important to remember that Hazlitt was responsible for economic content at the *New York Times* when the US economy was ensnared in the Great Depression, and amid policy debates over the appropriate response to the dire situation. In his capacity as an economic reporter, Hazlitt gave a fair hearing to both sides of the debate even when it starts to become evident which side Hazlitt finds more persuasive. An excellent example of this can be seen in Hazlitt, "The Road to Recovery: Spending or Saving," *New York Times*, January 6, 1935.

15. See, e.g., Hazlitt's (1935c) in-depth review of Pareto's *Mind and Society*.

also picked up an understanding of the market as an economic process, which stood in direct contrast to frameworks that were preoccupied with an equilibrium state of affairs. These insights from Wicksteed would govern Hazlitt's thinking on economic policies, and they also complemented what Hazlitt later learned from reading Mises.[16] In short, Wicksteed was a British "Austrian," as was Lionel Robbins at this time, who also had a significant impact on Hazlitt's introduction to Austrian economics. In the early 1930s, Hazlitt and Robbins began exchanging letters and discussing various in-depth economic issues, and Hazlitt started referring to Robbins in his editorials and reviewed two of his books in the *New York Times,* hence also exposing his work to the general public (Hazlitt 1937, 1939). In their correspondence, Robbins urged Hazlitt to read Mises and said that Mises's *Socialism* was "far and away the greatest work on social sciences which has appeared in the last twenty-five years."[17] Thus, from both Anderson and Robbins, Hazlitt was exposed to Mises and became versed in the Austrian tradition, which remained his framework of analysis throughout his career and was evident in his editorials and books.

The two reviews we have in mind that played a critical role in introducing the Austrian School of Economics to a wider US audience were Hazlitt's (1938, 1944) reviews of Mises's *Socialism* (1922)[18] and Hayek's *Road to Serfdom* (1944). In a letter describing the *Road to Serfdom* review process, Hazlitt states that the editor of the *New York Times Sunday Book*

---

16. As Wicksteed ([1910] 1933, 236) argues, "A market is the machinery by which those on whose scales of preferences any commodity is relatively high are brought into communication with those on whose scales it is relatively low, in order that exchanges make take place to mutual satisfaction until equilibrium is established. *But this process will always and necessarily occupy time*" (emphasis added). Wicksteed, in other words, is postulating a market *process* that has a tendency toward equilibrium, provided no additional changes in tastes, technology, or resource availability are introduced. As Robbins states in his introduction to *The Common Sense,* "Wicksteed's approach is by no means the same as Pareto's. His analysis of the conditions of equilibrium is much less an end in itself, much more a tool with which to explain the tendencies of any given situation. He was much more concerned with economic phenomena as a process in time, much less with its momentary end-products" (xix).

17. Hazlitt to Robbins, November 30, 1934, Henry Hazlitt Archives, DOC18151_3.pdf. In the Hazlitt Archives, there are about twenty-six letters between Hazlitt and Robbins from 1934 to 1981. The correspondence includes rather routine conversation to discussions of Robbins's *Great Depression* and *An Essay on the Nature and Significance of Economic Science,* and Hazlitt's various book reviews and his critique of government policies.

18. Hazlitt argues that "no open-minded reader can fail to be impressed by the closeness of the author's reasoning, the rigor of his logic, the power and unity of his thought." The book examines socialism from every possible angle, and Mises does so with such "power, brilliance and completeness" that *Socialism* "must rank as the most devastating analysis of socialism yet penned." Mises "has written an economic classic in our time."

Review section "intended to run my review on page 33 or so," but Hazlitt's prestige at the *Times* coupled with his description of the *Road to Serfdom* as "one of the most important books of our generation" persuaded the editor to put it on page 1. Based on this front page of the *Sunday Book Review*, Max Eastman, who was then affiliated with *Reader's Digest*, read the book and asked *Reader's Digest* to produce a condensed form. The book became a publishing sensation thereafter.[19] The editor of the University of Chicago Press, John Scoon, describes that "but by the time we had seen Henry Hazlitt's front page review in the Sunday Times Book Review we had ordered a second printing of 5,000 copies. In a few days we had requests for German, Spanish, Dutch and other translation rights, and on September 27 [four days after Hazlitt's review] we ordered a third printing of 5,000 copies, upping it to 10,000 the next day." Scoon emphasized that *Reader's Digest* created a significant spurt in book sales, which helped lead to nearly fifty thousand copies sold in just one year.[20]

Similarly, Hazlitt played an essential role in promoting the new free market think tank in 1955, the Institute for Economic Affairs. Hazlitt is said to have much to do with "putting the Institute of Economic Affairs on the map" by devoting a *Newsweek* column to review its first book, *The Convertibility of Sterling*, by George Winder. Hazlitt's coverage of the book created a tremendous catalyst and "ensured that it sold out within three months" (Cockett 1995, 109, 133). In his capacity as a leading journalist in the top newspapers, Hazlitt utilized his position to spread the ideas of free market economics.

Hazlitt also helped promote the ideas of a less well-known Austrian economist, Albert Hahn, by reviewing Hahn's book *Common Sense Economics* (1956) in *Newsweek*.[21] Various correspondences show that Hazlitt frequently received copies of books and inquiries from publishers to

---

19. Hazlitt to Henry Regnery, January 30, 1975, Henry Hazlitt Archives, DOC17860_3 .pdf. Hazlitt discusses how *Reader's Digest* introduced the condensation with a box quoting Hazlitt's review of the book comparing it with John Stuart Mill's essay *On Liberty*. Hazlitt tells Regnery that "all this followed solely because of the prestige of the front page of *Times* Sunday Book Review." He also says, "My review stimulated Max Eastman to get the book." In other correspondences, Hazlitt indicates his close connection to Eastman, stating that, for example, "I know him well," and recognizing Eastman during Hazlitt's seventieth birthday dinner as a fellow fighter in the battle of ideas.

20. John Scoon to C. Hartley Grattan, May 2, 1945, reproduced in Caldwell 2007.

21. In a letter to Hazlitt on December 15, 1956, found in the Henry Hazlitt Archives (DOC8868_3.pdf), Abelard Schuman Publishers sent a copy of Hahn's book to Hazlitt, and Hazlitt follows up with Hahn on March 5, 1957 (DOC13321_3.pdf), enclosing a review of the book published in the March 6 issue of *Newsweek*.

examine and review books or other requests such as asking Hazlitt to help with promoting certain economic material. In fact, in a letter responding to the economist David McCord Wright, Hazlitt writes that he is "astonished that an economist and author of your standing should have any difficulty in finding a publisher" and that "I shall see whether I can interest any publisher from this and hope I may be writing something positive to you soon."[22] Similarly, Hazlitt succeeded in getting Yale University Press to publish Mises's *Omnipotent Government* and later several others, including *Human Action*. In a letter describing his relationship with Mises, Hazlitt indicated that it was through his editor of the editorial page, Charles Merz, that Hazlitt was able to get Yale interested in publishing Mises's books.[23] In this way and in many other ways, Hazlitt used his esteemed journalistic positions and connections to steer these ideas and make them public—hence acting as an intellectual middleman.[24]

It is important to stress that Hazlitt did not see the Austrian School as exotic but as the continuation of the tradition of classical economics, although improved by the developments in value theory made in the late nineteenth and early twentieth centuries. The distinction that Hazlitt makes between "orthodox" economics and the economic theories of the New Deal "brain trust" as well as the ascendant new economics of Keynes and his followers in the 1940s–1960s parallels a distinction Peter Boettke (2012) has recently been making between "mainline" and "mainstream" economics. In that work, Boettke refers to mainstream economics as designating what is currently fashionable among the scientific elite of the profession. On the other hand, mainline, or what Hazlitt labeled "orthodox economics," refers to a set of propositions about social order from Smith and

---

22. Hazlitt to David McCord Wright, January 26, 1961, Henry Hazlitt Archives, DOC20100_3.pdf.

23. Hazlitt seemed to have had a close relationship with Merz, who was Hazlitt's boss for over six years. Hazlitt says that Merz "never pulled rank on me; he never gave me anything in the form of an order; he simply acted as if we were running the Editorial page in cooperation; and he always gave my suggestions as opened-minded consideration as he gave his own" (Hazlitt to Mrs. Charles Merz, Henry Hazlitt Archives, DOC16167_3.pdf).

24. In addition to his journalistic positions, Hazlitt was actively involved in the intellectual scene through his memberships in organizations such as the prestigious Authors' Club, the International Advisory Council for the American Economic Education Foundation, and various other organizations. Hazlitt's letters also show that he was always in contact with or was frequently contacted to meet with publishers, professional economists, or other journalists like Walter Lippmann. Hazlitt was also invited to speak at various events not only in New York but also overseas, often in London.

David Hume onward that focus on core principles about how a free economy operates and the perversities that result from too much government intervention in the economy.[25] Hazlitt argued that the accumulating criticisms from historians, philosophers, and intellectuals of the free market economy did not challenge the truth content of classical economic doctrine. These criticisms of orthodox economics, according to Hazlitt, were based on economic fallacies.[26] This is also evident in his earlier review essay on Lionel Robbins's *Economic Planning and International Order* (1937), where Hazlitt (1937, 82) says that Robbins "uses the tools of classical economic analysis like a fine surgeon; he moves deliberately from step to step with a relentless logic; and he writes with lucid and compact prose." Hazlitt concludes that the critics of orthodox classical economic doctrine—the planners—will "have a very difficult time" answering Robbins's argument.

During the Great Depression and then World War II, there was a leftward drift by members of the intelligentsia, but Hazlitt emphasized the importance of holding to orthodox economic doctrine and reminded his readers of basic economics. It is crucial to understand that during this time, a time before the popular figures of free market economics such as Mises, Hayek, Milton Friedman, and others had become known, it was solely Hazlitt who provided the substantive arguments of classical economics to challenge the New Deal policies in the public discourse. The departure from classical economics at this time was radical—take, for example, Rexford Tugwell, the key policy adviser to Franklin Delano Roosevelt and the architect of the New Deal. Tugwell wrote in his diary in 1934 describing a speech he was to give, "There is much to be said for

---

25. However, lest the reader believe that Hazlitt directed his critique only at those who advocated an expanding role of the state in economic affairs, it is instructive to read his review of Albert Jay Nock's *Our Enemy the State*, where Hazlitt (1935b) argues that Nock's analysis is marred by inconsistencies and contradictions. Hazlitt understood the Bastiat dictum that the worst thing that can happen to a good cause is not to be artfully criticized but to be ineptly defended.

26. One of Hazlitt's targets was Stuart Chase, who is often credited with the phrase "New Deal" that came to be identified with FDR's policies during the Great Depression. In one review of a book by Chase, Hazlitt (1935a) states, "Mr. Chase's logic wobbles, but his sentences march." Chase was strongly influenced by Henry George, Thorstein Veblen, and the Fabians, and his background training was in both economics and engineering. His long political and intellectual influence ran from FDR to Lyndon Johnson's Great Society program. The sort of economics of abundance that Chase represented, and his call that to fix the problem of poverty amid plenty required government activism and indeed government control over the economy, was in direct opposition to the lessons that Hazlitt thought economic doctrine had established.

economic isolation, that it is here to stay, and that therefore laissez-faire is dead," and in an earlier speech, he says, "The jig is up. The cat is out of the bag. There is no invisible hand. There never was" (see White 2012, 111). The explicit rejection of classical economic theory and with that the doctrine of free trade and self-regulation of the market economy, and the advancement of theories emphasizing the underconsumption explanation of the Depression, were very much part of the Roosevelt administration economic policy doctrine.

The *General Theory* provided a sophisticated restatement of the critique of laissez-faire doctrine and addressed the depth and length of the depression in the United States and the United Kingdom. Keynes captured the excitement of the intellectual youth at the time, as David Colander and Harry Landreth (1996, 9) note, "It was, with few exceptions, the young untenured professors who converted. . . . the relationship between Keynes and the young revolutionaries has few precedents in the history of economic thought." There are of course subtle and important differences between the older institutionalist and underconsumption theorists such as Tugwell, and the emerging new economics of Keynes, but from a broad-brush perspective the critical idea was the abandonment of the doctrine of laissez-faire and the embrace of the idea of government intervention in the operation of the economy to address the issues of unemployment and economic instability.

This was Hazlitt's intellectual landscape in the 1930s and 1940s, when he was writing economic editorials for the *New York Times*. Hazlitt was witnessing the shift from a classical- or "orthodox"-dominated economic worldview to a Keynesian hegemony that he saw as an intellectual error, and thus Hazlitt viewed as his task, from his influential perch at the *New York Times*, to defend in editorials and book reviews orthodox economics and criticize the departures from this as represented by the New Deal. A review of Hazlitt's columns during this time will indicate just how firmly and consistently Hazlitt challenged the New Deal policies, ranging from columns confronting the administration in "Fetish of Low Interest Rates" (July 29, 1946) to a piece on a former financial adviser of Roosevelt's ("James P. Warburg's Money Plan," May 13, 1934), to a direct response to Eleanor Roosevelt on cutting wage hours in "Enough to Buy Back the Product" (September 24, 1945). In fact, Hazlitt (1945) is characteristically straightforward in his response: "Mrs. Eleanor Roosevelt, in a column that probably set a record for the number of antique economic fallacies packed into that many lines of type, proved to her own satisfaction that we can realize our fondest dreams if only we stop technical progress" and continues with a logical and simplistic example of the problems and distortions created with a policy that cuts worker hours. This response captures the core elements of Hazlitt's editorials and writing style of coherence, clarity, and moderate wit. Paul Milazzo (2012, 2) writes that Hazlitt's columns in the *New York Times* "provide unparalleled quotidian account of the Roosevelt's Administration's economic policies. Collectively, they convey perhaps the broadest, most substantive case against the political economy of the New Deal, one the Administration often felt compelled to answer, and that informed the conservative critique of liberalism for decades to come."

In this sense, Hazlitt as a figure who was the voice of free market economics during the Great Depression and the World War II era is often significantly underplayed because, we hypothesize, historians outlining the American conservative movement pick up the narrative only after Mises and Hayek, and eventually Milton Friedman, rise to become prominent voices in the 1950s and 1960s. There is, in our opinion, a failure to contextualize the contributions that Hazlitt made as an economic commentator during the New Deal. Although many works recognize him for his role in popularizing the free market literature, he is not attributed with a central role in providing the substantive movement in free market economics, despite his defense of this position before the popularity of other free market figures emerged.

The extent to which the intellectual ground shifted under Hazlitt also became evident during his reporting on the Bretton Woods agreement in July 1944. World War II was not yet over, but the major industrial nations sought to create international agencies to manage and provide economic security to the global financial market. Forty-four nations were represented at the meetings, and Keynes clearly emerged as the intellectual leader. The Bretton Woods agreement established the International Monetary Fund and the International Bank for Reconstruction and Development. To Hazlitt, "all the wrong decisions were made" at these meetings.

His editorials for the *New York Times* reflected his opposition to what was being agreed to, which Hazlitt argued was nothing short of "institutionalized inflation." When the agreement was signed, however, Hazlitt was told by Arthur Sulzberger, editor of the *New York Times*: "Now, look, Henry, we've let you write your editorials condemning the decisions of the delegates to Bretton Woods as they were announced." But now that the agreement about the form of organization and common monetary policy had been adopted, "I don't see how *The Times* can any longer oppose it. It is up to us to go along." Hazlitt said he could not bring himself to write such an editorial, as he thought the Bretton Woods system would produce immense harm.[27]

Hazlitt's analysis of Bretton Woods was spot on, as he predicted that unavoidable inflation would occur worldwide and then Bretton Woods would collapse. By its very construction, the collapse of Bretton Woods was inevitable because establishing fixed exchange rates (which is what Bretton Woods did) meant that countries could not have both a free flow of capital and an independent monetary policy. Economists today note that the system was not in de facto full operation until after 1958, when Western European industrial countries made their currencies convertible; with this calculation, the regime actually lasted only twelve years, not thirty.[28]

With the breakdown of the Bretton Woods agreement and the subsequent stagflation of the 1970s, Hazlitt's editorials were collected into a volume *From Bretton Woods to World Inflation: A Study of Causes and Consequences* (1984). But for our purposes, the precise content of Hazlitt's argument is not as important as what the episode taught Hazlitt about the shifting intellectual landscape.[29] He had been critical of Keynes's economics throughout the 1930s and 1940s, but now he realized how widespread Keynes's influence had in fact grown in policy circles and the general intellectual climate of opinion. Exposing what he considered Keynesian fallacies became a primary aim of his economic writings.[30]

---

27. "My Life and Conclusions," p. 40, Henry Hazlitt Archives, DOC24289.pdf. See also Tucker 1999, 173–74. There are some discrepancies between Hazlitt's autobiographical account and other interviews he gave. His opposition to Bretton Woods did not lead to his firing at the *New York Times* as he points out in earlier interviews he gave, but it did increase the intellectual tensions he felt between himself and the general editorial staff at the paper. He moved to *Newsweek* in 1946, primarily to move from the anonymity of unsigned editorials multiple times a week to being responsible for one signed column a week. See Milazzo 2011, xxviii.

28. Michael Bordo (1993) discusses this in "Bretton Woods International Monetary System," in the volume *A Retrospective on the Bretton Woods System: Lessons for International Monetary Reform*.

29. Although it is interesting to note that in 1984, Friedman wrote to Hazlitt to congratulate him on a letter to the editor Hazlitt published in the *Wall Street Journal* on Bretton Woods. As Friedman says in his letter, "As you know, you and I differ somewhat about both the desirability and the feasibility of a real gold standard under current circumstances but *I certainly agree fully with your analysis of Bretton Woods*" ("Letter from Milton Friedman to Henry Hazlitt, dated August 10, 1984," Henry Hazlitt Archives, DOC12523_3.pdf; emphasis added).

30. Hazlitt was also more drawn into the larger movement of the reclaiming of true liberalism, which resulted in his involvement with the Mont Pèlerin Society and the Foundation for

The *New York Times* agreed to give Hazlitt alternate days off in 1945 so he could write *Economics in One Lesson* (1946). The book became a publishing sensation, rising to number six on the *New York Times* best seller list for nonfiction; even though the publisher ran out of stock, the book sold over seven hundred thousand copies in its original edition, and multiple millions when subsequent editions are accounted for, including translations.

Although Hazlitt was able to utilize his prestige and positions at the *New York Times*, and later at *Newsweek*, to advance many ideas, what is just as remarkable is Hazlitt's ability to communicate the economic ideas.[31] Hazlitt (1946, xii) saw his task as simply providing a readable exposition of "unblushingly 'classical,' 'traditional' and 'orthodox'" economics. In developing his approach, Hazlitt is explicit that he engaged in a "modernization, extension and generalization" of the approach found in Frédéric Bastiat's 1850 essay "What Is Seen and What Is Not Seen" (Bastiat [1850] 1995). For Hazlitt, the field of public economics (economic policy) ignored elementary truths because of the circumstances of the Great Depression and World War II and relied on intellectual justification by the new economics of Keynes and the Keynesians. Hazlitt's writing approach was to provide a commonsense or intuitive understanding of the basic lessons in economics. His writing is characterized by exquisite simplicity and clarity. Rather than dive into the complexities of economic theories, Hazlitt bestows basic economic reasoning on his readers by providing plenty of simple hypothetical and real-world examples to illustrate his points and eliciting rhetorical questions to guide readers in their reasoning.

Economic Education, and is reflected in works such as *The Free Man's Library* (1956). His argument in the introduction to that work echoes many of the arguments one can read back into his various book reviews from the *Nation* forward about the shifting meanings of liberalism and individualism. What now threatened Western democratic states was not totalitarian philosophies but an intellectual drift that failed to appreciate the connection between personal and economic liberties. Writers and thinkers believe that they can defend unequivocally the freedom of thought and speech, but not economic liberties. And Hazlitt sought to demonstrate to his brethren in the intelligentsia that "Liberty is a whole, and to deny economic liberty is finally to destroy all liberty."

31. In fact, it is because of Hazlitt's exceptional strength in writing coupled with his comprehensive economic reasoning that he is such a unique figure. Mencken's remarks about Hazlitt reproduced in the epigraph to the present essay demonstrate exactly this point when Mencken (1933, 385) refers to Hazlitt as "the only competent critic of the arts that I have ever heard of who was at the same time a competent economist, of practical as well as theoretical training, and he is one of the few economists in human history who could really write."

Perhaps the success of *Economics in One Lesson* can be attributed to utilizing this approach. In this best-selling book, Hazlitt takes the basic idea of direct and indirect effects and provides numerous applications from price controls, to restrictions on trade, to public spending, and so on. The book is characterized by the classic Hazlitt voice of *illustrating* the basic principles of economics without necessarily teaching us about any formal models of, say, supply and demand. That is, Hazlitt developed a method of logical analysis that walks the reader through the intuition of a certain policy. He uses a plethora of examples to again *show* us the laws of economics without explicitly stating them. His precision in this every step provides a clear reading of the message and highlights why certain people may respond to a policy in a certain way. Readers are not left wondering *why*, say, farmers responded in a certain way to a policy because Hazlitt has walked us through the logic of the *why*. In this way of writing, Hazlitt foresees possible objections and potential uncertainties that readers may have, and addresses these in his analysis. Hazlitt's writings thus appear persuasive, but not overly argumentative, as his main tone is *explaining* or illustrating the idea. A special emphasis is placed on the role of special interest groups in enacting these policies—and he ties in the special interest economics with his main lesson, that the art of economics consists of "tracing the consequences of that policy not merely for one group but for all groups" (Hazlitt 1946, 5). By introducing the role of special interest groups, Hazlitt concedes that a certain group of people may benefit from the law, but it comes at the expense of others—and this analysis appeals to intuition and simultaneously reinforces his clear and explanatory approach to understanding policies and also highlights the political economy approach.

The clarity and success of Hazlitt's writing style in conveying his point of view is generally recognized even when scholars may strongly disagree with Hazlitt's content. Take, for example, a relatively recent commentary by Brad Delong (2005), who while criticizing Hazlitt for failing to address problems of the market system (such things as externalities), nevertheless admits that *Economics in One Lesson* is an excellent book because it "brilliantly and coherently restates the Classical view."

A further point on the success of *Economics in One Lesson* is that in addition to his seductive, concise, and illustrative writing style, Hazlitt's chapters on the policies that he is analyzing are examples of economic policies occurring at that time. He discusses such things as unionization, the minimum wage, and other labor laws as well as make-work projects, commodity-price fixing in the agriculture sector, taxes on income, and various other policies that were enacted or proposed during the New Deal. Thus, even though the principles of economics are universal, this is a book about the economics of his time, which addresses the most pressing issues of his day.[32] In this respect, Hazlitt's book is both timely and timeless.

In his review of Hazlitt's book in the *American Economic Review*, the Princeton economist Archibald McIsaac (1947, 426) states that "Mr. Hazlitt has thrown down a vigorous, skillful, and provocative challenge to sophisticated formulations of theory and policy, and it must be conceded that all too often the forest has been neglected as a consequence of preoccupation with the trees." McIsaac, however, argues that Hazlitt's analysis does not apply to either an economy trapped in a less-than-full employment equilibrium or to a wartime economy, and that in the emergency times of depression and war, Hazlitt's commonsense economics must give way to more-nuanced economics. Nevertheless, even the sophisticated economist can learn a thing or two from reading Hazlitt's "smoothly written, swiftly moving and persuasive" addition to the economics literature (428).

In 1946, Hazlitt moved from the *New York Times* to *Newsweek*, where for the next twenty years he wrote a weekly column, Business Tides, applying *the lesson* to every contemporary economic policy issue of the day. As Milazzo (2011, xxx) writes, with his column: "Hazlitt condemned state intervention in the market, championed free trade, questioned underconsumption as a catalyst for recession, celebrated entrepreneurial creativity, and viewed inflation, rather than unemployment, as first among economic evils. He also emphasized how the spontaneous order of the price system conveyed vast quantities of information among countless market actors, allocating scarce capital, labor and resources far more efficiently than top-down planning mechanisms ever could." The topic of inflationary policies and the negative consequences of inflation constituted more than one-third of his *Newsweek* columns.[33] And given the weight he put on inflation, the main target of his animus was Keynesian

---

32. The New Deal polices and examples he gives in the book are just as relevant to policies today.

33. This preoccupation with the costs of inflation also explains why Hazlitt engaged in a battle with Friedman over the quantity theory of money throughout their relationship. Hazlitt learned his critique of the mechanical interpretation of the quantity theory of money from Benjamin Anderson, and that critique was reinforced by the writings of Mises (see Blanchette 2005). Hazlitt describes the trip overseas to the first Mont Pèlerin meeting where every night he and Friedman would debate monetary policy and inflation, never in an angry way, but in a very intense manner, to the great disinterest of all the other economists around the table.

economics. Hazlitt waged his battle of economic ideas wherever and whenever he could, which included not only his weekly column but numerous books—including his *Failure of the "New Economics"* (1959), where he provides the first line by line critical evaluation of Keynes's *General Theory of Employment, Interest, and Money*.[34]

3. Against the New Economics

During the 1950s the Keynesian hegemony of the economics profession was entrenched and permeated professional journals, classrooms, and the intellectual culture in general. After Keynes's death in April 1946, various tributes pointed out the worldwide influence that his work had enjoyed among academic specialists, intellectuals, politicians, and the general public. Keynes's importance as an economist in the twentieth century was compared with that of Adam Smith in the eighteenth century and Karl Marx in the nineteenth century. Smith had provided a devastating criticism of the mercantilist system, Marx a thorough analysis and critique of the capitalist order, and Keynes had put an end to the argument for laissez-faire.

Keynes's work demanded critical examination. Hazlitt was not only a well-read (although self-educated) economist, he was by professional training also a literary critic—he had even published *The Anatomy of Criticism* (1933a), an exercise in trying to steer a course between pure objectivism and relativism in analysis. Hazlitt's work on thinking, reading, and argument (*Thinking as a Science*) had given him a perspective on how one analyzes works of literary value. This is what he attempts to do with respect to the *General Theory* and Keynesian economics more broadly in his *Failure of the "New Economics"* and then bolstered by a reference volume containing the best of the specialist literature on the problems with Keynesianism, *The Critics of Keynesian Economics* (1960). In these works, Hazlitt sought to make an original contribution to economics by reasserting classical principles of economics and steering this understanding into the minds of the public. "In the history of

---

34. This even included an effort in the early 1960s to establish a new graduate school for economic education—the American School of Economics—that involved the efforts of not only Hazlitt and Hans Sennholz but Mises, Hayek, Rothbard, and several other prominent classical liberal thinkers in the social sciences and humanities. The discussions lasted three years, but the school never materialized. See the Hazlitt Archives under the heading "American School of Economics."

thought," Hazlitt (1959, 5) wrote, "great new contributions have often been made as a sort of by-product of what were originally intended to be merely refutations."

In making this intellectual move, Hazlitt clears the way for his presentation of the particular brand of "orthodox" economics he believes provides the most coherent challenge to the new economics of Keynes and the Keynesians—the economic analysis of the manipulation of money and credit found in Mises and Hayek, and all that implied about capital and interest theory, price theory and the market process, and deficit finance and principles of public finance. Hazlitt's "orthodox" economics involved a core body of thought from Smith, Say, Ricardo, and Mill, refined and developed by Menger, Böhm-Bawerk, Wicksteed, Mises, and Hayek, but also recognizing the contributions of early twentieth-century neoclassical writers such as Frank Knight and Jacob Viner.

Countering the fashionable Keynesian heresy of his day was Hazlitt's intent, and it did not surprise him in the least that by the late 1950s, his brand of "orthodox" economics was increasingly becoming out of step, although he claims he did not understand at the time just how out of step he had become either within the economics profession or in the intellectual culture in general. As the reviews of Hazlitt's *Failure of the "New Economics"* and the companion volume *The Critics of Keynesian Economics* came in from professional journals, it became more evident how "orthodox" economists could ignore the Keynesian heresies only at the risk of themselves being ignored, or challenge them only at the risk of losing status.[35] Economics, to Hazlitt, was losing its way as a scientific discipline.

Joseph McKenna's (1960, 190) review of *The Failure of the "New Economics"* in the *American Economic Review* concludes that "although Hazlitt clears up many minor points in the *General Theory*, his analysis

---

35. The relative stature of Hazlitt as someone worthy of attention is reflected by the fact that Abba Lerner (1960) reviewed *The Failure of the "New Economics"* in the *Review of Economics and Statistics*, but the fact that Hazlitt had become so out of step is also revealed in the content of the review. Lerner points out that he had in earlier work acknowledged that Hazlitt's *Economics in One Lesson* was among the best critical works against certain economic fallacies, although that was because Hazlitt was writing with respect to an economy already at full employment. He had hoped that Hazlitt would one day write a book that focused on economies in depression, which Lerner said would be economics in a second lesson. Unfortunately, Lerner states about *The Failure of the "New Economics"* that Hazlitt does not write the second lesson because he never learned it. Since Hazlitt never learned the second lesson, he is completely oblivious to the possibility of the third lesson, which is that when the institutional structure is such that Keynesian policies cannot guarantee full employment, government has to play an even more active role.

of the major ones is completely unsatisfactory. In short, those who agree with Hazlitt's preconceptions will find many excuses for their views; those seeking enlightenment must look elsewhere." Dudley Dillard's (1961, 424–25) review of *The Critics of Keynesian Economics* (also in the *AER*) states the criticism of Hazlitt and "orthodox" economics more forcefully:

> The political temper of modern democratic societies renders Hazlitt's position un-realistic in the sense that it calls for a more or less complete return to the never-never land of nineteenth-century laissez faire. Henry Hazlitt reminds one of the Japanese soldier who was found on an isolated Pacific isle a decade or more after the end of the second world war, unwilling to accept the fact that the war was long since over, and lost. Courage and perseverance in the face of opposition are qualities not to be taken lightly, but there is also merit in knowing that the war is over and in what century one is living.

Keep in mind that Dillard's review is of a collection of readings that include not only the writings of Mises, Hayek, and Hazlitt but also the works of Say, Mill, Viner, and Knight. There were critics of Keynes—ancient as well as modern—but they were ignored as relics of an earlier era, an era wedded to those "habitual modes of thought" that had led us to a situation of mass unemployment in the 1930s and saw no solution to the problem. But what if, as Hazlitt thought, those "habitual modes of thought" reflected the core of the scientific teachings of the discipline of economics, and as such provided the explanation for the problem of unemployment and its solution in a way that enabled democratic societies to avoid their own worst excesses? It is this conviction that motivated Hazlitt's own literary efforts and his activities as an intellectual middleman.

The rule by technically trained experts to use the public budget to ensure full employment revealed both a "pretense of knowledge" and a failure to understand the logic of "democracy in deficit," according to Hazlitt.[36] As Hazlitt (1959, 324) points out, the Keynesian economist/macroeconomic

---

36. I am consciously alluding to the title of Hayek's Nobel Prize lecture, "The Pretense of Knowledge," which was directed at the Keynesian exercise of macroeconomic management, and to the title of the book by James Buchanan and Richard Wagner, *Democracy in Deficit* (1977), which explores the political legacy of Keynes with respect to the budgetary policy. Hazlitt was already looking to see how the institutional structure of governance could be revised to guard against opportunist behavior in his work *A New Constitution Now* (1942), a point that was picked up in the review of that book by Jerome G. Kerwin (1943) published in the *American Political Science Review*.

manager must believe that "there exists a class of people (perhaps economists very much resembling Lord Keynes) who are completely informed, rational, balanced, wise, who have means of knowing at all times exactly how much investment is needed and in exactly what amounts it should be allocated to exactly which industries and projects, and that these managers are above corruption and above any interest in the outcome of the next election."

Challenging this idea and reviving classical economics would unite many of those involved in the free market counterrevolution that took place in the economics profession in the 1970s and 1980s. Hazlitt's explicit opposition to the post–World War II consensus in economic method, theory, and policy came with a price in terms of speeding along the decline in his reputation and status as the preeminent economic journalist in the United States. Consider how in the 1960s he lost his position at *Newsweek*. Osborn Elliott, then editor of *Newsweek*, replaced Hazlitt with three more-contemporary economic commentators (including Friedman), and, as Elliott (1980, 66) put it, it was about time he replaced the "antediluvian economics of Henry Hazlitt with something closer to current-day reality." The importance of this decision is to demonstrate just how much the intellectual climate had shifted toward new economics, but even more so, Hazlitt's endurance and dedication to reviving and defending orthodox economics.

In retrospect, though, we can read back into Hazlitt's *Failure of the "New Economics"* many of those subsequent developments from microfoundations, to expectations, to rules versus discretion, to political economy. His "novel" theory—novel, that is, if you do not read the classics—emerged as he said it would through his critique. Whereas Keynes had been able to tap into the greatest resentment of capitalism (inequality and the idle rich) and merge it with the greatest fear of capitalism (mass unemployment and insecurity) to forge a paradigm of managed capitalism that would minimize resentment and eliminate fear, Hazlitt offered a picture of the long-run folly of managed capitalism in terms of fiscal sustainability and the collapse of the monetary system through inflation.

4. The Ethics of the Liberal Order

Throughout the 1960s, 1970s, and 1980s, Hazlitt continued his intellectual crusade against inflation and the growing involvement of government in the economy, although he was not content to fight his battle solely in the realm of economic policy and commentary. As we turn to Hazlitt's next effort to move beyond his role as a public intellectual, it will perhaps be useful to remember that Hazlitt originally sought to pursue a career as a professional philosopher. Hazlitt throughout his career at the *Nation* as well as the *New York Times* maintained an active interest in philosophical treatises. Besides the review of Vilfredo Pareto for the *Times* mentioned earlier, during his time as a literary adviser at the *Nation*, Hazlitt reviewed works by Bertrand Russell, John Dewey, and his old professor at City College, Morris Cohen.

Over the years, Hazlitt became friends with all the leading classical liberal and libertarian thinkers. Milton Friedman in a letter dated June 10, 1969, about a review Hazlitt had written of Friedman's book, told him that "there are not very many people whose judgment I value as I do yours."[37] And, on the occasion of Hazlitt's seventieth birthday celebration, Mises referred to Hazlitt as "the economic conscience of our nation" and compared him favorably with Edwin Cannan and Frédéric Bastiat. Hayek said that he knew of no better modern source to learn the basic truths of economic science than the writings of Hazlitt.

Hazlitt, however, was not only friends with these economists, he was a close student of their works, and it is important to remember that as a teenager, Hazlitt was a devoted student of the works of Herbert Spencer, and also read the Scottish moral philosophers in-depth, especially David Hume. Hazlitt combined all this reading and study into *The Foundations of Morality* (1964). In *Thinking as a Science*, Hazlitt (1916, 217) had already pointed out that "no science is more provocative of thought than ethics." The question of good or bad acts—of just or unjust conduct—is the most subtle and elusive one that we can try to answer.

The Foundations of Morality sought to summarize and update the argument of the British utilitarians, beginning with Hume and Smith and continuing with Bentham, Mill, and Sidwick. But it is Hume's insistence on the utility of acting in accordance with general rules that provides the basis of Hazlitt's analysis. And it is the work of Mises on social cooperation—what Mises termed the "law of association"—that provided the more contemporary argument for the position that Hazlitt was to develop and juxtapose with modern ethical theory.

One core problem with ethical theory is that no two people will find happiness or ultimate purpose in precisely the same way. We cannot

---

37. Henry Hazlitt Archives, DOC82_3.pdf.

resolve this problem by appeal to a deity any more than we can rely on our moral intuitions. But Hazlitt argues that an answer can be found by focusing on social cooperation under the division of labor. "For each of us," he argues, "social cooperation is the great means of attaining nearly all our ends.... It has the great advantage that no unanimity with regard to value judgments is required to make it work. But it is a means so central, so universal, so indispensable to the realization of practically all our other ends, that there is little harm in regarding it as an end-in-itself, and even in treating it as if it were *the* goal of ethics" (Hazlitt 1964, 36).

Hazlitt's work on ethics in this sense complements his understanding of economics. As is discussed in classical economics, the division of labor is the greatest example of social cooperation, and it massively improves the productive capacity of each of us. For our purposes, what matters for Hazlitt is what general rules we are to live by, that will enable us to live better together so we can realize the benefits from social cooperation. Those general rules are embedded in the private property system. "All production, all civilization, rests on recognition of and respect for property rights" (Hazlitt 1964, 303). Free enterprise, competition, the division of labor, and wealth creation are not separate institutions but all grounded in private property rights and mutually reinforce one another. The free enterprise system, as Hazlitt points out, presupposes the acceptance of moral rules of just conduct. But the workings of the free market, the vibrancy of competition, the productivity gains from the division of labor, and the generalized benefits from social cooperation also serve to preserve and promote that morality. "Thus, social cooperation," Hazlitt argues, "is the essence of morality" (359).

It probably should be expected that this attempt to ground social ethics in basic economic reasoning would draw the ire of ethicists, but one harsh critic of Hazlitt was none other than another classical liberal economist, Frank Knight. Knight titled his *Ethics* review essay on Hazlitt's book, "Abstract Economics as Absolute Ethics."[38] Despite the fact that Knight

---

38. Despite the critical nature of his review, for the purposes of the present essay it is important to emphasize the following: (1) that a thinker of the stature of Knight would seriously engage the ideas of an economic journalist writing on an topic removed from economics; (2) the length of the essay, which ran for fourteen journal pages, two columns per page; and (3) the placement in a highly respected specialized outlet, *Ethics*. Knight would also address Hazlitt's book in a critical examination of Hayek's *Constitution of Liberty*, in the *Journal of Political Economy* (1967). In that discussion, Knight, while still critical of Hazlitt, does say the book presents strong, and largely sound, debating points in making the case for liberalism, although Hazlitt is far too extreme for Knight's tastes and sensibilities.

(1966, 163) says that Hazlitt's work "has good workmanship and much of the makings of a good treatise on socio-political ethics," it ultimately exhibits the same faults as other efforts at restating the case for classical liberalism. Knight argues that "what Hazlitt has done is to take the vastly simplified postulates that are legitimate and necessary for the first stage of economic analysis—but which should never be taken as describing reality, and still less as normative—and treat them as universal ideals" (177).

A more favorable reading of Hazlitt's *Foundations* can be found in Leland Yeager's *Ethics as Social Science: The Moral Philosophy of Social Cooperation* (2001).[39] As Yeager states in his preface, Hazlitt's *Foundations of Morality* is "the best single book on ethics that I know of." Yeager continues, "It seems to me that Hazlitt has received nowhere near the credit that he deserves for his scholarly accomplishments, and for no better reason than that he lacked the usual academic credentials and platform." But, Yeager concludes, Hazlitt "was a profoundly educated man, but mostly self-educated" (vii).

The dilemma that Knight (1967, 794–795) put before us is not that the arguments that cut against Hazlitt (and the entire tradition of classical or orthodox economics) and claim that laissez-faire must be overturned for government control and scientific planning are persuasive. According to Knight, they are not. Knight, in fact, siding with the teachings of orthodox economics, believes that such claims are "nonsense," but he asserts that the defenders of market freedom have inadequately dealt with the dark side of human nature. "Men are, and ought to be free," Knight understands, and that freedom within the economic realm means freedom of exchange. An exchange is an exchange is an exchange, Knight emphasized in many of his works; it is voluntary and mutually beneficial, otherwise it would not have taken place. The principles of economics are applied common sense derived from the facts of nature.

Humankind exhibits two natural propensities: (1) to truck, barter, and exchange, as Adam Smith taught us; and (2) to rape, pillage, and plunder, as Thomas Hobbes warned. Which propensity is realized in lived history is a function of the rules of the social game that are in operation in that particular time and place. If the rules encourage our social nature, then individuals will be able to realize the gains from social cooperation under

---

39. In fact, in *Ethics as Social Science*, Yeager builds on the work of Hume, Smith, Mill, Mises, Hayek, and Hazlitt and provides a modern defense of rule or indirect utilitarianism in contrast to contractarianism, natural rights theory, and moral intuitionism. His analysis is, in essence, the message that Hazlitt tried to articulate in 1964.

the division of labor. If those rules encourage our antisocial nature, then those benefits from social cooperation will go unrealized. That the "antisocial side of human nature must be taken into account in any serious and intelligent discussion of economic policy" (Knight 1967, 795) is a point that Hazlitt's *Foundations of Morality* would agree on despite Knight's objection that this problem is ignored. It is not ignored, and in fact, one could reasonably argue that it was precisely the core point of the book—the necessity to discover, implement, and establish mechanisms of enforcement for the rules that encourage social cooperation by curbing our predatory nature, and the "shocking" revelation that private property provides the institutional foundation for such a social order.

Hazlitt's discussion anticipates not only the work in political economy on governance and the institutional structure required to sustain a private property market economy but also the evolution of the tacit norms and mores on which the formal structure of the rules of governance rests and without which the system cannot be sustained. For any modern social scientists working on questions of development and institutional transformation, this will sound all too familiar. We are not claiming that Hazlitt influenced the modern discussion on these topics, but the ideas that Hazlitt worked with are clearly reflected in that literature, and he was emphasizing these points when few other authors were in the disciplines of philosophy, politics, and economics.

5. Conclusion

Henry Hazlitt was a unique public intellectual who utilized both his uncanny ability to communicate the ideas of orthodox economics to the general public and his prominent positions and connections to promote certain writers and ideas. At the same time, Hazlitt's success in this garnered respect and attention from professional economists, although Hazlitt mostly saw himself as advancing the understanding of classical economics and applying the basic reasoning to current issues. Perhaps the most eminent and immeasurable aspect of Hazlitt is that he was *the* voice of orthodox economics at a time when the tides had turned against these ideas and writers of the ideas. From his prolific articles and the publication of his first book in 1916 to his final books in 1984, Hazlitt sought to write works advancing the understanding of orthodox economics that would seek approval from specialists while generating a wide readership among intelligent laymen.

The evidence that we have tried to marshal to support our conjecture that Hazlitt occupied a unique position in mid-twentieth-century intellectual life in the United States as a public intellectual consisted of pointing not just to his prominent position in the world of journalism—both as a literary critic and as an economist—but also to the attention his written work commanded in the specialized professional journals in economics and philosophy, as well as the active correspondence he engaged in throughout his life. The company Hazlitt kept was not just that of the New York intelligentsia but included many of the leading minds in the social sciences during his lifetime.

In the battle of ideas, Hazlitt's remarkable ability to translate the complexities of economic theories to simple and lucid "commonsense" principles was a seductive weapon that Hazlitt used to explain classical economics and to steer readers to other writers and economists, such as his reviews did for Hayek and Mises. In this way, Hazlitt influenced the intellectual climate for many decades, as was also noted by Friedman when he wrote to Hazlitt saying, "I think you grossly underrate the results of your own efforts. The facade of opposition to sensible arrangements seems to me to be cracking, though I readily grant that the cracks are not much wider than can be seen with the microscope."[40] The only other case comparable to Hazlitt in the history of economics is perhaps Bastiat.[41] Unfortunately, Hazlitt has suffered a similar fate. This should not be surprising, since Hazlitt tied his own work so closely to that of Bastiat. In *History of Economic Analysis* (1954, 500), Joseph Schumpeter writes that Bastiat has been given "undue prominence" and that his case is simply one of "the bather who enjoys himself in the shallows and goes beyond his depth and drowns." Schumpeter summarily dismisses Bastiat by stating: "I do not hold that Bastiat was a bad theorist. I hold that he was no theorist."

Schumpeter's judgment of Bastiat is certainly subject to challenge, especially when one moves away from the simplistic reading of Bastiat and focuses instead on the nascent opportunity cost reasoning, the invisible-hand-style argument, and the public choice analysis evident throughout his writings. Although Hazlitt has not been subject to such a harsh dismissal in a leading work on the history of modern economic thought,

---

40. Friedman to Hazlitt, May 8, 1953, box 28, folder 3, Friedman Papers.

41. Lippmann clearly occupied a similar place, although less in the field of economic theory than in political economy and political science. But Lippmann's work is still celebrated today among academics and public intellectuals, whereas Hazlitt has faded into obscurity.

his fate has been worse—which is to be ignored. Rather than an "undue prominence" as a result of relentless critics as Schumpeter maintains was Bastiat's fate, Hazlitt has failed to inspire critics, having been thought to have been so soundly defeated in his own day that he suffers "undue neglect." It is our hope that this essay, as well as recent and forthcoming work by Paul Milazzo and Angus Burgin, will lead to a reassessment of Hazlitt's contributions both as economic thinker and as communicator, as well as an intellectual middleman for "orthodox economics" during the ascendency of the new economics of the post–World War II era.

References

Anderson, B. (1911) 1966. *Social Value*. New York: Augustus Kelley.
———. 1917. *The Value of Money*. New York: Macmillan.
———. (1949) 1979. *Economics and the Public Welfare: A Financial and Economic History of the United States, 1914–1946*. Indianapolis, Ind.: Liberty Fund.
Bastiat, Frédéric. (1850) 1995. "What Is Seen and What Is Not Seen." In *Selected Essays in Political Economy*. Irvington-on-Hudson, N.Y.: Foundation for Economic Education.
Blanchette, J. 2005. "Anderson, Hazlitt, and the Quantity Theory of Money." *Journal of Libertarian Studies* 19 (1): 25–36.
Boettke, P. 2012. *Living Economics: Yesterday, Today, and Tomorrow*. Guatemala City: Universidad Francisco Marroquin Press.
Bordo, M. 1993. "Bretton Woods International Monetary System." In *A Retrospective on the Bretton Woods System: Lessons for International Monetary Reform*, edited by M. Bordo and B. Eichengreen. Chicago: University of Chicago Press.
Buchanan, J., and R. Wagner. 1977. *Democracy in Deficit: The Political Legacy of Lord Keynes*. New York: Academic Press.
Burgin, A. 2012. *The Great Persuasion: Reinventing Free Markets since the Great Depression*. Cambridge: Harvard University Press.
Caldwell, B. 2007. *The Road to Serfdom: Text and Documents—the Definitive Edition*. Vol. 2 of *The Collected Works of F. A. Hayek*. Chicago: University of Chicago Press.
Cockett, R. 1995. *Thinking the Unthinkable*. London: Fontana.
Colander, D., and H. Landreth. 1996. *The Coming of Keynesianism to America*. Cheltenham, UK: Edward Elgar.
Delong, Brad. 2005. "Economics in One Lesson." *Brad Delong* (blog), April 10. http://delong.typepad.com/sdj/2005/04/economics_in_on.html.
Dillard, D. 1961. Review of *The Critics of Keynesian Economics*. *American Economic Review* 51 (3): 423–25.
Elliott, O. 1980. *The World of Oz*. New York: Viking.
Hazlitt, H. 1916. *Thinking as a Science*. New York: Dutton.

———. 1933a. *The Anatomy of Criticism: A Trialogue.* New York: Simon and Schuster.
———. 1933b. "Crises Are Not 'So Simple.'" *Nation*, May 24.
———. 1935a. "The Government's Role in Business." *New York Times*, September 22.
———. 1935b. "Mr. Nock Cries a Pox on the State." *New York Times*, October 20.
———. 1935c. "Pareto's Picture of Society." *New York Times*, May 26.
———. 1937. "Economic Planning as a Panacea." *New York Times Book Review*, August 1.
———. 1938. "A Revised Attack on Socialism." *New York Times*, January 9.
———. 1939. "Lionel Robbins on Class Conflict." *New York Times Book Review*, October 22.
———. 1942. *A New Constitution Now.* New York: Whittlesay House.
———. 1944. "An Economist's View of 'Planning.'" *New York Times*, September 24.
———. 1945. "Enough to Buy Back the Product." *New York Times*, September 24.
———. 1946. *Economics in One Lesson.* New York: Harper Brothers.
———, ed. 1956. *The Free Man's Library.* Princeton, N.J.: Van Nostrand.
———. 1959. *The Failure of the "New Economics."* Princeton, N.J.: Van Nostrand.
———, ed. 1960. *The Critics of Keynesian Economics.* Princeton, N.J.: Van Nostrand.
———. 1964. *The Foundations of Morality.* Princeton, N.J.: Van Nostrand.
———. 1984. *From Bretton Woods to World Inflation: A Study of Causes and Consequences.* Chicago: Henry Regnery.
———. 2011. *Business Tides: The Newsweek Era of Henry Hazlitt.* Auburn, Ala.: Ludwig von Mises Institute.
Kerwin, J. G. 1943. Review of *A New Constitution Now.* *American Political Science Review* 37 (2): 334–36.
Knight, F. 1966. "Abstract Economics as Absolute Ethics." *Ethics* 76 (3): 163–77.
———. 1967. "Laissez Faire: Pro and Con." *Journal of Political Economy* 75 (6): 782–95.
Lerner, A. 1960. Review of *The Failure of the "New Economics."* *Review of Economics and Statistics* 42 (2): 234–35.
McIsaac, A. 1947. Review of *Economics in One Lesson.* *American Economic Review* 37 (3): 424–28.
McKenna, J. 1960. Review of *The Failure of the "New Economics."* *American Economic Review* 50 (1): 188–90.
Mencken, H. L. 1933. "Ten Years." *American Mercury*, December, 385–87.
Milazzo, Paul. 2011. Introduction to *Business Tides.* Auburn, Ala.: Ludwig von Mises Institute.
———. 2012. "Editorializing the New Deal: The New York Times Era of Henry Hazlitt." Working paper, Ohio University.
Schumpeter, J. 1954. *History of Economic Analysis.* New York: Oxford University Press.
Sowell, T. 1981. *Markets and Minorities.* New York: Basic Books.
Tucker, J. 1999. "Henry Hazlitt: The People's Austrian." In *Fifteen Great Austrian Economists*, edited by Randall Holcombe, 167–79. Auburn, Ala.: Ludwig von Mises Institute.

White, L. 2012. *The Clash of Economic Ideas.* New York: Cambridge University Press.

Wicksteed, P. (1910) 1933. *The Common Sense of Political Economy.* 2 vols. London: Routledge.

Williams, W. 1982. *The State against Blacks.* New York: McGraw-Hill.

Wilson, W. 1997. *When Work Disappears: The World of the New Urban Poor.* New York: Vintage.

Yeager, L. 2001. *Ethics as Social Science: The Moral Philosophy of Social Cooperation.* Cheltenham, UK: Edward Elgar.

Federal Reserve Bank Presidents as Public Intellectuals

Rob Roy McGregor and Warren Young

In his remarks to an MIT forum on public intellectuals and the academy, Alan Lightman identified two types of public intellectual, one in the tradition of Ralph Waldo Emerson and one with the "mission" of Edward Said. The former "communicates his ideas to the world, not just to fellow intellectuals"; the latter "actively" disturbs the "status quo" (Lightman 1999).

Over the past decade, the role of academic economists as "public intellectuals" has received increasing attention (Hubbard 2004; Lebaron 2006; Lepper 2007). Those individuals chosen as Federal Reserve Bank presidents also took on the role of public intellectual, as they usually had to explain economic policy in the context of both regional and national economic developments to a much wider audience than their fellow professionals. In other words, they had to bring academic discussion and debate over economic theory and policy into the public domain when speaking to or writing for the public at large. Indeed, the translation of complex theoretical and policy issues into terms understood by the public was a key role taken on by those presidents opposing what could be called the "mainstream" view that characterized the late 1970s and early 1980s.

In this essay, we explore the role of Reserve Bank presidents in public discourse, focusing on their public pronouncements and efforts at analyzing and explaining economic events and policies to professional and academic audiences and the public at large, and their own positions at the

---

Correspondence may be addressed to Rob Roy McGregor, Department of Economics, UNC Charlotte, 9201 University City Boulevard, Charlotte, NC 28223-0001; e-mail: rrmcgreg@uncc.edu.

History of Political Economy 45 (annual suppl.) DOI 10.1215/00182702-2310989
Copyright 2013 by Duke University Press

Federal Open Market Committee, in the late 1970s and early 1980s. The period was a time of intense political pressures on the FOMC (Chappell, McGregor, and Vermilyea 2005; Kettl 1986; Wells 1994; Woolley 1984). Although the Federal Reserve has always taken pride in its independence, the record of committee deliberations from this period indicates that members were mindful of the preferences of the president, the Congress, and the public, even though there is no indication that the committee ever felt compelled to follow instructions from any outside authority (Chappell, McGregor, and Vermilyea 2005). Nevertheless, because the message communicated most consistently was that growth was too slow and unemployment too high, the FOMC over the period worried that a determined anti-inflationary monetary policy would prompt a recession, and it is clear that most members were unwilling to risk the backlash that might occur in the face of such a recession (as documented by Chappell, McGregor, and Vermilyea 2005). This perspective was, in fact, *mainstream*, receiving the support of the executive and legislative branches, public opinion, and most members of the economics profession (Hetzel 1998). As we show, the Reserve Bank presidents we examine clearly *communicated* their ideas and worldviews to the public at large and, in some cases, *actively* took issue with the "mainstream" that characterized the "institutional consensus" of the Federal Reserve.

The rest of the essay is organized as follows. Information about the organizational structure and institutional practices of the US Federal Reserve System is presented first. The backgrounds of the presidents we have chosen—of the St. Louis, Philadelphia, and Minneapolis Feds—are then presented. Two challengers of the mainstream perspective were St. Louis Fed president Lawrence Roos and Minneapolis Fed president Mark Willes, while the mainstream view was held by Philadelphia Fed president David Eastburn. In each case, we focus on the pronouncements of these presidents as *individual* public intellectuals. This is based on (1) their respective *individual policy views* as *published* in material directed at *professional* and *academic audiences*, (2) interviews and articles *other* than in academic outlets, and (3) their public speeches and remarks on economic issues.

Institutional Background: The Federal Reserve System

The Federal Reserve System consists of a seven-member Board of Governors headquartered in Washington, DC, and twelve district Federal

Reserve Banks headquartered in Atlanta, Boston, Chicago, Cleveland, Dallas, Kansas City, Minneapolis, New York, Philadelphia, Richmond, St. Louis, and San Francisco. The members of the Board of Governors and the presidents of the district Federal Reserve Banks are chosen by different means. Members of the Board of Governors are appointed by the US president and confirmed by the Senate to serve fourteen-year terms. The district Reserve Bank presidents, on the other hand, are chosen to serve five-year terms by the boards of directors of the district banks, subject to approval by the Board of Governors. The members of the Board of Governors and the presidents of the district banks serve on the policymaking Federal Open Market Committee. The FOMC's monetary policy decisions are formally made by majority vote among the committee's voting members (the seven governors, the New York Fed president, and four of the remaining eleven district Reserve Bank presidents, who rotate voting privileges in a prescribed way). The difference in appointment mechanisms for governors and Reserve Bank presidents has prompted research about whether the FOMC voting behavior of these groups differs in a systematic way, with the preponderance of the evidence suggesting that Reserve Bank presidents prefer tighter monetary policy than governors (for a review of the literature, see Chappell, McGregor, and Vermilyea 2005).

The Board of Governors has regulatory and supervisory responsibilities that cover the domestic operations of US banks and bank holding companies, the US operations of foreign banking organizations, and the foreign activities of US banking organizations. The Board of Governors also has the authority to set reserve requirements on certain classes of deposits and to approve the discount rates proposed by the district Reserve Banks. The Reserve Banks themselves are the operating arms of the Federal Reserve System, responsible for such tasks as holding reserves for depository institutions in their districts, making discount loans to such institutions, and supervising and examining bank holding companies and state-chartered member banks in their districts to ensure their safety and soundness and compliance with banking regulations. In addition, each district Reserve Bank maintains an independent research staff that monitors and analyzes national and regional economic conditions. Moreover, the Reserve Bank presidents have frequent contacts with district businesspeople who provide their perceptions about business conditions. This type of anecdotal economic information from each Federal Reserve district is presented in the Beige Book prepared in advance of each FOMC meeting. During the discussions of economic conditions that are a routine part of FOMC meetings, the Reserve Bank presidents typically address their district conditions as well as national conditions.

The chairman of the Federal Reserve plays key roles in FOMC deliberations as an agenda setter and as a consensus builder. He is the most prominent spokesman for the committee in political and public arenas, and he is responsible for allocating Board of Governors staff resources to rank-and-file governors; both of these roles may give him some leverage over the FOMC (Woolley 1984). Nevertheless, while the power of the chairman is widely recognized, his is not the only voice in the monetary policy decision process. Moreover, although there is at the FOMC an ethic that favors keeping disagreements private and closing ranks in public, dissenting members do from time to time feel compelled by conscience to speak publicly about why they differ from the majority of the committee. In part because they have independent staff support, the Reserve Bank presidents are especially well positioned to present alternative views about monetary policy. This has its value within an institution like the Federal Reserve System; as Marvin Goodfriend (2000, 9) notes, "The diversification of research within a system of central banks brings a variety of analytical perspectives to policy deliberations that is invaluable in our increasingly complex economy." Moreover, it can be argued that failing "to air differences among Committee members would deprive markets of useful information, and it would put the public at a permanent disadvantage in understanding monetary policy" (16–17). Indeed, some observers have stressed the importance of the presidents' role in public discourse (Poole 2007; Nash 2010). For example, Betty Nash (2010, 11) notes that "the Reserve Bank presidents frequently give speeches, in which they may detail ideas about monetary policy, whether or not they've dissented. In this fashion, they plant ideas in the public discourse. These discussions also appear to be a way of informing the market, by conditioning expectations." We next describe how selected district Reserve Bank presidents participated in the public discourse of the late 1970s and early 1980s.

Presidents and Pronouncements

The period we examine saw the Great Inflation of 1965–79 end with the 1979–82 Volcker Disinflation. We have noted above that the era was one of intense political pressure on the Federal Reserve and that the Federal Reserve was anxious to protect its independent status. As we document below, the three district Federal Reserve Bank presidents we consider often spoke to their audiences about the importance of insulating monetary policy as much as possible from day-to-day political pressures. In the realm of economic theory and policy, the era saw the Keynesian consensus challenged first by monetarist analysis and then by new classical analysis. The stable Phillips curve of the 1950s and 1960s had suggested that permanently lower unemployment might be purchased at the price of modestly higher inflation. In the late 1960s, though, Milton Friedman (1968) and Edmund Phelps (1967, 1968) had questioned the likelihood of a permanent trade-off between inflation and unemployment, arguing that in the long run any attempt to exploit the Phillips curve trade-off would lead to higher inflation but no permanent reduction in unemployment. By the mid- to late 1970s, experience appeared to be confirming the Friedman-Phelps conjecture that the long-run Phillips curve might be vertical. As Henry Chappell, Rob Roy McGregor, and Todd Vermilyea (2005) have documented, although not all FOMC members in the 1970s accepted the idea of a vertical long-run Phillips curve, they nevertheless appreciated that the inflation-unemployment trade-off might be more favorable in the short run than in the long run and that expectations of inflation might affect what monetary policy could achieve. As we also document below, the public comments of our three protagonists often touched on the related question of how costly it might be to reduce inflation by application of restrictive monetary policy.

David Eastburn and the Philadelphia Fed

David Eastburn, a PhD economist, began his career as a research statistical clerk at the Philadelphia Fed after graduating from Amherst College in 1942. He then advanced through the ranks, holding positions as an economist and head of research before being named president in 1970, an office he held until his retirement in 1981. He did graduate work in the evenings at the University of Pennsylvania, earning MA (1945) and PhD (1957) degrees in economics. During his years as Philadelphia Fed president, Eastburn served as a member of the FOMC, voting every third year in the rotation group that also included the Boston and Richmond Federal Reserve Banks. His FOMC voting record indicates that he tended to prefer easier monetary policy than many of his colleagues (Chappell, McGregor, and Vermilyea 2005).

Eastburn fit comfortably into the mainstream of the 1970s. His worldview is summed up by William Eagleson (2008, 140) as follows:

> Dave was not a doctrinaire economist and was not sympathetic to ideological approaches to complex problems. He had an economist's respect for the efficiencies of a market economy, but did not think that markets should be worshiped slavishly in pursuit of some greater good and without concern for those who may be affected adversely in the short term. He sought harmony between economic man and social man, and believed it necessary for the viability of a free society, as well as a moral imperative, that life's losers not be cast aside like outdated clothing or an obsolete machine. These are the values of a *liberal* in the finest sense of that word.

Indeed, the evidence we find in his speeches is consistent with Eagleson's characterization of his views. Eastburn believed that market failures did require some degree of government intervention in the market economy. He was concerned about the problems caused by inflation and recognized that monetary discipline was necessary to control inflation, but he worried about the output and (especially) the jobs that might be lost if monetary policy were too restrictive for too long.

In a February 1975 address to a conference on futurism held at Eastern College, Eastburn (1975b) did not address monetary policy but focused instead on the problems of resource exhaustion, environmental deterioration, and inequality. He stated his view that the market system and technology—aided by government interventions to deal with problems of market failure—could help slow the use of scarce resources, encourage the development of alternative resources, and solve the problem of environmental deterioration. He was less favorable to income redistribution, arguing that the problems caused by inequality were better addressed by economic growth. Eastburn also observed that there had been a decline in economic freedom that was likely to continue, but he felt that this need not be a bad thing as long as the government played its increasing role in the economy well enough.

Eastburn (1975a) addressed the political context of monetary policy decisions in an August 1975 lecture delivered at the University of Wisconsin's Graduate School of Banking. The Fed, he argued, must be part of the political process because it must be responsive to the public. At the same time, though, it must be insulated from short-run political pressures to debauch the currency. Indeed, the tension between being responsive to the public and being insulated from short-run political pressure, Eastburn (1975a, 4) said, "characterizes much of what happens in the Fed." In this context, he discussed the challenges posed by the Fed's dual mandate and stated his preference for "stronger Government programs to deal with unemployment by other means. These include liberalized unemployment compensation and more vigorous commitments to public service jobs, more effective training, and a more enterprising minimum-income program" (4). Eastburn went on to say that the Fed's organizational structure provided adequate insulation from political pressures, but he noted that the Fed's traditional caution about what information it releases and when it releases that information was not always helpful. To address this shortcoming, he argued for greater transparency of monetary policy:

> There are a few modifications that would be helpful in this regard. The first has to do with making information about monetary policy decisions more readily available. The Fed now announces its Open Market decision 45 days after the fact. This departure from secrecy has done much to dispel the belief that financial markets would be unduly disturbed or that large financial firms would gain an unfair advantage in money markets. In my view, the next step is to move to a 30-day delayed announcement. If this action has no damaging impact, the immediate announcement of policy decisions should be considered. More information of this nature would promote better understanding of the Fed and its decision-making process. (7)

Eastburn concluded by saying that the Fed "must be increasingly open, responsive, and flexible" if it is to make monetary policy effectively in an increasingly politicized environment (9).

Eastburn worried that high inflation threatened to undermine corporate social responsibility. In November 1978 remarks to the Business Honor Society Colloquium at La Salle College, published in early 1979 as a Philadelphia Fed *Business Review* commentary, Eastburn (1979a) argued that inflation put pressure on real corporate profits and thereby threatened the wherewithal for corporate social action, thus making corporations less willing to undertake activities to improve social conditions. In this speech, he called for corporations voluntarily to fight inflation so that monetary and fiscal policies would not have to shift to an overly restrictive stance that "would require a recession or at least very slow growth for a long period" (4).

Eastburn's reluctance to risk a deep and prolonged recession was also evident in remarks he made later in 1979 before the Financial Analysts of Philadelphia. In that talk, he acknowledged that monetary discipline was necessary to get inflation under control, but he cautioned that in imposing monetary discipline the Fed needed to avoid creating a serious recession. He also noted that the Fed had chosen a partially accommodative policy stance in response to OPEC oil price shocks and wage pressures to avoid the recession that might have occurred in the absence of accommodation. Eastburn (1979b, 7) went on to state his support for at least partially validating cost-push pressures, but he thought that the degree of validation should just "not [be] as much as in the past." He did discuss the role of inflation expectations in creating the problem of stagflation, recognizing that lowering inflation would require the Fed to slow money growth for long enough to reduce inflation expectations, but he thought that the Fed faced serious challenges to implementing a successful disinflationary strategy:

> Whether the American people will sit still for a gradualist solution to inflation remains to be seen. Whether the Fed will be able to exercise the persistence and constancy which a gradualist solution requires remains to be tested. Certainly, if any institution can perform this role, the Fed, with its independence from short-run political influences, is in a position to do it. (9)

It is worth highlighting that these remarks, made in September 1979, came on the eve of the Volcker Disinflation. During 1979–82, the Fed was able to pursue a monetary policy course that brought inflation down from over 10 percent to about 4 percent, even in the face of what at that time was the most severe recession since the Great Depression, with the unemployment rate peaking at nearly 11 percent in late 1982.

Lawrence Roos and the St. Louis Fed

Lawrence Roos, a graduate of Yale University, was named president of the St. Louis Fed in 1976, an office he held until his retirement in 1983. Prior to his appointment, he had been executive vice president of the First National Bank in St. Louis. During his years as St. Louis Fed president, Roos served as a member of the FOMC, voting every third year in the rotation group that also included the Atlanta and Dallas Federal Reserve Banks. His FOMC voting record indicates that he tended to prefer tighter monetary policy than many of his colleagues (Chappell, McGregor, and Vermilyea 2005).

In a December 1976 speech to the Memphis Rotary Club, Roos (1976, 1) explained why he chose to accept the St. Louis Fed presidency:

> Approximately nine months ago I left the world of commercial banking to become President of the Federal Reserve Bank of St. Louis. I did so, not only because of the challenge of being part of the Fed System which plays such an important role in the financial affairs of the United States and the Free World. Rather, I joined the Fed because I'm sincerely concerned about the future of our way of life. I am convinced that the greatest threat to the survival of our free society is runaway inflation . . . and I believe that the best chance we have of avoiding a return to double-digit inflation is through a sound monetary policy formulated by an independent Federal Reserve System.

After discussing the damage that inflation can do (1) and arguing that inflation is a monetary phenomenon (2–3), he went on to lay out what he felt was at stake in the fight against inflation and issued his listeners a call to action (5–6):

> We *can* put an end to spiraling prices; we *can* stop the growth of government; we *can* resist the siren song of more and more government spending and more and more government controls. But it means that we must be prepared to stand up for the principles that have made America great. . . . I urge you as civic leaders to speak out for what you know is right. By doing so, and *only* by doing so, can we secure the future of our generation and the prosperity of generations of Americans to follow.

Roos (1977a) believed that inflation had to be overcome by the application of sound monetary policy. As he explained to a 1979 conference of the American Bankers Association, he saw Federal Reserve independence as a necessary safeguard against the inflationary bias inherent to the political process:

> In almost every case where independent central banks have been placed under the control of politically-motivated forces, short-term considerations have taken priority over the longer-term national interest and responsible monetary policy has given way to inflation-generating expediency.

If we are to avoid this happening here, each of us must take part in the struggle to preserve sound monetary policy. We can best do this by supporting the full independence of the Federal Reserve System and, in turn, making certain that the Fed acts flexibly, responsibly, and steadfastly in the conduct of our Nation's monetary policy. (Roos 1979a, 9–10)

During his tenure as St. Louis Fed president, Roos persistently pressed the monetarist perspective—not only to his FOMC colleagues but also to the audiences at his speeches—as money growth and inflation increased and the committee targeted the interest rate instead of money growth. In a January 1977 address to the St. Louis Downtown Rotary Club, he argued that the Fed's monetary policy decisions "determine the fundamental rate of inflation" (Roos 1977b, 2) and denied that unemployment and inflation must necessarily be traded off against each other. Specifically, he stated that unemployment could be reduced without causing more inflation, noting that job training programs could help, but that "providing better information on local, industrial, and sectorial employment opportunities" would help more (4). He also advocated removing labor market restrictions that set floors under wages and reforming unemployment compensation (5). Finally, Roos argued that the Fed played its role by keeping inflation under control: "A steady, noninflationary pace of economic activity offers workers and business people their best opportunity to plan for themselves and their futures without constantly having to protect themselves from unpredictable inflation" (6).

Two years later, in a February 1979 address before the New York Society of Security Analysts, Roos proposed that the FOMC could better deal with inflation by adopting a monetarist operating procedure. He argued that excessive money growth is the underlying cause of inflation and that episodes of inflation and deflation had been caused by targeting interest rates rather than money growth. He then described what had happened during the 1970s when interest rate and money growth targets had clashed:

Two conclusions can be drawn from these observations. First, it is evident that in periods of incompatibility, the Federal funds rate reigns as the primary target in the conduct of monetary policy while adherence to monetary aggregate ranges is secondary. Secondly, the principal thrust of monetary policy has been to stabilize the Federal funds rate and to resist both upward and downward pressures, even if by doing so the aggregates fell outside of their ranges. Monetary policy, either by design or by default, has been fashioned to stabilize interest rates, even if it has meant destabilizing money growth. (Roos 1979b, 4)

Roos proposed that the FOMC "should abandon the stabilization of interest rates as the primary goal of monetary policy and move gradually toward a freely-fluctuating Federal funds market" and that the committee "should concentrate instead on establishing and adhering to long-term money supply growth rates that are consistent with national economic policy" (7).

After the October 1979 announcement that the FOMC was adopting a new operating procedure designed to improve control over money growth, Roos (1980, 6) first took up the task of explaining the new procedure, telling the St. Louis Society of Financial Analysts that any "analysis that relies on daily fluctuations in the federal funds rate or weekly changes in money supply figures, always of doubtful value, now under the new Fed procedures, is worthless" and that only "patterns that change in the longer term can indicate which way the Fed is heading." A year later, when addressing the Institutional Investor Bond Conference in New York, he urged patience and persistence in the fight against inflation, saying that the "biggest problem we face today comes from those who advocate abandoning our anti-inflationary effort and returning to expansionary policies that they mistakenly believe would bring relief from the temporary pain of high interest rates and sluggish economic activity" (Roos 1981, 8).

By 1982, the Fed had succeeded in bringing down average money growth, with the effective M1 money supply growing "around 4.6 percentage points slower in 1981 than its average annual growth over the preceding five years" (Goodfriend 1997, 13, citing data constructed by Alfred Broaddus and Goodfriend [1984]). The pattern of money growth had been erratic even as money growth had slowed, however, and this contributed to "unusually high and unpredictable interest rates" (Roos 1982b, 2). In a March speech to the St. Louis Rotary Club, Roos laid out the choice to be made that year:

> We can opt for what might seem the easy way out of our present predicament by expanding money growth and encouraging more spending by the federal government. . . .
>
> An alternative option is to stick with the policies that have already brought about a decline in inflation, and to endure whatever pain is necessary to permanently eliminate inflation. (6)

Later in 1982, in a speech to the New York Society of Security Analysts, Roos (1982a, 4, 5) defended monetarism against its critics, arguing that the recent evidence was consistent with the monetarist propositions that "inflation is primarily a monetary phenomenon" and that "accelerations in money growth produce accelerations in nominal GNP and that decelerations in money growth produce slower growth in nominal GNP." He concluded by reflecting on the progress made in monetary policy operating procedures during his tenure as St. Louis Fed president:

> In closing, I would simply like to remind you that current monetary policy procedures, in particular, the use of monetary aggregate targets, arose in response to the adverse consequences of earlier policy procedures. The belief that the Federal Reserve could control interest rates, a notion that dominated monetary policy actions when I first joined the Federal Reserve System seven years ago, was in my opinion responsible for nearly 15 years of accelerating inflation, 15 years of rising interest rates, and 15 years of worsening financial conditions. . . .
>
> The credibility of monetary policy in this nation has been partially restored. Let us stay with what is working and reject what has been found wanting. Only by so doing can we restore the non-inflationary stability so essential for future economic growth and prosperity. (11–12)

By the time Roos left office in 1983, inflation had been brought down from over 10 percent to about 4 percent. Moreover, this roughly six-percentage-point disinflation occurred rapidly and—despite the severity of the recession—at lower cost than might have been expected for such a sizable reduction in inflation; specifically, Jeffrey Lacker and John Weinberg (2007, 214) report that "the reduction in output during the Volcker disinflation amounted to less than a 4 percent annual shortfall relative to capacity," whereas at the time a "common range of estimates was that the 6 percentage-point reduction in inflation that was ultimately brought about would require output from 9 to 27 percent below capacity annually for up to four years."

Mark Willes and the Minneapolis Fed

Born in Salt Lake City, Utah, Mark Willes received his bachelor's degree from Columbia University and his PhD in economics and finance from Columbia's Graduate School of Business in 1967. He was appointed an assistant professor at the Wharton School, University of Pennsylvania. While there, he also did consulting work for the research department of the Federal Reserve Bank of Philadelphia, eventually becoming its director and, later, first vice president for operations of the Philadelphia Fed, interestingly enough, serving under President David Eastburn.

Willes was president of the Minneapolis Fed from April 16, 1977, to June 30, 1980, and he served as a voting member of the FOMC between March 1978 and February 1979. During his tenure, he strongly advocated the main tenets of what came to be known as the new classical macroeconomics, that is, rational expectations and the neutrality view, and their implications for economic modeling and policy analysis, as reflected in his writings (e.g., 1978, 1979, 1980a, 1980b). This is also reflected in his input into FOMC discussion in general, and how he presented his position specifically, both in FOMC voting and to the public at large. Willes's FOMC voting record indicates that he tended to prefer tighter monetary policy than many of his colleagues (Chappell, McGregor, and Vermilyea 2005).

Willes's interest in policy issues developed during 1967–71. His 1967 Columbia PhD thesis was titled "The Inside Lags of Monetary Policy," and he published some of his empirical findings in a paper in the *Journal of Finance* (1967).

In a series of articles in the Philadelphia Fed's *Business Review* during 1968–71, Willes dealt with monetary and fiscal policy lags and rules, and "the fight against inflation," such as his March 1968 article, "Lags in Monetary and Fiscal Policy," and his September 1970 article, "Lags, Fine Tuning, and Rules of Monetary Policy." In the February 1971 issue of the *Business Review*, he set out three possible approaches in the "fight against inflation": traditional monetary and fiscal policy, voluntary wage-price guidelines, and compulsory wage and price controls. He noted that there was a change in expectations formation such that it was "likely that . . . expectations about aggregate demand, unemployment and prices might be quite different in times past. This makes the use of parameter estimates of the relation between unemployment and inflation based on historical experience of questionable value in the current situation. Conditions are certainly ripe for the kind of developments predicted by those theories which suggest only a fleeting tradeoff between inflation and unemployment" (Willes 1971a, 10–11n7).

In a 1971 paper in the *Journal of Money, Credit, and Banking*, Willes (1971b, 630) was explicit about the limitations of countercyclical policy—both fiscal and monetary. He focused on the issue of lags in the attempt to counter short-run economic fluctuations and also dealt with the efficacy of utilizing lags and forecasting turning points, when determining policy actions.

From 1972 to 1977, Willes served as first vice president of the Philadelphia Fed, in charge of operations. As such, as required by the role at all district Federal Reserve Banks, he was responsible for financial services, information technology, strategic planning, human resources, and administrative services, in effect somewhat isolating him from the ongoing developments in economic theory and policy debates. The transition to the Minneapolis Fed presidency brought him to the cutting edge of the "rational expectations revolution." As he recalled in an interview with James Fogerty in December 1992:

> When I came to Minneapolis, I asked the guys to just bring me up to date on what had been going on for the last five years. It turned out that I'd fallen into a hotbed of rational expectations and all the things that they were doing in that area. With Tom Sargent over at the University and Bob Lucas in Chicago, and so on, I was not only fascinated by what they were doing, but felt like they were doing things that ought to be much more in the public discussion, as it relates to policy, than it clearly was at that point. So I rather happily took on the chore of not only injecting that into the policy discussions in Washington, but talking about it in speeches and in the press, and we wrote some articles which we published, and so on, all of which was designed to get the discussion out of strictly the academic environment into the public domain, so people could talk about it, and hopefully have some impact on the way people thought about monetary policy, given the implications of that kind of view of the world.

Only a few months after assuming the position of Minneapolis Fed president in April 1977, in a May 24 speech to a group of bankers titled "A New Policymaker's View of Inflation," Willes (1977d) said: "Being a new member of the FOMC has some significant advantages. One of the most important is that it is not possible to blame me for past policy mistakes. And mistakes there have been, even in recent years. . . . What I can and would like to do . . . is give you some idea of my view on what is surely one of the great economic issues of this decade—the issue of unemployment versus inflation. That view will guide me as I participate in the deliberations of the Open Market Committee. . . . My participation in that committee is my most important responsibility . . . while . . . a member of the FOMC I represent the country at large and not just banking or other groups in the Ninth District."

He continued, "I can state my view in a very few words: the over-riding economic problem today is inflation. . . . I do not deny that we have a serious unemployment problem . . . the problem may be, however, a little less serious than it appears" because of its changing composition and compensation patterns. He went on to say, "Our very generosity has aggravated the . . . problem . . . our definition of full employment has changed. . . . some unemployment is the result of generous . . . compensation and other benefits" (Willes 1977d).

He then expressed what he took to be the central message of his speech, that there was "no tradeoff between inflation and unemployment." As he put it: "Tolerating inflation . . . will not reduce unemployment. . . . More inflation does not mean less unemployment. . . . In fact . . . inflation may ultimately cause unemployment to rise" (Willes 1977d).

In June 1977, in a talk on labor statistics and economic policy, Willes (1977c) asserted that "as we are all painfully aware, the Keynesian policy prescription has not seemed to live up to its promise. Policies designed to stimulate aggregate demand seem to have a . . . larger effect on prices than on unemployment."

In remarks on "economic education" in October 1977, Willes recalled that as director of economic research at the Philadelphia Fed, he realized "that the Keynesian system just wasn't adequate to explain the problems that we faced" and came to believe in "monetarism." He continued: "That was fine until I came here to Minneapolis. I now have a staff that says that both of my former views are wrong. It is really the rational expectations view of the world that describes how things work. . . . I think that the kind of intellectual evolution that I've gone through, to a rather remarkable degree, approximates the kind of evolution that is taking place" in economics (1977b). Whether rational expectations constituted an "evolution" or "revolution" in economic thought has been discussed elsewhere (Young, Leeson, and Darity 2004); suffice it to say here that Willes actually thought the rational expectations approach to be *orthogonal* to the "Keynesian revolution," as we show below.

In November 1977, in a lecture at the University of Minnesota titled "Effective Economic Policy: Some Key Requirements," he said: "It is of course primarily to the academic community and other research groups that we look for . . . the insights that allow us to improve our understanding of how the economy works. . . . Unfortunately . . . they sometimes develop such a vested interest in their own views of the world that they are unwilling or unable to seriously and openly consider different theories and ideas. . . . Academic debates often generate more heat than light, and the public is the loser" (Willes 1977a). He went on to put the work done by Sargent and Wallace at the Minneapolis Fed into this perspective. As he put it:

> If we are to have effective economic policy you must have a coherent theory of how the economy works. . . . Keynes . . . said "practical men, who believe themselves to be quite exempt from any intellectual influences, are usually the slave of some defunct economist." Unfortunately, many "practical men" are now slaves of the ideas of Keynes himself. Policies based on his theories cannot deal effectively with today's economic conditions. Somehow the monetarist view of . . . Friedman doesn't seem completely convincing either. Perhaps the rational expectationists here . . . have the ultimate answer. At this point only Heaven, Neil Wallace, and Tom Sargent know for sure. I must say I am very impressed with their work; they have made a substantial—and stimulating—contribution to research being done at the Minneapolis Fed. I only hope that it receives the benefit of open and genuine debate so that it is either confirmed and extended or is replaced by something better. (Willes 1977a)

In a talk at St. John's University in Collegeville, Minnesota, in December 1978, he set out what he took to be the central message of the rational expectations approach, so as to lower "the costs of fighting inflation." In his words, "all that's necessary is that people use information efficiently so that they avoid making systematic errors . . . to allow people to make more accurate forecasts . . . which makes it easier to fight inflation . . . new policies should be announced in advance . . . [and] . . . the government must . . . stick to its announced policies fastidiously."

In June 1979, in his statement to the Inflation Task Force of the House Budget Committee, Willes said:

> Economists at the Federal Reserve Bank of Minneapolis have, since early in this decade, been conducting research that has resulted in a serious challenge to the traditional ways government conducts economic policy, including anti-inflation policy. . . . We have also tested different theories of how the economy works and have developed new theories and new economic models that, we think, can better explain both inflation and fluctuations in economic activity. . . . Although our conclusions are still controversial, they are rapidly gaining acceptance.

In December 1979 Willes completed the final draft of his essay "Rational Expectations as a Counterrevolution," which first appeared in *Public Interest* (1980b) and was reprinted in the widely read volume *The Crisis in Economic Theory* (1981). In December 1979 he also gave a talk at the Allied Social Science Association meeting in Atlanta titled "The Future of Monetary Policy." In this, he dealt with the policy implications of the rational expectations research program as manifest in the work undertaken at the Minneapolis Fed from 1974 on. He made the important point that its results were "often misinterpreted. Many interpret [it] as saying that monetary policy does not matter. . . . This, however, is the wrong implication . . . The results are strong indictment of ad-hoc macroeconomic models. . . . Ad-hoc macroeconomic models are not explicit enough to capture the impact of monetary policy" (Willes 1980a).

In his piece on the "counterrevolution" that appeared in *Public Interest* in 1980, Willes (1980b, 81–90) counterpointed the rational expectations approach to the "Keynesian revolution" and defended its precepts against attacks on it, for example, by mainstream economists, such as James Tobin (92), and in the popular press, such as in *Business Week* in 1978 (93).

Beige Books and FOMC Input: Roos, Eastburn, and Willes, 1978

The views of the "constituencies" of the district Federal Reserve Bank presidents were reflected both in their public speeches and in their FOMC input. To assess the former, that is, what was "on the minds" of business leaders, bankers, managers, and others who were the audience of, and interacted with, the presidents before and during their public presentations, we examined the Beige Books—the monthly regional economic assessments—of the three Reserve Banks for 1978. We also examined transcripts of monthly FOMC meetings during 1978, when Eastburn, Roos, and Willes served on the FOMC as voting or alternate voting members.

Both the Beige Books and FOMC meetings that year were characterized by concern about inflation and inflationary expectations, on the one hand, and the possibility of recession, on the other. These concerns and policy prescriptions were not expressed in a monolithic manner.

At the January 1978 FOMC meeting, Willes noted that "the businessmen that are talking to me are very concerned about inflation" and "expectations of inflation" (January 17, 1978, 19). Eastburn, an alternate voting member, for his part, mentioned the "concern about inflation" while attributing an "intractable nature" to it (22). Roos, on the other hand, then a voting member, raised questions about the most efficacious FOMC policy to deal with inflation and inflationary expectations that affected his specific district and the US economy as a whole, noting that "the growth rate in money having persisted above our [FOMC] ranges for nearly 12 months or more now . . . is recognized, at least in our neck of the woods . . . as a harbinger of inflation" (31).

The February FOMC meeting saw Eastburn talking about the "connection between . . . uncertainty about inflation" and its impact on unemployment in the context of supply and demand shocks, which, in his view, accelerated inflation expectations and increased uncertainties about inflation. Moreover, according to Eastburn, research undertaken at the Philadelphia Fed implied that this would, in turn, affect "real output and unemployment" (February 28, 1978, 21). Roos reinforced Eastburn's assessment of the impact of inflation uncertainty, saying "one of the big problems we face is inflation and one of the big inhibiting factors that is stopping businessmen from engaging in capital formation projects is their . . . uncertainty with regard to inflation." Roos went on to say, critically, that "somewhere along the line, monetary policy ought to concern itself with inflation. If that is literally something that is only occurring to us currently . . . I don't understand the rules of this game because we've all been talking about it for some time" (30). In his comments that followed those of Roos, Willes said that "the major difference we [the research staff at the Minneapolis Fed] have with the staff forecast, is on their expectation of inflation" (30).

At the March meeting, in response to the presentation by the FOMC staff economist James Kichline about the US economic and financial situation, Roos asked if "any consideration" had been given to the impact of "monetary expansion." In his reply, Kichline said that that was indirectly taken into account both in the price forecast generated by "the quarterly model" and in the "judgmental forecast" made by the staff economists at the Board of Governors (March 21, 1978, 27). Roos also called for the FOMC to be "really serious about doing something . . . on correcting inflation" (34). Eastburn also spoke about the problem of inflation and said, "I think we need to emphasize inflation . . . but preferably stress the point that . . . inflation does lead to recession . . . so the posture that we ought to have is to . . . indicate to the public that we're clearly going to avoid overkill" (29). Willes, for his part, focused on the effectiveness of the Carter administration's anti-inflationary policy and the information aspect of FOMC decision making, projections, and the issue of transparency. As he put it, "People look at what we do . . . they try to evaluate how well we do it," so that the public should have access to information "in order to see why and what we did" (46). In answer to the point Willes made, Paul Volcker, then vice chair of the FOMC, said that there was a distinction between "expressing alarm" about inflation, as against "the Federal Reserve . . . in its august majesty" projecting what inflation "is going to be" (41). Willes immediately responded, saying that "what happens now is that it all seems patently inconsistent to the public because we appear to be tightening when there's no reason and we appear to be easing when there's no reason. I think it would be a great advantage, in terms of our ability to do our work, to have those kinds of statements out in the public domain" (47).

In April, the Minneapolis Fed Beige Book reported that "directors believe inflationary expectations have been revised upward" and that "the major concern in the District right now is inflation." It went on to say that "businesses have revised inflationary expectations upward," blaming "food price increases, higher import costs due to a weakened dollar, and increased unit labor costs" as "reasons for this revision." It also maintained that the prevailing opinion of businessmen was that "governmental plans for voluntary restraint" regarding price increases "will be disregarded" (April 12, 1978). The St. Louis Fed Beige Book reported, "One representative [among area retailers] noted that fear of inflation by consumers may inhibit their spending while another observed that consumers are nervous and seem only willing to buy at special sale events" (April 12, 1978). The Philadelphia Fed Beige Book noted "widespread uncertainty among entrepreneurs about future business conditions, and particularly about the future course of inflation. Businessmen appear to be unwilling to commit themselves to investment projects in the face of such economic uncertainty" (April 12, 1978).

At the April FOMC meeting held a week later, Roos talked about the goals of monetary policy in terms of confidence and credibility, saying that "if our credibility is that bad, it is of our own doing. . . . I think here's an excellent opportunity to announce . . . what our monetary aggregate policy is and to attempt to stick with it" (April 18, 1978, 10). Eastburn asked if there was a "delayed impact of the earlier increases in money supply" on the inflation rate, as much of the price increases were considered "exogenous" and input as such to the econometric model of the Federal Reserve, according to Kichline (18–19). Willes expressed the rational expectations position as developed by his own staff at the Minneapolis Fed. As he put it, "There is a growing acceptance of the notion that expectations of businessmen and consumers have a certain degree of self-fulfilling activity in them. People sign contracts, and conduct behavior, that in effect, helps validate their expectations" (19). As manifest in the April Minneapolis Fed Beige Book, Willes went on to report the high inflationary expectations of businessmen in his district and said, "Now it doesn't make a whole lot of difference whether their expectations are soundly based or not, in the sense that if that is their expectation and they operate on that expectation, it has very serious implications both for inflation and, of course, for the kind of recession that would put in place."

The May meeting saw Roos complaining about the lack of interaction between the Board of Governors and district Reserve Bank research staffs (May 16, 1978, 17). Eastburn, for his part, talked about the "possibility of bringing on recession via monetary policy," albeit he did not foresee this; rather, he thought the risks to be "all on the inflationary side" (18). Willes reiterated the position he took the month before about the high inflationary expectations of businessmen, when he said that it "doesn't make any difference whether" they were "soundly based or not . . . if that feeling is widespread, they will make decisions that will in effect generate those kinds of rates" (16).

The summer meetings of the FOMC were characterized by a continuing concern with inflation, inflationary expectations, and the possibility of recession if certain policies were implemented. In September, Eastburn again queried the "optimistic" economic projections by the Board of Governors' research staff and went on to say, "I think it is quite remarkable . . . that we have even the moderate growth that's forecast. I think we're doing quite well, given the inflation rate" (September 19, 1978, 15). Willes reasserted that inflation "was still clearly the number one economic problem," going on to stress that he could not see people believing that the Fed would deal with it "unless we do something to get the rate of growth of money down" (26). Roos agreed with Willes and said that "we can reduce aggregates growth without causing recession."

In October, the Minneapolis Fed Beige Book reported that "throughout the District we are hearing reports that loan demand has not slowed despite high nominal interest rates." It went on to say, "With the current inflationary psychology, borrowers apparently are attempting to stay ahead of expected price increases." It continued on to state, as Willes had put it at the FOMC meeting three weeks earlier, that in the view of businessmen in the District, inflation was "the economy's number one problem" (October 11, 1978). The Philadelphia Fed Beige Book reported ongoing upward pressure on the prices of raw materials and finished products (October 11, 1978), while the St. Louis Fed Beige Book noted that area businessmen "continue to speak of inflation as a major concern" (October 11, 1978).

In November, the Minneapolis Fed's Beige Book was more explicit about the problematic efforts to "combat" inflation and reported that "the outlook is clouded by uncertainty regarding the likely impact of government moves to combat inflation," going on to say that "few observers are sanguine about the future or the economic ramifications of recently announced wage-price guidelines" and that some observers "feared" that "the President's wage-price guidelines would harm the real economy" (November 15, 1978). The Philadelphia Fed Beige Book also included comments about the Carter administration's anti-inflation program, reporting that "most merchants contacted feel the program will be largely ineffectual, particularly with regard to wage guidelines, but plan to try to cooperate with the program. They feel that price inflation will be somewhat slower next year so that the price guidelines will not be binding" (November 15, 1978).

At the November FOMC meeting, Eastburn said that "we are in for a recession" (November 21, 1978, 9). Roos, for his part, was a bit more optimistic, under the condition that monetary policy be conducted according to FOMC targets (16), while Willes reiterated his position on changing assumptions in modeling, especially regarding expectations formation, each set of assumptions generating or not resulting in "a recession forecast" (17). In December, Willes stressed the need to avoid recession (December 19, 1978, 14). Roos, for his part, was more critical of FOMC policymaking overall, when he said, "Have we actually, in our own practices, ever discussed or agreed upon what our ultimate economic objectives would be and then attempted to make our monetary policy decisions consistent with the achievement of those objectives? Or have we really sort of played around with our monetary policy and then asked of our people to project what they think will be the result of that monetary policy. This has disturbed me" (55). Roos went on to raise the issue of monetary aggregates targeting (59). Finally, Eastburn reported on research done at the Philadelphia Fed about the relationship between short-run and long-run policy objectives (60).

The Federal Reserve Bank President: Public Bureaucrat and Public Intellectual

Given the *dual* responsibilities of the Federal Reserve Bank presidents—to their respective districts and to the Federal Reserve System—some degree of cognitive, or even functional, dissonance on their part could be expected. In the cases presented here, however, the individuals were able to appreciate the concerns of their local constituencies—as reflected in the respective Beige Books—and that of the nation as a whole, and translate these concerns in both their input to the FOMC, on the one hand, and their public pronouncements, on the other hand, thereby fulfilling the *dual* function of public bureaucrat, for which they were chosen, *and* public intellectual, which they chose to be. This gave them a *unique* role in the discourse and debate over economic policy in the period under consideration.

For example, despite their *differing* economic worldviews—ranging from mainstream to monetarist to new classical—all three district Federal Reserve Bank presidents dealt with here expressed concern about the *same* economic problems, such as unemployment and especially inflation facing their districts and the nation as a whole, both in their public pronouncements and at the FOMC. Indeed, while the delay in publishing minutes of its deliberations prevented identification of *dissent* at the FOMC, the public speeches and writings of the presidents, as presented here, on the other hand, provide some indication of the degree of consensus or dissent, reflecting both their concerns and those of their district constituencies *at the time*. In retrospect, the fact that these individuals took on the responsibility of publicly expressing their views—and not only behind the closed doors of the FOMC—provided fertile ground for public expression by presidents who followed them, up to the present day.

References

Board of Governors of the Federal Reserve System. 1978. *FOMC: Transcripts and Other Historical Material, 1978.* http://www.federalreserve.gov/monetarypolicy/fomchistorical1978.htm.

Broaddus, Alfred, and Marvin Goodfriend. 1984. "Base Drift and the Longer Run Growth of M1: Experience from a Decade of Monetary Targeting." *Federal Reserve Bank of Richmond Economic Review* (November–December): 3–14.

Chappell, Henry W., Jr., Rob Roy McGregor, and Todd A. Vermilyea. 2005. *Committee Decisions on Monetary Policy: Evidence from Historical Records of the Federal Open Market Committee.* Cambridge: MIT Press.

Eagleson, William B., Jr. 2008. "David P. Eastburn: A Biographical Memoir." *Proceedings of the American Philosophical Society* 152 (1): 135–40.
Eastburn, David P. 1975a. "The Fed in a Political World." *Federal Reserve Bank of Philadelphia Business Review* (October): 3–9.
———. 1975b. "Is There a Future for Economic Man?" *Federal Reserve Bank of Philadelphia Business Review* (April): 3–7.
———. 1979a. "Commentary: Voluntary Inflation Restraint and Corporate Social Responsibility." *Federal Reserve Bank of Philadelphia Business Review* (January–February): 3–4.
———. 1979b. "Current Monetary Dilemmas: How Effective Is Orthodoxy in an Unorthodox World?" *Federal Reserve Bank of Philadelphia Business Review* (November–December): 5–9.
Federal Reserve Bank of Minneapolis. *Beige Book Archive.* http://www.minneapolisfed.org/bb/index.cfm?.
Friedman, Milton. 1968. "The Role of Monetary Policy." *American Economic Review* 58 (1): 1–17.
Goodfriend, Marvin. 1997. "Monetary Policy Comes of Age: A Twentieth Century Odyssey." *Federal Reserve Bank of Richmond Economic Quarterly* 83 (1): 1–22.
———. 2000. "The Role of a Regional Bank in a System of Central Banks." *Federal Reserve Bank of Richmond Economic Quarterly* 86 (1): 7–25.
Hetzel, Robert L. 1998. "Arthur Burns and Inflation." *Federal Reserve Bank of Richmond Economic Quarterly* 84 (1): 21–44.
Hubbard, R. Glenn. 2004. "The Economist as Public Intellectual." *Journal of Economic Education* 35 (4): 391–94.
Kettl, Donald F. 1986. *Leadership at the Fed.* New Haven: Yale University Press.
Lacker, Jeffrey M., and John A. Weinberg. 2007. "Inflation and Unemployment: A Layperson's Guide to the Phillips Curve." *Federal Reserve Bank of Richmond Economic Quarterly* 93 (3): 201–27.
Lebaron, Frédéric. 2006. "'Nobel' Economists as Public Intellectuals: The Circulation of Symbolic Capital." *International Journal of Contemporary Sociology* 43 (1): 87–101.
Lepper, Larry. 2007. "The Spread of Economic Ideas: The Role of the Economist as Public Intellectual." Paper presented to the Asia-Pacific Economic and Business History Conference, University of Sydney, February 12–14.
Lightman, Alan. 1999. "The Role of the Public Intellectual." Paper presented to the MIT Communications Forum, "Public Intellectuals and the Academy," December 2.
Nash, Betty J. 2010. "The Changing Face of Monetary Policy." *Federal Reserve Bank of Richmond Region Focus* (Third Quarter): 7–11.
Phelps, Edmund S. 1967. "Phillips Curves, Expectations of Inflation, and Optimal Unemployment over Time." *Economica* 34 (135): 254–81.
———. 1968. "Money-Wage Dynamics and Labor Market Equilibrium." *Journal of Political Economy* 76 (4, pt. 2): 678–711.
Poole, William. 2007. "Understanding the Fed." *Federal Reserve Bank of St. Louis Review* 89 (1): 3–13.

Roos, Lawrence K. 1976. "Inflation and Federal Reserve Independence." Speech to the Memphis Rotary Club, Memphis, Tennessee, December 7. *Statements and Speeches of Lawrence K. Roos*, FRASER, Federal Reserve Bank of St. Louis, http://fraser.stlouisfed.org/publication/?pid=482&tid=85.

———. 1977a. "Should Monetary Policy Be Made More Responsive to the Political Process?" Speech at Arkansas State University, Jonesboro, June 2. *Statements and Speeches of Lawrence K. Roos*, FRASER, Federal Reserve Bank of St. Louis, http://fraser.stlouisfed.org/publication/?pid=482&tid=85.

———. 1977b. "Unemployment and Inflation." Speech to the Downtown Rotary Club, St. Louis, Missouri, January 6. *Statements and Speeches of Lawrence K. Roos*, FRASER, Federal Reserve Bank of St. Louis, http://fraser.stlouisfed.org/publication/?pid=482&tid=85.

———. 1979a. "Let's Get Off the Roller Coaster." Address before the Thirty-First Annual National Credit Conference of the American Bankers Association, Phoenix, March 19. *Statements and Speeches of Lawrence K. Roos*, FRASER, Federal Reserve Bank of St. Louis, http://fraser.stlouisfed.org/publication/?pid=482&tid=85.

———. 1979b. "Monetary Policy . . . a Better Way." Speech to the New York Society of Security Analysts, February 5. *Statements and Speeches of Lawrence K. Roos*, FRASER, Federal Reserve Bank of St. Louis, http://fraser.stlouisfed.org/publication/?pid=482&tid=85.

———. 1980. Speech to the St. Louis Society of Financial Analysts, January 3. *Statements and Speeches of Lawrence K. Roos*, FRASER, Federal Reserve Bank of St. Louis, http://fraser.stlouisfed.org/publication/?pid=482&tid=85.

———. 1981. "Monetary Policy . . . A Time for Resolve, not Retreat." Speech to the Institutional Investor Bond Conference, New York, October 15. *Statements and Speeches of Lawrence K. Roos*, FRASER, Federal Reserve Bank of St. Louis, http://fraser.stlouisfed.org/publication/?pid=482&tid=85.

———. 1982a. "Does Money Still Matter?" Speech to the New York Society of Security Analysts, October 6. *Statements and Speeches of Lawrence K. Roos*, FRASER, Federal Reserve Bank of St. Louis, http://fraser.stlouisfed.org/publication/?pid=482&tid=85.

———. 1982b. "1982: A Critical Year." Speech to the St. Louis Rotary Club, March 11. *Statements and Speeches of Lawrence K. Roos*, FRASER, Federal Reserve Bank of St. Louis, http://fraser.stlouisfed.org/publication/?pid=482&tid=85.

Wells, Wyatt C. 1994. *Economist in an Uncertain World: Arthur F. Burns and the Federal Reserve, 1970–78*. New York: Columbia University Press.

Willes, Mark H. 1967. "The Inside Lags of Monetary Policy: 1952–1960." *Journal of Finance* 22 (4): 591–93.

———. 1968. "Lags in Monetary and Fiscal Policy." *Federal Reserve Bank of Philadelphia Business Review* (March): 3–10.

———. 1970. "Lags, Fine Tuning, and Rules of Monetary Policy." *Federal Reserve Bank of Philadelphia Business Review* (September): 12–20.

———. 1971a. "The Fight against Inflation." *Federal Reserve Bank of Philadelphia Business Review* (February): 3–11.

———. 1971b. "The Scope of Countercyclical Monetary Policy." *Journal of Money, Credit, and Banking* 3 (3): 630–48.

———. 1977a. "Effective Economic Policy: Some Key Requirements." Lecture at University of Minnesota, Minneapolis, November 17. Willes File: Speeches, Research Library, Federal Reserve Bank of Minneapolis.

———. 1977b. Speech to the annual meeting of Minnesota State Council on Economic Education, October 25. Willes File: Speeches, Research Library, Federal Reserve Bank of Minneapolis.

———. 1977c. "Labor Statistics and Economic Policy." Speech to the North American Conference on Labor Statistics, Bloomington, Minnesota, June 15. Willes File: Speeches, Research Library, Federal Reserve Bank of Minneapolis.

———. 1977d. "A New Policymaker's View of Inflation." Speech to the North Dakota Bankers Association Convention, May 24. Willes File: Speeches, Research Library, Federal Reserve Bank of Minneapolis.

———. 1978. "The Recession Obsession." Speech at St. John's University, Collegeville, Minnesota, December 6. Willes File: Speeches, Research Library, Federal Reserve Bank of Minneapolis.

———. 1979. "Rational Expectations as a Counterrevolution." Final Draft. December 21. Willes File: Speeches, Research Library, Federal Reserve Bank of Minneapolis.

———. 1980a. "The Future of Monetary Policy." *Federal Reserve Bank of Minneapolis Quarterly Review*, Spring.

———. 1980b. "Rational Expectations as a Counterrevolution." *Public Interest*. Special issue, 81–96.

———. 1992. Interview with James Fogerty, Minnesota Historical Society, December 8, Federal Reserve Bank of Minneapolis website: http://www.minneapolisfed.org/about/role/history/willes.cfm.

Woolley, John T. 1984. *Monetary Politics: The Federal Reserve and the Politics of Monetary Policy*. New York: Cambridge University Press.

Young, Warren, Robert Leeson, and William Darity. 2004. *Economics, Economists, and Expectations*. London: Routledge.

Age of Certainty: Galbraith, Friedman, and the Public Life of Economic Ideas

Angus Burgin

In the summer of 1973, while watching John Dean's testimony in the Watergate trial at his vacation house in rural Vermont, John Kenneth Galbraith received an unexpected telephone call. On the other end of the line was Adrian Malone, a producer with the BBC who had become known for developing multipart historical documentaries of notable ambition and expense (Galbraith 1981c, 528). Most recently Malone had completed *The Ascent of Man*, a thirteen-part series on the history of science that had attracted glowing reviews and turned its central figure, Jacob Bronowski, into a household name. Malone was now shifting his attention to the history of the social sciences and commencing the project of presenting the subject's notoriously abstract themes to a mass audience on the small screen. Malone informed Galbraith that he would be the ideal person to guide such an enterprise. The reasons for this choice, as a later proposal noted, were readily evident: Galbraith was "that rare being, a practical philosopher." He was "an authority who stands outside, but is respected by those with political power," benefited from "a world-wide reputation," and maintained the capacity to "entertain ideas and experiments from both

Correspondence may be addressed to Angus Burgin, Johns Hopkins University, Department of History, 3400 North Charles Street, 338F Gilman Hall, Baltimore MD 21218; e-mail: burgin@jhu.edu. I am grateful to Kelly Kelleher Richter and Paige Glotzer for their invaluable research assistance and to two anonymous readers for *History of Political Economy* for their helpful comments and suggestions.

ends of any spectrum, radical or reactionary." Galbraith transcended the conventional divisions between academia and politics, and between abstract debates in the social sciences and a mass audience. Malone, who was a vocal admirer of the eighteenth-century French philosopher, declared his chosen star a "modern Voltaire."[1]

For Galbraith, deciding how to respond to Malone's offer was not easy. There were, of course, many reasons to find it appealing. Unlike many of his fellow economists, Galbraith was not known for his distaste for celebrity: as a frequently photographed confidante to Jacqueline Kennedy Onassis and a television presence on *Today*, *Firing Line*, and the political coverage on the network news, he had already become known in the popular press as a "resident pundit" and "house liberal" who was in danger of "overexposure" (Meyer 1977). Accusing his academic colleagues of confusing obscurity with rigor, Galbraith had instead directed his writings toward a mass public, and his many appearances on the best seller lists were a testament to his successes. He found television's capacity to reach a still-broader audience alluring and may have seen some romantic appeal in the prospect of traveling the world as a television star. At the same time, accepting the offer would force him to leave Harvard only two years before he reached retirement age, which might imply an unwanted hint of bitterness at an economics department within which he had long been marginalized (Parker 2005, 517). He would need to teach himself an elaborate new medium at an age when he had expected to be spending more time in rural repose and skiing in Gstaad. And for a figure who had already achieved international literary renown, tackling such an unusual enterprise entailed some risk of appearing a fool. Colleagues who expressed skepticism of his mass-market books were likely to find television more dubious still. "It's the instinctive reaction of writers—perhaps they feel threatened," he later recalled. "The feeling is that if something is done in pictures, done visually, it's inherently inferior than if it had been done in words, in print."[2]

Flattered and intrigued by the opportunity, Galbraith decided to set aside his reservations and accept it. In doing so, he became the first econo-

---

1. "A PRE-OFFER," box 567, folder "BBC program correspondence: BBC: early [1973]," John Kenneth Galbraith Papers, John F. Kennedy Library, Boston (hereafter cited as Galbraith Papers).

2. Cecil Smith, "John Galbraith Feels Certain about Success of 'Age of Uncertainty,'" Miami Herald TV Preview (undated), box 566, folder "BBC program: articles [general]," Galbraith Papers.

mist to engage in an ambitious, long-form attempt to relay economic ideas to a popular audience via a visual medium. He was well aware that this challenge would not be easily met. Malone had been clear from the outset that television was a "blunt instrument," requiring a simplified form of exposition that did not easily align with Galbraith's patrician persona and ironic sensibility (Parker 2005, 517). But Galbraith also knew that the discipline of economics, despite its reputation for tedious abstraction, had become a site of intense public interest and engagement. With the profession buoyed by the prestige of its new association with the Nobel Prize and made relevant by debates over inflation and stalled economic growth, the time seemed right for an economist to explain the discipline to those who sensed its importance but did not have the time or patience to learn much of it in books.

Galbraith was not the only one in his profession to sense the propitiousness of the moment and the potential of the medium. He commenced work on the documentary series that would become *The Age of Uncertainty* in an era when a growing number of corporations, advocacy organizations, and think tanks were engaging in concerted attempts to convince popular audiences of the merits of free market ideas. Sensitive to their own perceived marginalization, they observed the production process for Galbraith's incipient series with evident alarm. Seeking to discredit and displace his arguments, they turned to Milton Friedman, who had in recent years become Galbraith's most prominent opponent in the public sphere. Like Galbraith, Friedman demonstrated a facility for popular journalism and routinely embraced opportunities to influence public opinion on matters of political concern. Although the two men were neighbors in Vermont and referred to each other as friends, their distaste for each other's views had become evident in their frequent sparring sessions in columns and editorials. It was therefore no surprise that Friedman, at the request of colleagues at a think tank in London, met the release of *The Age of Uncertainty* with a public lecture that was intended to discredit its claims. And not long thereafter—at the urging of a public television executive who had been converted to his views—Friedman developed and released a competitive multipart documentary of his own, *Free to Choose*, which would (in conjunction with a companion volume) become the most popular and widely disseminated introduction to his ideas.

At this moment of unusually intense debate over economic policy, the most prominent public exemplars of left- and right-wing economic views therefore found themselves engaged in competing attempts to reach a mass audience through the maturing medium of television. An exploration of their efforts helps address several crucial aspects of the popularization of economic ideas over the final decades of the twentieth century. Such efforts, it will become apparent, were deeply embedded in institutional structures that varied quite extensively for economists of differing views. Although writers of books rely on networks of colleagues, assistants, editors, and publishers, the act of writing itself is often solitary, and social connections can be relegated to an ancillary or intermediary role. The apparent intimacy of television, by contrast, obscures the enormous administrative and technical complexity of the production process. Beginning in its earliest stages, a television documentary series requires substantial funding, specialized expertise, and the support of programming executives. Even the inceptions of Galbraith's and Friedman's series were not attributable to them: both were approached and propositioned by individuals within the industry who had become enchanted with their ideas. And the quality of the productions remained largely at the mercy of colleagues who possessed technical competencies that Galbraith and Friedman were not fully equipped to evaluate. This rapidly evolving media environment required institutions to play a thicker and more constitutive role than had been the case in a public sphere that depended primarily on literary production. The advocacy of economic ideas now involved much more than simply stating them.

The medium itself also posed a unique set of problems, which rewarded certain modes of presentation while rendering others ineffective. Print effaces the personal and allows for the construction of an identity that transcends physical appearance and comportment. Television is not so kind. Now, new details mattered: height, accent, inflection, eye contact, clothing, and spontaneity of exposition. Economists who appeared regularly on television became personalities, and their audiences came to see their self-presentations as deeply entwined with their representations of their ideas. But even as the medium made economists' personal traits more vivid, it had the capacity to render their ideas more turgid. Its format is unforgiving toward theory, jargon, or extended exposition. A discipline that functions by abstracting from the social accords at best uneasily with a medium that thrives on personalizing the abstract. Even those historians of economic thought who are most attuned to problems of transmission tend to focus on written exposition, but in this new era the personal instantiation and visual expression of economic ideas would play a crucial role in conditioning their reception.

To emphasize the importance of the visual is not to imply the insignificance of language. Here, as elsewhere, rhetoric mattered. Television producers are impatient with elaborate caveats and justifications, and seek to induce performers to arrive quickly at a compelling distillation of their ideas. The contrast between Galbraith's and Friedman's responses to this imperative was stark. In *The Age of Uncertainty*, Galbraith attempted to bring to television the ironic sensibility, attuned to paradox, that had long served him well in his literary productions. His elaborate contrasts and attempts at mordant humor withered on the screen, and he found himself criticized by television audiences for the very academicism that he had long deplored. Friedman instead relied on a simple exposition of the market metaphor, rendering it tangible through carefully chosen human examples that appeared to validate his ideas. The rediscovery of the market unfolded, in part, as a plebiscite on these dueling representations of the economic world.

The eventual outcomes, of course, were lopsided: as Galbraith's public career continued its gradual eclipse, Friedman rapidly ascended to become the leading economic prophet of the final decades of the twentieth century. Galbraith may have labeled this the "age of uncertainty," but it would prove kindest to those economists who offered the absence thereof.

When Galbraith and Malone began work on *The Age of Uncertainty*, they were seeking to adapt an approach to long-form documentary that had been refined by the BBC in the previous half decade—in Kenneth Clark's pioneering history of art, *Civilisation* (1969); Alistair Cooke's history of the United States, *America* (1972); and Jacob Bronowski's history of scientific thought, *The Ascent of Man* (1973)—to new subject matter. These massively expensive and thematically rich series had taken advantage of the increasing prevalence of new technologies, including higher-band UHF signals and color (introduced by BBC2 in 1964 and 1967, respectively), to take on subjects of greater visual complexity and topical ambition than were conventionally associated with the medium (Briggs 1985, 360; Crisell 1997, 115, 117). Seeking to tie a broad and diffuse range of historical material together, the director Michael Gill had relied on jet travel in *Civilisation* to adopt a striking technique: a central narrator would simply materialize at the location under discussion, instantly traversing vast distances multiple times in a single show (Barnouw 1993, 315). Enormous time, effort, and resources were leveraged to develop programs that elided their necessity by projecting an impression of ease.

The effect was miraculous, and audiences that had been habituated to the parochial television offerings of the time observed these expansive new productions with awe. The most cynical among them wondered why such ambitious cultural programming seemed always to originate from the BBC. As a review of *The Age of Uncertainty* in the January 19, 1977, issue of *Variety* observed, "Adult education as riveting entertainment is seemingly an English video patent." A critic in the *Washington Post* was less circumspect: series like *America* and *Civilisation*, he remarked, made one wonder why there was "so much idiocy on American TV" (Mitchell 1974).

Malone, as his colleague Geoff Haines-Stiles later recalled, was a man of "grandiose ambitions" who believed himself to be engaged in the development of a new cultural form: the "creative documentary," a mode of presentation that was "just different from other forms of communication" and capable of achieving "some things that books can't" (Dornfeld 1998, 44). At times this self-conception inspired Malone to drift into descriptive excess, as in his peculiar assertion in an offering sheet that if "Voltaire lived today he would want to do a thirteen part television series along the intellectual lines of Candide." But television executives found his goal of doing "for social evolution what 'The Ascent of Man' did for cultural evolution" compelling, and Malone had little difficulty in convincing the BBC to provide primary support for his proposed $2 million budget.[3] Time-Life, which had cosponsored *The Ascent of Man*, proved more skeptical of the project, for reasons related to Galbraith's political inclinations rather than the subject matter itself. As its executives observed to Malone, Galbraith would have difficulty finding underwriters for a series that would likely yield conclusions unpopular with corporate decision makers.[4] PBS, however, saw the long-form documentary as a format that differentiated the still-nascent network from its commercial competitors and offered to contribute $720,000 to the development of the series (Dornfeld 1998, 42; Kelley 1977). In conjunction with the $300,000 contributed by the Canadian Broadcasting Corporation and $150,000 from the Ontario Educational Communications Authority, this ensured that the necessary funding had been raised.[5] These resources would enable three years of

---

3. "A PRE-OFFER," Galbraith Papers.

4. Adrian Malone to John Kenneth Galbraith, December 14, 1973, box 567, folder "The Age of Uncertainty: BBC program correspondence: BBC: early [1973]," Galbraith Papers.

5. Graham Fraser, "Be Patient, Good Viewer, and Uncle Ken Will Make It All Make Sense" (publication and date unknown), box 581, folder "The Age of Uncertainty: BBC program reviews: Canadian," Galbraith Papers.

work on the series, with a full production team assembling thirteen episodes out of scenes shot from locations around the world.

When the series finally appeared on English television in 1977, public expectations were high. In a sometimes lightweight popular culture, the *Birmingham Evening Mail* remarked that Galbraith was likely to serve as a new "'heavy' star" ("Figuring to Be a Star" 1977). The *Daily Mail* added that Galbraith would receive the "superstar treatment" in BBC2's "prestige series of the year" (Rees 1977). Malone's vision was still grander: he saw the series as one that should remain relevant for "at least ten to twenty years."[6]

Galbraith therefore found himself "puzzled," and a little dismayed, when the initial reviews registered a response that ranged from tepid to scathing.[7] Conservative publications lambasted Galbraith's perspective: the *Daily Telegraph* called the series a "hymn of hate," and the *Spectator* brushed it aside as a "banality" (Last 1977; Ingrams 1977). Other critics observed that Galbraith had failed to make a smooth transition from the written word to television: the *Crew Chronicle* preferred the book version of the series, flatly stating that it was "better in print," and the *Times* concluded that the only virtue of the programs was "as a commercial on behalf of" the transcripts serialized in the *Listener* ("TV Series Better in Print" 1977; Church 1977). One British reviewer noted that "little is left unshaken of Prof. Galbraith's reputation as a scholar, if not as a television personality."[8] Witnessing the reception in England, the *New York Times* acerbically noted that the series was "not, in any case, the subject of dinner table banter" (Kilborn 1977). Although a few British critics expressed more favorable views of the series, it was difficult for those assessing the response to the series not to conclude with the *New York Times* that "this time" the BBC's "formula" had failed (O'Connor 1977).

There was no single reason for the series' perceived failure: as with many productions of this kind, its problems were complex and interrelated. They began, however, with Galbraith's attempt to address abstract social theories through a historical analysis. The series proceeded as a march through great thinkers, from Adam Smith and the classical economists through Karl Marx and John Maynard Keynes up to contemporary

---

6. "A PRE-OFFER," Galbraith Papers.
7. John Kenneth Galbraith to Aubrey Singer, May 5, 1977, box 567, folder "The Age of Uncertainty: BBC program: correspondence: BBC, July 1977–February 1976," Galbraith Papers.
8. Colin Welch, "The Rich Wot Gets the Blame," box 566, folder "The Age of Uncertainty: BBC program articles [general]," Galbraith Papers.

times, providing Galbraith's abbreviated assessments of their theoretical contributions and the contexts in which they wrote. There was never any question that this would be the animating concept behind the series: its predecessors at the BBC had all structured their episodes around an advancing chronology, and Galbraith himself saw it as an opportunity to provide needed attention to an often-overlooked subject. "The history of economic thought has been a declining subject both in the universities and in the public eye," he told *Focus* magazine in 1976. "This will be something to revive interest" ("John Kenneth Galbraith" 1976). In a letter to the *History of Economic Thought Newsletter*, he expressed optimism that the series would draw attention to issues that had long been neglected by economics departments that had become ever more narrowly focused on the problems of the present day.[9]

Galbraith, however, had risen to fame as an overtly partisan political economist, creating an awkward problem for his attempts to adopt a more-distanced historicism. Malone addressed this by seeking to avoid any overt sense that the series was structured around the star's contemporary political views. "The feeling should be of objectivity, assuming no god-given truths," he wrote in an early outline.[10] And Galbraith tried to adapt himself to this new role: as the series was released, he emphasized his detachment from contemporary politics and referred to himself as "essentially a middle-of-the-road figure" (Henry 1977a). But shortly after the first episodes were released, conservative commentators began expressing their dissatisfaction with perceived distortions of the historical record. Was not the treatment of Marx notably more charitable than those of his classical predecessors?[11] Why did Galbraith draw attention to the foibles of the capitalists that Thorstein Veblen criticized but not the obvious personal shortcomings of Veblen himself (Jewkes 1977)? Where could one find all the equations that might be expected in a history of economic thought (Minogue 1977)? And in the episodes exploring the economics of more recent times, why were the theories of Milton Friedman ignored?[12] As the "high priest of wage and price controls," a "fervent Democrat," and the

    9. John Kenneth Galbraith, "Note on 'The Age of Uncertainty' for the History of Economic Thought Newsletter," box 577, folder "The Age of Uncertainty: BBC program: History of Economic Thought Newsletter, Spring 1977," Galbraith Papers.
    10. Adrian Malone, series outline, box 577, folder "The Age of Uncertainty: BBC program: outline," Galbraith Papers.
    11. Welch, "Rich Wot Gets the Blame."
    12. Galbraith responds to this question in a letter to the editor of the *Wall Street Journal*, April 4, 1977, box 983, folder "Letters to the Editor: Wall Street Journal."

house economist of the Kennedy family, it was difficult for many to see the series as anything other than a vehicle for Galbraith's well-known and distinctive economic views (Lyon 1976; Reed 1977). Perhaps in an attempt to acknowledge and defuse impressions of partiality, the series adopted the subtitle from the Bronowski series: "A Personal View." But the "problem" that many perceived, as *Newsweek* wrote, was that "the view is *highly* personal" (Ruby 1977, 61; emphasis added). The *Boston Globe* put it more bluntly: "Galbraith is not scholarly, not abstract, above all not objective" (Henry 1977b). Kenneth Minogue (1977, 1978), a market-oriented political theorist at the London School of Economics, excoriated the series as "trial by caricature" for which the operative principle was "distortion of the past for the purpose of flattering the present." In *The Age of Uncertainty*, Galbraith attempted to suppress his views in search of historical credibility that proved difficult for him to achieve.

He therefore found himself trapped in a muddled space between the poles of advocacy and objectivity that had riven economics since its professionalization nearly a century before (Furner 1975). The foundational tension was evident in the choice of a title: this was a series that would draw its attention to "uncertainty," or the instability of established theories and solutions, rather than posing its own. The grand narrative that Galbraith established was one of decline, as the theories of earlier political economists were swept aside in the wake of failed predictions and unexpected events. (In the halls of the BBC, the production became colloquially known as *The Descent of Man* [Rees 1977].) It was intended, as Galbraith noted in a contemporary interview, to reveal "how *sure* capitalists were of capitalism," "how sure the socialists were of socialism," how sure the European countries were of their dominant political position, and how sure the ruling classes of earlier generations were of the permanence of the social order. In exposing these fallacies, Galbraith hoped to draw attention to the conceptual instability of a postmodern age. He represented this as a great virtue of the series, which situated itself against those who "make the firmness of their avowal a substitute for the certainty of their position," exchanging "strong affirmation for lack of information" (Cross 1977, 24–25). But why was Galbraith, one of the most formidable intellectual gladiators in the op-ed pages of his time, suddenly arguing against a posture of certainty in the face of incomplete information? The title was surely an "irony," the *Washington Post* observed, "for a man who is rarely in doubt" (Nossiter 1977). This new posture, while perhaps more nuanced, posed some rhetorical challenges: as the world confronted successive waves of economic crisis in the late 1970s, audiences proved reluctant to listen to a prophet who now dwelled on the absence of readily available solutions. Milton Friedman, in viewing the series, drew attention to the limitations of Galbraith's critical-historical posture. "I looked in vain for a central idea," he observed. "All I could see was a man sneering at conventional solutions, without offering any of his own" (quoted in Holden 1980).

Galbraith's historical subject matter posed another problem: how does one find visual material to accompany discussions about the history of economics? As one critic observed, "Art and science lend themselves to pictures," providing ample fodder for Clark and Bronowski, "but economics—the dismal science—does not" (Meyer 1977). There were no rich tapestries or complex inventions for the camera to linger on during Galbraith's extended narrations. The search for visual expression posed an insuperable challenge, as the *New Statesman* observed, for a discipline in which the "greatest exponents have scarcely been able to express their ideas in intelligible prose" (Porteous 1977). In deciding how to overcome this problem, Galbraith and Malone made a crucial decision. Rather than relying primarily on shots set on contemporary locations and historical images and video, they would hire actors to reenact many of the scenes and situations that Galbraith described. Much of the series was devoted to elaborately costumed actors silently enacting their relations in exaggerated poses while Galbraith described the leading economic theories of the time. Thus viewers were shown a re-creation of the famous banquet at Delmonico's in which actors dressed as waiters served stuffed life-sized dolls circling a table, in an elaborate play on Henry Ward Beecher's reference to the diners' "continually stuffed bodies"; or extended studio images from a metaphorical carnival, to demonstrate the so-called carnival ride set off by the rise of money.[13]

The reliance on exaggerated historical reenactments prevented Galbraith from adopting a posture of empiricism: rather than a detached observer of economic truths, he appeared as a roving master of elaborate visual fictions. The opening scene of *The Age of Uncertainty*, in a stunning moment of trompe l'oeil, overtly cast him as a conjurer of artifices rather than a teller of social-scientific truths. Galbraith began by speaking about the role of economic ideas in history in terms that most viewers would have presumed to be his own before he slyly revealed them to have

---

13. John Kenneth Galbraith, transcripts, "The Morals & Manners of High Capitalism" and "The Rise and Fall of Money," *The Age of Uncertainty*, BBC.

been written by Keynes. Galbraith then stated, as the camera receded to reveal a stately Oxbridgian backdrop, that he was addressing his audience from Keynes's rooms at King's College. The camera, however, continued to recede, demonstrating that this too was a mirage, and he was instead delivering his lines from a tiny set in the midst of a vast black box theater. This was all, Galbraith announced, a "theatrical impression," one of the many that would be used to illuminate his views. "The illusions of the theatre—and film—have long been used to give substance to abstraction, visual form to ideas." As he stated these words, a set of costumed characters moved beneath his feet in rehearsed postures over a map of Europe. They were the "participants in the parade," subjected to "the carnival of boom and slump," and Galbraith was the showman who assembled and ordered the spectacle for the viewers watching from the quiet of their homes.[14] Most documentaries elide the process of their own construction, and few commence with such an overt statement of narrative control. This, it seemed, would be a reflexive documentary: one that engaged in a metacommentary on its own construction and thereby encouraged readers to reflect on the partiality of its representation (Nichols 1991, 56). Galbraith, who already attracted some derision as a literary practitioner of an increasingly mathematical profession, would appear here as a weaver of narratives rather than a conduit for facts. He would not take advantage of the appearance of empiricism afforded by the visual form.

Few viewers, however, saw the reflexivity of *The Age of Uncertainty* as a sign of methodological sophistication; instead, most simply wondered why the costumes and sets were so unconvincing and the acting was so bad. The depiction of symbolic royalty, capitalists, and peasants in metaphorical dances on a giant map of Europe struck many, in the words of one critic, as "so puerile as to make me cringe with embarrassment."[15] Galbraith, who had granted authority to the BBC for the visual aspects of the series at the outset, hinted at some skepticism of their creations. "Let's never forget that one word is worth a thousand pictures," he observed in the first episode, not yet aware of the number of reviewers who would leverage that comment to explain the series' flaws.[16] Observers complained

---

14. John Kenneth Galbraith, transcript, "The Prophets and Promise of Classical Capitalism," *The Age of Uncertainty*, BBC.
15. Blaik Kirby, "Galbraith Series a Yawn," box 581, folder "The Age of Uncertainty: BBC Program Reviews: Canadian," Galbraith Papers.
16. John Kenneth Galbraith, transcript, "The Prophets and Promise of Classical Capitalism," *Age of Uncertainty*.

that the visual accompaniments to Galbraith's words were "gimmickry" ("Making It Clear as Mud" 1977), a "nuisance" (Birtchall 1977), and signs that the documentary series was a "Play School version" of Galbraith's ideas.[17] Many, including the author and critic Martin Amis (1977), mocked the elaborate set pieces as signs of decadence. "While Galbraith drawled wryly on, we were offered a restful collage of diagrams, cartoons, allegories, emblems, stills, mock-ups, toytowns, old things superimposed on new things, new things superimposed on old things, modern chaps dressed up in antique garb, modern chaps not dressed up in antique garb," he wrote. "Soon, no doubt, these boys will have appropriate footage for such concepts as 'a' and 'the,' so that the viewer can simply flop back and let his eyes do the listening." The extravagant and self-conscious visuals in *The Age of Uncertainty* seemed to have done little to make Galbraith's arguments more rhetorically compelling for his audience. In America, George Stigler (1977) wrote that the documentary had fulfilled his "fears about the effective use of television" as a medium for economics, as Galbraith "made no observable attempt to use visual methods to illuminate ideas": in England, one observer noted that Galbraith's visuals seemed as though they had been "mischievously" devised by a conservative think tank "to distract attention from his message."[18] Silent reenactments and composed dances, it seemed, were a disruptive complement to Galbraith's narrations; in a series on the social sciences, viewers manifested a preference for visual economy rather than excess.

Perhaps the most surprising aspect of the viewer response to the series, however, was the perception of Galbraith himself. In searching for a star, the producers had high expectations: the goal, Malone told a reporter, was to find someone "whose opinions have mattered for the past twenty years, and will go on mattering for some time to come" (Rees 1977). Among those who met this standard, Galbraith enjoyed the added advantage of international celebrity and a charismatic persona. His frequent presence around famous women had earned him the reputation, as one publication noted, as a "fascinating cavalier" (Field 1971). Perhaps alone among economists, his television appearances brought frequent references to his "sex-appeal" ("Now for the Sexy Ken Galbraith Show" 1977). *Cosmopolitan* named him one of the "sexiest men in the world" (Henry 1977a), journalists described him as "a kind of donnish Gary Cooper" (Rees 1977), and

17. Untitled article in *Sunday Telegraph*, January 16, 1977, box 1021, folder "The Age of Uncertainty: BBC program: reviews: [American]," Galbraith Papers.
18. Welch, "Rich Wot Gets the Blame."

female viewers wrote letters to the *Times* dwelling on "his sensitive hands and his ravaged sardonic features" (Jemal 1977). One source of this fixation was his striking height: at well over six and a half feet tall, he physically embodied his academic stature and appeared always to be "looking down at" those around him (Hampshire 1977). Few scholars, at first blush, seemed so well suited to translate their discipline to a television audience.

During his extended monologues in *The Age of Uncertainty*, however, it soon became clear that Galbraith maintained a professorial demeanor that did not translate easily to a mass audience. His producers had observed the problem when Galbraith first submitted his proposed scripts. "There wasn't a sentence that didn't have three or four ideas in it," Malone later recalled. "Sometimes they got so dense that the viewer would miss the point" (Parker 2005, 517–18). Attempts to expunge complexity were not entirely successful: in viewing the final product, Martin Amis (1977) marveled at Galbraith's ability to state "the obvious as though it were excruciatingly, ticklishly oblique." In contrast to the spontaneous enthusiasms of Bronowski, Galbraith seemed to deliver his lines in a "monotonous drone" (O'Connor 1977). Critics found him "fidgety" and "vague" (Henry 1977a); "eccentric" and "wooden" (Stigler 1977); "dry," and, perhaps most damningly, "intellectual."[19] Even his defenders grew tired, at times, of his aura of "self-celebration" (Reed 1977). These personality traits attracted some ridicule in the British press and were not well-received in an American context that had long been noted for its anti-intellectualism. The best-known economic advocate of the poor seemed, in his public appearances, wholly alien to the people whose interests he was ostensibly defending. "If Galbraith would just stoop a little to hide his embarrassing height," one journalist suggested, "adopt a humble, self-effacing personality, and disguise himself as one of those 'people's' corn-belt Republicans, maybe someone would listen to him" (Smith 1978). Galbraith was condemned to purveying a populist message in elitist form.

Conservative intellectuals, who expressed anxiety about the impact of *The Age of Uncertainty* in the months leading up to its release, drew on a rapidly developing network of intellectuals, politicians, magazines, and policy institutions to critique the series and diminish Galbraith's credibility. In their narrative, he received privileged treatment from a public media

---

19. "Fidgety" was the judgment of Bill Marvel ("The Economist Takes to the Tube," box 1021, folder "The Age of Uncertainty: BBC program: reviews: [American]," Galbraith Papers); "eccentric" was Welch's term ("Rich Wot Gets the Blame"); and Kirby ("Galbraith Series a Yawn") said "dry" and "intellectual."

apparatus that uncritically supported the views of a liberal establishment. (Galbraith did not contest the notion that he was among the establishment, but insisted that he was on its "raffish fringe" [Stanley 1977].) Exploiting vulnerabilities exposed during the Nixon administration, they castigated the Corporation for Public Broadcasting for deviating from its mandate, dating from the Public Broadcasting Act of 1967, to maintain "strict adherence to objectivity and balance in all programs or series of programs of a controversial nature." The meaning of this requirement had never been entirely clear: did it entail balance across all programs on the schedule, or balance within each program itself? And how was balance to be defined across the infinitely broad spectrum of possible views (Ledbetter 1997, 97)? Galbraith was quick to point out to critics the range of conservative perspectives that were reflected on public television on shows such as William F. Buckley's long-running program *Firing Line* and Louis Rukeyser's *Wall Street Week*.[20] But well before *The Age of Uncertainty* appeared, his critics were already logging their dissatisfactions with his work in the *Congressional Record*. Barry Goldwater was sure that it would be "socialistic propaganda" and castigated the use of "taxpayer money" to launch an attack on "the economic system upon which this country is built."[21] In the same year that the series was released, Senator Orrin Hatch (R-UT) pushed unsuccessfully to have a Public Broadcasting Fairness Act write tangible requirements for "balance" into law (Ledbetter 1997, 98). The effect of all this was to leave public television executives highly skittish about any subject deemed politically controversial. As a result of these concerns, executives at the public television station in Los Angeles decided—without raising the possibility to Galbraith or the BBC—to append to each episode a brief critique of Galbraith's analysis from a conservative perspective. To achieve this goal they turned to the Hoover Institution, which compiled a list of twelve prominent pundits, celebrities, and experts who were willing to add a few recriminations to counterbalance Galbraith's views.

These appendages to the series, like the criticisms of Galbraith from the conservative press, dwelled repeatedly on several themes. Galbraith, they argued, was a member of an academic elite who sought to run the country themselves. Ronald Reagan had become expert in this rhetorical mode

20. John Kenneth Galbraith, draft letter to Barry Goldwater (undated), box 577, folder "The Age of Uncertainty: BBC program: Goldwater's objection to PBS financing BBC series Congressional record," Galbraith Papers.
21. Barry Goldwater, *Congressional Record* 121:15, June 17, 1975, S19253.

during his gubernatorial battles with the University of California. Galbraith's series, he asserted in the final appended critique, implied "that leadership is best left to development by a group of wise mandarins on college campuses." Decades of conservative populism had inspired him and his colleagues to associate arguments from the academic left with expressions of elitism. Presumably Reagan's sympathies could be trusted to lie with a broader public instead.[22] Even as some of Galbraith's critics castigated him for his connections to the establishment, others tried to radicalize his views in order to marginalize them from mainstream policy debates. William F. Buckley Jr. represented Galbraith as an "avowed socialist" in the thrall of "his lifelong mistress, the state."[23] *The Age of Uncertainty*, Albro Martin asserted in his remarks, "mocks the history of America, demeans it, makes it something to be ashamed of."[24] Drawing on an argument that Friedrich Hayek had long promulgated, commentators also interpreted his views as the product of a misguided rationalism. Galbraith seems, Reagan argued, "to believe that it is a simple matter to identify what the community interest is."[25] Here Reagan cast himself as the defender of complexity: the virtue of capitalism, in his view, was that it bypassed many of the thorny problems of collective action by simply deferring to consumer choice. In *Encounter*, Kenneth Minogue drew attention to Galbraith's assertion in the book version of *The Age of Uncertainty* that "few social problems, if any, are difficult of solution," in order to highlight the imputed arrogance of planning. "Professor Galbraith believes that social and political problems are essentially simple," he wrote; "I believe them to be essentially complex" (Minogue 1978).

The final, and perhaps most effective, argument that critics leveraged against Galbraith was that he did not have sufficient credibility within the discipline to author a series of this kind. Galbraith maintained a public persona that was more common in Britain than the United States, deriving his authority from both elite social connections and an ability to engage with questions of public policy in terms that a layperson could understand. Many American economists remained skeptical of this

22. Ronald Reagan, response to episode 12, box 567, folder "The Age of Uncertainty: BBC program: correspondence with KCET," Galbraith Papers.
23. William F. Buckley Jr., response to episode 1, box 567, folder "The Age of Uncertainty: BBC program: correspondence with KCET," Galbraith Papers.
24. Albro Martin, response to episode 2, box 567, folder "The Age of Uncertainty: BBC program: correspondence with KCET," Galbraith Papers.
25. Ronald Reagan, response to episode 12, box 567, folder "The Age of Uncertainty: BBC program: correspondence with KCET," Galbraith Papers.

model, seeking instead to justify their public authority in terms of technical accomplishments as judged by a small community of disciplinary peers (Fourcade 2009). Those who disagreed with Galbraith were quick to use such arguments to discredit his views among those who might otherwise be receptive. Milton Friedman was uniquely well positioned to launch just such an attack. His recent receipt of a Nobel Prize had provided him with an impeccable disciplinary signifier of technical accomplishment that Galbraith conspicuously lacked. Unlike most recipients of the prize, Friedman had also demonstrated—in both his *Newsweek* columns and *Capitalism and Freedom*—a capacity for engaging economic questions in a language that a broad public could understand. His celebrity was fast approaching Galbraith's own: media outlets covered him as the Harvard economist's "principal bete noir" (Nadel 1977) and adopted the two of them as "helpful reference points at opposite ends of the spectrum" (Curley 1980). Galbraith himself joked that, in the face of the publicity surrounding Friedman, *The Age of Uncertainty* was just his bid for "a little equal time."[26] Friedman was capable of matching Galbraith in public stature while arguing that only his had been legitimately earned.

A year before the release of *The Age of Uncertainty*, the market-oriented Institute of Economic Affairs in London recruited Friedman to give a public lecture on Galbraith to a group of businessmen, journalists, and political leaders at a church in Westminster.[27] The goals, presumably, were to undermine Galbraith's credibility and provide an array of useful arguments to conservative intellectuals before the series aired. The extent to which Friedman's analysis anticipated, and perhaps helped form, later criticisms of Galbraith's series is striking. Galbraith was an "arrogant" elitist who believed that all questions should be solved by an intellectual "aristocracy" of which he was a notable member. He was (ironically, given his famous distaste for the profession) an "advertiser par excellence" whose views achieved wide acceptance because they were "easy to understand," in contrast to the more challenging complexities of free market economics. And he pretended to be a scientist seeking answers when he was, in truth, a "missionary seeking converts." His theories had never been empirically "demonstrated" and had "never found any acceptance in the *academic* world" (Friedman 1977, 17, 30–31, 35–36). Friedman posi-

26. Don McGillivray, Southam News Services, "Economists Need Watching" (publication and date unknown), box 581, folder "The Age of Uncertainty: BBC program reviews: Canadian," Galbraith Papers.

27. "Economics Viewed as a Martial Art," *Times* (London), September 2, 1976.

tioned himself, in contrast, as a populist who deferred to the opinions of the masses by leaving decisions to the decrees of a marketplace that was outside his control. While Galbraith attempted to persuade others by filtering simplistic arguments through his formidable literary imagination, Friedman cast himself as the defender of his own discipline's scientific and empirical foundations. Galbraith, who owned a house near the Friedmans in Vermont and had long been a personal friend, saw this assault as yet another public skirmish in an ongoing political war. But, in contrast to his iconoclastic opponent, he had never held out much hope that his message would achieve traction in the public arena. He acknowledged an "affinity for lost causes" and implied in private correspondence that this new television series might be yet another. While many of his friends considered Friedman's London lectures bad form, Galbraith claimed to have been patiently explaining to them that this was merely "what a man must do to win the Nobel Prize."[28]

Days after *The Age of Uncertainty* first aired in England, Milton Friedman received a call at his new home in San Francisco. After nearly three decades at the University of Chicago, he had recently resigned his post to accept a temporary visiting position at the Federal Reserve Bank of San Francisco followed by a permanent appointment at the conservative Hoover Institution (Friedman and Friedman 1998, 471). Having purchased an apartment with the proceeds from the Nobel Prize, Friedman now faced the prospect of life in a new city without all of the regular commitments that affiliation with a university economics department entailed. He was free to pursue his own interests for the foreseeable future to a degree that academia rarely allowed. But the person on the other end of the line, an executive at a small public radio station in Erie, Pennsylvania, was proposing to fill this newfound free time with a radical departure from his previous work. Would Friedman, as the leading free market advocate in the public sphere, consider making a television documentary about his own ideas?

It was a prospect that Friedman had begun considering not long after learning that Galbraith was at work on a series for the BBC. In private correspondence, Friedman wrote that it would be "highly desirable to

---

28. "Readable Economics," *Auckland Chronicle*, 1977, box 1072, folder "[General: 1977]," Galbraith Papers; John Kenneth Galbraith to John Wood, February 15, 1977, box 149, folder 5, Milton Friedman Papers, Hoover Institution Archives, Stanford, California (hereafter cited as Friedman Papers).

have a good deal more exposure of the ideas of liberty and freedom on television." He had lobbied for the idea among program officers at market-oriented foundations, telling them that one of "the most effective things they could do would be to sponsor a regular program, preferably on commercial TV, presenting economic ideas in a serious way."[29] PBS executives, under political pressure to maintain "balance" as the release of Galbraith's series approached, expressed their own enthusiasm at the idea of providing Friedman with a venue to express his contrary views. "I can only say again how anxious we are," a vice president at the network wrote to Friedman in the summer of 1976, "to discuss with you at greater length the possibility of putting together some form of commentary or critical analysis or even 'counter programming' vis-a-vis the Galbraith series."[30] Even conservative politicians, when confronted by the Galbraith series, independently arrived at the conclusion that Friedman should develop a set of competing documentaries of his own.[31] Although Friedman had not yet made any specific plans, upon picking up the phone in January 1977 he was prepared to listen.

The executive on the other end of the line, however, was very different from the one who had first approached Galbraith nearly four years before. *The Age of Uncertainty* was developed from the outset by leading figures in the small community of producers and technicians who had invented the long-format public television documentary, and their work had attracted impressive audiences and critical accolades (Dornfeld 1998, 43). Robert Chitester, the executive who contacted Friedman, ran a small public-television station that was barely a decade old, and his most substantial programming success had been a series on tropical fish called *From Guppies to Groupers*. And unlike the team that had contacted Galbraith seeking to develop an "objective" overview of the history of social science, Chitester wanted to sponsor the series for overtly political reasons. A onetime Democrat who had distributed leaflets for McGovern in 1972, he had experienced a dramatic political conversion after reading *Capitalism and Freedom* only months before he first contacted Friedman. Chitester quickly concluded that "economic freedom had to exist, or the rest of the freedoms could not," and his social philosophy became "settled" in a way that it "had never been before" (Cox 1980, 43). The book became Chitester's "Bible," and his "faith

29. Milton Friedman to Roy A. Childs Jr., March 18, 1976, box 11, folder 4, Friedman Papers.
30. Charles Lichenstein, July 27, 1976, box 149, folder 5, Friedman Papers.
31. Jack Kemp to John C. Kerr Jr., January 9, 1978, box 224, folder 3, Friedman Papers.

in the market" became "absolute." He dreamed of serving as an evangelist to bring Friedman's news to a broader public than could be reached through his books and *Newsweek* articles alone. But Chitester was also a slightly peculiar character, who attended meetings with open shirts and forced colleagues to warn potential business partners that they would likely find him "eccentric" (Bernstein 1980, 108–9). This was a longshot bid.

Although Friedman was intrigued by the prospect and flattered by Chitester's enthusiasm, he initially expressed skepticism about the proposal. His *Newsweek* columns and well-received appearances on *The Phil Donahue Show* had brought him to a broader public, but he still agreed with Hayek that he could change popular opinion more effectively by "persuading economists" rather than the "public at large." But here, as with the development of *Capitalism and Freedom* decades earlier, Rose Friedman pushed him to expand his rhetorical horizons (Bernstein 1980, 109). Her job was perhaps made easier by the near-complete freedom granted to them by Friedman's new research position. After four meetings at the Friedmans' apartment, they agreed to develop the series. Chitester, in a state of "euphoria," quickly began planning for the enterprise.

The "basic idea," as Friedman informed his colleagues, was "really to put *Capitalism and Freedom* on TV."[32] But newspapers that picked up on the enterprise immediately saw it as a direct response to *The Age of Uncertainty*. As "the two men do not form a mutual admiration society," the *New York Post* observed, it "should surprise no one" that "Milton is about to try something" at which Galbraith had "failed" ("Nobel Winner Set for TV Show" 1977).

Whereas Galbraith's series had obtained all its financing from public television outlets and struggled to maintain even a modicum of corporate support, Chitester and Friedman decided to raise all of their $2.8 million in projected costs entirely from outside funders. Chitester set up a nonprofit entity with a board well stocked with Fortune 500 executives to assuage potential concerns about donations to a small public radio station. From the beginning, foundations and corporations proved enthusiastic about contributing to the enterprise, which allowed them to make a nonprofit donation to support the propagation of ideas they supported while receiving exposure among a wealthy public-television audience. The Olin Foundation provided space at the New York Athletic Club for an initial meeting to develop the concept for the project, and its $250,000 contribution was soon

---

32. Milton Friedman to Arnold Moore, October 4, 1977, box 224, folder 7, Friedman Papers.

accompanied by $500,000 from the Sarah Scaife Foundation, $300,000 from the Reader's Digest Association, $240,000 from Getty Oil, and donations from eleven other underwriters ranging from General Motors and Bechtel to a charity fund managed by a maker of pressure cookers (Bernstein 1980, 108–11). William Jovanovich of Harcourt Brace Jovanovich, who sympathized with Friedman's ideas, provided financing for a preliminary lecture series under favorable terms (Friedman and Friedman 1998, 477). In courting support, Friedman and Chitester could afford to be selective: they discouraged contributions from major corporations, and particularly oil companies, to maintain representation from "small industries" and to "avoid any impression whatsoever that the program represented paid apologies for a particular segment."[33] Chitester relied on the idea that PBS, with its budget squeezed and its ideological orientation under constant scrutiny, would find it impossible to turn down a fully paid-for documentary series presented by a Nobel laureate. Friedman later recalled his prescience in believing that "the pressure to provide some balance to Galbraith's clearly ideological series would make it impossible for them to refuse to broadcast a program . . . which presented the other side" (Friedman and Friedman 1998, 474). Friedman's series was made possible by a potent combination of ideologically committed staff and a rapidly developing network of corporation and foundation support. This infrastructure, in combination with political pressure from conservatives in Congress and relentless critiques of media bias, established a model that would prove central to the propagation of free market ideas in the decades that followed.

Although Friedman acknowledged that his series was inspired by Galbraith's prior effort, he quite explicitly avoided using its format as a model. (In correspondence he conspicuously cited Bronowski as the closest analogue to the format he was trying to capture.)[34] Several qualities would quite sharply differentiate his approach from Galbraith's. First, his series would not be presented under any pretense of neutrality; instead, he would unabashedly try to convince viewers of his philosophical perspective. Chitester marketed it as such to prospective funders, writing to Charles Koch that it would be "a strong statement on the need for a free market."[35] Rose Friedman publicly acknowledged that they were inspired to develop

---

33. Robert Chitester to George Schultz, October 7, 1977, box 61, folder 6, Friedman Papers; Friedman to Moore, Friedman Papers.
34. Milton Friedman to Arthur Nielsen, June 28, 1977, box 225, folder 1, Friedman Papers.
35. Robert Chitester to Charles Koch, October 6, 1977, box 61, folder 6, Friedman Papers.

the show out of a "missionary instinct" (Bernstein 1980, 110, sidebar). And Friedman himself quite frankly stated that it was not "a series in economics" but "a personal statement of my own social, economic, and political values."[36] Second, the series would not dwell on historical subjects. Rather, it would be presented from a contemporary perspective, and its footage would focus entirely on real-world images of people and organizations who exemplified the point that he was trying to make. Rather than jumping around the world from instant-to-instant, each program would be rooted on a single problem and a few discrete locations, allowing Friedman to draw out his perspective with carefully chosen examples at somewhat greater length. Finally, the documentary footage would consume only a half hour, rather than a full hour, with the rest of the program consisting of Friedman in debate with a small group of individuals who expressed varying degrees of sympathy to his point of view.

Each of these decisions had important effects on the structure and reception of the series and help illuminate the posture that Friedman adopted in attempting to persuade a broader public of his views. Friedman was acutely conscious that public interest in economic ideas relied partly on an appearance of controversy. When a journalist asked him why economics was turning into a combative branch of show business, he immediately replied that "nobody wants to hear economists talk about subjects on which they are agreeing."[37] He sensed that any interest that the series inspired would result from the clarity of his policy prescriptions, rather than the skill with which they were effaced. At the same time, he believed that an appearance of empiricism was crucial to convincing others of his views. Friedman may have readily announced his iconoclasm, but he repeatedly insisted that it was founded on a careful scientific analysis of all the available data. As work began on the series, he expressed a strong desire to avoid all "gimmicks" and insisted that his "own participation and the impact of ideas should not be diluted by obviously artificial activities." One searches in vain for any signs of reflexivity in *Free to Choose*. Instead, Friedman constantly thrust himself among the subjects of his analysis, leveraging the distinctive ability of visual observation to persuade. And he emphasized, in particular, the texture of everyday life. "If we are to rest our case on spectaculars, I am afraid government would not come out badly," he wrote to one funder. Voyages to the moon and military endeavors had a certain

---

36. Milton Friedman to John A. Howard, March 11, 1980, box 224, folder 2, Friedman Papers.

37. "Economics Viewed as a Martial Art."

aesthetic appeal. Instead, he wanted to focus on the successes of corporations in transforming the practices of "everyday humdrum life."[38] Thus when speaking about welfare, Friedman dwelled on images from a single public housing project where he argued that government policies had helped make poverty more intractable; when discussing schools, he focused on a wealthy public school to criticize the taxing of the poor to fund an educational system that delivered superior outcomes to members of the middle class.[39] Every argument was supported by real-world footage that provided anecdotal validations of his claims.

The extended discussion sessions at the end were intended, in part, to satisfy what he saw as the public desire for sharp disagreement and verbal sparring. They also implicitly addressed the mandate for public television to include balanced views (without requiring any appended rebuttals) and helped validate its star's claims that he was engaged in an earnest and tough-minded search for the truth. (The *Wall Street Journal*, not realizing that Friedman added these sessions voluntarily and that Galbraith had been required to include rebuttals, implied bias in noting that "the TV people subjected Mr. Galbraith to no such scrutiny" [Malabre 1980].) Perhaps most importantly, however, they took advantage of Friedman's unique proficiency at interpersonal debate. Galbraith himself acknowledged, when asked to participate in these discussions, that this was a mode at which Friedman was superior. Applying the principle of "comparative advantage," he informed Friedman that he preferred to relay his ideas in prose, as "I am far better than you in writing, and you are far more expert in debate."[40] Friedman—who filmed all of the discussion sessions over a few days at the University of Chicago and sought to minimize any editing—found himself on the defensive more often than not in his public appearances, as his interlocutors pushed back against his sometimes convenient decisions about what information to emphasize and what to obscure.[41] But the sessions provided viewers with the excite-

38. Milton Friedman to Anthony Jay and Michael Peacock, December 18, 1977, box 224, folder 3, Friedman Papers; Milton Friedman to Denis M. Slavich, August 30, 1977, box 225, folder 6, Friedman Papers.
39. Milton Friedman, transcripts, "From Cradle to Grave" and "What's Wrong with Our Schools?," in *Free to Choose* (television series), WQLN.
40. John Kenneth Galbraith to Milton Friedman, September 27, 1979, box 200, folder "Friedman, Milton /1984–1978," Galbraith Papers.
41. See, for example, the discussion with Peter Jay in "Created Equal" and the discussion with Albert Shanker and others in "What's Wrong with Our Schools," *Free to Choose* (television series), WQLN.

ment of competitive punditry, and allowed Friedman to display the formidable forensic skills he had developed on shows like *Firing Line* and *Donahue* and two decades of frequent public appearances before often-hostile crowds.

Friedman's self-presentation throughout the series posed a sharp contrast with Galbraith's. The differences began with their height: while Galbraith towered over his subjects, projecting an aura of lofty superiority, Friedman looked up at the world with what one friendly reviewer referred to as "elfin charm" from nearly twenty inches below (Malabre 1980). Whereas Galbraith read from elaborately prepared scripts, Friedman was entirely extemporaneous: he began preparing his comments on the set as the crews were setting up their equipment and performed even the precisely timed dubbing sessions entirely off the cuff (Friedman and Friedman 1998, 483, 491). Claiming that he was too "literal-minded" to understand Galbraith's "more subtle allusions," Friedman abandoned any pretense of literary style in favor of simple exposition.[42] While Galbraith's producers labored to shorten his sentences and simplify his ideas, Friedman's praised their star for his reliance on "good, clean, two-syllable words" (Bernstein 1980, 110, sidebar). All "jargon" was avoided in *Free to Choose*, a reviewer in *American Film* wrote, in favor of "short sentences, simple ideas, and unsubtle illustrations" (Mayer 1980). Friedman's effect on viewers was evident in the letters that began to arrive as the series aired. A college student expressed his gratitude for Friedman's ability to develop arguments in terms that seemed "spontaneous" and "understandable" to the "layman viewer."[43] Another told him that it was "rare to find a brilliant intellectual who is so able at expressing his ideas so that the average person can understand."[44] Others expressed confusion at how such a coherent message could elude the understanding of academics and policy elites. "It really is so simple," one wrote, in a message that was echoed by many of her peers.[45] The clarity and consistency of Friedman's message convinced many viewers that there were clean solutions to problems that other opinion leaders continued to represent as messy. While Galbraith dwelled on the collapse of the certainties of earlier eras, Friedman was busy propounding replacements to suit the needs of his own.

---

42. Milton Friedman to John Kenneth Galbraith, October 1, 1978, box 200, folder "Friedman, Milton: 1984–1978," Galbraith Papers.
43. Devin Warner to WQLN, July 20, 1980, box 226, folder 1, Friedman Papers.
44. Ann Hanley to Milton Friedman, April 17, 1980, box 8, folder 4, Friedman Papers.
45. Joan Person to Milton Friedman, April 18, 1980, box 8, folder 4, Friedman Papers.

Friedman wanted his message in the series to continue reaching young audiences long after its network runs had concluded. Following its release to largely positive reviews, he devoted close and sustained attention to increasing its availability for students in high schools and colleges. Friedman had long been intrigued by the idea that college lectures should be videotaped by the most effective instructors in their fields and widely distributed, rather than entrusted to the inferior talents who inhabited most university positions.[46] In *Free to Choose*, he now possessed a set of videos that were far more lavishly illustrated and produced than was possible in any conventional set of lectures. The challenge was how to price them for broad distribution in the era that preceded the widespread availability of inexpensive videocassettes. Video copies of *The Age of Uncertainty* had languished on the shelves largely because of high prices, yielding sales figures that distributors described as "troubling and slow."[47] Friedman's sympathizers at the Americanism Educational League thereby devised a system in which they purchased over a dozen copies and loaned them out to colleges and universities for free. Within months they were lending them to over eighty colleges; six years later, the number was in the hundreds, and they informed Friedman that nearly all their copies were "out on loan all of the time."[48] Friedman also deemed high schools "a particularly critical area for affecting long-range public opinion" and courted support from foundations for a project to develop filmstrips and elaborate curricular materials for use across the country.[49] And when the opportunity presented itself, he bought back the rights to the series to make it available on videocassette at minimal prices (Friedman and Friedman 1998, 502). While Galbraith assiduously cultivated his connections to people in positions of political influence, Friedman insisted from the outset of his work on *Free to Choose* that "our fundamental appeal must be to the young and not to those already in the establishment."[50] Ever the econo-

---

46. See, for example, Milton Friedman to Larry Moss, August 23, 1978, box 224, folder 7, Friedman Papers.

47. Letter from Gale Livengood, box 577, folder "The Age of Uncertainty: BBC program: materials sent by Charles Benton: December 1977 (1 of 2)," Galbraith Papers.

48. Milton Friedman to John Sloan, July 29, 1987, box 225, folder 1, Friedman Papers.

49. Milton Friedman to Richard M. Larry, Sarah Scaife Foundation, January 16, 1981, box 224, folder 5, Friedman Papers.

50. Milton Friedman to Robert Chitester, December 7, 1978, box 223, folder 5, Friedman Papers.

mist, he believed that reaching this audience would require close attention to pricing and opportunity costs, and worked assiduously to ensure that both remained low.

Although *Free to Choose* contained few novel arguments and little new information, the documentary series and companion volume soon became the most popular distillation of Friedman's economic and political views. In conjunction they provided perhaps the clearest exemplar of his fully developed persuasive technique. In the series Friedman self-consciously sought to avoid the rhetorical shortcomings of his political allies and exploit those of his political foes. He believed that market advocates should represent their views as simple in concept, populist in tone, empirical in methodology, and capable of solving the great problems of the modern world. This message found an eager audience among corporate executives and think tanks, and Friedman exploited these networks to disseminate his ideas among those whose opinions were not yet fully formed.

Galbraith, as one might expect, was horrified by Friedman's means of persuasion. He found the arguments Friedman adopted "simplistic" and perhaps even "purely rhetorical," relying "almost wholly on passionate assertion and emotional response" (Galbraith 1981b). He marveled at the "radicalism" of economic ideas in the early 1980s, labeling himself a dispositional "conservative" by comparison (Galbraith 1981d) and expressing new sympathy for the rapidly receding "responsible right" (Galbraith 1981a). But even as he disparaged what he saw as the reductive extremity of Friedman's ideas, he acknowledged that they had shifted public opinion far more effectively than his own. Friedman, he wrote in the late 1980s, was "perhaps the most influential economic figure of the second half of the twentieth century" (Galbraith 1987, 271). Galbraith may never have accepted Friedman's economics, but he developed a reluctant admiration for Friedman's ability to convince others of his views.

Any study of the public life of economic ideas must confront problems of rhetoric and transmission, and engage with activities that extend far beyond the journals, lecture halls, and seminar rooms that have long formed the backbone of disciplinary history. *The Age of Uncertainty* and *Free to Choose* reveal the extent to which the nature of these public activities had changed over a single generation. During the final quarter of the twentieth century, the advocacy of economic ideas relied more heavily than ever before on dense layers of intermediary institutions. Those who compared the qualities of the respective series' early production teams might have assumed that Galbraith's establishment credentials lent him every advantage, and Friedman himself did not hesitate to draw on that argument when it served his ends. But the production of *Free to Choose* relied on an advocacy network that proved, even at this early stage, remarkably effective. In contrast to Galbraith's persistent failure to attract corporate sponsorship, Friedman had little trouble financing his series entirely through business and foundation support. Even as the expensive reels of Galbraith's series languished on distributors' shelves, Friedman enjoyed help from organizations that developed extensive curricular materials and made pedagogical usage of the series free. And while Friedman's series was released to a largely genial critical reception, Galbraith's was met with a carefully orchestrated hostile response. The Institute for Economic Affairs arranged for public lectures, including Friedman's, that would discredit Galbraith's ideas; the Hoover Institution helped assemble the critical respondents whose views were appended to each episode; and publications including *Barron's*, the *Daily Telegraph*, and the *National Review*, in conjunction with a number of Friedman's fellow members of the Mont Pèlerin Society, met the release of the series with a set of sharply critical reviews. Friedman could rely on a network of allied institutions to provide the forms of support that this new era of advocacy required.

Free to Choose was a popular success for many reasons, including Friedman's disciplinary credibility, his populist persona, and the financial and promotional support provided by sympathetic institutions. At the center of his appeal, however, lay the force of the market metaphor. While Friedman's rhetoric aligned well with the requirements of late twentieth-century modes of transmission, Galbraith never found a way to distill his views in such simple and broadly applicable terms. As one journalist wrote before the release of either documentary, to be an "economic superstar" it was necessary to arrive at a "fixed view of the world, learn to state it forcefully and cast unremitting scorn on those who disagree."[51] This may have been cynical, but it was not entirely untrue. The reductivism of economic debate in recent years can be attributed, in part, to the pattern of consumer demand.

51. "Economics Viewed as a Martial Art."

References

Amis, Martin. 1977. "Capitalism and the Camera-Angle." *Sunday Times*, January 16.
Barnouw, Erik. 1993. *Documentary: A History of the Non-fiction Film*. 2d rev. ed. New York: Oxford University Press.
Bernstein, Peter. 1980. "The Man Who Brought You Milton Friedman." *Fortune*, February 25, 108–11, 122.
Birtchall, Tony. 1977. "Economic Delivery." *Journal* (Newcastle-upon-Tyne), February 24.
Briggs, Asa. 1985. *The BBC: The First Fifty Years*. Oxford: Oxford University Press.
Church, Michael. 1977. "Coming Clear." *Times*, January 25.
Cox, Patrick. 1980. "Public Television Maverick." *Reason*, October, 43–44.
Crisell, Andrew. 1997. *An Introductory History of British Broadcasting*. London: Routledge.
Cross, Robert. 1977. "Dialog: John Kenneth Galbraith." *Chicago Tribune Magazine*, May 15, 24–25, 43–44.
Curley, Anne. 1980. "TV Gets a New Uncle Milty." *Milwaukee Journal*, January 11.
Dornfeld, Barry. 1998. *Producing Public Television, Producing Public Culture*. Princeton: Princeton University Press.
Field, Leslie. 1971. "The Secrets . . . of a Woman's Kind of Man." *Daily Mail*, November 27.
"Figuring to Be a Star." 1977. *Birmingham Evening Mail*, January 6.
Fourcade, Marion. 2009. *Economists and Societies: Discipline and Profession in the United States, Britain, and France, 1890s to 1990s*. Princeton: Princeton University Press.
Friedman, Milton. 1977. *Friedman on Galbraith: And on Curing the British Disease*. Vancouver, B.C.: Fraser Institute.
Friedman, Milton, and Rose D. Friedman. 1998. *Two Lucky People*. Chicago: University of Chicago Press.
Furner, Mary. 1975. *Advocacy and Objectivity: A Crisis in the Professionalization of American Social Science, 1865–1905*. Lexington: University Press of Kentucky.
Galbraith, John Kenneth. 1981a. "All Quiet on the Conservative Front." *Washington Post*, April 29.
———. 1981b. "The Conservative Onslaught." *New York Review of Books*, January 22, 30–36.
———. 1981c. *A Life in Our Times: Memoirs*. New York: Ballantine.
———. 1981d. "Musings of a (Relative) Conservative." *New York Times*, January 4.
———. 1987. *Economics in Perspective: A Critical History*. Boston: Houghton Mifflin.
Hampshire, Stuart. 1977. "Watch This Man." *Vogue*, May, 241, 283.
Henry, William A., III. 1977a. "Galbraith's First Law Put to the Test." *Boston Globe*, May 22.
———. 1977b. "Uncertainty? Not Galbraith." *Boston Globe*, May 20.

Holden, Anthony. 1980. "The Free Market Man." *Observer*, February 17.
Ingrams, Richard. 1977. "More Banality." *Spectator*, February 12.
Jemal, Biddy. 1977. "BBC2's Most Fascinating Man." Letter to the editor. *Sunday Times*, January 23.
Jewkes, John. 1977. "Critic of Capitalists." *Daily Telegraph*, February 7.
"John Kenneth Galbraith Tells *Focus* about His Upcoming Series on Economics: *The Age of Uncertainty*." 1976. *Focus*, August. Box 566, folder "The Age of Uncertainty: BBC program: articles: Focus, August 1976," Galbraith Papers.
Kelley, David. 1977. "Distorted Picture: A Hard Look at Galbraith's 'Age of Uncertainty.'" *Barron's*, July 18.
Kilborn, Peter. 1977. "Galbraith on TV." *New York Times*, March 20.
Last, Richard. 1977. "Galbraith Sustains a Hymn of Hate." *Daily Telegraph*, January 18.
Ledbetter, James. 1997. *Made Possible by . . . the Death of Public Broadcasting in the United States*. London: Verso.
Lyon, Jim. 1976. "Seeing the Light at Last." *Vancouver Sun*, May 15.
"Making It Clear as Mud." 1977. *North-western Evening Mail*, January 15.
Malabre, Alfred L., Jr. 1980. "The Milton Friedman Show." *Wall Street Journal*, January 11.
Mayer, Martin. 1980. "Uncle Miltie's Money Talk." *American Film*, April, 10–12.
Meyer, Karl E. 1977. "The Revelation according to Prophet Galbraith." *Socialist Review*, May 28. Box 1021, folder "The Age of Uncertainty: BBC program: reviews: [American]," Galbraith Papers.
Minogue, Kenneth. 1977. "Galbraith's Wit and Unwisdom: Ordeal by Caricature." *Encounter*, December, 14–18.
———. 1978. "The Galbraithian Fallacy." *Encounter*, April, 88–89.
Mitchell, Henry. 1974. "The Way BBC Works." *Washington Post*, March 8.
Nadel, Gerry. 1977. "Galbraith's No Nobel Laureate, but He Is a TV Star." *Fort Wayne Journal-Gazette*, April 24.
Nichols, Bill. 1991. *Representing Reality: Issues and Concepts in Documentary*. Bloomington: Indiana University Press.
"Nobel Winner Set for TV Show." 1977. *New York Post*, December 6.
Nossiter, Bernard D. 1977. "Galbraith and the BBC: Entertaining Economics." *Washington Post*, January 8.
"Now for the Sexy Ken Galbraith Show." 1977. *Daily Mail*, January 6.
O'Connor, John J. 1977. "TV: Galbraith Offers 'A Personal View.'" *New York Times*, May 19.
Parker, Richard. 2005. *John Kenneth Galbraith: His Life, His Politics, His Economics*. New York: Farrar, Straus and Giroux.
Porteous, John. 1977. "Money Talks." *New Statesman*, February 25.
Reed, Clayton. 1977. "Show Biz." *St. Petersburg Times*, August 28.
Rees, Jenny. 1977. "The Most Unlikely Superstars of All . . ." *Daily Mail*, January 8.
Ruby, Michael. 1977. "The Galbraith Show." *Newsweek*, May 23, 61–64.

Smith, R. C. 1978. "John Kenneth Galbraith, Some of Us Hear You!" *Charlotte News*, August 31.
Stanley, Don. 1977. "Galbraith: Goad and Gadfly." *Vancouver Sun*, May 13.
Stigler, George. 1977. "The Heckler: John Kenneth Galbraith's Marathon Television Series." *National Review*, May 27, 601–4.
"TV Series Better in Print." 1977. *Crew Chronicle*, March 2. Box 1021, folder "Books: The Age of Uncertainty, 1977," Galbraith Papers.

Economic Indicators as Public Interventions

Gil Eyal and Moran Levy

The main argument of this essay is that the term *public intellectual* is too narrow for historical research about the public influence of economists and economic expertise. We propose, instead, the concept of *public interventions* to inform a more comprehensive approach, one that broadens the analytical frame by multiplying the relevant actors, modes, and targets of intervention yet could still include within it research on public intellectuals narrowly construed. As an empirical example, we suggest that the design and diffusion of economic indicators—specifically, the GDP and the myriad indicators compiled in recent years as part of proposals to replace it with a better representation of human welfare—could be analyzed as a specific mode by which economists intervene in and shape the public sphere. This argument, about the profound influence wielded by those who design economic indicators, has of course been made by many others—especially feminists—before us (Alonso and Star 1987; Berkowitz 1996; Block and Burns 1986; Folbre 1989; Waring 1988). Its significance here is merely in demonstrating the wide terrain that opens up for historical and sociological analysis once we broaden our scope from intellectuals to interventions.

Correspondence may be addressed to Gil Eyal, Department of Sociology, Columbia University, 606 West 122nd Street, New York, NY 10027; e-mail: ge2027@gmail.com. The authors would like to thank Nitza Berkowitz, Daniel Breslau, Marianna Laura Heredia, Tiago Mata, Yuval Yonay, and the three anonymous reviewers for *HOPE*.

History of Political Economy 45 (annual suppl.) DOI 10.1215/00182702-2311007
Copyright 2013 by Duke University Press

The approach we propose is inspired by Michel Foucault's (2000) distinction between the "universal" and "specific" intellectual; Pierre Bourdieu's ([1992] 1996) replacement of the latter by a "collective intellectual"; and the approach to the public sphere urged by the contributors to *Making Things Public* (Latour and Weibel 2005). Additionally, our suspicion that the concept of public intellectual is too narrow for capturing the specific way in which *economists* intervene in public affairs follows in the footsteps of the many sociologists of economics who have tried to analyze how economic expertise is deployed to shape public affairs, or how it "preforms" the economy (Breslau 1998, 2003; Callon 1998; Foucault 1991; Fourcade 2009; MacKenzie, Muniesa, and Siu 2007; Mitchell 1998; Rose, O'Malley, and Valverde 2006; Yonay 1998).

In the first section of this essay, we elaborate this argument in theoretical terms. We provide a brief genealogy of the concept of public intellectual, to explain why it is too narrow for present purposes. Then we draw on Foucault, Bourdieu, and others to develop an analytical framework for research on interventions, distinguishing between agencies, modes, and targets of intervention. In the second section, we argue that this approach, focusing on interventions rather than intellectuals, is especially suited for guiding research on the public deployments of *economic* expertise. In the third section, we offer a brief history of the origins of the GDP (and of the system of national accounts more generally), aiming to substantiate our treatment of it as a specific target of public intervention by economists. The fourth and final section analyzes the now four-decades-long collective attempt to provide a summary index of human welfare and economic progress that could replace, supplement, or correct GDP, as such public interventions.

From Public Intellectuals to Public Interventions

A concept like public intellectual cannot be just picked up ready-made to be used for analytical purposes. It trails behind it a long history of uses and abuses that is activated every time one deploys it unawares. The concept of intellectual in its modern meaning was invented during the Dreyfus affair (1894–1906). It was not coined for analytical or diagnostic purposes but as a political mobilizing device, a rallying call designed to bring into being the very category it was naming. Moreover, it was an exercise in self-definition, since those who issued the call considered themselves to be the best representatives of the category and addressed it to the likeminded (Bauman 1987, 2–8). The later career of the concept involved a continuous tangle between those who wanted to give it objective analytical meaning and extend it to wider circles of the educated, and those who sought to redraw the boundary between who is and who is not a "true" intellectual. This boundary work (Gieryn 1999) often took the form of accusations that intellectuals have betrayed their "true" mission (Benda [1927] 1928), and it ultimately informed a problematic of *allegiance* that pervaded all the later attempts to give the concept an objective analytical meaning (Eyal and Buchholz 2010).

Within this history, the concept of public intellectual plays a very specific role. The first point to note is that it is a very recent construction. As can be seen in figure 1, the conjunction *public intellectual* hardly existed before 1987, when, no doubt, the publication of Russell Jacoby's book *The Last Intellectuals* marked the moment when the term came into ever-widening circulation.[1]

The second point to note is a certain touch of redundancy in the conjunction *public intellectual*: are not intellectuals precisely those who in their writing and speaking appeal to a broad public? Is not the notion of public intervention and public audience already contained in the term *intellectual*? What exactly is *done* by adding the qualifier *public*? This peculiarity can be understood only against the background of the history of the concept, as noted above. This history is characterized by continuous attempts to extend the category of intellectuals to characterize a larger "new class" composed of experts, reaching a peak in the late 1970s (Bruce-Briggs 1979; Gouldner 1979; Konrad and Szelenyi 1979; Walker

---

1. For comparison's sake, the term *intellectuals* without qualifiers entered English-language discussions during the first decade of the twentieth century (following the Dreyfus affair), enjoyed a steady climb, and peaked around 1970. Discussions of "intellectuals" then declined till 1985, when they picked up again and by 1995 returned to 1970 levels. We suspect that the coining of the term *public intellectual* revived the interest in intellectuals more generally, for reasons explained in the text above: see the Ngram we constructed using Google Books at books.google.com/ngrams/graph?content=public+intellectual%2Cintellectuals&year_start=1880&year_end=2000&corpus=0&smoothing=1 (accessed November 8, 2012). To test whether these results are robust, we also conducted a similar search on *JSTOR*. We found that the conjunction *public intellectual* appears in the title of 67 articles, the first of which is from 1988 and is a review of Jacoby's book. It had never been used in the title of an article before. The conjunction appears in the full text of 2,769 articles, only 62 (2.2 percent) of which precede 1987. A textual check shows that in the majority of these 62 articles the conjunction does not identify an individual or a social role but is a different, unrelated usage (e.g., "public intellectual life" or something similar).

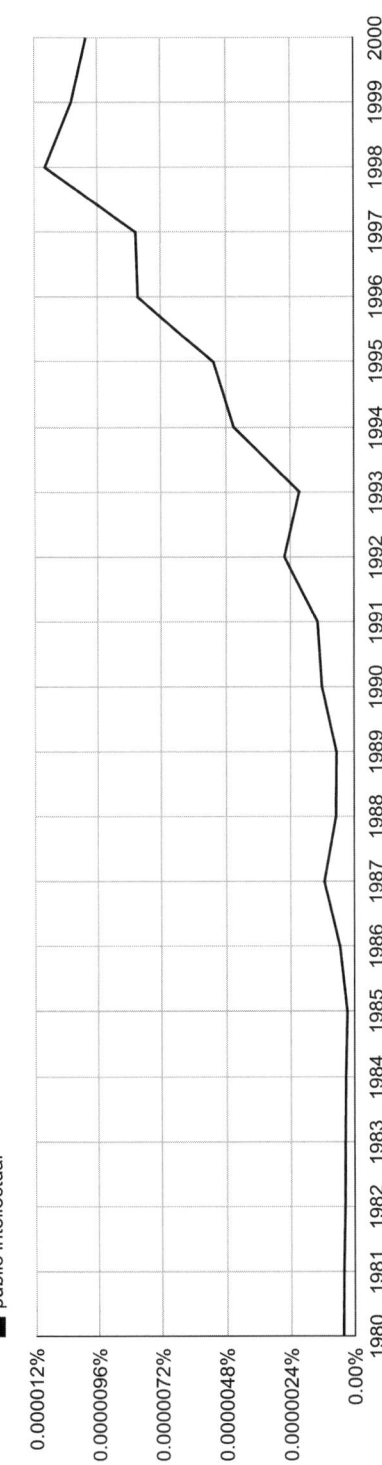

Figure 1 Frequency of appearance of *public intellectual* in Google Books from 1980 to 2000. Ngram created by the authors using Google Books (accessed November 8, 2012)

1979). Adding the qualifier *public*, therefore, was boundary work meant to exclude experts from the category and to signal that true intellectuals are *not* experts: they are not entangled in mundane technical affairs but address a broad public, owing allegiance only to truth and universal values. Since this conjunction first appeared in a book titled *The Last Intellectuals*, a book that belonged in the genre of jeremiad (mixture of lament and accusation) about the decline of true intellectuals and betrayal of their original mission (Posner 2001), it activates not only boundary work from experts but also a whole narrative about decline, "endangered species," the threat of betrayal (by turning expert), extinction (by a society of expertise), and consequently a debate about whether public intellectuals are disappearing or reappearing on the Web and the blogosphere (Donatich 2001; Fuller 2004; Kellner 1997). Using this term with respect to economists—who are first and foremost technical experts, whatever else they are, and for whom the diagnostic problem is *not* to understand a decline in their public role, but on the contrary a broadening and increase of their influence (Markoff and Montecinos 1993)—dooms the analysis in advance. It privileges a narrow focus on speech acts that have been intentionally framed as nontechnical (via their mode and site of delivery, via the prominence claimed by their authors), although in reality they always reference the technical, whether explicitly or implicitly, and could not be efficacious without it.

Fortunately, the history of writing about intellectuals affords us with a more productive alternative, represented by Foucault's (2000, 128) distinction between the universal and specific intellectual. While the classic "universal" intellectual fits the mold of what is meant by "public intellectual"—the prototype is represented by the engaged man of letters (Émile Zola, Jean-Paul Sartre) who speaks in the name of truth and universal values—the specific intellectual is an *expert*. Foucault's example of a "specific intellectual" is Robert Oppenheimer. Oppenheimer, says Foucault, was an individual whose narrow technical work as expert acquired universal dimensions when it threatened the whole human species with extinction, and who consequently was compelled to intervene in public affairs. Foucault concludes, therefore, that there is no reason to draw a strong distinction between intellectuals and experts: "The intellectual is simply the person who uses his knowledge, his competence and his relation to truth in the field of political struggles." Put differently, what is common to all who may be termed "specific intellectuals" is not that they correspond to a specific social type (since experts come in many different forms and shapes), but the *movement* by which their local and technical knowledge acquires a more general and public value and becomes the basis for an intervention in public affairs. The case of Oppenheimer, once again, is instructive. Oppenheimer did not begin as the independent, engaged critic that he came to embody later. He started as an expert working in the service of the state, first at the Manhattan Project, and then as chairman of the General Advisory Committee to the Atomic Energy Commission (AEC). It was from this position that he began lobbying for international arms control, that is, that he began intervening in public affairs. Eventually, his activism led to the revocation of his security clearance in 1954 during the heyday of McCarthyism, and he became a bona fide dissident intellectual. What is interesting about Oppenheimer surely is not this final result but the movement that took him from technical concerns and state service to increasingly independent intervention in public affairs. What Foucault did was not to add another type but to draw analytic attention to the enduring element in the concept of intellectual, the part that is indifferent to boundary work and classificatory struggles, and that could serve as a basis for reconstructing the concept.

Once we focus on this enduring element, namely, the movement by which knowledge acquires value as intervention in public affairs, we can see that given the right preconditions or precipitating events many different actors and social types could play this role. In fact, why should the agents of intervention be only individuals? Why not also groups, collectives, even organizations? This was Bourdieu's ([1992] 1996) criticism of Foucault. In contemporary conditions, he said, the agent of public intervention is most often a "collective intellectual," a group of experts working together. The same message comes from the literature on "epistemic communities" (Haas 1992). Broadening the field of investigation in this way reveals the "public intellectual" to be merely shorthand for one specific actor laying claim to one specific mode of intervention—typically the manifesto, the signed petition, the polemical op-ed piece (and now the blog), the gesture of "revelation," prophesying, "speaking truth to power," as well as propounding "transformative ideas" (Bell 1960; Gouldner 1975–76; Bauman 1987)—in one specific type of public arena.

Instead of research focusing on a certain social (and normative) type, asking whether individual economists fit this mold, as some essays in this volume do, it would be far more profitable to analyze the movement by which economic knowledge and expertise are mobilized to inform a value-laden intervention in the public sphere. In this essay, we would like to draw on earlier work (Eyal and Buchholz 2010) to propose a conceptual framework suitable for this type of analysis:

1. *Agencies of intervention*: The term *public intellectual* tends to privilege the actions and pronouncements of a few prominent figures. As noted earlier, this inevitably leads to boundary work, and can often degenerate into hagiography or into its opposite, a narrative of decline and betrayal. Instead, we suggest several ways of widening the category of relevant actors into multiple agencies of intervention: first, we follow Bourdieu in considering not only individuals but also collectives of practitioners, networks constituting epistemic communities, even organizations such as think tanks. Second, inevitably this means that the analysis includes not only the glamorous and well-known individuals but the crowds of more "gray" practitioners, who often work together in such collectives away from the spotlight enjoyed by prominent figures. Yet, arguably, the public impact of their collective work is no less profound. Finally, we analyze all these agencies—individuals and collectives—in relation to one another, as coexisting and interdependent in a field of competition and contestation over the claim to represent publicly relevant knowledge or the proper mode of engaging with public affairs (Sapiro 2009).

2. *Modes of intervention*: The term *public intellectual*, as noted above, privileges a particular way of making such claims and of influencing public affairs. Public intellectuals intervene by means of writing op-eds, speaking in public, petitioning, or blogging. Put differently, they intervene by making their *opinion* known and seeking to influence the opinions of others. This seems to us an impoverished vision of what it means to intervene in public affairs. Often "it is precisely the most technical social science that has the most important political effects, even more so because those political effects are generally not recognized as such" (Breslau 1998, 39–40). We think that Foucault's point about "specific intellectuals" was precisely about a movement that takes one from the problems and contestations encountered at the technical level to the "political effects" of these technicalities. It follows that intervention could be also in the form of a report, a technical document, expert testimony, even an experimental demonstration (properly publicized), or—as we shall emphasize here—in the form of a "politics of measurement," by modifying how matters of public concern are quantified, measured, and represented (Porter 1995; Breslau 1998; Alonso and Star 1987; Block and Burns 1986). The crucial point is that the format or mode of intervention can take many different forms besides the

publication of one's written or spoken opinion, and that often the most efficacious interventions either come black-boxed as charts, figures, numbers, and other technical devices, or they are counter-strategies that aim precisely to open up these black boxes and make the technical public and political.

3. *Arenas/targets of intervention*: The concept of public intellectual carries with it a certain normative (Habermasian) vision of its target as a public sphere of *opinion* or a sphere of public opinion. This is the main reason why the concept of public intellectual often comes coupled with a narrative of decline and betrayal, especially in the United States, because influencing, orchestrating, even creating public opinion has become the business of think tanks and they are much better at it than intellectuals. It is not a coincidence that the concept of public intellectual was coined in the mid-1980s, a time marked by the ascendency of second-generation think tanks in the American polity, who have professionalized the work of producing opinions and of producing individuals who present an opinionated posture as a way of living—pundits, commentators, "talking heads"[2]—as well as the work orchestrating and creating "public opinion" using modern PR techniques. These organizations crowd out, speak over, or buffer the interventions of independent intellectuals (Medvetz 2012).[3] But there is a more fundamental (and less American-centric) reason why this vision of a public sphere of opinion is inadequate. The posture of the public intellectual references an agora populated by reasonable citizens, who are presented with conflicting opinions and are capable of adjudicating between them according to the force of the better argument. The conversation in this agora hardly ever gets technical, and when it does, the suspicion is that somebody is obfuscating, evading the debate, using scientific jargon and technical details as ideology (Habermas 1970). Modern-day politics, however, are increasingly about technical affairs of which "the public" is ignorant. This has led Walter Lippmann to declare the public a "phantom" and others in the interwar years to say that public opinion does not exist or that democracy founded on public opinion is a sham masking the rule of

---

2. In a play on the old Weberian distinction, we could say that intellectuals live "for opinion," while pundits (and think tanks) live "of opinion."

3. Philip Mirowski and Edward Nik-Khah (in this volume) demonstrate the extent to which actors within this buffer zone can completely block, distort, or disarm the interventions made by scientists and academics.

experts (Lippmann 1922, 1927; Dewey 1927; Marres 2005; Binkley 1928). The point, however, is more subtle. The point is that "opinion" is a very limited way of understanding what constitutes the target of public intervention. Concerning technical matters of public concern, intervention cannot be efficacious without being equipped with all that makes expertise strong, and that opinion by itself lacks, namely, techniques, instruments, demonstrations, figures, charts, numbers.[4] We show, indeed, in the next section, how public intervention is crafted by collectives of experts and laypeople, who educate themselves about a technical matter of public concern (the experts need educating too! They are often quite ignorant about newly emerging matters of concern) and equip themselves with the knowledge and the technical means to craft an intervention. This means, however, that we have to think in terms of a very different image of the public sphere. It cannot be this open homogeneous space of pure discussion. But nor can it be the closed, quasi-private space of the laboratory. We must think of it as a channel, or more precisely multiple channels, in Bruno Latour's (2005, 19) terms, "the frail conduits through which truths and proofs are allowed to enter the sphere of politics." Put differently, if there are public interventions it is because there are already established "ports into the Leviathan," so to speak; there are already institutionalized conduits by means of which particular types of expertise are permanently connected to the state. In our new and admittedly strange topology, the public sphere, or spheres, is not outside the state but within its boundary, within fuzzy and thick interfaces where expertise and the state interpenetrate and blend into each other (Mitchell 1991; Rose 1992). These interfaces constitute multiple public spheres of sorts, that is, targets of public intervention that are directly continuous with the work of experts. The conversation in this space is almost always technical, but not because it is obfuscating; on the contrary, as Latour (1987) puts it about science, "when controversies flare up, the literature gets technical," namely, it is precisely in the technical details that one finds the politics, the opinions, and the values. Recall the example of Oppenheimer: he first intervened in public affairs not from outside the state but from

---

4. This observation is closely related to Posner's (2001, 72) argument that the production and circulation of public intellectual commentary suffers from a "market failure" because of low barriers to entry and poor quality control that is unable to encourage market exit.

inside it (the Manhattan Project) or from inside its boundary (the advisory committee to the AEC). Perhaps what befell Oppenheimer the man is less significant than the institutional link he helped forge, the fact that the Advisory Committee to the AEC constitutes an institutional interface between nuclear physics and the state. The intervention of physicists in public affairs about nuclear matters need not come from "outside." It is an extension of their work as advisers for the AEC, and it would most likely flow through institutionalized channels and grooves. It would not be mere "opinion," but would most likely come equipped with charts, statistics, experiments, and calculations.

Ultimately, our point is not that there are no individuals who could be reasonably identified as "public intellectuals" (although never without implicit or explicit boundary work excluding others from the same status), nor do we wish to reject the use of the biographical or prosopographical method in historical analysis, nor are we suggesting that there is no point in analyzing a media "space of opinion" (Jacobs and Townsley 2012) where such individuals may possess significant symbolic capital. Our point is that the analytical problem indexed by the concept of intellectual—namely, the problem of how knowledge is mobilized to influence public affairs—is better served by broadening the analytical lens to include not only prominent individuals but also gray practitioners and collectives (hence even biographies of prominent intellectuals must be analyzed in the context of a whole field of competing and interdependent agencies); not only op-eds and "ideas" but also technical means of shaping, representing, and intervening in public affairs (hence no prosopography of an "epistemic community" is complete without examining the devices and networks it mobilizes or takes apart as part of its advocacy); not only the mediatized sphere of opinion but also the multiple "ports into the Leviathan" established by specific types of expertise. All these considerations, we argue, are doubly relevant when it comes to economists and the question of how economic expertise is mobilized to influence public affairs.

Why Thinking in Terms of Interventions Is Especially Suited for Analyzing the Public Impact of Economists and Economic Expertise

We organize our comments here through the trio of agencies, modes, and targets of intervention.

There are, no doubt, a few prominent economists who enjoy media celebrity and opine about public affairs from the pages of the *New York Times* or in best seller books, but they are the exception. The self-perception of economists is as technical experts, and many wield public influence not as intellectuals but as advisers, "chief economists" of firms and banks, technocrats, and technical innovators. Moreover, by its very nature, the work of economic calculation is collaborative and requires academic or government economists to join forces with "economists in the wild" (Callon 1998), such as accountants, statisticians, risk analysts, and so on. In short, economics by its very nature entails multiple and varied *agencies* of intervention.

Some economists, no doubt, write op-eds, as do many other academics (Jacobs and Townsley 2012), but to limit analytical attention to this *mode* of intervention is to lose sight of what is most distinctive about economic expertise and how it is inserted into the public sphere through formulas, charts, accounting conventions, index numbers, and so on. In recent years, this point has been made most forcefully by the "performativity" school. To say that economics is performative is to argue that it does not describe or explain the economy from outside but weaves a network that reaches all the way from the citadels of academia through "economists in the wild," to the economic actors themselves, equipping them with calculative prostheses on which they rely in making decisions (Callon 1998). This argument, as we shall see, is in surprising agreement with Wesley Mitchell's and Irving Fisher's respective visions for how the index numbers and statistical aggregates they produced were expected to affect economic reality (Breslau 2003, 405). Performativity, therefore, has the double sense of (1) giving form, pre-forming; the waffle does not exist independently of the waffle iron, and things economic—as distinct from what is considered "noneconomic"—do not exist independently of the grid of knowledge that disentangles and frames them so they become calculable (see also Eyal 2012); and (2) but to perform is also to act, to intervene; the statements of economics are not descriptions, they are ways of "doing things with numbers" (to paraphrase the British philosopher J. L. Austin). The relationship between economic knowledge and economic reality is not one of description or explanation but, as Daniel Breslau (2011) puts it, "applied Platonism." When economists are consulted about the design of electricity markets, for example, they compare existing markets with the "platonic" model of perfect market competition and ask what institutional arrangements and/or calculative devices would permit these markets to approximate the functioning of the ideal model. The model itself is not modified by the contrast with reality, but on the contrary, reality is modified to approximate the model by equipping economic actors with the means and motivations to calculate as if they inhabit the virtual terrain of perfect competition. Similarly, the Black-Sholes formula is not a representation of existing reality but a tool used to price an option within given limitations of information (i.e., it disentangles the option so that calculation is possible), so that the behavior of market actors can approximate the model of perfect competition (MacKenzie 2007; MacKenzie and Milo 2003). I do not think, however, that the argument of "performativity" rests on whether the introduction of calculative devices and/or institutional arrangements modifies economic processes in a way that confirms or disconfirms the economic theory from which they derive (what MacKenzie [2007] calls "Barnesian performativity" and "counter-performativity," respectively). A tool may be "right for the job" or not. It may do the job well or sloppily. But we do not say that the tool has been confirmed or disconfirmed. The performativity of economics rests on the fact that its concepts and formulas are used as tools to shape the behavior of economic actors. The tools are measured not by their "truth" (which belongs to the Platonic realm of the ideal model) but by their relative ability to bring about the closest possible approximation to the desirable output of the ideal model, namely, governability—orderly coordination of the autonomous activities of multiple calculative agencies, predictability, self-correction, responsiveness to the "light hand" of a governor who modifies incentives only gradually and piecemeal. So most of the time economists intervene in public affairs not by writing or commenting to a general audience but through a far more "technical" mode of intervention, namely, by equipping economic actors and governors with calculative tools designed to bring about governability, or by taking apart such calculative devices to expose the assumptions about public affairs built into them. The case of index numbers—the topic of the next section—is a good example of this mode of intervention.

Moreover, even when economists *do* write or comment to a general audience, it is not always insightful to think of them as public intellectuals. The idea of public intellectuals assumes that speech is meant to inform, educate, influence, and persuade. As noted earlier, it is intimately tied to the concept of *opinion*. But is this really the best way to construe, let us say, what Ben Bernanke has to say about the economy, whether in a press conference, a carefully worded Fed dispatch, or even an op-ed piece? (McGregor and Young, this volume). Speaking or writing in these cases has a completely different value than "opinion." It is not description or even prescription but *action*, a policy tool. It is part of a game in which the audience construes what is said as intended to signal certain intentions or actions on the part of the Fed. So the statements are prepared in advance by Fed policymakers reflecting how they expect the audience will construe each and every specific expression, qualifier, adjective, or number. Of course, this process of careful preparation and calibration is something of which the audience is well aware and takes into its interpretation, which means that the drafting has to take into account this double hermeneutic layer, and so on and so forth. The same goes for the "chief economists" of large banks, who are regularly interviewed in the press to give their opinion or assessment of the state of the economy. They, too, calculate in advance what they say because they know that a crowd of investors and brokers is listening to the very "tone" of their message, and like good economists they are well aware of all the unintended and perverse consequences that can follow. Economics may be highly mathematized; it may even claim to have absorbed the mathematics of information and communication games (Mirowski 2002); but at the core of its form of expertise there is also a fairly imprecise and nonmathematical language game. Its tool kit, especially for "economists in the wild," is chock-full of flowery adjectives that would make a wine critic blush (as in speaking of a "soft" market or a "sluggish" recovery), and it is characterized by special attention to how things can be done by words, and how to keep the audience continually guessing. This sort of speech is snake-charming the economy. It is certainly a form of public intervention of sorts. But even when it appears on the op-ed page of the *New York Times* it is not "opinion," not the public intellectual speech variant.

Finally, most of the time the *target* of economists' interventions is not the open, homogeneous sphere of public opinion but the multiple frail conduits by which economic expertise is linked with politics and the state, the multiple institutional arenas where economic things become public. In the next section, we pay close attention to how one such institutional arena—the system of national accounts—emerged, and what types of public intervention become possible along this conduit. The general point is that economic expertise is not something that is formulated in the academy and then "applied" elsewhere. It is a network that stretches from the academy through businesses and quasi-governmental organizations, along a permanent "port" into the state. The largest employer for new US economics PhDs is the US government (18 percent in 1997), followed by the International Monetary Fund, World Bank, and the Federal Reserve. The only discipline better represented in government is physics (Siegfried and Stock 1999). More importantly, economic expertise is absolutely essential to how modern, liberal societies are governed (Miller and Rose 1990). "Economy" originally meant the correct manner of governing individuals, goods, and wealth, and "political economy" was concerned with how to introduce this economy (frugality, rationality, calculability) into the general running of the state (Foucault 1991, 92). Even when economics are seemingly technical and neutral, they are often about a problem of *government* broadly understood, namely, about the art of governing people, things, and relations and leading them toward a convenient end—equitable distribution, efficiency, growth, and so on. Economists, therefore, are different from most other experts. Whether or not they are employed by the state, economists' technical field of expertise is never very far from politics and the public sphere, because it is about how to arrange things, relations, incentives, and rules so as to produce governability, and because liberal states govern by means of calculation. The more technical economists' work is, the more it is about "governing by numbers" (Desrosières 2008; Miller 2004; Porter 1995). So our point is that most economists, most of the time, intervene not in the public sphere of opinion but through the multiple arenas where economic expertise intersects with the state and where numbers are produced through which liberal societies are governed.

Once again, our point is not to argue that there are no prominent economists who write or speak about public affairs in the mediatized public sphere, but that the analytic question about how economic expertise intervenes in public affairs should not be reduced to this rather narrow view. Moreover, comparative work on the economics profession (Fourcade 2009) demonstrates that the extent to which the public stance of economists corresponds to this image of the "public intellectual" is highly variable and dependent on specific institutional constellations, on the relations between the state, business, the academy, and the media, and the political cultures of expertise to which they gave rise. To be an economist and to intervene in public affairs means something quite different if you are an American, French, or British economist. The "centrality of market institutions to US political culture" and the consequent "definition of the economist by a technical, measurable form of competence" has meant that American economists intervene in the public sphere primarily by producing a "vast array of practical instruments that are widely used in policy and business" or by mobilizing economic knowledge as a "marketable political commodity that helps different groups with public claims fight one another" (8–9). French economists, in contrast, are shaped by a "national political culture and institutional makeup centered on the administrative exercise of public power" wherein they play the role of technocrats, and where economic knowledge is produced directly as part of the formulation of state policy, so economists intervene in public affairs by formulating policy, for example, by working for the Commissariat général du plan (11). In the United Kingdom, finally, a "political culture centered on small, tightly knit elite societies that traditionally enjoy great authority in producing public discourse" meant that a greater premium was placed on the "ability to communicate economic ideas in plain and eloquent language" through both interpersonal networks as well as writing directly to the general, educated public (9–11). Put differently, if British economists tend to fit more the image of the "public intellectual" as the engaged man of letters (as is evident in the essay on John Maynard Keynes by Roger Backhouse and Bradley Bateman, and the essay on Lionel Robbins by Susan Howson, both in this volume), this is because of the specific constellation connecting Oxbridge with the civil service and with elite media outlets and clubs. In this restricted milieu, an audience exists for the speech variant that is closest to the image of the "public intellectual." The American case, in comparison, best approximates the format of public intervention as technical performativity we discussed earlier: the tight linkage between research departments, businesses, and regulatory agencies providing the ideal ecology for it.

This is, of course, a simplified summary of a much more complex analysis. In reality, the different formats of intervention are co-present in each national case. The bifurcation of economics in France, for example, between state technocrats and academicians leads the latter to attempt to influence state policy by writing op-ed pieces in the major newspapers, while *clubs de réflexion* bring together academic economists, senior civil servants, journalists, and business and union leaders, forming a horizontal network through which economic ideas can influence the governing elites (Fourcade 2009, 232–33). This merely vindicates, however, our main point, namely, that once we consider how economic knowledge is mobilized to intervene in public affairs we are confronted with a plurality not only of agencies and formats of intervention but also of public arenas or spheres where such interventions take place. Economists intervene in public affairs when they write "directly" to the public in op-ed pieces or generalist books, but also when they have the ear of business leaders and civil servants in more-rarefied forums; when they produce position papers for think tanks or are trained by these to become "talking heads"; when they become advisers or advocates or expert witnesses on behalf of consumer organizations; and also when they work for state agencies or businesses to design markets or devise economic indicators.

The GDP as an Institutionalized Interface between Economic Expertise and Statecraft

The preparation of economic indicators and summary indexes may seem a dreary technical activity with none of the glamour associated with public intellectuals, yet it is a key form in which economic expertise intervenes in public affairs. Our example in this essay is the prodigious and, by now, four-decades-long collective attempt to provide a summary index of human welfare and economic progress that could replace, supplement, or correct the GDP. This collective attempt has recently achieved some evident success and publicity through the agency of the French government and the work of the Commission on the Measurement of Economic Performance and Social Progress (CMEPSP), headed by the economists Joseph Stiglitz, Amartya Sen, and Jean-Paul Fitoussi (2009). Yet it is important to note that the Stiglitz-Sen-Fitoussi project is but the most recent and most famous example of what had begun already in 1972 with James Tobin and William Nordhaus's work on the Measure of Economic Welfare (MEW) and was continued by a host of other economists working inside and outside academia, in nongovernmental organizations and think tanks, as well as in state economic and statistical agencies and international agencies ranging from the Organisation for Economic Co-operation and Development to the United Nations Development Programme (Afsa et al. 2009). In their report, Afsa et al. (2009) compile information on thirty extant indexes, but note that many more exist, which they could not cover.

We would like to begin, however, with a short history of the GDP itself. We argued earlier that economic expertise does not intervene in public affairs from without. It is plugged into the body of the Leviathan through various permanent ports, institutionalized interfaces between economic expertise and statecraft. The GDP, or more precisely the system of national accounts, represents such an institutionalized interface. To understand current efforts at public intervention by economists who prepare summary indexes, we first need to describe the terrain on which they take place, the quasi-public sphere that is the system of national accounts.

In a very general sense, economic indicators such as the GDP work in the same way as the Black-Scholes formula, or the other calculative devices we described under the heading of technical performativity. In a perfect market, economic actors would have perfect and complete information about economic activities and enough time to peruse and evaluate this information to arrive at the optimal investment decision. GDP, CPI, or an index of aggregate productivity trends are tools meant to equip the economic actor with computational proxies for the information that is lacking or cannot be evaluated within human finite time. But this analogy to performativity is incomplete and does not capture the historically specific way in which economic indicators such as the GDP developed and how they function in the public sphere.

The GDP owes its origins, in fact, to a transition from the point of view of the economic actor to that of the economic *governor*. The production of statistical series of economic aggregates at the National Bureau of Economic Research (NBER) began in the 1920s guided by Wesley Mitchell's theory of the business cycle. Mitchell thought that if business managers and other economic actors were equipped with these aggregate indicators as calculative devices, they would make sound investment decisions because they would take "the entire picture of the business economy in their calculations." Consequently, the business cycle would be eliminated or at least moderated (Breslau 2003, 405). Mitchell's ambition, therefore, was precisely to achieve what today is called "performativity." Economic expertise would equip business managers with index numbers so that they would be better able to calculate, better able to act as rational economic actors and thus render markets governable. But this is not how Mitchell's numbers ended up being used. Historians of the system of national accounting do not locate its origins in NBER's efforts during the 1920s but in the governmental reaction to the stock market crash of 1929 (Vanoli 2005, 16–18, 26–27). Simon Kuznets's (1934) classic estimate of total national income produced and national income paid out, to which current measures of GDP owe their provenance, was compiled in response to a request by the US Senate to estimate the extent to which the economy contracted during the Great Depression, 1929–32. The Senate directed the Department of Commerce to provide the estimate, but when it became evident that it did not have the means to do so, the request was forwarded to Mitchell at NBER, who suggested Kuznets.[5] Thus the origins of the GDP are when the techniques developed at NBER were called on to equip the economic governor with the means "to see where the economy has been and ... where it is going and the kinds of policies necessary for governments, and private groups or individuals to achieve their objectives" (Kendrick 1996, 2; Kapuria-Foreman and Perlman 1995, 1541; Kenessey 1994, 12–13). Similarly, the Bureau of Economic Analysis (2000) celebrates the GDP as "one of the great inventions of the 20th century" and

---

5. Kuznets delegated the task to two of his best students—Robert Nathan and Milton Gilbert—both already employed by the Department of Commerce.

speaks of it as a "beacon that help[s] policymakers steer the economy toward the key economic objectives."

The Senate wanted to know, in short, how bad the depression was, whether recovery was under way, and what else could be done. For this purpose, however, it needed more than just descriptive statistical aggregates. These had to be linked to one another as a system of causal variables within a framework that explained how they related to one another and what levers they provided for policy. Ultimately, this framework was provided by Keynes, but before Keynes—and in an important sense this provided the ground on which Keynes's theory was built—it was provided by the introduction of accounting methods and tools, especially double-entry bookkeeping, turning economic statistics into "social accounting" (later "national accounting") and turning the statistical series into a system of controlling accounts. Kuznets drew on the work done by Irving Fisher to introduce accounting methods into economics. Thus in 1934, before the publication of the *General Theory*, Kuznets's empirical analysis had already begun measuring these causal variables, to which Keynes would give a more solid theoretical grounding. Theory and measurement would be adjusted to one another, says Zoltan Kenessey (1994, 112), because they responded to the same policy needs. What needs to be added is that they were also formulated from the same point of view of "social accounting," the point of view of the economic governor now conceived as the accountant balancing the books of the national economy (see also Vanoli 2005, 19).

There is a tight linkage, indeed, between the GDP, the application of accounting methods to economic analysis, Keynesianism, and the invention of the "economy" as an object of knowledge and government. As Breslau (2003, 380, 407–8) and Mitchell (1998) convincingly demonstrate, the term *the economy* simply did not appear in economic texts before the 1940s, certainly not in the sense given to it today as a bounded totality of economic activity abstracted from social life. *The economy* postdated the huge effort of compiling national statistical series of production, prices, wages, and so on, and only through this effort could it come to designate the aggregate of a nation's productive activities. An essential part of the whole exercise was to define what is considered economic activity and what is not, something that did not bother at all the earlier political economists. Kuznets and colleagues "pre-formed" the economy by disentangling what they considered obvious evidence of "participation . . . in the economic activity of the nation," that is, "work for wages, profit or salary, or . . . capital investment in industry" from what they considered to be "non-economic" activities. The most obvious of these was the exclusion of unpaid domestic work, but Kuznets and colleagues also excluded other items that previous economists have included in their own estimates, such as "imputed net rental," that is, income accruing to people living in their own homes (Kuznets 1934, 4). By the same token, however, only through the huge effort of producing the concepts and measures of "social accounting" could the "national economy" come to be understood as the object of "macroeconomics," that is, of a causal theory that treated it as a relatively bounded system of interrelated flows. The true beginnings of modern macroeconomics, said Hicks, was not the *General Theory* (1936) but Keynes's pamphlet *How to Pay for the War* (1940), which worked out a national accounting structure for the British economy (quoted in Kurabayashi 1994, 96–98), thereby specifying in measurable forms the Keynesian variables. This was the context in which the GDP or GNP finally came into being. While the term *GNP* was already used during the 1930s, and Kuznets's analysis certainly gestured at it, World War II provided the final impetus for the formation of a system of national accounts, and the annual measurement and publication of GDP figures, in both the United States and Britain. In both cases, the GDP and related measures were required in order to address questions touching on the war effort: How to pay for the war? How to determine the correct balance between defense and civilian spending ("guns or butter tradeoff")? How to avoid spiraling inflation at the end of war? What would be the effect of demobilization on employment? (Kurabayashi 1994, 95; Kenessey 1994, 111; Vanoli 2005, 21–23).

From this beginning, the system of national accounts evolved into an "articulated macro level statistical response to the operational demands of a Keynesian economics" (Ward 2004, 10). At the heart of later critiques of the GDP there would be precisely this point that it is not simply an objective measure of the economy but a translation of the concern with full employment and growth—central to Keynesian theory, but also intimately tied to the postwar context in the United States and the UK and to the ideological struggles of the Cold War—into a quantitative standard. The universalization of this standard by the United Nations in the 1950s thus biased economic policies in ways that were often harmful to third world countries and to substantive conceptions of human welfare (7, 63–67), a point made and bemoaned even by Kuznets himself (Kapuria-Foreman and Perlman 1995, 1532–33).

We have engaged in this rather brief history of the origins of the GDP and the system of national accounts in order to give substance to our claim that the system of national accounts is a public sphere of sorts, and that consequently the design of alternatives to the GDP could be analyzed as a form of intervention in public affairs. Economic indicators like the GDP are tools meant to provide decision makers with a bird's-eye view of the economy and permit them to make rational decisions, but they are also "black boxes" that obscure from view the assumptions, policy choices, and history of usage they encapsulate. Thus Keynes's (1936, 383) oft-quoted adage that "practical men, who believe themselves to be quite exempt from any intellectual influence, are usually the slaves of some defunct economist" is particularly apt when considering the impact of economic indicators generally, and of the GDP specifically.[6] As noted above, it encapsulated within itself a Keynesian conception of macroeconomic management, a certain role for the economic governor, and a restrictive definition of human welfare and the activities contributing to it. No less importantly, the activities of compiling, calculating, and using the GDP occupy a multitude of economists both inside and outside government: to the 18 percent of new economics PhDs being employed in government (Siegfried and Stock 1999), we would add a probably equal proportion of new PhDs employed in the private sector whose concrete working activities would consist primarily of perusing daily the indicators and tables produced by the system of national accounts, and another large proportion of academic economists who use these as the primary data for their research. The activities of compiling, calculating, and using the GDP thus constitute a permanent port through which economic expertise is constantly brought to bear on some of the most central issues in the public sphere—how to define and measure the public good, or human welfare—that the state is entrusted with protecting and increasing. Once this port exists, it becomes possible,

---

6. A good example is the indicator of aggregate productivity trends. As Fred Block and Gene Burns (1986) show, it was compiled as part of an underconsumptionist explanation for the Great Depression. Productivity gains, it was argued, would lead to weakening demand if wages do not rise as fast, or prices decline accordingly. Then, through the efforts of the Department of Labor, a specific version of the indicator became institutionalized as the linchpin in the post–World War II bargain between organized labor and big corporations. The indicator thus encapsulated within itself a theory not only of economic processes but no less importantly of the "subject" of government, if you will: namely, a conception of the proper role of the economic governor in steering and stabilizing the economy, encapsulated in the wage and price guidelines issued by the Council of Economic Advisers during the Kennedy administration. When the indicator begun showing declines in aggregate productivity in the late 1960s, this "fact" framed political debates and empowered wage restraint policies, even though, as Block and Burns show, slightly different versions of the indicator would have produced dramatically different trends. Decision makers were the "slaves" of the defunct economists who constructed the specific version of the indicator and of the underconsumptionist theory encapsulated in it.

and indeed inescapable, to intervene in public affairs by changing some aspects of the economic expertise flowing through it. No surprise, then, that seemingly technical and abstruse debates about how to calculate the GDP can involve quite vehement disputes, reflect policy disagreements, pitting one against the other divergent political ideologies and the interests of nation-states (Popkin 2000; Lower 1990; Ward 2004, 64–67; Aukurst 1994, 43).

Alternatives to the GDP as Public Interventions

"Economists all know," declared Nordhaus and Tobin (1972, 4), that "maximization of GNP is not a proper objective of policy . . . and yet their everyday use of GNP as the standard measure of economic performance apparently conveys the impression that they are evangelistic worshipers of GNP." To correct this impression and to respond to the "limits to growth" critics, they constructed a Measure of Economic Welfare (MEW) that was largely a rearrangement of the items of the national accounts so that what it measured was not output but household consumption (5). They used this measure to reply to the critics of growth-oriented policies—since the MEW grew at a rate only slightly below the GNP. Growth is not obsolete, they declared: "The broad picture of secular progress which the [GNP and similar measures] convey remains after correction of their most obvious deficiencies" (24). This essentially conservative move, however, became the first salvo in a much longer offensive that consistently tracked the two issues tackled by Tobin and Nordhaus, namely, the irrelevance of output measures for estimating human welfare and the problem of sustainability (4). Why is it that a relatively conservative or defensive position in the public debate about limits to growth has become the forerunner of a much more radical effort—as we show below—to revise economic priorities, an effort that now counts Tobin and Nordhaus as its founding fathers in its retrospective histories? The answer is obvious. It has nothing to do with *what* Tobin and Nordhaus said, but with *how* they said it. What mattered to those who followed in their footsteps was the fact that Tobin and Nordhaus showed, from within NBER, that it is possible to construct an alternative *number*. What counted most, what was innovative, was the *mode* of intervention in public affairs, not the specific position they took in the debate.

Tobin and Nordhaus opened the floodgates. In the years immediately following there were several attempts to produce an alternative index of welfare, one that would show—contra Tobin and Nordhaus—that growth as measured by the GDP was increasingly irrelevant to the more fundamental goal of human welfare. Among these were the Japanese Net National Welfare (NNW) indicator in 1973, the Economic Aspects of Welfare (EAW) index (Zolatas 1981), the Physical Quality of Life Index (PQLI) (Overseas Development Council 1980), and the Index of Sustainable Economic Welfare (ISEW) (Daly and Cobb 1989), which later became the Genuine Progress Indicator (GPI) (Talberth, Cobb, and Slattery 2007). By far the most successful and influential of these, however, is the Human Development Index (HDI) produced by the United Nations Development Programme (UNDP) from 1990 onward.

The story of how the HDI came about is told by Frederick Wherry (2004, 161). The main driving force behind the HDI was Mahbub ul Haq, a British-trained Pakistani economist who worked at the World Bank (1970–82), served as Pakistan's minister of planning and finance (1982–88), and then was drafted as special adviser to the UNDP (1989–96). Haq—a close personal friend of Amartya K. Sen, later winner of the Nobel Prize in economics—wanted "to shift the focus of development economics from national income accounting to people centered policies" (Fukuda-Parr 2003, 303, 305). That is, he wanted to intervene in public affairs and set a new agenda of policy priorities.

Haq, however, did not create the HDI by himself. Compiling the HDI was collective work by the Human Development Report Team with a staff of five statisticians and economists, and a much larger group of consultants drawn from the Society for International Development (SID), an international nonprofit acting as knowledge broker to foster sustainable development. Sen was the most famous of these consultants, but all the others were also highly respected economists and development professionals (Wherry 2004, 161). Today, the Human Development Report Team consists of eighteen regular staff members who are statisticians, economists, MBAs as well as one anthropologist.[7]

Even though the team was assembled under the auspices of the UNDP, an administrative unit of the UN, it cultivated a measure of social, physical, and administrative distance from it. Wherry (2004, 163–64) shows quite convincingly that the initial Human Development Report Team that first compiled the HDI enjoyed a semi-outsider status that permitted it to

---

7. See the list of team members, along with links to capsule biographies of each member, at hdr.undp.org/en/contacts/about/ (accessed November 8, 2012).

act independently to reshape the agenda of development discourse and policy. The consultants and the staff were newly recruited to the UN and knew each other from SID. As one of them recollected, the team "wasn't a UNDP or a UN thing ... it was very outside of the UN, [and it was] full of a lot of people who are not accountable to the UN." The team occupied offices physically separate from UNDP and enjoyed a protective umbrella supplied by the chief administrator of the UNDP, Bill Draper, a former venture capitalist. In this sense, the initial team with its consultants was more akin to an "epistemic community" than a bureaucracy.

This semiseparation at the institutional and personnel level was balanced by continuity at the level of the actual product of the group's work. The *Human Development Report* and the HDI were crafted so they bore "strong family resemblance" to the World Bank's *World Development Report*, and also to the GNP. On this latter issue there was dissension within the group. Sen and others were concerned that the full complexity of human capabilities could not be captured in a single index, but Haq responded to their doubts by insisting that "only a single number could shift the attention of policy-makers from material output to human well-being as a real measure of progress." He argued emphatically that "we need a measure ... of the same level of vulgarity as the GNP—just one number—but a measure that is not as blind to the social aspect of human lives as the GNP is." And "vulgar," or simplistic, indeed it is. The HDI is a composite weighted index combining scores for economic growth (GDP), health (life expectancy at birth), and education (adult literacy rate and student enrollment rates). It thus captures a very general notion of "welfare" as material well-being and of "capabilities" as being healthy and educated. Despite Sen's doubts, Haq was convinced that a single, composite index number would be much more effective than the written reports in "convincing the public, academics, and policy-makers that they should evaluate development by advances in human well-being and not only by advances in the economy" (Wherry 2004, 165–66; Fukuda-Parr 2003, 303, 305). Put differently, Haq's judgment was that in order to achieve the public aims of Sen's intellectual work, the format of intervention had to be changed from one that corresponded to the classical image of the public intellectual (which Sen embodies to great effect) to the different format of an index number, however simplistic and "vulgar," ultimately because it can be plugged into already existing institutions and networks of policymaking.

If the classic public intellectual is an outsider, a prophet, Haq and the Human Development Report team positioned themselves as insiders/outsiders, structurally equivalent to what Georg Simmel (1950) identified as the position of the "stranger." We think this sort of insider-outsider status is typical of "specific intellectuals" and in fact illustrates our point that intervention happens through an established port or interface. Wherry (2004, 164) comments insightfully that this "insider-outsider" status is what permitted the team to formulate the HDI as a bold departure from business as usual—because they were independent of the administrative routines and political pressures of the UN—yet, also as a highly effective intervention in development discourse and policy, because they acted under the auspices of UNDP and enjoyed the legitimacy, resources, and attention it commanded. If they had been either insiders (burcaucrats) or outsiders (public intellectuals), they would not have been able to craft this effective intervention in public affairs. It was the *movement* of bringing the outsiders in, and the insiders out, along preexisting conduits represented by SID and by the system of national accounts that explains the HDI's success as public intervention.

And success (or notoriety) it did enjoy. The first report in 1990 provoked a firestorm of criticism (and attention) precisely because of the table comparing where countries ranked on the HDI—the United States, second in GNP per capita, fell to nineteenth behind most of the advanced industrialized countries, while Cuba shot up forty-four places higher than where it ranked by GNP. Yet the report and the index were adopted by the UN and were plugged into its normal operations. By 2000, the UNDP was printing one hundred thousand copies of the report in ten different languages for distribution. Many national governments now produce their own "human development" report, in hopes of improving their ranking (Wherry 2004, 153, 166–67). The assessment of many observers is that the HDI managed to change public discourse about development, shifting it from being centered on growth and bringing attention to other dimensions of development. It was an effective intervention in public affairs.

However successful, the HDI was also deeply flawed. Its measurement of welfare was crude, failing to account for income distribution, subjective dimensions of welfare, and the critical literature pointing to the importance of nonmarket services (Waring 1988), and it did not touch at all on the matter of sustainability. Hence its publication merely led to even more new indexes. Information about a few representative examples is summarized in table 1. A few points regarding the agencies, modes, and targets of intervention are noteworthy.

The first point is that the work of constructing and deconstructing economic indicators, as reflected in HDI and these later indicators, is

Table 1 Projects Proposing Replacements or Corrections of the GDP

Index	Organization	Staff	Type and Construction
Human Development Index (HDI)	United Nations Development Programme (UNDP)	Human Development Report Team composed of statisticians, economists, business specialists, and anthropologists	Composite weighted index: GDP + life expectancy at birth + average of adult literacy rate (2/3) and student enrollment rate at first, second, and third level (1/3). Each is rescaled based on its likely range of variation and then combined.
Happy Planet Index (HPI)	Centre for Well-Being, New Economics Foundation (NEF), nonprofit	Economists, research staff with degrees in operations research, psychology, and political science	A composite efficiency measure that multiplies life expectancy at birth (taken from HDI) by subjective life satisfaction measure (from Gallup or the World Values Survey), and divides these by ecological footprint (from the Global Footprint Network), measured in units of land required to provide for resource requirements and absorb CO_2 emissions per capita. This index is intended to measure the efficiency with which countries convert the earth's resources into well-being for their citizens.
Genuine Progress Indicator (GPI)	Redefining Progress, a public policy think tank, nonprofit	Environmental economists, theologians, lawyers, former politicians	Composite weighted index aiming to measure sustainable welfare by adding the value of nonmarket services generating welfare (such as domestic labor, public goods, and education) to private consumption (weighted by an index of income distribution), and then deducting from it the private and public costs of natural deterioration caused by economic activity. Then deducting or adding from the result the value of net capital investment and the balance of foreign trade.
Environmental Performance Index (EPI)	Earth Institute, Columbia University, and the Center for Environmental Law and Policy, Yale University	Economists, statisticians, research staff draw on reports from economists and environmental scientists	Composite weighted index based on time series. Score in each area is based on gap between current results and policy target. Scores are then weighted and aggregated into scores for "eco-system vitality" and "environmental health," which are combined into the final score. This index is not intended to replace the GDP, but could be combined with either a "corrected GDP," a composite index, or a dashboard of indicators approach.
Report	Commission on the Measurement of Economic Performance and Social Progress (CMEPSP), French government	Economists, statisticians, state officials	No index yet, but a report pointing out the deficiencies of composite indexes and suggesting a comprehensive revision of the system of national accounts including correcting the GDP, measuring well-being in objective and subjective ways, and measuring sustainability.

collective, interdisciplinary, and long-term. Stiglitz, Sen, and Fitoussi provide the intellectual glamour and public face of the CMEPSP, but there are twenty-two other economists and social scientists on the commission, including Kenneth Arrow, Kemal Dervis, Daniel Kahneman, and Robert Putnam. More importantly, a team of nine Rapporteurs consisting of leading French statisticians and economists provides much of the deeper analysis on which the work of this commission relies (Stiglitz, Sen, and Fitoussi 2009). And if the work of the commission, which for the moment culminated merely in a report and recommendations, were to be translated into a revision of the system of national accounts, a new synthetic index and a "dashboard" of additional relevant indicators as foreseen, it would surely take a small army of not only junior economists and statisticians but also environmental scientists, policy analysts, psychologists, sociologists, and the all-important accountants to compile it. Similarly, the Happy Planet Index (HPI), which purports to measure "the relative efficiency with which nations convert the planet's natural resources into long and happy lives for their citizens," is compiled at the Centre for Well-Being at the New Economics Foundation (NEF), by a large team of fellows and researchers with backgrounds in economics, operations research, experimental psychology, political science, and so on.[8] The Genuine Progress Indicator (GPI) is a composite index developed on the basis of the earlier ISEW. It is compiled by a team of economists and environmental experts at Redefining Progress, a public policy think tank in Oakland, California.[9] The Environmental Performance Index (EPI)—"a composite index tracking a diverse set of socioeconomic, environmental, and institutional indicators that characterize and influence environmental sustainability at the national scale"—is compiled jointly by the Earth Institute at Columbia University and the Center for Environmental Law and Policy at Yale University. A core team of five investigators draws on several dozen expert contributors, some of whom are economists and many are environmental scientists.[10] In short, the production of indexes and economic indicators is the work of collectives composed of a large number of individuals representing different disciplines, forms of expertise, and institutional affiliations.

   8. For more on the Happy Planet Index, visit its website at www.happyplanetindex.org/ (accessed November 8, 2012).
   9. For more on Redesigning Progress, visit its website at rprogress.org/index.htm (accessed November 8, 2012).
   10. The 2012 report of the EPI can be found at epi.yale.edu/sites/default/files/downloads/2012–epi-full-report.pdf (accessed November 8, 2012).

The second point is about the format of public intervention in these examples, which is not an op-ed, a petition, a book, or a blog, but typically a number. Granted, the number is usually surrounded by a whole lot of words: programmatic launch statements, "discussion," technical clarifications, and so on, but ultimately the whole endeavor of producing summary index numbers would not make sense if the participants did not believe that, so to speak, a single number is worth a thousand words. Unlike HDI, the numbers now incorporate a measure of sustainability. The GPI incorporates the estimated costs of air pollution and destruction of the natural environment. The HPI measures the ecological efficiency with which well-being is provided by incorporating a measure of "ecological footprint" in the denominator. The EPI measures the degree to which a country is moving toward the policy goals of environmental health and ecosystem vitality.

The exception that proves the rule is the report coauthored by Stiglitz, Sen, and Fitoussi. They explicitly reject the idea that their target should be a single index number. There is a sense that this report, coming two decades after the HDI, now marks the end of an era. As noted earlier, the French team compiled information on thirty extant indexes, but noted that many more exist (Afsa et al. 2009). In such a saturated field, it is perhaps no longer a meaningful intervention to produce one more number, one more acronym, which most likely will disappear among the many similar sounding indexes, or at best would be incorporated like the HDI alongside the GDP, but only as supporting cast. Instead, Stiglitz, Sen, and Fitoussi (2009) did two things. First, they compiled an exhaustive and critical review of all extant indexes, including the GDP, and the different approaches taken in compiling them. Pointing out the deficiencies, they argue for the need to create a new international system of national accounts capable of calculating a corrected measure for GDP (which would include nonmarket services), objective and subjective measures of well-being, and a measure of sustainability. Put differently, their report opens up the "black boxes" of which economic indicators, both mainstream and alternative ones, are made, pillages their components, and proposes a new set of accounts that would pre-form "the economy" in a different way. This new system of national accounts would define, for later decision makers, not only the facts on which they base their calculations but also their own proper role as governors of economic life. This is exactly what is being attempted also by the other three measures surveyed here, although in more piecemeal fashion. The task of the economic governor, they argue, is not to maximize growth but to maximize sustainable welfare and well-being, and to achieve this goal the government needs an appropriate index—indeed, a whole new system of national accounts – that brings into calculation what were previously deemed incalculable externalities.

The third point is about the target of intervention common to these projects. To our mind, they all are built around a similar inside-outside movement as we saw with the HDI. It is true that the GPI, HPI, and EPI are produced by either independent nonprofit organizations (essentially, think tanks) or university institutes, and thus they exhibit a measure of independence and distance from national or international bureaucracies. At the same time, however, they seek to plug their indexes into the existing ports or conduits through which economic expertise flows into the state, and therefore they cultivate social ties that facilitate this plug-in. Redefining Progress, where the GPI is calculated, although it was begun by a renegade environmental economist and a theologian, is now a respected public policy think tank, with a former Republican congressman as executive director, a host of corporate funders, and former managers from PG&E, Apple, and other corporations on its board of directors.[11] It has offered its GPI as a "guide for public policy" and had some success persuading the state of Maryland to adopt it.[12] An affiliated think tank, GPI-Atlantic, has taken up the same cause in Nova Scotia, Canada, and provides regional government there with policy briefs as well as with a comprehensive system of Nova Scotia GPI Accounts (Pannozzo and Colman 2009).

The New Economics Foundation (NEF), where HPI is produced, characterizes itself as a "think and do tank" that is in the business of "promoting innovative solutions that challenge mainstream thinking on economic, environment and social issues." It is one of the biggest think tanks in the UK with a permanent staff of fifty and a continuous set of activities apart from compiling the GPI, including advocacy among

---

11. Our information regarding Redefining Progress comes from Source Watch, which is published by the Center for Media and Democracy and can be found at www.sourcewatch.org/index.php?title=Redefining_Progress (accessed November 8, 2012). According to the website of the Center for Media and Democracy, Source Watch is a "collaborative resource for citizens and journalists looking for documented information about the corporations, industries, and people trying to influence public policy and public opinion" (www.sourcewatch.org/index.php/SourceWatch).

12. See the description of Maryland's GPI at www.green.maryland.gov/mdgpi/ (accessed November 8, 2012).

members of Parliament and seeding other grassroots organizations such as Jubilee 2000, the Ethical Trading Initiative, and so on. While it targets some of its campaigns to policymakers, it operates at a much more populist and grassroots level than Redefining Progress. When HPI was first constructed in 2006, the report was published on the Web, and NEF proudly reports that within two days it was downloaded by a million users in 185 countries. The whole initiative to form NEF came out of The Other Economic Summit (TOES), which challenged "the right of the G7 leaders to speak for the economic future of the planet." It was supposed to be a permanent economic secretariat for TOES, but evolved into something much more far-ranging. NEF emphasizes that its proposals are often designed and run in participation with "local people" and that it "work[s] with all sections of society in the UK and internationally—civil society, government, individuals, businesses and academia."[13]

The Earth Institute at Columbia University, which partners with the Yale Center for Environmental Law and Policy to calculate the EPI, is not your garden-variety academic institute. It is led by one of the best-known and better politically connected US economists, Jeffrey Sachs. It is a mammoth enterprise comprising thirty centers and a staff of 850. Earth Institute experts advise national governments and the United Nations on issues related to sustainable development, combining expertise in economics with basic science and advocacy. Its advisory board includes economic luminaries such as Kenneth Arrow, celebrities such as Bono, and financiers such as George Soros.[14] In short, while it is physically located at a university, and while its activities center on an academic core, it is best analyzed as inhabiting an interface between academia, government, business, and the media, as do other think tanks (Medvetz 2012).

CMEPSP, of course, differs from these three organizations by being conducted officially under the auspices of the French government, but it is plain that it enjoys a similar insider-outsider status as did the HDI team. The involvement of the French president served, in fact, to buffer the initiative from bureaucratic pressures, and the intellectual glamour commanded by Stiglitz, Sen, and Fitoussi did the rest. The report identifies its audience as composed of political leaders and relevant policymakers, who

---

13. www.happyplanetindex.org/about (accessed March 22, 2013). A history of NEF can be found on the organization's website at www.neweconomics.org/content/history-nef (accessed November 8, 2012).

14. For a complete list of its advisory board members, see earth.columbia.edu/articles/view/1006 (accessed November 8, 2012).

use the indicators to formulate policies, as well as the academic community and the national statistical offices, and only lastly civil society organizations to the extent that they are producers and users of statistics (Stiglitz, Sen, and Fitoussi 2009).

It is clear from the emphasis on doing, on solutions, on policymakers, on the users of statistics, and on working with local people, that the target of intervention is not *opinion* but a semitechnical, semipolitical network into which these organizations aim to plug their indicator. Or more precisely, some of these organizations indeed pay a good deal of attention to mobilizing and shaping opinion. NEF has a charter that supporters can sign online. NEF, Redefining Progress, and the Earth Institute all employ communications and public affairs staff who work to guarantee media space and attention to the research staff. Many on their staff write blogs and op-eds. But compared with the effort to have the GPI, HPI, or EPI adopted as a basis for analysis and policy, this work at the level of opinion is the least original and least important aspect of their intervention in public affairs. Some of these organizations identify themselves as belonging to a burgeoning new field of "green economics," understood as an alternative to neoclassical or mainstream economics. Green economics are, quite plainly, neither a purely academic pursuit nor pure advocacy or opinion but a technical network of experts, organizations, and calculative devices that extends along the same conduit or port by which economic expertise is plugged into the state, namely, the system of national accounts. This network typically uses as its input government data and components from the system of national accounts, and its output as well is meant to plug back into government policy in the form of index numbers, policy position papers, and, most ambitiously with CMEPSP, a complete overhaul of the system of national accounts to reflect a new epistemic and moral agenda. Taken as a whole, this network definitely fits Peter Haas's (1992, 3) concept of "epistemic community," namely, a far-flung network of "professionals with recognized expertise and competence in a particular domain and an authoritative claim to policy-relevant knowledge within that domain or issue area," who are tied together by shared truth claims and a public moral stance (see also Adler and Haas 1992; Keck and Sikkink 1998; King 2005). In this field at least, this network or epistemic community is a far more effective "collective intellectual" than public intellectuals addressing public opinion, as it gradually has been changing not only the agenda of public policy but its very infrastructure.

References

Adler, E., and P. M. Haas. 1992. "Conclusion: Epistemic Communities, World Order, and the Creation of a Reflective Research Program." *International Organization* 46 (1): 367–90.

Afsa, Cédric, et al. 2009. "Survey of Existing Approaches to Measuring Socio-economic Progress." Commission on the Measurement of Economic Performance and Social Progress. www.stiglitz-sen-fitoussi.fr.

Alonso, William, and Paul Star. 1987. *The Politics of Numbers*. New York: Sage Foundation.

Aukurst, Odd. 1994. "The Scandinavian Contribution to National Accounting." In Kenessey 1994, 16–65.

Bauman, Zygmunt. 1987. *Legislators and Interpreters: On Modernity, Post-modernity, and Intellectuals*. Cambridge: Polity.

Bell, Daniel. 1960. *The End of Ideology*. Glencoe, Ill.: Free Press.

Benda, J. (1927) 1928. *The Treason of the Intellectuals*. New York: William Morrow.

Berkowitz, Nitza. 1996. "On 'The Homemaker and National Accounting.'" [In Hebrew.] *Theoria ve-Bikoret* 9:189–97.

Binkley, Robert C. 1928. "The Concept of Public Opinion in the Social Sciences." *Social Forces* 6 (3): 389–96.

Block, Fred, and Gene A. Burns. 1986. "Productivity as a Social Problem: The Uses and Misuses of Social Indicators." *American Sociological Review* 51 (6): 767–80.

Bourdieu, Pierre. (1992) 1996. "For a Corporatism of the Universal." In *The Rules of Art: Genesis and Structure of the Literary Field*, 337–48. Stanford: Stanford University Press.

Breslau, Daniel. 1998. *In Search of the Unequivocal: The Political Economy of Measurement in US Labor Market Policy*. London: Praeger.

———. 2003. "Economics Invents the Economy: Mathematics, Statistics, and Models in the Work of Irving Fisher and Wesley Mitchell." *Theory and Society* 32 (3): 379–411.

———. 2011. "What Do Market Designers Do When They Design Markets? Economists as Consultants to the Redesign of Wholesale Electricity Markets in the US." In *Social Knowledge in the Making*, edited by Charles Camic, Neil Gross, and Michele Lamont, 379–404. Chicago: University of Chicago Press.

Bruce-Briggs, B., ed. 1979. *The New Class?* New York: McGraw Hill.

Bureau of Economic Analysis. 2000. "GDP: One of the Great Inventions of the 20th Century." *Survey of Current Business*, January. www.bea.gov/scb/account_articles/general/0100od/maintext.htm.

Callon, Michel. 1998. "Introduction: The Embeddedness of Economic Markets in Economics." In *The Laws of the Markets*, edited by Michel Callon, 1–57. Oxford: Blackwell.

Daly, H., and J. Cobb. 1989. *For the Common Good*. Boston: Beacon.

Desrosières, Alain. 2008. *Gouverner par les nombres*. Paris: Presses Des Mines, Paristech.

Dewey, J. 1927. *The Public and Its Problems*. Athens: Ohio University Press.

Donatich, J. 2001. "The Future of the Public Intellectual: A Forum." *Nation*, February 12, 25–35, www.thenation.com/doc/20010212/forum.
Eyal, Gil. 2012. "Spaces between Fields." In *Pierre Bourdieu and Historical Analysis*, edited by Phil Gorski, 158–82. Durham, N.C.: Duke University Press.
Eyal, Gil, and Larissa Buchholz. 2010. "From the Sociology of Intellectuals to the Sociology of Interventions." *Annual Review of Sociology* 36:117–37.
Folbre, Nancy. 1989. "Women's Work and Women's Households: Gender Bias in the US Census." *Social Research* 56 (3): 545–69.
Foucault, Michel. 1991. "Governmentality." In *The Foucault Effect: Studies in Governmentality*, edited by G. Burchell, C. Gordon, and P. Miller. Chicago: University of Chicago Press.
———. 2000. "Truth and Power." In *Power*, vol. 3 of *Essential Works of Michel Foucault*, edited by P. Rabinow and J. D. Faubion, 111–33. New York: New Press.
Fourcade, Marion. 2009. *Economists and Societies*. Princeton: Princeton University Press.
Fukuda-Parr, Sakiko. 2003. "The Human Development Paradigm: Operationalizing Sen's Ideas on Capabilities." *Feminist Economics* 9 (2–3): 301–17.
Fuller, S. 2004. "Intellectuals: An Endangered Species in the Twenty-First Century?" *Economy and Society* 33:463–83.
Gieryn, T. F. 1999. *Cultural Boundaries of Science: Credibility on the Line*. Chicago: University of Chicago Press.
Gouldner, Alvin W. 1975–76. "Prologue to a Theory of Revolutionary Intellectuals." *Telos* 26:3–36.
———. 1979. *The Future of Intellectuals and the Rise of the New Class*. New York: Seabury.
Haas, P. M. 1992. "Introduction: Epistemic Communities and International Policy." *International Organization* 46 (1): 1–35.
Habermas, Jürgen. 1970. "Technology and Science as Ideology." In *Towards a Rational Society*, 81–127. Boston: Beacon.
Jacobs, Ronald, and Eleanor Townsley. 2012. *The Space of Opinion: Media Intellectuals and the Public Sphere*. Oxford: Oxford University Press.
Jacoby, Russell. 1987. *The Last Intellectuals*. New York: Basic Books.
Kapuria-Foreman, Vibha, and Mark Perlman. 1995. "An Economic Historian's Economist: Remembering Simon Kuznets." *Economic Journal* 105 (433): 1524–47.
Keck, M., and K. Sikkink. 1998. *Activists beyond Borders: Advocacy Networks in International Politics*. Ithaca: Cornell University Press.
Kellner, D. 1997. "Intellectuals, the New Public Spheres, and Techno-politics. *New Political Science* 41–42:169–88.
Kendrick, John W. 1996. *The New System of National Accounts*. Dordrecht: Kluwer.
Kenessey, Zoltan. 1994. *The Accounts of Nations*. Amsterdam: IOS Press.
Keynes, J. M. 1936. *The General Theory of Employment, Interest, and Money*. London: Macmillan.
King, M. R. 2005. "Epistemic Communities and the Diffusion of Ideas: Central Bank Reform in the United Kingdom." *West European Politics* 28 (1): 94–123.

Konrad, G., and Ivan Szelenyi. 1979. *The Intellectuals on the Road to Class Power.* New York: Harcourt Brace Jovanovich.

Kurabayashi, Yoshimasa. 1994. "Keynes' *How to Pay for the War* and Its Influence on Postwar National Accounting." In Kenessey 1994, 93–108.

Kuznets, Simon. 1934. "National Income, 1929–1932." *National Bureau of Economic Research Bulletin*, no. 49 (June 7): 1–12.

Latour, Bruno. 1987. *Science in Action: How to Follow Scientists and Engineers through Society.* Cambridge: Harvard University Press.

———. 2005. "From Realpolitik to Dingpolitik." In Latour and Weibel 2005, 14–41.

Latour, Bruno, and Peter Weibel, eds. 2005. *Making Things Public: Atmospheres of Democracy.* Cambridge: MIT Press.

Lippmann, Walter. 1922. *Public Opinion.* New York: Free Press.

———. 1927. *The Phantom Public.* New Brunswick, N.J.: Transaction Books.

Lower, Milton D. 1990. "A Type-of-Product System of National Accounts." *Journal of Economic Issues* 24 (2): 371–79.

MacKenzie, Donald. 2007. "Is Economics Performative? Option Theory and the Construction of Derivatives Markets." In MacKenzie, Muniesa, and Siu 2007, 54–86.

MacKenzie, Donald, and Yuval Milo. 2003. "Constructing a Market, Performing Theory: The Historical Sociology of a Financial Derivatives Exchange." *American Journal of Sociology* 109 (1): 107–45.

MacKenzie, Donald, Fabian Muniesa, and Lucia Siu. 2007. *Do Economists Make Markets? On the Performativity of Economics.* Princeton: Princeton University Press.

Markoff, J., and Veronica Montecinos. 1993. "The Ubiquitous Rise of Economists." *Journal of Public Policy* 13 (1): 37–68.

Marres, N. 2005. "Issues Spark a Public into Being: A Key but Often Forgotten Point of the Lippmann-Dewey Debate." In Latour and Weibel 2005, 208–17.

Medvetz, Tom. 2012. *The Rise of Think Tanks in America: Merchants of Policy and Power.* Chicago: University of Chicago Press.

Miller, Peter. 2004. "Governing by Numbers: Why Calculative Practices Matter." In *The Blackwell Cultural Economy Reader*, edited by Ash Amin and Nigel Thrift, 179–90. Malden, U.K.: Blackwell.

Miller, Peter, and Nikolas Rose. 1990. "Governing Economic Life." *Economy and Society* 19 (1): 1–31.

Mirowski, Philip. 2002. *Machine Dreams: Economics Becomes a Cyborg Science.* Cambridge: Cambridge University Press.

Mitchell, T. 1991. "The Limits of the State: Beyond Statist Approaches and Their Critics." *American Political Science Review* 85 (1): 77–96.

———. 1998. "Fixing the Economy." *Cultural Studies* 12 (1): 82–101.

Nordhaus, William, and James Tobin. 1972. "Is Growth Obsolete?" In *Economic Growth*, vol. 5 of *Economic Research: Retrospect and Prospect*, edited by William Nordhaus and James Tobin, 1–80. New York: NBER.

Overseas Development Council. 1980. *The United States and World Development.* New York: Praeger.

Pannozzo, Linda, and Ronald Colman. 2009. *New Policy Directions for Nova Scotia: Using the Genuine Progress Indicator to Count What Matters.* GPIAtlantic. www.gpiatlantic.org/pdf/integrated/new_policy_directions.pdf.
Popkin, J. 2000. "Data Watch: The U.S. National Income and Product Accounts." *Journal of Economic Perspectives* 14 (2): 215–24.
Porter, Theodore. 1995. *Trust in Numbers.* Princeton: Princeton University Press.
Posner, R. 2001. *Public Intellectuals: A Study in Decline.* Cambridge: Harvard University Press.
Rose, N. 1992. "Engineering the Human Soul: Analyzing Psychological Expertise." *Science in Context* 5 (2): 351–69.
Rose, N., P. O'Malley, and M. Valverde. 2006. "Governmentality." *Annual Review of Law and Social Science* 2:83–104.
Sapiro, Giselle. 2009. "Modeles d'intervention politique des intellectuels: Le cas français." *Actes de la recherche en sciences sociales* 176–77:8–31.
Siegfried, John J., and Wendy A. Stock. 1999. "The Labor Market for New PhD Economists." *Journal of Economic Perspectives* 13 (3): 115–34.
Simmel, Georg. 1950. "The Stranger." In *The Sociology of Georg Simmel,* edited by Kurt Lewin, 402–8. New York: Free Press.
Stiglitz, Joseph E., Amartya Sen, and Jean-Paul Fitoussi. 2009. *Report by the Commission on the Measurement of Economic Performance and Social Progress.* www.stiglitz-sen-fitoussi.fr.
Talberth, John, Clifford Cobb, and Noah Slattery. 2007. *The Genuine Progress Indicator 2006: A Tool for Sustainable Development.* Oakland, Calif.: Redefining Progress.
Vanoli, André. 2005. *A History of National Accounting.* Amsterdam: IOS Press.
Walker, P. 1979. *Between Labor and Capital.* Hassocks, U.K.: Harvester.
Ward, Michael. 2004. *Quantifying the World: UN Ideas and Statistics.* Bloomington: Indiana University Press.
Waring, Marilyn. 1988. *If Women Counted: A New Feminist Economics.* New York: Harper.
Wherry, Frederick F. 2004. "International Statistics and Social Structure: The Case of the Human Development Index." *International Review of Sociology* 14 (2): 151–69.
Yonay, Yuval. 1998. *The Struggle over the Soul of Economics.* Princeton: Princeton University Press.
Zolotas, Xenophon. 1981. *Economic Growth and Declining Social Welfare.* New York: New York University Press.

Becker and Posner: Freedom of Speech and Public Intellectualship

Jean-Baptiste Fleury and Alain Marciano

Gary S. Becker and Richard A. Posner have known each other for over forty years. They have taught at the same university, were involved in the same projects, and worked on similar topics at about the same period, and they share similar—if not identical—views on what economics is and what economists should do. But they never, strictly speaking, worked together in the sense that they never coauthored scientific work. The closest they have come to joint, collaborative work is when, as *public intellectuals*, they addressed the wide audience of Internet surfers through the then rather original project of *The Becker-Posner Blog*. Part of this essay provides a historical analysis of what Becker and Posner did in their blog. But we argue that the blog cannot be understood without an analysis of the routes Becker and Posner followed before arriving on the Internet. Indeed, the blog was not their first try as public intellectuals. Before that, both Becker and Posner had been writing (separately) for nonacademic audi-

Correspondence may be addressed to Jean-Baptiste Fleury, Université de Cergy-Pontoise, THEMA, UMR CNRS 8184, F-95000 Cergy-Pontoise, France (e-mail: jbfleury@gmail.com); and to Alain Marciano, Université de Montpellier 1, Faculté d'Economie, Avenue Raymond Dugrand, CS 79606, F-34960 Montpellier cedex 2, France (e-mail: alain.marciano@univ-montp1.fr). We thank the participants of the 2012 conference, in particular, Roger E. Backhouse, Peter Boettke, Gil Eyal, Craufurd Goodwin, Edward Nik-Khah, and Emily Skarbek, for their comments and remarks. We are grateful to the two anonymous referees as well as the editors of this volume, Tiago Mata and Steven G. Medema, for their helpful suggestions. We also thank Yann B. Giraud, for comments, and Gary S. Becker, Kieran Healy, Lawrence Lessig, Richard A. Posner, and Steven Shepard for answering various queries.

History of Political Economy 45 (annual suppl.) DOI 10.1215/00182702-2311016
Copyright 2013 by Duke University Press

ences, experiencing various ways to be a public intellectual and developing different views on its significance and implications for academics. In particular, they realized and appreciated the freedom that writing for a nonacademic audience allows compared with writing for university colleagues; they appreciated the freedom to test (more) provocative ideas and (more) radical policy recommendations without being as rigorous as in academic writings. From this perspective, certainly, the blog was even more interesting and powerful than mass-market books, columns, and journal articles. The blog is a flexible medium that allows them to express their different sensibilities and disseminate their provocative views. But it came after Becker and Posner had had long independent experiences as public intellectuals. Thus the purpose of the present essay is to discuss how Becker and Posner became intellectuals, which resources they used to engage nonacademic audiences, and with what purposes.

Gary Becker: A Social-Minded Scholar

Autobiographical accounts (e.g., Swedberg 1990) tell us that Becker felt the need to engage with society's problems as a young teenager, stimulated by the conversations he had with his family. Then, as an undergraduate at Princeton, he was interested in mathematics and in social problems (28), but he had no faith in economics. The reason he invoked was that it "wasn't really dealing with important social problems" (29). He converted in 1953 when, as a graduate student, he came to Chicago and took Milton Friedman's course. "No course had anywhere near the influence that Friedman's did," Becker (1991, 143) wrote, precisely because of the emphasis "on applications of the theory to the real world" (142) through concrete illustrations, from "why companies often sell several products tied together in a package" to "why people buy lottery tickets" to "the determinants of parental demand for children." Becker understood that economic theory was not necessarily "an end in itself or a way to display pyrotechnics" but could be "worthwhile only insofar as it helped explain different aspects of the real world" (142). Thus it comes as no surprise that Becker chose to study "discrimination" for his PhD dissertation. It was an excellent way for Becker to show how useful economics could be applied to a concrete problem, and a particularly topical one in the desegregation context of the aftermath of the US Supreme Court decision in 1954 in *Brown v. Board of Education* (Fleury 2012). Similarly, in the 1960s, Becker's contributions to the emerging theories of human capital and crime consisted in reframing in economic terms problems—education, health, and delinquency—that were central to the policies of the Johnson and Nixon administrations (Fleury 2010). Again, in the 1970s, the economic analyses Becker made of marriage and the family were related to important changes—in particular, the place of women—in American society. Even Becker's most recent work about addiction or Social Security reform and disaster management will confirm the centrality and resilience of his interest in topical problems.

What evolved over the years is the nature of his engagement with these issues and the audience for which he wrote. Surprisingly for a social-minded scholar like him, only incidentally did Becker comment on concrete policy programs in his scholarly works that preceded the late 1960s. The study of "concrete" problems was a way to show that most if not all (policy) questions usually outside the scope of economics could be actually studied by using the rationality assumption and that the ad hoc assumptions made in traditional economics and other social sciences were superfluous. At the end of the 1960s, a change occurred as Becker moved from Columbia to Chicago, where he rejoined George Stigler, who recruited him back, and Friedman. Both of them were convinced by the power of ideas, interested in analyzing concrete real-world problems, and convinced by the role of think tanks. But Friedman found it crucial to address a broad nonacademic audience—since 1966, he had been writing a column for *Newsweek*, and since 1968 he had been participating, with Paul Samuelson, in a biweekly Economics Cassette Series, which consisted of half-hour talks about the day's issues. Stigler, for his part, had no faith at all in what he called "preaching," that is, speaking to the general public, but believed in the importance of talking to politicians and decision makers, through congressional hearings and consulting for big companies, and to other social scientists by showing the usefulness of economics to reshape their views about markets and democracy (see Nik-Khah 2010 and Nik-Khah and Van Horn 2012). In the late 1960s, thus, Becker started to pay more and more attention to the policy dimensions of the problems he studied, starting with his 1968 paper on crime, which developed an economic framework aimed at understanding and measuring crime with the objective of "determining optimal policies to combat illegal behavior" (Becker 1968, 208).[1] Also significant is the research program on the economics of the family he developed in the 1970s, which included empirical

---

1. Still underdeveloped in the 1968 piece, ideas about a policy reform based on the compensation of "enforcers" (such as the police) were developed in a 1974 paper by Becker and Stigler in the *Journal of Legal Studies*.

evaluations of the effects of various welfare programs (such as compensatory education programs, Head Start, AFDC, and the reform of marriage contracts) on divorce and intergenerational inequality, as well as how parents redistribute wealth to their children and contribute to their education.

However, academic journals did not seem to be the best place for delivering concrete policy advice. Except perhaps for the few proposals about crime control, his scholarly articles remained relatively timid in terms of "concreteness." When speaking to economists in scholarly papers, Becker would put forward the methodological powers of economics and insist on how this framework could lead to testable predictions. By contrast, writing for noneconomists would allow Becker to express his views on policy programs and offer reform proposals. And throughout the 1970s, Becker's interest in writing for a wide audience developed as he came increasingly involved with think tanks and other policy advising activities. In 1971, Becker was invited to attend his first Mont Pèlerin Society meeting—Friedman was then its president. Becker also became a member of the Domestic Advisory Board of the Hoover Institution in 1973. Later, in 1977, he (and Posner) appeared on the initial roster of Stigler's Center for the Study of the Economy and the State, whose primary ambition was to study regulation and governmental control. Every subsequent paper of his appeared as a working paper for the center. In 1978, when Stigler was president of the Mont Pèlerin Society, not only did Becker's name appear in the "new board members proposals" section, but he was also invited to present a paper at the society's meeting.[2] Titled "The Effect of the State on the Family," the paper was tailored for a broad—not only academic—audience, and its content, which summarized the findings of his research program on the negative impact of government intervention on family decisions, showed that the framework he had developed was indeed suitable for policy advising. No surprise, then, that Becker was increasingly willing to devote some time to this activity (Becker, e-mail to authors, January 31, 2012).[3]

Yet, until the mid-1980s, besides the few and discontinuous involvements with the people from the Mont Pèlerin Society and other think tanks, Becker had not much ventured outside academe. In his own words,

2. Becker joined its executive board in 1985.
3. After the publication of his 1983 paper on political competition, Becker pointed to Friedman: "I now feel more comfortable intellectually supporting such type of government limitations" (Becker to Friedman, December 29, 1982, box 20, folder 30, "Gary Becker," Milton Friedman Papers, Hoover Institution, Stanford).

he "had never written one single word in the popular media, not a word, be it a newspaper, magazine, or the like" (Becker 2009, 268). But it did not last: in 1985, he was offered a position as a columnist for *Business Week*. The recently (on November 1, 1984) appointed chief editor, Stephen B. Shepard, believed that the economic situation—the stock market had taken off after nearly fifteen years of stagnation—justified a need for economic expertise and chose to initiate a strategy of development of *Business Week*'s Economic Viewpoint column. Until 1985, the magazine had only one outside columnist, the supply-side economist Paul Craig Roberts. Shepard was looking for columnists to balance Roberts's opinions. Becker's name was suggested by Bill Wolman, the magazine's chief economist, and Seymour Zucker, senior editor for economics (Shepard, e-mail to authors, September 7, 2011). The latter eventually contacted Becker to offer him a monthly column, rotating with Roberts, Alan Blinder, and Robert Kuttner.

Initially, Becker thought of rejecting the offer mainly because, despite his interest in such activities, he wanted to remain focused on his research agenda and thought that he would not have enough time and energy to pursue both. He eventually accepted, first, under the influence of close friends from whom he asked for advice and who encouraged him: Ted Schultz, Stigler, and, most importantly, Friedman. The latter had the experience to understand Becker's reaction. Friedman had at first turned down the proposal to write a column for *Newsweek*, made in 1966—because, like Becker, of the interference with his research agenda and a fear of lacking interesting subjects. Ultimately, his wife and his son persuaded him to accept. Also, he was convinced (contrary to Stigler) that columns in magazines and newspapers were a more efficient way to influence public policy than other types of interventions, such as, for instance, congressional hearings. *Business Week*'s offer was made to Becker just one year after the abrupt end of Friedman's columns. To Friedman, it was a way to ensure continuity in diffusing the Chicago message to the general public.[4] He could not but welcome it.

Even more decisive was the role played by Guity Nashat, Becker's second wife. An Iranian native, Nashat completed a PhD in history at the University of Chicago and, in the mid-1980s, was an assistant professor at the University of Illinois at Chicago (the Circle Campus) working on the

---

4. Actually, the *Business Week* project mimicked *Newsweek*'s economic columns in gathering authors with different views, and in the case of *Newsweek*, had opposed Friedman to Paul Samuelson and, later, Lester Thurow (Friedman and Friedman 1998).

history of Iran with a focus on the place of women in Iranian society (see, e.g., Nashat 1980). Before going to the United States, she had studied at the American University in Cairo and later at the Columbia School of Journalism and gained professional experience in journalism. Nashat was also more politically active than her husband at the time. She thus immediately perceived the importance of those columns, and, as Becker acknowledged in an autobiographical account, through his wife's encouragement he "overcame [his] reluctance to do the *Business Week* columns" (Becker and Becker 1997, 2). She offered to help him write the columns, and indeed, she read the various drafts of every column that Becker wrote during his nineteen years at the magazine, "offer[ing] suggestions to help make them more effective" and "propos[ing] many topics, especially those dealing with contemporary issues of public policy" (2).[5] She convincingly argued that these columns "would provide an excellent vehicle for influencing government policy as well as for communicating his ideas to a wide audience" (2). And this is exactly why Becker took on the *Business Week* columns: as an opportunity to formulate concrete policy proposals, at a time when his participation in think tanks and other policy advising activities also increased.[6] His desire to influence policy has implications in terms of what topics were discussed in the columns and also in terms of how these columns were written.

Becker did not write only about issues on which he had already published as a scientist, like crime, discrimination, human capital, or the family. Of course, his policy proposals were related to topics derived from his scholarly work, for instance, the hiring of bounty hunters to collect the debts of "deadbeat dads" for single mothers (an application of his and Stigler's idea of the compensation of enforcers), the creation of an enforceable yet perfectly negotiable marriage contract, and the increase in severity of punishments; and these concrete proposals added to Becker's comments on the negative effects of social welfare programs on family decisions. Yet the columns also dealt with other topics with which Becker was not so familiar, such as immigration, international trade, stock markets, antitrust, taxes, capitalism versus communism, government regulation, and welfare

---

5. Logically, Guity Nashat was credited as coauthor of *The Economics of Life* (1997), the book that gathered Becker's 1985–95 *Business Week* "economic viewpoints." Indeed, "*The Economics of Life* is a Becker double-decker, giving us the insights of the two Beckers" (Foldvary n.d.).

6. Becker became a member of the Academic Advisory Board of the American Enterprise Institute in 1987 and an adviser for the Japanese Ministry of Finance in 1988.

programs, as well as environmental problems. In such cases, Becker's angle and recommendations conveyed a traditional Chicago message and sometimes rested on the results of a Chicago-friendly study (by, say, Friedman, Robert Barro, Kevin Murphy, Michael Grossman, Sam Peltzman) about the negative effects of regulation and welfare programs, as well as the organizing role of the market and free competition, for instance, when advocating for the selling of immigration rights, the privatization of public companies, a "pay as you go" social security system, the development of student loans, and school vouchers.

Despite this connection to research, what is striking about these columns is Becker's focus on policy recommendations and reform proposals, rather than economic analysis. One may even note that, on several occasions, Becker's columns were only remotely related to economic reasoning, especially on the subject of crime and the family. Yet one should not conclude that when he was writing for a nonacademic audience Becker was distancing himself from economics. What should actually be stressed is that the columns were used to popularize a totally different definition of economics compared with the one we find in his academic works. Here, he never insisted on the predictive powers of economics, its logical consistency, and ability to encompass all aspects of human behavior. Rather, as revealed by a partly *ex post* but nonetheless significant characterization of his work as a public intellectual, Becker wrote:

> Economics analyzes how markets, public policies, and other events affect the behavior of individuals and organizations that try as best they can to improve their situations by competing against each other for incomes, jobs, customers and even prestige and power. Markets and prices help reconcile the unbounded desires of individuals and organizations to make themselves better off and the very finite resources available to satisfy these desires. (Becker and Becker 1997, 4)

Thus the columns were written to promote the idea that economics is a science that explains the importance of markets for organizing society and designing optimal public policies. That idea served as the backbone of the pieces Becker wrote for *Business Week* and allowed him to make his proposals compelling. This was not only the role of a public intellectual but also a reason for his success. From this perspective, the failure of George Stigler as a columnist (he lasted less than a year) proved Becker right. Although Stigler made provocative analyses, he "did not take a strong stand on policy questions," probably a consequence of his distrust of "preaching" (Becker and Becker 1997, 6).[7] As a result, he did not receive many letters, and this lack of feedback led him to quit. For his part, Becker believed that adopting a strong angle would stimulate reactions and debate. Becker's columns did generate a lively correspondence, ranging from insults to constructive debate, a "contact with readers [that] has been one of the unexpected pleasures from writing these columns" (Becker and Becker 1997, 10). And if the price to pay was sometimes a certain degree of unrealism, this was not a problem either. On the contrary, Becker believed that "the sometimes new and frequently 'unrealistic' proposals . . . will be accepted in the future" (8). The public intellectual wrote precisely to make his ideas public. And that is what Becker did.

Becker's work as a columnist lasted nineteen years. His success was validated when he was awarded the 1992 Nobel Prize, which certainly provided additional incentives to address a broad audience and offer opinions on and proposals of reforms for many public policies. It is likely that Becker's stature as a public figure has had a feedback effect on his work as a scholar from the 1990s on: some characteristics of his work as a public intellectual might be found in some of his work as a scholar. More precisely, a few clues indicate that Becker the scholar might have also turned into a provider of new ideas and intuitions to be deepened and studied more rigorously by others. First, most of his papers since the early 1990s have been written with younger scholars (Kevin Murphy, Luis Rayo, Casey Mulligan). Second, Becker has increasingly published short and "simplified" papers, providing an introductory analysis to a new phenomenon. Examples are the 1991 piece on restaurant pricings and social interactions, as well as his "simple theory of advertising" published in the *Quarterly Journal of Economics* (Becker and Murphy 1993). Moreover, although Becker has remained involved in "technical" papers, the number of less-mathematized ones has increased. These developments in Becker's work as a scholar and as a public intellectual provide an interesting entrée to understanding Becker's subsequent activity: the blog.

---

7. In 1987, Stigler was contacted by *Business Month* (previously *Dun's Review*) to write a column, rotating with Robert Solow. This offer was part of the aggressive strategy of the newly appointed editor John van Doorn to boost the magazine's advertising revenues by providing "top notch" editorials ("Putting a New Twist on Business Journalism" 1988). Stigler quit in 1988 because "nobody had criticized it. They didn't get any letters to the editor" (Freedman 1997).

Posner: What It Means to Be a "True" Public Intellectual

Between 1968—when he was appointed associate professor for the first time at the Stanford Law School—and the mid-1980s, Posner was focused on trying to reach an academic audience. The number of academic articles he wrote—over one hundred in that period—vastly outnumbered the three contributions he made to strictly nonacademic journals, to which one can add two articles that were pitched to an audience "between" the academic and nonacademic: "Some Thoughts on Legal Education" (1972) and "Reflections on Consumerism" (1973b), both of which appeared in the *University of Chicago Law School Record*, the "magazine for alumni and friends" of the law school.

Toward the end of the 1970s, Posner started to address a nonacademic audience. In 1977, Posner, William H. Landes—an economist who completed his thesis under Becker's supervision and was one of the first contributors to an "economic analysis of law"—and one of their students, Andrew Rosenfield, created Lexecon Inc. A consulting firm, it aimed at explaining "basic economics (and even econometrics) and showed [attorneys] how they could use economics to help structure and strengthen legal arguments" (Landes 2009, 67). Then, a few years later, in 1981, Posner was appointed by Ronald Reagan to the US Court of Appeals for the Seventh Circuit. Certainly, writing legal opinions and making judicial decisions—especially at one of the highest levels in the judicial hierarchy—as well as advising attorneys do not equate to writing articles for newspapers or magazines. Yet one cannot doubt that, first, it suggests a taste for addressing wider, various, nonacademic audiences, and second, in a legal system in which the names of judges are linked to the decisions they make, there is probably no other activity that can satisfy such a taste and allow someone to reach a wide audience.

These activities may have served as a substitute for being a public intellectual, or maybe they simply were too time-consuming. It is hard to tell. It nonetheless remains that, until the second half of the 1980s, Posner's contributions to magazines and newspapers were scarce, nonsystematic, and restricted to legal topics. One (coauthored with Landes) article for *Regulation Magazine* (1986) was about punitive damages. In the *New Republic* (Posner 1987b) appeared a paper on judicial decision making. For the *Wall Street Journal*, in 1990, he wrote a review of Sheldon M. Novick's 1989 book on Oliver Wendell Holmes and a note on antitrust. It slightly changed in the early 1990s, when Posner became a regular contributor to the *New York Times Book Review* and to the *New Republic*—for which he mainly wrote reviews of legal books; to the *Washington Post*; and among other newspapers, the *New York Times*. Yet, by comparison with Becker and even if one recalls that we are talking about "the wonder of the legal world" (Dworkin 2000), a judge who delivered twenty-five hundred judicial opinions over forty years at the US Court of Appeals, who was described as a "hyperactive" scholar (Brooks 2002), as well as "America's most prolific writer on legal subjects" ("Sense and Nonsense" 2003), the fact is that Posner wrote few pieces for magazines, journals, or newspapers.

The genuine change occurred during the 1990s, when Posner started to write "books on a variety of legal subjects [and] in numbers that would be amazing even if he had no other responsibilities" (Dworkin 2000).[8] Now, if one stresses that Posner, like Becker, was publishing books in a field that does not care much about books, this should be interpreted as Posner's major means used to enlarge his audience.[9] Certainly, one could object that, when asked who was his "intended audience" when he wrote *How Judges Think?* (2008), Posner answered by saying that "most people write for themselves. Academic writing, which is what this was, is not focused on an audience. I try to write very simply. Beyond that, I don't have a precise sense of audience" (Posner 2009, 1808). The statement might be exact for what is one of Posner's most recent books, focused on a relatively specific topic, written when his reputation is already made and the scholar and the character are perfectly well known. However, the same can hardly be said of the books Posner wrote in the 1990s. Revised versions of his academic writings, these books were described as tailored for a *nonacademic* audience.[10] For instance, in *Sex and Reason* (1992), Posner wrote that he was presenting, "in a form accessible to the legal profession," the "principal findings of . . . a literature to which medicine, biology, sociobiology,

---

8. Posner has written fifty-four books since the beginning of his academic career, including revised editions. The figure remains remarkable, and it has been noticed: "Judge Richard Posner . . . is . . . the author, seemingly, of more books written while in active judicial service than many judges are of opinions" (Leonard H. Becker 2001).

9. Posner (2009, 1808) even declared, "I don't think that judges do much reading—at least, not much secondary reading. The ordinary judicial job itself requires a great amount of reading. Most judges probably figure that that is enough."

10. *Aging and Old Age* was based on presentations made in various *academic* seminars among others, the Tanner Lectures on Human Values he gave at Yale University in 1994. *The Problematics of Moral and Legal Theory* was based on the 1997 Oliver Wendell Holmes Lectures he gave at the Harvard Law School and on an eponymous article published in the *Harvard Law Review*.

psychiatry, psychology, sociology, economics, jurisprudence, theology, philosophy, history, classics, anthropology, demography—even geography and literary criticism—have all contributed" (2). Similarly, in *Aging and Old Age* (Posner 1995a), he said that he had written the book to make "intelligible" to "different audiences" (2) knowledge included in disciplines "ranging from evolutionary biology and cognitive psychology to philosophy and literature" (1). Obviously, in his books, Posner was translating knowledge from a vast range of diversified disciplines and passing it to a broad and nonacademic audience. In a way, this activity of translation has always characterized his academic work, which, in the form of review articles, scientific books, or textbooks—like his seminal *Economic Analysis of Law* (1973a)—can be described as introducing and therefore passing the technical knowledge of economics to law scholars.

That he dealt with "almost absurdly wide ranging" subject matters (Ryerson 2000) for which answers remain imprecise, unclear, and debatable could not bother him. First, for personal reasons and capacities, Posner does not hesitate to acknowledge loving "variety, which may be another name for being impatient," and "loving [his] work and having plenty of energy and concentration and only limited family responsibilities, and having the ability that many intelligent people lack of switching from project to project without loss of momentum."[11] Second, he uses his time wisely. As he explains, "You need good work habits, such as: not procrastinating; careful prioritizing; and accepting assistance, in my case from law clerks and student research assistants. The trick is to delegate the truly delegable parts of one's work but retain full control over the nondelegable."[12] Third, one should not forget to insist on the role of economics, which, as a scientific method, allowed him to go beyond the nominal boundaries of his discipline. In the case of aging, for instance, "economics can do a better job of explaining the behaviors and attitudes associated with aging, and of solving the policy problems that aging presents, than biology, psychology, sociology, philosophy or any other single field of natural or social sciences" (Posner 1995a, 2). This is certainly no surprise for someone who believed that the use of economics to analyze the functioning of the legal system is legitimate because economics could be defined only in terms of method, as "a powerful tool" (Posner [1973] 1986, 3), as an open-ended set of concepts such that "when used in sufficient density

---

11. The quotation is from the January 14, 2002, entry in an online diary that Posner kept on slate.com (www.slate.com/articles/arts_and_life/diary/features/2002/_34/entry_1.html).

12. www.slate.com/articles/arts_and_life/diary/features/2002/_34/entry_1.html.

these concepts make a work of scholarship 'economic' *regardless of its subject matter or its author's degree*" (Posner 1987a, 2; emphasis added).

Thus, for Posner, economists—that is, scholars trained in economics or not but nevertheless using economic assumptions and models—were virtually *never* outside their domain of expertise. This idea had permeated Posner's scholarly work almost since the beginning, but it progressively led Posner to think about the proper role of a public intellectual, about what public intellectuals should or should not do. In another collection of revised articles, *Overcoming Law* (1995b), Posner sketched a dichotomy between the intellectuals who use economics and the others: contrary to the latter, the former are able to make scientific and indisputable claims. This dichotomy was deepened in his Oliver Wendell Holmes Lectures given at the Harvard Law School in 1997, in which Posner extended the distinction to *public* intellectuals: only the claims made using economics could be valid outside academia; those who did not use economics, but philosophy or moral theory, were only to make useless, unscientific analyses. Significantly, Posner named those intellectuals "professors of morals" or "academic moralists" and used the label to designate in particular Ronald Dworkin, one of his earliest opponents, a legal philosopher and a *public intellectual*. The relatively violent reply by Dworkin (1998, 1718), who criticized "Richard Posner's jeremiad" and his "spectacularly unsuccessful" arguments, led Posner to write an article and then a book titled *The Problematics of Moral and Legal Theory* (1999b). That Posner chose to go beyond a set of articles and write a book about exactly this topic illustrates that he not only wanted to give more details about what are good and bad "public intellectuals" but also aimed at making his views on the role of public intellectuals known outside academe.

He was even clearer about the role of public intellectuals and how they should engage the public during another controversy with Dworkin just after—and because of—the publication of Posner's *Affair of State: The Investigation, Impeachment, and Trial of President Clinton* (1999a). Posner "began writing [it] in October 1998 when the crisis was very much *in media res* . . . and . . . finished on February 16, 1999, four days after the Senate trial ended" (4). But it was also one of the only attempts by a scholar to understand the legal dimension and consequences of the affair. Indeed, Posner was surprised by the "deafening" (241) silence of the academic legal profession about Bill Clinton's conduct during his testimony to the grand jury. Rather than restraint, this silence pointed to a form of incapacity—the "debacle" of the "*academic* practitioners of 'soft' subjects in the humanities or the social sciences" (233; emphasis added). Intellectuals could be good; this was not sufficient to be a good *public* intellectual. A scientific methodology was also required.

One of those criticized for their silence, Dworkin (2000) attacked Posner in a sharp review for the *New York Review of Books*, precisely because the judge should have remained silent and, by failing to do so, had made a double ethical fault.[13] This led, again, Posner to answer Dworkin in an article—also published in the *New York Review of Books*—and then, following the suggestion of his editor at Harvard University Press, a book. *Public Intellectuals: A Study of Decline* (2001) was not simply another book on public intellectuals: it was meant to be the ultimate book on the topic, in which Posner established again and more firmly the norm of what is a good or "true" and, complementarily, a bad or "false" public intellectual. The former develops positive analysis and makes positive statements based on the use of scientific methods, namely, economics or statistics. By contrast, the latter are simply "engaged in naïve extrapolation" because they lack a "causal theory"; their opinions are normative, personal, and subjective, and of a poor quality, as Posner kept on stressing in further newspapers and magazine articles tellingly titled "In over Their Heads When Intellectuals Tackle Issues beyond Their Expertise, They Often Finish Way Off Base" (2002a) and "The Professors Profess. Ordinary People Can Say Stupid Things. Brilliant People Do It Brilliantly" (2002b).

Beyond the lack of an *internal* control mechanism, provided only by a sufficiently powerful analytical framework such as economics, one excellent reason explains, according to Posner, why such "false" public intellectuals could survive and flourish: the lack of an *external* mechanism to discipline them. Since academic knowledge got increasingly specialized, the expertise and legitimacy of many public intellectuals were, in many cases, impossible to question. Moreover, public intellectuals were not accountable for the explanations and recommendations they formulated. The cost of making foolish recommendations grounded

---

13. Posner (1999a, 241) wrote: "Harsh words about Clinton might also have been expected from Professor Dworkin, who is a lawyer as well as a philosopher and who is well known for advocating that law be reconceived as a branch of moral philosophy. These expectations would have been disappointed." Dworkin (2000) replied that Posner "misstated the rule: Canon 3(A)6 of the Code of Conduct for United States Judges prohibits federal judges from commenting publicly on 'pending or impending' cases." Also, Posner's "own ethics, in publishing a book about Clinton's impeachment so soon after the event, are open to question, because judges are not meant to enter political controversies" (Dworkin 2000).

in inconsistent reasoning was very low. Since public intellectuals were only part-time columnists, the cost of being fired or fooled was low, as were the costs of leaving public intellectual life altogether. Finally, there was no peer review process, and one's reputation was hardly engaged. The high number of specialized comments, as well as the diversity of support (printed media, interviews, etc.), made them hard to monitor.

Considering such lack of incentives to provide accurate reasoning and predictions, the market for public intellectuals performed less well than other markets for what Posner (2002b) called "symbolic goods," such as scholarly work: "Academics are smart and fast, and, in nonscientific fields such as law and history, they can be glib. . . . But when academics speak off the cuff, especially about matters outside their areas of expertise, quality tends to go to hell." Yet his book also offered a few modest solutions to improve the market for public intellectuals, mostly centered on a monitoring system that would improve the public intellectual's accountability. He notably proposed to require university faculty members "to post annually, on the university's web page, all the nonacademic writing, in whatever form or medium published, and public speaking that they have done during the preceding year" (Posner 2001, 390). This reform would be "a deterrent to irresponsible interventions by academics in public controversies" and would act the same way as how trial judges and lawyers control professional experts (390). Another reform sketched by Posner would consist in forcing public intellectuals to disclose any conflict of interest, as well as the income they receive from their activity as a public intellectual, including their consulting activities for think tanks, which would have some interests in advocating certain policies. In short, Posner dreamed of a *Journal of Retractions*, in which public intellectuals would "periodically review their predictions and other statements and report which one had turned out to be true and which false" (396). As we will see in the next section, *The Becker-Posner Blog* offered an interesting opportunity to implement and test similar types of reforms.

The Becker-Posner Blog: "Here's What I Think and Why"

The creation and launching of the blog in 2004 seems to be, at the same time, the product of coincidences and the desire both for Becker and for Posner to remain active as public intellectuals. First, let us recall that, although the earliest blogs were created in the 1990s, it was only in the mid-2000s that blogging became a recognized activity and bloggers were eventually viewed as influential people. More precisely, 2004 is the year that marked the end of the "ancien régime" of the media, after bloggers revealed the weakness of the documents used in a CBS show about George W. Bush's National Guard service during the Vietnam War (see Munger 2008).

The year 2004 was also a turning point in Becker's and Posner's careers as public intellectuals. On July 12, Becker wrote his last Economic Viewpoint column in *Business Week*, anticipating coming changes in the magazine's editorial team.[14] But the pleasure and interest felt during those nineteen years as a columnist could not be easily forgotten. Becker rapidly "missed writing regularly." He then invited Posner to a debate through this new technique, blogging, that he perceived as "the wave of the future" (Becker, e-mail to authors, January 31, 2012) and a way to satisfy his hunger for addressing real-world problems. Yet Becker's project might not have met with immediate enthusiasm had Posner not already published some posts on Lawrence Lessig's blog. One of Posner's former clerks at the Court of Appeals, and now a law professor at Harvard Law School, Lessig was particularly interested in new communication technologies and their effect on intellectual property law. In 2001, he founded Creative Commons, a nonprofit organization aimed at expanding the range of the public domain. In 2002, he received the Advancement of Free Software award, for promoting the understanding of the political dimension of free software, was named one of the top fifty visionaries from the world of research by the magazine *Scientific American*, and launched his own blog.[15] In August 2004, as he used to do with various people when on vacation, Lessig asked Posner to host the blog for a few days. Posner very much liked the experience (Lessig, e-mail to authors, October 9, 2011).[16] He found it "fun," enough to take it to heart, writing twenty-six (some of them long) posts in seven days and answering a few comments. But when

---

14. Shepard, who had hired Becker in 1985, left in 2005, and the Economic Viewpoint column, which was then held by Robert Barro, Laura Tyson, Jeffrey Garten, and Robert Kuttner, ended in December of that year.

15. See, on the website of the GNU operating system, "2002 Free Software Awards" (www.gnu.org/award/2002/2002.html). Lessig was given the award because he "argued against interpretations of copyright that could stifle innovation and discourse online" (http://www.scientificamerican.com/article.cfm?id=the-scientific-american-5-2002-11-11&page=2).

16. Posner never hesitated to use new communication technologies. He wrote a weeklong diary for slate.com and agreed to appear in Second Life (see nwn.blogs.com/nwn/2006/12/the_second_life.html).

Lessig invited him to host his own blog, Posner accepted by joining Becker and creating a blog with him. Lessig then helped Becker and Posner with the basic Web administration work, notably registering the name of the domain (becker-posner-blog.com) and mobilized some Creative Commons human and material resources to develop the blog. Thus, if, as Posner told us, the blog was "all Becker's idea" (October 4, 2011), Lessig also "can claim credit for only one thing that [Posner's] done: The Posner-Becker [sic] Blog."[17]

At the end of November 2004, the word was spreading that Becker and Posner were going to start their blog "soon."[18] One week later, on December 4, 2004, it started with an "introduction," in which it was emphasized how important, and why, blogging already was. It is, they wrote,

> a major new social, political, and economic phenomenon. It is a fresh and striking exemplification of Friedrich Hayek's thesis that knowledge is widely distributed among people and that the challenge to society is to create mechanisms for pooling that knowledge. The powerful mechanism that was the focus of Hayek's work, as of economists generally, is the price system (the market). The newest mechanism is the blogosphere.[19]

At that time, the blog had already attracted a certain amount of attention, with thirty subscribers, and they increased to sixty-eight on December 5, 2004, the official launching date of *The Becker-Posner Blog*.[20] Comments, posted by ordinary people, students, and scholars as well, were more numerous (156 after the introductory note and 127 after the first

---

17. Lawrence Lessig, "Project Posner," October 18, 2006, lessig.org/blog/2006/10/project_posner.html.

18. See the reference to *The Becker-Posner Blog* in the assorted entries for Monday, November 29, 2004, in the archives of *The Volokh Conspiracy* (blog), www.volokh.com/archives/archive_2004_11_28.shtml#1101750671; crookedtimber.org/2004/11/29/legitimation-effects/.

19. Gary Becker and Richard Posner, "Introduction to the Becker-Posner Blog," *The Becker-Posner Blog*, December 4, 2004, www.becker-posner-blog.com/2004/12/introduction-to-the-becker-posner-blog.html.

20. Evan Schaeffer, another blogger, joked about the visibility of the blog, noting on December 13, 2004: "Recently, someone stopped me on the street to ask, 'Hey, Evan, what do you think about the new Becker-Posner blog?' The question didn't surprise me: who's not thinking about *The Becker-Posner Blog*?" ("*The Becker-Posner Blog* and My Own Shitty Writing Style," December 13, 2004, www.legalunderground.com/2004/12/becker_posner_b.html). In the discussion that follows, we write in the past tense because our narrative is about the blog as it existed between its inauguration and 2009; it is important to point out that the blog is still an active concern.

post). Some of them were enthusiastic and others critical.[21] After the first post, Kieran Healy, then assistant professor of sociology at the University of Arizona, ironized that "the blog is an elaborate hoax" and "that the reader is being gamed," not only because of "the absurd suck-up comments from law students" but also because "the *real* Richard Posner is one of the preeminent legal minds of our time" and thus "can hardly be responsible for *this*" (our emphases).[22] "This" referred to one post by Posner about preemptive war that another blogger considered a "toy numerical example"[23] and that went as follows:

> Suppose there is a probability of .5 that the adversary will attack at some future time, when he has completed a military buildup, that the attack will, if resisted with only the victim's current strength, inflict a cost on the victim of 100, so that the expected cost of the attack is 50 (100 x .5), but that the expected cost can be reduced to 20 if the victim incurs additional defense costs of 15. Suppose further that at an additional cost of only 5, the victim can by a preventive strike today eliminate all possibility of the future attack. Since 5 is less than 35 (the sum of injury and defensive costs if the future enemy attack is not prevented), the preventive war is cost-justified.[24]

Healy's irony was lost to commenters, who seriously replied by emphasizing how Posnerian such reasoning was and suggested that it had to be debated as if it were scientific. This revealed, at least to some commenters, how flawed were the analyses and demonstrations made in the posts. Typically, this was why the *Anti-Becker-Posner Blog* was created in May 2005,

---

21. Greg Newburn noted: "It's fascinating that the Internet and, more specifically, blogs, allow people from all disciplines and backgrounds to comment on the ideas of heavyweights like Becker and Posner. When was the last time a 'regular guy' got to comment on, say, a law review article by a Nobel Laureate? Who says technology is divisive? This is amazing!" Michael Kim wrote: "This blog will be on my daily must reading." And Art de Vany congratulated them: "Gary and Richard: What a great idea for the two of you to comment on the world's events from the deeper perspective of economics and law that you have done so much to advance." Note that a lot of comments are lost because the blogs on which they were published have been shut down since 2004.

22. Kieran Healey, "Posner and Becker Comedy Gold," *Out of the Crooked Timber of Humanity, No Straight Thing Was Ever Made* (blog), December 6, 2004, crookedtimber.org/2004/12/06/posner-and-becker-comedy-gold/.

23. John Quiggin, "Consequentialism for Beginners," *John Quiggin* (blog), December 8, 2004, johnquiggin.com/2004/12/08/consequentialism-for-beginners/#more-171.

24. Richard Posner, "Preventive War," *The Becker-Posner Blog*, December 5, 2004, www.becker-posner-blog.com/2004/12/preventive-war—posner.html.

whose tagline reads, "Correcting the mistakes, omissions, and downright nonsense on the Becker-Posner-Blog." However, such an objective would have made perfect sense if Becker and Posner had intended to write with the rigor that some expected from academics like them.[25] Actually, the promoters of the *Anti-Becker-Posner Blog* missed the point: in their blog, Becker and Posner were not interested in being theoretically sound and correct, which was one reason the economist and the judge were able to publish posts at such a regular pace. It was a pace that the authors of the *Anti-Becker-Posner Blog*, in their concern for accuracy, could not keep up, and they gave up the blog in June 2005. Indeed, Becker and Posner kept on using the same "consequentialist-for-beginners" analyses as they used in their first posts. Omissions and shortcuts were not a problem because, to them, the blog provided a space that, to a wider extent than with other media, they could experiment and refine their thoughts, a space in which theoretical arguments, observations of the outside world, and policy views would evolve together and influence one another in a way flexible enough so as to allow for the use of price theory without the strong limitations imposed by the criteria of academic research, but rigorous enough so as to give them the legitimacy to make provocative analyses and claims.[26] To use a categorization put forward by Deva Woodly (2008), they followed a "here's what I think and why" standard (117), in which the objective is to "frankly disclose their political leanings and affections" (116), and what matters is to be "insightful" (117). In our words, Becker and Posner engaged in "casual economic thinking."

One of the first consequences of this approach of blogging relates to their way of using data. Some posts would disseminate the results of an empirical study or a report, much like Becker's previous columns. But such data would also be used casually to substantiate Becker's or Posner's arguments. Thus the rather loose use of figures in their examples, a recurrent feature of their posts, gave the blog its provocative tone. It is obviously a

---

25. To illustrate this expectation, one may note a remark made by an associate professor of political science at George Washington University, Henry Farrell, who welcomed Becker and Posner's venture precisely because it came from two top academics. Recall that Posner was the first federal judge to blog, and Becker was the first Nobel Prize laureate in economics to blog. Among noted economists, he was preceded only by Brad DeLong, who has blogged since 1999, and Tyler Cowen and Alex Tabarrok, who created *Marginal Revolution* in 2003 (Mata 2011).

26. One may wonder if their blog is really a blog at all. We thank Emily Skarbek for having emphasized this point. Indeed, the posts read too long, are not reactive, and lack the puns and witticisms of the blog form. Actually, the pieces Becker and Posner write are more like traditional columns that happen to be posted on the Internet than genuine blog posts.

freedom that was impossible to have in traditional media, much less in academic papers. This is illustrated by Posner's evaluation of the benefits of the New York trans-fat ban proposal (December 17, 2006), arguing that the decision would save five hundred lives—"an upper bound," since "it seems *unlikely* that removing trans fats from restaurant meals alone would cause a 2 percent drop in heart disease" (emphasis added)—each year and that the "*consensus* economic *estimate* of an American life" is $7 million (emphasis added). For these reasons, Becker confessed to preferring writing the blog over any other media, so he "doesn't have to deal with copy editors," which he replaced with his own assistants, when facts or other things needed checking (Becker, e-mail to authors, January 31, 2012). Similarly, Posner confirmed that there is no editor for the blog (Posner, e-mail to authors, June 14, 2012). Thus Becker and Posner did not only like but also used without restraints the freedom that blogging allowed by comparison with other media, not to say academic publications.[27]

From this perspective, it is significant to note that, in addition to the blog, Becker and Posner kept addressing a broad audience through print media, for instance, the *Wall Street Journal*, and even online ones (the *Atlantic Monthly* and the *Hoover Digest*). Yet, within these other media, Becker and Posner would more tightly conform to defined style and constraints, and thus these columns would appear closer to previous op-eds by both authors. They put forward the less controversial of their proposals—such as the need for economic growth in Pakistan to prevent terrorism. By contrast, in the blog, they could allow themselves to reach conclusions too provocative—as when they argued in favor of racial profiling and preventive war—to be printed or published elsewhere. In other words, the blog pushed to the limit the habit of controversy that characterized their past work. A good instance is provided by Becker's arguments about the death penalty. On the blog, he wrote that "public policy on punishments cannot wait until the evidence is perfect. Even with the limited quantitative evidence available, there are good reasons to believe that capital punishment deters murders."[28] And, quite significantly, when he moved from the blog to the paper, that is, when this debate was partially reprinted in the book *Uncommon Sense* (Becker and Posner 2009), Becker was less controver-

---

27. Ironically, it was for indulging in that same freedom that Posner had criticized public intellectuals. We thank Paul Dudenhefer for this point.

28. Gary Becker, "More on the Economics of Capital Punishment," *The Becker-Posner Blog*, December 18, 2005, www.becker-posner-blog.com/2005/12/more-on-the-economics-of-capital-punishment-becker.html.

sial, conceding that "perhaps given the strength of the emotional opposition to capital punishment, and the limited quantitative evidence supporting the deterrent effect . . . it is best not to use such punishment unless the evidence gets stronger" (309).

The liberty to be as casual as they wanted also rubbed off on their choice of topics. Becker and Posner did not hesitate to address the controversies of the day independently of whether or not they had specialized knowledge of them. Their blog mixed discussions about issues on which they had already written—for instance, education, global warming, capitalism, immigration, marriage, and supply-side economic policies in the case of Becker, law and regulation in the case of Posner—with issues that neither Becker nor Posner had ever addressed, such as racial profiling, the involvement of the Muslim community in the 2005 French riots, terrorism prevention, the Iraq War, pharmaceutical patents, the fat tax as well as trans-fat bans, organ sales, and intellectual property.[29] For Posner, the blog was more than a place to translate knowledge in the most balanced way possible; it was also a place devoted to opinions and policy recommendations; it was, for Becker, a place that allowed him to introduce more basic economic thinking and new theoretical intuitions that were not found in his previous columns because of space constraints and the kind of audience that was targeted.[30] Evidence is provided by the introduction of *Uncommon Sense*, which spends much more space than the beginning of Becker's *Economics of Life* to introduce economics (its definition) as well as some important conceptual tools such as rents, externalities, agency costs, and full prices (prices including search costs). This also suggests that, just as Posner did not worry too much about his audience when he wrote his previous books, Becker and Posner did not give much thought about the audience their blog might attract: depending on the kind of post, Becker and Posner could have raised the interest of former *Business Week* readers who wanted strong policy opinions and concrete policy reforms, but also students and scholars in economics and law in search of theoretical intuitions on how to tackle a topical issue; too, a post could have interested companies looking for innovative and provocative pundits for hire, since Becker had also participated in Steve Levitt's Greatest Good consulting company (co-created with Lexecon's Andrew

---

29. In the case of the Iraq War, however, this perhaps resulted from Becker's involvement as a member of the Advisory Committee to the secretary of defense from 2001 to 2004, which gave him an opportunity to expand the applications of his views about crime and punishment.

30. Posts are longer than Becker's past printed columns.

Rosenfield), devoted to applying innovative economics tools to business problems.

Quite surprisingly, for scholars interested in blogging because of the lack of constraints it offers, Becker and Posner allowed readers to comment on their posts and did not regulate those comments.[31] This seems to imply that the readers of the blog were allowed to control what Becker and Posner had written, by identifying mistakes and inconsistencies in their comments. At first, one might think that comments were viewed by Posner as playing the role of the kind of external mechanism that Posner thought necessary to discipline the pronouncements of public intellectuals and that, according to him, was lacking so far. Comments, in other words, could improve and refine the content of the posts. This was obviously how readers interpreted this possibility, repeatedly underlining the inconsistencies of Becker's and Posner's arguments vis-à-vis their previous writing, as the website offers a complete record of all Becker's and Posner's posts. However, for their part, Becker and Posner did not actually use comments as a corrective device. In effect, comments were not used by Becker or Posner to change their beliefs and casual thinking. Actually, and although Becker and Posner almost systematically wrote replies to (some of) the comments a few days after the initial post, they did not modify their analyses, but restated what they had already said in the initial post, by striking directly at the heart of the misunderstanding or using more compelling illustrations.[32] Even Becker's disagreements with Posner, which were more numerous than Becker had initially expected, did not lead one of them to change radically his mind (Becker, e-mail to authors, January 31, 2012).

No surprise then if Becker and Posner, from the second half of 2009 on, stopped replying to—and even "ceased reading" (Posner, e-mail to authors, June 14, 2012)—comments and that the blog, like the columns, became more "a regular monologue than an ongoing dialogue between

---

31. Such openness is far from systematic in the blogosphere. Greg Mankiw does not permit comments on his blog, and *Marginal Revolution*, which began in 2003, did not appear to permit comments until around January 2006; Paul Krugman's and Brad DeLong's blogs permit comments, but the authors do not reply explicitly to them.

32. Let us mention only one of Becker's replies (dated November 2006) about women, marriage, and rationality, which reads: "I repeat what I have said in my post: I have considerably more confidence than some of the posters that young women can make at least as considered decisions with respect to marriage as young men" (Becker, "Reply on Polygamy," *The Becker-Posner Blog*, November 12, 2006, http://www.becker-posner-blog.com/2006/11/reply-on-polygamy--becker.html).

author and readers" (Woodly 2008, 117). To Posner, the explanation was the "sheer lack of time" (Posner, e-mail to authors, June 14, 2012). It also revealed that comments were not a way to change their minds and improve their posts. Comments and answers were, rather, a dissemination device. Accordingly, allowing people to comment on their posts was a strategic choice, because it increased the circulation of Becker's and Posner's ideas among commenters. Even if one reader never completely agreed with the message, the resulting discussion prevented Becker's and Posner's idiosyncratic approach from being neglected, as provocative as the analysis might be. And then, progressively, the initial argument made by Becker or Posner rapidly ceased to be at the heart of the discussion, as an independent discussion emerged between commenters who tried to convince each other about the validity of their own views on Becker's and Posner's views. This way, the message disseminated in the blog got more attention than it would have if communicated through a more traditional outlet. Thus, whatever ability it had to influence and shape the public debate came from the blog's specific combination of provocative arguments and the possibility of commenting on them thoroughly without any form of regulation. Interestingly, Daniel W. Drezner and Henry Farrell (2008) argue that it is their ability to frame a problem that confers blogs their influential power over journalists, leaders of opinion, and government officials. Becker often framed a problem with references to the organizing power of markets, while Posner often framed the problem as a cost-benefit calculation.

Conclusion

Although they may have disagreed about what a public intellectual is supposed to expect from his or her engagement—to offer policy recommendations and proposals to the public (Becker) or to bring them knowledge to confirm their beliefs (Posner)—and even if they may not have used the same resources, from early on in their careers Becker and Posner nonetheless had the same objective: to promote and disseminate their ideas and their views of the world. Writing for magazines, newspapers, and now the Internet allows them to put forward provocative claims and radical policy recommendations without the constraints and limitations of academic writing. Being a public intellectual gives them the freedom to address a great variety of topics and allows them to potentially influence public policies related to those topics. From this perspective, it is no surprise that Becker and Posner eventually ended up on the Internet, authoring a blog.

Compared with their previous works as public intellectuals (books, columns), the blog provides a unique place to shape their opinions through theoretical intuitions, casual empiricism, and policy views. Blogs may attract less attention and be less directly influential than standard media, but they provide a potentially huge network for disseminating their ideas and therefore can be indirectly influential. More specifically, it is by allowing readers to comment on their posts that Becker and Posner introduced an innovation in the way public intellectuals interact with their audience and disseminate their message. Yet, in 2009, Becker and Posner ended one form of interaction, when they stopped replying to the comments. This is not surprising from the perspective of how Becker and Posner see public intellectualship. But the regular decrease in the number of comments per post might eventually call into question the specific disseminating powers of the blog compared with traditional media.

References

Becker, Gary S. 1968. "Crime and Punishment: An Economic Approach." *Journal of Political Economy* 76 (2): 169–217.

———. 1978. "The Effect of the State on the Family." Unpublished document.

———. 1991. "Milton Friedman." In *Remembering the University of Chicago: Teachers, Scientists, and Scholars*, edited by Edward Shils, 138–46. Chicago: University of Chicago Press.

———. 2009. "Gary S. Becker." In *Lives of the Laureates: Twenty Three Nobel Economists*, edited by William Breit and Barry T. Hirsch, 251–72. Cambridge: MIT Press.

Becker, Gary S., and Guity Nashat Becker. 1997. *The Economics of Life*. New York: McGraw and Hill.

Becker, Gary S., and Kevin Murphy. 1993. "A Simple Theory of Advertising as Good and Bad." *Quarterly Journal of Economics* 108 (4): 941–64.

Becker, Gary S., and Richard Posner. 2009. *Uncommon Sense*. Chicago: University of Chicago Press.

Becker, Gary S., and George J. Stigler. 1974. "Law Enforcement, Malfeasance, and Compensation of Enforcers." *Journal of Legal Studies* 3 (1): 1–18.

Becker, Leonard H. 2001. "A Legal Recounting." *Nation*, November 12.

Brooks, David. 2002. "Notes from a Hanging Judge." *New York Times*, January 13.

Drezner, Daniel W., and Henry Farrell. 2008. "Introduction: Blogs, Politics, and Power: A Special Issue of Public Choice." *Public Choice* 134:1–13.

Dworkin, Ronald. 1998. "Darwin's New Bulldog." *Harvard Law Review* 111 (7): 1718–38.

———. 2000. "Philosophy and Monica Lewinsky." *New York Review of Books*, March 9.

Fleury, Jean-Baptiste. 2010. "Drawing New Lines: Economists and Other Social Scientists on Society in the 1960s." In *The Unsocial Social Science? Economics and Neighboring Disciplines since 1945*, edited by Roger E. Backhouse and Philippe Fontaine. *HOPE* 42 (supplement): 315–42.
———. 2012. "Wandering through the Borderlands of the Social Sciences: Gary Becker's Economics of Discrimination." *HOPE* 44 (1): 1–40.
Foldvary, Fred E. n.d. "The Becker Double Decker." *Progress Report*. www.progress.org/fold82.htm (accessed November 2, 2012).
Freedman, Craig. 1997. "An Insider's View: A Conversation with Claire Friedland." Mimeo, Macquarie University.
Friedman, Milton, and Rose Friedman. 1998. *Two Lucky People*. Chicago: University of Chicago Press.
Landes, William. M. 2009. "The Art of Law and Economics: An Autobiographical Essay." *American Economist* 41 (1): 31–42.
Mata, Tiago. 2011. "Invasion of the Bloggers: A Preliminary Study on the Demography and Content of the Economic Blogosphere." In *Handbook of Economic Methodology*, edited by John Davis and Wade Hands, 514–24. Cheltenham, UK: Edward Elgar.
Munger, Michael C. 2008. "Blogging and Political Information: Truth or Truthiness?" *Public Choice* 134:125–38.
Nashat, Guity. 1980. "Women in the Islamic Republic of Iran." *Iranian Studies* 13 (1–4): 165–94.
Nik-Khah, Edward. 2010. "George J. Stigler." In *The Elgar Companion to the Chicago School of Economics*, edited by Ross B. Emmett, 337–44. Cheltenham, UK: Edward Elgar.
Nik-Khah, Edward, and Robert Van Horn. 2012. "Inland Empire: Economics Imperialism as an Imperative of Chicago Neoliberalism." *Journal of Economic Methodology* 19 (3): 259–82.
Posner, Richard A. 1972. "Some Thoughts on Legal Education." *University of Chicago Law School Record* (Winter): 19.
———. 1973a. *Economic Analysis of Law*. Boston: Little, Brown.
———. 1973b. "Reflections on Consumerism." *University of Chicago Law School Record* (Spring): 19.
———. (1973) 1986. *Economic Analysis of Law*. 2nd ed. Boston: Little, Brown.
———. 1987a. "The Law and Economics Movement." *American Economic Review* 77 (2): 1–13.
———. 1987b. "What Am I? A Potted Plant?" *New Republic*, September 28.
———. 1990. "Review of Honorable Justice: The Life of Oliver Wendell Holmes." *Wall Street Journal*, August 9.
———. 1992. *Sex and Reason*. Cambridge: Harvard University Press.
———. 1995a. *Aging and Old Age*. Chicago: University of Chicago Press.
———. 1995b. *Overcoming Law*. Cambridge: Harvard University Press.
———. 1999a. *An Affair of State: The Investigation, Impeachment, and Trial of President Clinton*. Cambridge: Harvard University Press.

———. 1999b. *The Problematics of Moral and Legal Theory*. Cambridge: Harvard University Press.

———. 2001. *Public Intellectuals: A Study of Decline*. Cambridge: Harvard University Press.

———. 2002a. "In over Their Heads When Intellectuals Tackle Issues beyond Their Expertise, They Often Finish Way Off Base." *Boston Globe*, January 27.

———. 2002b. "The Professors Profess. Ordinary People Can Say Stupid Things. Brilliant People Do It Brilliantly." *Atlantic Monthly*, February.

———. 2008. *How Judges Think?* Cambridge: Harvard University Press.

———. 2009. "A Conversation with Judge Richard A. Posner." *Duke Law Journal* 58:1807–23.

Posner, Richard A., and William M. Landes. 1986. "New Light on Punitive Damages." *Regulation Magazine* 10 (1): 33–36, 54.

"Putting a New Twist on Business Journalism." 1988. *Magazine for Magazine Management* 17 (3).

Ryerson, James. 2000. "The Outrageous Pragmatism of Judge Richard Posner." *Lingua Franca* 10 (4): 26–34.

"Sense and Nonsense." 2003. Review of *Law, Pragmatism, and Democracy*, by Richard Posner. 2003. *Economist*, June 19.

Swedberg, Richard. 1990. *Economics and Sociology*. Princeton: Princeton University Press.

Woodly, Deva. 2008. "New Competencies in Democratic Communication? Blogs, Agenda Setting, and Political Participation." *Public Choice* 134 (1): 109–23.

Private Intellectuals and Public Perplexity: The Economics Profession and the Economic Crisis

Philip Mirowski and Edward Nik-Khah

1. Agnotology and the Modern Public Face of Economics

It is beginning to dawn that the Great Recession of 2007–? has not only been a crisis of economic contraction and financial failure but has also precipitated a profound crisis of epistemic and scientific dimensions.[1] As Maureen Tkacik (2010) puts it, the general public responded to events by wanting to feel less stupid but were then shocked by how stupid those in positions of authority appeared to be. As all manner of glib expositors flooded the airwaves and the blogosphere, many people reasonably began to wonder if any experts were trustworthy under any circumstances. In particular, economists' rationalist insistence on their deep mathematical technologies of taming uncertainty ran up smack against their plaintive pleas that no one could have predicted the crisis. It was worse when economists with stellar credentials tended to wander aimlessly from one "culprit" to another—from improvident borrowers to "animal spirits" to "toxic assets" to ratings agencies to clueless regulators to sovereign investment funds to an obscure shadow banking sector and beyond—revealing not

---

Correspondence may be addressed to Philip Mirowski, History and Philosophy of Science, 452 Geddes Hall University of Notre Dame, Notre Dame, IN 46556; e-mail: Mirowski.1@nd.edu. We wish to thank Duke's Center for the History of Political Economy for research support.

1. For some clear statements of this realization, see Davies and McGoey 2012, Tkacik 2010, and Ferguson 2012.

only that they had been blindsided but that they came equipped with no fixed conception of the right places to look for possible sources of breakdown: maybe they never entertained the real possibility of breakdown in the first place. The spectacle of the flailing economists prompted some to wonder aloud whether the profession was rendering the public more stupid rather than more informed. Certainly the orthodox professionals never publicly entertained the possibility of the culpability of the economics profession in the run-up to the crisis.

Our primary thesis is that the crisis has revealed a severe epistemological contradiction at the heart of the modern economics profession, as well as highlighted a new set of practices and institutions that have developed since 1980 to paper over the contradiction. Both the current authors have argued elsewhere that the orthodox profession has become more "neoliberal" over time in a very precise sense: following the work of Friedrich Hayek and the Mont Pèlerin Society, orthodox economics has shifted from earlier portrayals of markets as allocation mechanisms for scarce means to given ends and toward versions of markets as ideal information processors.[2] We take that proposition as given here, because we aim to explore one of its most important implications: namely, that it sets up a treacherous dynamic interplay between the economics profession and the public, brought to the surface by the crisis. In a phrase, neoliberal theory in the context of economic crisis creates problems for economists' self-image as public intellectuals.

In the neoliberal playbook, intellectuals are inherently shady characters precisely because they sell their pens for hire to private interests: that is their inescapable lot in life as participants in the marketplace of ideas. It is "The Market" as superior information processor that ultimately sorts out what the masses should deem as Truth, at least in the fullness of time. This informs Robert Barro's position that, as long as they keep paying us, we must be right. This stance creates a problem for the economics profession, because it drives a wedge between trusting economists to clarify issues of great public import and trusting The Market to arrive at time-tested knowledge. This epistemic tension becomes a full-blown contradiction when the issue becomes the possibility of the breakdown of The Market itself. If one adopts the hard neoliberal horn of the dilemma, then the intricate operation of The Market is truly inscrutable, unknowable by any

---

2. This narrative was first broached in Mirowski 2002 and made much more precise in Mirowski 2009 and Mirowski and Plehwe 2009, and much elaborated in Nik-Khah 2011.

individual person, and thus economists are charlatans who keep pretending to know what they can never know. From this perspective, The Market has never actually failed, even in the current crisis; all that has happened is that economists have befogged our understanding of the necessary accommodations that must occur in order for the Spontaneous Order to come to terms with current events. Economists have been engaging in their usual obfuscation and are now being pared away by Occam's razor. Clearly, in this neoliberal frame, economists (with few exceptions) end up looking like part of the problem, not generally part of the solution. Yet, if one instead occupies the more "moderate" horn of the dilemma, then orthodox economics theory was never fundamentally falsified, because it was the markets themselves that bore inherent flaws, which only the economists can be trusted to rectify. However, this bumps up hard against the empirical phenomenon apparent for all the public to see: the orthodox profession was blindsided by the depth and pervasiveness of the crisis, and has been perplexed and befuddled as to any consensus diagnosis of the crisis, much less appropriate measures to rectify it. And worse, there is no limit to how "deep" the market failures go. There is no reason not to think that "market failure" itself betokens failure of the orthodox economics profession as well (Ferguson 2012).

Neither horn of this dilemma is very tolerable, so in the aftermath of economic collapse the economics profession has sought to have it both ways: the lesson they would want to draw from the crisis is that the public should trust *both* The Market and the economics profession to rescue them from economic disaster (Davies and McGoey 2012, 77). This happened on both the notional left and the notional right. Pace Robert Barro, this contradiction has proved to be a source of growing dissatisfaction with economists on the part of the public. Our contribution to this distressing situation is to document how some elements within the economics profession have sought to sustain this impossible straddle, in order to modulate between the two opposed horns of the dilemma.

The hypothesis we propose to pursue is that there have surfaced in the crisis some relatively systematic attempts to pump doubt and confusion into public discourse; in other words, some "explanations" of manifestations of the crisis and its aftermath have been launched as trial balloons *not* expressly for purposes of further test and elaboration by sanctioned professional economists but as calculated interventions in public discourse. The orthodox economist cannot help but try to get his audience to simultaneously trust markets and trust economists, denying the implicit divergence. Older notions of the role of the "public intellectual" referred to someone who serves to both personify and clarify positions of great import in public debate (Posner 2003); but one of the signal contemporary postmodern developments has been the genesis and nurture of intellectuals poised and primed to muddy up the public mind and consequently foil and postpone most political action, and hence to preserve the status quo ante.

The literature that discusses this feature of public discourse travels under the rubric of *agnotology*: the focused study of the intentional manufacture of doubt and uncertainty in the general populace for specific political motives.[3] This literature refers to phenomena very different from an older "sociology of propaganda," which was an artifact of Cold War theories of totalitarian societies. Agnotology instead studies a pronounced market-based set of procedures, as opposed to propaganda, which tends to emanate from a single source. It situates the practice of the manufacture of doubt as rooted in the professions of advertising and public relations, with close connections to the organization of think tanks and lobbying firms. Its essence is a series of techniques and technologies to both *use* and *influence* independently existing academic disciplines for fostering impressions of implacable controversy where actual disputes are marginal, wreaking havoc with outsider perceptions of the configuration of orthodox doctrines, and creating a parallel set of spokespersons and outlets for ideas that are convenient for the behind-the-scenes funding interests, combined with the inflation of disputes in the name of "balance" in order to infuse the impression in outsiders that nothing has been settled within the core research community. The ultimate purpose of erection of this Potemkin controversy is to stymie action. The earliest examples of agnotology were focused on instances deployed in the natural sciences, most specifically, on the political controversies over the cancer consequences of tobacco smoke, Star Wars antimissile systems, the theory of evolution, the efficacy of pharmaceuticals, and the causes and consequences of global warming (Oreskes and Conway 2010; Michaels 2008; Proctor 2012; Sismondo 2011).[4]

---

3. The term was coined in 1992 by the linguist Iain Boal, and first used to designate a new approach to science studies in Proctor and Scheibinger 2008. For a primer that provides the motivation for agnotology, see the introductory chapter of that volume. For the present purposes, we note only that it should be sharply distinguished from *agnoiology*, "the doctrine of things of which we are necessarily ignorant" (27).

4. In other words, think tanks have been able to recruit esteemed members of the scientific community in good standing to volunteer in various agnotological projects, to better cultivate

The stance adopted in this essay is that if agnotological procedures can be found regularly deployed in physics and biology and climate science, then we should not think it beyond the pale that they can be readily found in economics as well.[5] Agnotology studies enumerate a number of hallmark techniques, from the accusation of opponents of dealing in "junk science" to the manipulation of the media through various public relations techniques, to the magnification of "uncertainties," the circumvention of various prior academic outlets and peer review structures, attacks on the legitimacy of existing experts, and appeals for "balance" to accord credibility to otherwise fringe explanations. Agnotology is both *social* and *constructivist*; it is not concerned with isolated lone mavericks, and it approaches truth as a flexible construct. Agnotological fomentation of ignorance happens on many different scales: incidents at the individual level are much easier to document and understand than those that happen at the scale of (let us say) the large subset of the profession devoted to macroeconomic theory. For instance, take the individual case of Joseph Stiglitz having to undergo a bit of targeted agnogenesis. Big money cascaded into financial economics in order to defend the sector from threats of regulation of derivatives in 2010–11. Many think tanks and public relations firms produced "position papers" arguing that any attempt to rein in derivatives would be disastrous. One such contract research house issuing papers was Keybridge Associates. Their report drew attention because of some very high-profile names attached to the document as "advisers": Professor Stiglitz for one, David Laibson of Harvard for another. The only problem was that, when the report was brought to the attention of those worthies, they felt impelled to go on record as repudiating the report (Sorkin 2011). What Keybridge had done was pay them a prior retainer for some other purposes, and then attached their names to documents that they would not normally endorse, without notifying them of its activities. Now, was Keybridge attempting to influence the positions of Joseph Stiglitz? No; rather, it was pursuing the standard agnotological procedure of

---

the ignorance that lies at the foundations of the neoliberal conception of social order. At the risk of venturing into thorny questions beyond the scope of the current essay, we reproduce the following quotation from Hayek's *Constitution of Liberty* (1960, 378; our italics): "There is not much reason to believe that, if at any one time the best knowledge which we possess were made available to all, the result would be a much better society. *Knowledge and ignorance are relative concepts.*"

5. See, in particular, Ferguson 2012, chap. 8. The first author has sought to make this case in greater detail in Mirowski 2011.

the manufacture of ignorance and confusion over what Stiglitz stood for in the minds of the public. The fact that this was just one element of a full-service agnotological offensive is demonstrated by another concurrent parallel activity, the manufacture of an astroturfed letter campaign to the Commodity Futures Trading Commission opposing rule changes to bank control of derivatives markets (Brush and Benson 2010). These are all standard practices from the agnotological playbook, orchestrated by firms located somewhere "outside" the academic sphere but "inside" the beltway. And, when it came to the regulation of derivatives, money talked.

There have been a plethora of similar agnotological initiatives over the past few years: the artificial brouhaha over whether spending austerity can actually produce economic growth, the meme that the Troubled Asset Relief Program procedure was totally successful and cost the taxpayer not a penny, and so on. Rather than survey a ragbag sequence of micro-level agnotological interventions in the crisis, having little common denominator from one instance to the next, the aim of this essay is to document two discrete cases of the manufacture of ignorance. In what follows, we document the fabrication and promulgation of two singular alternative narratives concerning the crisis, honed and simplified so they can fit on a placard or a stump speech teleprompter. In the first case, economists promote a universal nostrum for everything that ails the body politic; in the second, the narrative has the fingerprints of think tanks all over it. In both cases, we observe how economists negotiate the straddle between trusting economists and trusting The Market. As Thomas Pynchon wrote in that great twentieth-century classic, *Gravity's Rainbow*, "If you have them asking the wrong questions, you don't have to worry about the right answers."

2. Incident One:
Market Designers Flip over the TARP

In this section, we examine the circumstances surrounding the promotion (and subsequent demise) of the idea that the government could deliver us from financial calamity by devising an auction to remove "toxic assets" from the balance sheets of large banks. Most relevant from the present perspective was that the role of volunteer hazmat team was to be played by a small band of "market designers"—game theorists and experimental economists who were experts in the construction and deployment of specialized auctions. Curiously, these theorists were called in to assist with the justification and passage of the Troubled Asset Relief Program (TARP) in the confusion of late 2008.

The plan to run an auction for toxic assets originated in the immediate aftermath of the March 2008 Bear Stearns collapse, and from the conviction among market participants and some Treasury and Federal Reserve staff that it would be wise to have a plan to "pull off the shelf" in the case of another Bear Stearns–type emergency (Swagel 2009; Sorkin 2009). After several rounds of discussion between staff at the Treasury and the New York and DC Federal Reserve Banks, Neel Kashkari and Phillip Swagel drafted a memo titled "'Break the Glass': Bank Recapitalization Plan."[6] In this memo, Kashkari and Swagel identified alternative emergency measures, argued in favor of using asset auctions to remove mortgage-related assets from bank balance sheets, and set forth a timeline for completing the asset purchases. Secretary of the Treasury Henry Paulson would eventually second their judgment to purchase on ideological grounds,[7] but at that juncture essentially ordered that the plan be set aside.

So when the emergency did eventually arrive, following the September collapse of Lehman Brothers, breaking the glass was something Paulson and Federal Reserve Chairman Ben Bernanke attempted to do. They began to make rounds to convince members of Congress of the need for an emergency asset purchase plan, solicited an auction plan from the New York Fed, and approached academic market designers to fill in the details.[8] But they almost immediately began to encounter difficulties. Bernanke gave a performance at Congress for which he was "much ridiculed": during a hearing on the impending asset purchase plan, Bernanke laid out a plan to purchase troubled assets from banks at "close to the hold-to-maturity price," a slippery magnitude that was highly disputable, but certainly meant paying prices much higher than currently prevailed in asset markets (Ferguson and Johnson 2009, 28–29).[9] Serious criticisms immediately surfaced: Doesn't this purchase plan just boil down to giving Wall Street a subsidy? Then why bother with the circumlocutions? Given the

---

6. A draft of the plan, dated April 15, 2008, is available at www.scribd.com/doc/21266810/Too-Big-To-Fail-Confidential-Break-the-Glass-Plan-from-Treasury.

7. "Secretary Paulson's intent to use TARP to purchase assets reflected a philosophical concern with having the government buy equity stakes in banks: he saw it as fundamentally a bad idea to have the government involved in bank ownership" (Swagel 2009, 50).

8. Oliver Armantier and James Vickery of the New York Fed delivered the baseline auction proposal on September 20; during the following week, the Treasury and the New York and Washington Feds reached out to the academic market designers Lawrence Ausubel, Peter Cramton, Jacob Goeree, Charles Holt, Paul Milgrom, Jeremy Bulow, and Jonathan Levin. See Armantier, Holt, and Plott 2011 and Klemperer 2010.

9. See "Bernanke's Comments" 2008. The concern was with "mark to market" accounting rules, under which low prices might make banks appear insolvent.

nature of the emergency, was it realistic to believe that a relatively small asset purchase plan would do the job? While these objections were gaining intensity in the public sphere, the Treasury worked behind closed doors to craft the original "Break the Glass" memo into a legislative proposal. The initial effort, which totaled only about two and a half pages, was viewed by many as so insubstantial as to be insulting; the House voted down the initial bill based on the proposal. Clearly the plan was in jeopardy.

It was in this context—with skepticism about the asset auctions abounding, and financial disaster looming—that market designers assumed a public role in the debate over TARP. Market designers soon found themselves in the public spotlight when Bernanke and Swagel referred to market designers' expertise when fielding concerns about the prices to be paid in their plan,[10] and in short order two of the academic market designers approached by the Treasury, Lawrence Ausubel and Peter Cramton, emerged publicly to defend the legitimacy of the asset purchase plan. They claimed they could design an auction that would improve on the Treasury's approach in the sense of establishing lower "competitive market prices," a prospect that did not sound very salubrious from the standpoint of Bernanke, Paulson, and the bevy of Wall Street lobbyists who had already gone on record with their concerns about the consequences of driving prices too low.[11] If these microeconomists were to be politically useful, they had better manage to get on the same page as Treasury officials and the Fed. Ausubel and Cramton (2008a) responded by creatively interpreting "competitive market prices" to mean prices that were "reasonably close to value," by which they meant basically the same thing as Bernanke's "hold-to-maturity" prices.[12] The plan purported to allow for the Treasury to manipulate its demand for securities, thereby manipulat-

---

10. For example: "Treasury is talking with the experts you would expect—prominent academics who have designed auctions. . . . Treasury is committed to get the market price as best it can" (Swagel, quoted in Greg Mankiw, "A Defense of the Paulson Plan," *Greg Mankiw's Blog*, September 25, 2008, gregmankiw.blogspot.com/2008/09/defense-of-paulson-plan.html). Whereas the quote is unattributed in this blog entry, Swagel (2009, 47) has subsequently made clear that he was its author.

11. For an example of the latter, see Tim Ryan's "Lesson from Saving and Loan Rescue" (2008). Ryan was the president and CEO of the Securities Industry and Financial Markets Association, a lobbying group.

12. In an NPR interview with David Kestenbaum, Cramton made it clear that he shared Bernanke's concern: "If the price [for a toxic asset] was too low then the banks would collapse and we would still have a mess." See the transcript of the interview ("Complicated Reverse Auction May Aid in Bailout"), October 10, 2008, www.npr.org/templates/story/story.php?storyId=95591129.

ing the price paid, while preserving the ability to claim that the prices paid were still "market" prices, at least in some sense, an intention that has been subsequently acknowledged:

> A concern of many at the Treasury was that the reverse auctions would indicate prices for MBSs so low as to appear to make other companies appear to be insolvent if their balance sheets were revalued to the auction results. This could easily be handled within the reverse auction framework, however. . . . we could experiment with the share of each security to bid on; the more we purchased, the higher, presumably, would be the price that resulted. (Swagel 2009, 56)

The claim that, armed with the right technique, the Treasury could in effect "go the market one better," while not baldly implausible, did look like they were claiming that the circle could, in fact, be squared: the government could pay greater than market prices, yet the act of doing so could be rendered "transparent" by the notional market setup.[13] But to the extent that it was possible to ignore this little detail, that would pave the way toward accepting the Treasury's position: issues ranging from executive compensation to reform of the structural composition of the financial sector to direct banishment of certain formats of derivatives immediately fell by the wayside. At a time when the most publicly visible economists were arguing against the TARP, the endorsement of these market designers was surely powerful.[14]

According to the market designers, if you understood the crisis from the correct microeconomic perspective you would come to realize how necessary their intervention was. Market designers claimed the problem stemmed from an absence of liquidity, not—crucially—pervasive insolvency. In their frame, banks possessed a variety of assets, some worthless but most others pretty valuable, and it was the inability to distinguish between the two that caused the crisis. By purchasing these assets, the government would reestablish liquidity, not merely by removing toxic assets from the banks' balance sheets but by releasing information that

---

13. Promoting confusion about what markets are supposed to be has become standard operating procedure among market designers. To wit: "In addition to markets, there is also the market, an abstraction as in 'the market economy' or 'the free market' or 'the market system.' The abstract market arises from the interaction of many actual markets" (McMillan 2002, 6).

14. The fact they were *academic* economists was significant. Swagel noted that Wall Street economists were also in favor of the TARP, but acknowledged that people would be suspicious of their judgments (Swagel, quoted in Mankiw, "Defense of the Paulson Plan").

would establish the assets' true values. One immediate consequence of this view was that the imposing magnitude of the toxic asset problem was not necessarily worrisome, nor was the possibility that the TARP program would be unable to remove the vast majority of the toxic assets from banks' balance sheets:

> The "losers" are not left high and dry. By determining the market clearing price, the auction increases liquidity. . . . The auction has effectively aggregated information about the security's value. This price information is the essential ingredient needed to restore the secondary market for mortgage backed securities. (Ausubel and Cramton 2008a, 2)

What mattered, they insisted, was "information": information would summon forth funds from private actors, thereby thawing frozen secondary markets. The basis for this claim was that the assets to be purchased had a true, objective value that was the same for all bidders, or in the argot of game theory, "common" valued. According to conventional theory, one should expect in such cases that purchasers of such assets should misjudge this objective value, resulting in a kind of undesirable behavior called the "winner's curse." Market designers believed they could mitigate such problems by designing markets that efficiently aggregate information and thereby assist market participants to discover the true value of items being sold. Although one way to read the market designers' argument was that one should generally trust existing markets to do the best job of aggregating information about assets, there were specific flaws (resulting from the nature of the commodity exchanged) that necessitated a suitably trained economist to provide a helping visible hand. In circumstances like these, with the largest financial firms in the nation perched on the precipice of default, the stakes were dangerously high, making their participation all the more crucial.

However, in practice, the auction design process would encounter serious difficulties. The Treasury had initially selected as a baseline auction a design that "although undoubtedly sub-optimal in the formal mechanism design sense, it was deemed simple, transparent, and robust enough to be implemented rapidly and effectively" (Armantier, Holt, and Plott 2011, 6). In a crisis, especially important was the speed of deployment, since from the perspective of the "Break the Glass" memo the Treasury had already lost a week because of the House's rejection of the first version of TARP. Unfortunately, the market designers responded to the Treasury's call for assistance by submitting wildly incompatible designs for the auctions, necessitating the Treasury to decide between the rival analyses (Ausubel and Cramton 2008c; Klemperer 2010; Armantier, Holt, and Plott 2011). By itself, the presence of rival proposals was not an insuperable obstacle, but complicating matters was that from the perspective of the Treasury one could not tell on paper what the best auction form was (Swagel 2009; Armantier, Holt, and Plott 2011). For example, one dispute broke out over whether to run an "open" or "sealed bid" auction. This had historically been one of the most basic issues that market designers grapple with. Which one was to be preferred was supposed to turn on which mechanism did the best job of aggregating information, but theory provided neither guidance about which form was better nor guidance about whether either form would bring new bits of useful information into the market. There were an enormous number of distinct heterogeneous securities (over twenty-three thousand types), but apparently there was no reliable price information from either markets (which had ground to a halt) or standard simulation methods (which had proved unreliable). Therefore, there was no reason for any market participant to generalize from information released by getting the price "right" for one security to the thousands of others available. The market designers placed in charge of implementing the auction acknowledged, "The relevant issues could not be addressed directly with economic theory" (Armantier, Holt, and Plott 2011, 4).[15] The dispute over auction forms raised a second and more serious problem: there was no good reason to believe that the auctions would do what the market designers said they would: namely, summoning a chain of events that would eventually bring the economy out of crisis by, in the first place, aggregating dispersed information. After all, no work had been done by market designers on how to fix a collapsing economy.

Since market designers could identify no single optimal auction, the Treasury decided to set up two teams and asked them to more fully develop their proposals. Whereas the "Break the Glass" memo called for announcing auction terms within two weeks of TARP's passage, followed by the commencement of auctions in another two weeks, it took until the end of October to even manage to narrow down the candidates to two alternatives (Swagel 2009, 55). Projections at that point had the first auctions beginning no earlier than December. Some Treasury staff became

---

15. More specifically, Armantier, Holt, and Plott (2011, 13) acknowledged that "there is no Bayesian Nash equilibrium bidding strategy for a similar auction that we can use as a benchmark. The reference price auction is beyond current theory."

increasingly nervous about performance, regarding the auction design process as a "science experiment" run amok: market designers had always insisted that the performance of the auctions was sensitive to even seemingly minor changes in rules, yet they could not even agree about how rule changes would affect performance. They wanted to implement both of the alternative auction forms and use the first set of auctions as trial runs, a prospect that surely failed to inspire confidence. And this in the midst of a collapsing world economy.

Meanwhile, markets themselves had turned against the TARP plan. Things initially had started out well for the Treasury. The first announcement of the toxic asset purchase plan led immediately (on September 18) to a gain on the Dow of 410 points, followed by another 369 points the very next day. Paulson (2010, 258, 264) observed that the Treasury's plan had "acted like a tonic to the markets." Unfortunately, matters went from bad to worse to catastrophic over the next two weeks, at least if one trusted the judgment of markets. The Dow plummeted, and credit markets remained frozen. While it was tempting to attribute the declines to the initial failure to pass TARP, its passage on Friday, October 3, made this a difficult position to maintain, since the declines continued unabated. When the declines resumed the following Monday and spread across the world, Paulson interpreted financial markets as having judged that "TARP would not provide a quick enough fix" (Paulson 2010, 334; see also Swagel 2009, 50). But by then, the handwriting was on the wall: Bernanke and various Treasury staff had been for at least a week expressing doubts that the asset purchase program would work; Paulson himself intimated to President George W. Bush that the Treasury would probably need to purchase equity in the banks on October 1, *two days before TARP's passage*. On October 13, Paulson informed the CEOs of Citigroup, Wells Fargo, JP Morgan, Bank of America, Merrill Lynch, Goldman Sachs, Morgan Stanley, Bank of New York Mellon, and State Street Bank that the Treasury now intended to emphasize capital injections—and he instructed these nine banks to accept them (Paulson 2010, 363–68; Swagel 2009, 50–52). By the end of October, Paulson canceled the auctions and instructed his staff to concentrate on capital injections instead (Paulson 2010, 389; Swagel 2009, 58). When markets judged the prospective market-based program to be faulty, the Treasury heeded the markets, not the economists.

To the Treasury, it ultimately didn't much matter whether it resorted to boutique auctions or capital injections: to be sure, Paulson and his staff might lose face through their reversal, but Paulson had been considering such action well before TARP passed. What mattered was political efficacy, not austere academic notions of "efficiency." The main policy objective was to stop the market freefall without succumbing to bank "nationalization," and the capital injection program basically accomplished that. But to the market designers, it made all the difference in the world. The market designers still under contract responded to the Treasury's volte-face in emphasis by insisting that there was no good reason the Treasury could not use auctions to purchase bank shares in addition to toxic assets (Ausubel and Cramton 2008b), a position they maintained until the Treasury made it clear it had no intention to seek release of any additional TARP funds, therefore foreclosing any prospect for using auctions for the remainder of the Bush administration.

Once that happened, things turned ugly: the market designers for hire themselves became some of the most fierce critics of TARP. In an interview for NPR Ausubel complained, "Instead of conducting transparent auctions, the Treasury is going to instead distribute suitcases of cash"; for Cramton, "It really is moving down the path to crony capitalism, in my mind, where the government is picking winners and losers in a nontransparent way."[16] This turnabout, however turncoat, was easy to pull off because both the market designers and the anti-TARP petitioners now claimed to have shared very similar assumptions about the economic role of government.[17] At times these shared views became apparent: during the period of the most heated disagreement, the Hoover and Cato economist Charles Calomiris stated to NPR that "if Larry (Ausubel) can convince me that he's got the right mechanism, that's great"; Calomiris went on to point out that he and Ausubel actually agreed on many things.[18]

In hopes of getting auctions back on the agenda for the incoming Obama administration, market designers publicly promoted what appeared to be a scientific demonstration that the Paulson Treasury had taken the wrong approach. Cramton claimed that his study had demonstrated "the auction was a success. The banks traded their toxic assets for solid capital, and the taxpayers got a fair deal." The fact that these "banks," "taxpayers," and

---

16. See the transcript of the NPR story, "Study Suggests Buying Toxic Assets Could Work," November 18, 2008, www.npr.org/templates/story/story.php?storyId=97161786. Ausubel and Cramton (2009, 1) repeat the "suitcase approach" charge.

17. Primarily economists associated with the University of Chicago and various neoliberal think tanks. The speedy production of this petition is discussed in some detail in Mirowski 2013.

18. Transcript of NPR interview, "Complicated Reverse Auction May Aid in Bailout."

"assets" were only sketchy constructs in a laboratory did not necessarily detract from the lesson and might even have served to highlight the difference between the naked politics of Paulson's Treasury and the calm, impartial science of the market designers. One could institute real markets in laboratories, removed from the noise of the real world, and these real markets deemed the market designers to have been correct. But what did getting a "fair deal" have to do with the market designers' theory of the crisis? At most it seemed only to address the issue of whether one could consider the price generated to be a legitimate "market" price—a matter that really could not be settled by an experiment, anyhow. This was a far different claim than the one they had originally made to the Treasury: in their initial submission, Ausubel and Cramton argued not for the information aggregation ability of markets in general but instead for a very specific kind of "clock auction." While their early public statements did take care to portray their auctions as marketlike, they tended to emphasize to the Treasury how their clock auction improved on other designs:

> A security's value is closely related to its "hold to maturity value," which is roughly the same for each bidder. Each bidder has an estimate of this value, but the true value is unknown. The dynamic auction, by revealing market supply as the price declines, lets the bidders condition their bids on the aggregate market information. As a result, common-value uncertainty is reduced and bidders will be comfortable bidding more aggressively without falling prey to the winner's curse—the tendency in a procurement setting of naïve sellers to sell at prices below true value.... A principal benefit of the clock auction is the inherent price-discovery feedback mechanism that is absent in any sealed-bid auction format. Specifically, as the auction progresses, participants learn how the aggregate demand changes with price, which allows bidders to update their own strategies and avoid the winner's curse.... Efficiency in the clock auction always exceeded 97%. (Ausubel and Cramton 2008c, 10)

In holding that the value of the toxic assets was "roughly the same for each bidder," this passage corresponds to the point made above, that market designers viewed the toxic assets as "common" valued, and that such cases posed for the market designer the task of figuring out how to aggregate information. It also makes explicit the mandate of Bernanke's warning to avoid purchasing assets at too-low prices (although market designers offered a different rationale for doing so—avoiding the winner's curse). But what is most notable about this passage is that it advocates a specific type of auction—a clock auction—and does so on the basis of its ability to avoid the winner's curse, as evident by its demonstrably superior "efficiency." The reason this claim is so notable is because it is incoherent on its own terms: it makes sense to attribute "97% efficiency" only in the case of private valued auctions, where bidders value assets idiosyncratically.[19] If toxic assets are common valued, meaning that all bidders value the assets identically, then all distributions are efficient *by definition*, and therefore the efficiency criterion is useless, or at best irrelevant. While the criterion does make sense in the case of private valued auctions, one can never suffer from the winner's curse in such cases, again *by definition*, and therefore the argument to prefer the clock auction on the grounds of information aggregation is nonsense. Since the market designers' claim that one could avert the crisis by increasing information about the value of assets implied that the assets must be common valued (or else the link between auction performance and crisis aversion is severed), the "efficiency" evidence is especially misleading.

Now, anyone who has taken a course in game theory during the past decade should immediately recognize that the claim advanced by Ausubel and Cramton to the Treasury in support of their "clock auction" was misleading. But perhaps the point of the exercise was never to get the particulars of the economics justification correct, and instead to get the Treasury to purchase their "clock auction." Sifting through all the coverage of the TARP plan, one comes across an acute observation made by a *Newsweek* reporter:

> [Ausubel and Cramton] hope to convince officials that not only does a reverse auction work, but, in the event the Treasury conducts one, to run it off their patented software platform. . . . Ausubel and Cramton own two auction-services companies, Power Auctions and Market Design, each of which handle the back end of auctions for companies and foreign governments. They've already helped the French government sell electricity off its grid and Dutch energy companies auction off natural gas. (Philips 2008)

---

19. And, indeed, the studies that Ausubel and Cramton draw on to get their 97 percent figure (Kagel and Levin 2001, 2009) provided experimental treatments of private valued auctions.

In fact, Power Auctions and Market Design held the patents for the stipulated clock auction. But the presentation delivered by Ausubel and Cramton for the Treasury listed several additional "Typical Auction Related Activities" (product design; definition of detailed auction rules; auction software specification, development, and testing; bidder training; establishment of an auction "war room"; operation of auction; postauction reports on success of auction and possible improvements for future auctions) for which Power Auctions and Market Design could provide assistance.[20] Of course we do not know the exact provisions that would have been contracted between the parties, since the Treasury scrapped the plan, but given the previous record of market designers, it is entirely reasonable to believe that they shaped their claims with an eye on landing lucrative contracts (Nik-Khah 2008). For years, market designers had made all sorts of fantastic claims for newfangled markets—They can reverse global warming! Improve access to health care! Redress racial and gender discrimination, without committing "reverse discrimination!" Even achieve "free lunch redistribution!"—so long as you hire their firms to build them to your exacting specifications (after all, "details matter"). They have almost always directed the pitch at cash-strapped governments, urging them in particular to sell off public assets to private oligopolistic concerns; in the case of toxic asset auctions, one need only invert the logic.

Unfortunately, no one provided an independent evaluation of market designers' claims. After all, there was a crisis a-brewing. Only a relatively small coterie of market designers ever got invited to participate in market design exercises, and most were partners in a handful of firms with interlocking directorates. In the case of the toxic asset auctions, the job of judging the proposals was assigned to Jeremy Bulow and Paul Milgrom, both partners with Ausubel and Cramton in Market Design. So much for Chinese walls and plausible deniability. It does not verge on the wildly conspiratorial to suggest that such arrangements create some perverse incentives when it comes to reining in some of the more fantastical claims (gaining popular acceptance for them improves the firm's prospects), a fact that has seemed only to encourage ever more extravagant claims:

20. Lawrence Ausubel and Peter Cramton, "Auction Design for the Rescue Plan," slide presentation, October 5, 2008, www.cramton.umd.edu/papers2005–2009/ausubel-cramton-auction-for-rescue-plan-slides.pdf.

The crisis was caused by mispricing: investment bankers were able to sell poor securities for full value based on misleading ratings. This mispricing was supported by the absence of a transparent secondary market for these mortgage-related securities. If we had transparent prices, a lot of the bad things that happened would not have happened. In particular the housing bubble would have been much less, and the investment bankers would not have been able to make such clever use of the rating agencies and create tens-of-thousands of senseless securities obfuscating prices. Even a tiny bit of good market design would have averted the financial crisis by preventing its root cause: the sale of subprime mortgages as near-riskless securities. (Cramton 2008, p. 1)

Calls for sensible regulation and market design were met with condescension before the credit crisis, a condescension that is being reevaluated now.[21]

Good auction design in complex environments . . . requires exploiting the substantial advances that we have seen in market design over the last fifteen years. The recent financial crisis is another example where the principles of market design, if effectively harnessed by regulators, could have prevented or at least mitigated the crisis. (Cramton 2010, 2)

Of course, there is no record of any market designers having actually intervened to prevent the crisis or helped anyone else to ameliorate it, but historical accuracy was never the name of the game, and no one bothers to check for evidence, anyhow: the latter statement was submitted to the NSF as part of a challenge grant proposal. The NSF already awarded its author $400,000 to pursue a related study.[22] And at a recent meeting of the Southern Economic Association, Cramton repeated his claim that market design could have solved the economic crisis. The officer in charge of NSF funding for economics was a copanelist, and she singled out market design as a perfect example of the kind of work the NSF likes to fund: referring to

---

21. "The Credit Crisis and Market Design," *Market Design* (Alvin Roth's blog), January 3, 2009, marketdesigner.blogspot.com/2009/01/credit-crisis-and-market-design.html.

22. News item, "Economics Faculty Have Been Awarded a $400,000 Grant by the National Science Foundation," October 12, 2009, www.bsos.umd.edu/news-and-events/hot-topics/economics-faculty-have-been-awarded-a-$400000–grant-by-the-national-science-foundation.aspx.

work done with the FCC, she gushed, "Auction theory has put $80 billion in the economy!"[23]

To understand what elevates the public activities of market designers from the realm of mere puffery and self-promotion to the level of agnotology, it is necessary to review how their public statements changed over the course of the crisis. Initially, market designers provided public defense of the Treasury plan in both its particulars (the decision to use reverse auctions) and its generalities (they signed a petition to Congress in support of the proposition that government could act beneficially to correct for market failures). Especially important was the seeming independence of the academic support—as Swagel rightly noted, Wall Street economists were cheerleaders for the TARP as well, but no one would pay attention to them. Inevitably, market designers had to walk a tightrope in order to participate, at times stressing their ability to deliver competitive (low) market prices, at others, higher than fire-sale prices. But in the short term, the academics gave the Treasury the arguments it wanted for instrumental ends—to get the TARP passed. Market designers then persisted with their advocacy for auctions even after Treasury insiders had themselves dismissed the plan as unrealistic; once the Treasury changed its plans, the market designers now devolved into free agents, turned on a dime, and attacked the Treasury. Their complaints, rendered loudly and often in the public sphere, resembled nothing so much as those being made by the *opponents* of TARP. If the public was tracking the record of the economists (which it was not—there was a crisis on), they would be justified in wondering: did these market designers have any clear idea what might have *caused* the crisis in the first place? Did they even have any expertise regarding the financial sector? What made this about-face so confusing is that the phantom public could not trace it to any major shift in the Treasury's position: the market designers had registered no dissent about Treasury's plan to inject capital into the banks, at least so long as it was poised to use their auctions to do so. But once they were out of the running for any auction contracts, and kicked out into the cold, market designers merely flipped and adopted the rhetoric of the TARP opponents. So how much of their analytical stance can be traced to the icy slopes of logic, and how much to the fickle fiduciary considerations of their patrons?

---

23. Session titled "Research Funding for Economists." See www.etnpconferences.net/sea/seaarchive/sea2011/User/Program.php?TimeSlot=4#Session11. The second author was present at that session.

3. Incident Two: The Federal Crisis Inquiry Commission, and the Neoliberal Saga of Fannie Mae and Freddie Mac as Prime Causes of the 2008 Crisis

In the early stages of the crisis, think tank economists came up with what would become the single most popular story on the right in America, wrapping the entire crisis up in a neat, tidy package. In this meme, the crisis was first and foremost a housing bubble, which when it burst, had some other unpleasant side effects; loans were extended to a bunch of deadbeats who should never been given a shot at home ownership in the first place; the reason that happened was the ill-conceived Community Reinvestment Act passed by the Democrats in 1977; and then the mortgage loans to the deadbeats were enabled by the Government Sponsored Entities (GSEs) Fannie Mae (Federal National Mortgage Association) and Freddie Mac (Federal Home Loan Mortgage Corporation). Hence, on both the demand and supply sides, the government had polluted the mortgage market, first causing the housing bubble, and then the subsequent collapse. It was all the fault of the government. Full stop.

It is indisputable that Fannie and Freddie had become untenable as vague "public-private" financial entities in the early phases of the crash, as the prices and collateral value of mortgage-backed securities tanked and, as such, were nationalized on September 6, 2008, by the Bush administration (Sorkin 2009, 227–29). Their previous status as purely governmental entities was therefore dubious, a minor glitch in the neoliberal demonization of the government. What is a bit more stunning is that the story that Fannie and Freddie had *caused the crisis* was first put forth a little more than a month later by think tank members Charles Calomiris (whom we encountered in the previous section) and Peter Wallison (American Enterprise Institute [AEI]) in the *Wall Street Journal* (Calomiris and Wallison 2008). As a trial balloon, it initially appeared rather unpromising, both to those with ringside seats at the subsequent collapse of Wall Street giants like ninepins and to various pundits on both sides of the political divide in 2008. For instance, in testimony at the October 23, 2008, session of the House Committee on Oversight and Government Reform, Alan Greenspan explicitly ruled out the hypothesis that Fannie and Freddie were the "primary cause" of the financial crisis, as did Christopher Cox, then chair of the Securities Exchange Commission (SEC). Paul Krugman, smelling a rat, came out fairly early against the whole idea:

Fannie and Freddie had nothing to do with the explosion of high-risk lending a few years ago, an explosion that dwarfed the S&L fiasco. In fact, Fannie and Freddie, after growing rapidly in the 1990s, largely faded from the scene during the height of the housing bubble. Partly that's because regulators, responding to accounting scandals at the companies, placed temporary restraints on both Freddie and Fannie that curtailed their lending just as housing prices were really taking off. Also, they didn't do any subprime lending, because they can't. (Krugman 2008)

Here is where considerations of agnotology kicked in. The think tank collective does not abandon a hypothesis simply because it appears to stumble on a few facts and encounters strenuous opposition.[24] Instead, they are flush and primed to send up multiple trial balloons, observe which way the prevailing winds are blowing, and then invest in further inflation for those that appear to take flight and festoon their political allies. The Fannie/Freddie meme was not the only causal narrative explored by the think tanks, but it sure looked good in crisis-aftermath America, especially after the efforts of various Koch-funded front organizations to commandeer the Tea Party movement began to realize results. The Cato Institute seconded the analysis with alacrity (White 2008). The AEI then threw its weight behind the Fannie/Freddie story, with Wallison (2008, 2009, 2010a, 2010b) as point man, and the echo chamber was revved up. Professional economists were recruited to bolster the narrative. The public choice crowd was quick to contribute to the effort (Congleton 2009). Mark Calabria (2011) from Cato was brought in to fluff up the numbers. Dependable fellow travelers like David Brooks, George Will, and Tyler Cowen chimed in with columns and blogs. Douglas Holtz-Eakin signed on, in a way to soon become important in the Financial Crisis Inquiry Commission. Edward Pinto (2009) at AEI was brought on board to crunch some numbers. Raghuram Rajan (2010) promoted a

---

24. We employ the term *collective* (and, below, *thought collective*) in the sense of Mirowski and Plehwe 2009. In what follows, we can only sketch this collective at work, although it is imperative to acknowledge it operates as a collective, and not the loosely correlated activities of some individuals. For the present purposes, we note that those participating in these efforts were guided by neoliberal ideas about the functioning of markets. We direct those interested in the larger context within which think tanks operate and its relationship to neoliberal approaches to knowledge and markets to Mirowski 2011, chap. 7, and Mirowski 2013, chap. 6.

more politically ambiguous and humanized version of the story in his *Fault Lines*. But the real agnotological breakthrough came when a respected journalist seemingly positioned outside the usual neoliberal precincts (indeed, hailing from within that brimstoned Mordor for the right, the *New York Times*) was somehow induced to write a book also casting Fannie and Freddie as the evil twins behind everything that went wrong in the crisis: Gretchen Morgenson and Josh Rosner's *Reckless Endangerment* (2011). This sparsely sourced and footnote-free book clearly depended heavily on Pinto for the few vague numbers it cited; it was much more expansive when it pursued searing indictments of political figures like Barney Frank, Robert Zoellick, and Andrew Cuomo. A few obscure economists at the Fed came in for especially vituperative comment. At this juncture the thought collective hit a home run: Michael Bloomberg was caught repeating the meme in his outbursts provoked by the Occupy Wall Street movement (Paybarah 2011). Persistence and repetition and emoluments had paid off—the Fannie/Freddie "explanation" had become embedded in the blogosphere and the cultural landscape, spread far and wide by the Republican presidential candidates and beyond. When the SEC brought charges against six former Fannie and Freddie executives in December 2011, Wallison was accorded column inches in the *Wall Street Journal* to crow that he and his comrades had been vindicated.

It was this sequence of events that prompted Joe Nocera (2011), also of the *New York Times*, to bemoan the spread of the Big Lie:

> Thus has Peter Wallison, a resident scholar at the American Enterprise Institute, and a former member of the Financial Crisis Inquiry Commission, almost single-handedly created the myth that Fannie Mae and Freddie Mac caused the financial crisis. His partner in crime is another A.E.I. scholar, Edward Pinto, who a very long time ago was Fannie's chief credit officer. Pinto claims that as of June 2008, 27 million "risky" mortgages had been issued—"and a lion's share was on Fannie and Freddie's books," as Wallison wrote recently. Never mind that his definition of "risky" is so all-encompassing that it includes mortgages with extremely low default rates as well as those with default rates nearing 30 percent. These latter mortgages were the ones created by the unholy alliance between subprime lenders and Wall Street. Pinto's numbers are the Big Lie's primary data point.

The literature attempting to refute this meme was even more prodigious than the usual crisis lit standards; it nearly defies cogent summary.[25] The vulnerability of those skeptical of the GSE meme was the fact that attack on the neoliberal Fannie/Freddie story was often confused with defense of the behavior and structure of Fannie and Freddie, something no politically savvy person of almost any stripe would countenance. Even its supposedly spineless regulator accused Fannie of accounting fraud in 2005 (Morgenson and Rosner 2011, 121). At the end of the day, Fannie and Freddie had made money through heavily promoted ambiguity concerning whether as a privatized entity it had enjoyed a government guarantee of its debt; of course the government takeover settled that question, but only at the expense of debilitating the rest of the banking sector. The fact that it was a cesspit of party political slush funds, machine cronyism, and cooked books did not dispel the undeniable stench of corruption, something Morgenson and Rosner made much of. The other drawback in refuting the neoliberal meme was that almost no one wanted to get bogged down in the minutiae of the extended history of the GSEs, nor in endless picky fights over the numbers, and other subtleties that often eluded the journalists and bloggers. For instance, it was demonstrably the case that Fannie and Freddie were the initial loci of the invention of securitization of mortgages decades ago, but that hardly saddled them with responsibility for every baroque development of securitization thereafter, many of which they avoided. A crisis story that could fit on a three-by-five card, yet revealed multiple layers of slippery ramification just below the surface, was the holy grail for the neoliberal thought collective. Yet, in the end, their three-by-five slogan was a ruse.

There are two pincers of the attack on the Fannie/Freddie meme: the first, concerning the Community Reinvestment Act (CRA), and the second, the weaknesses in the proposition that Fannie and Freddie somehow caused or motivated the housing bubble and subsequent crisis. With regard to the CRA, the largest players in the subprime market were private-sector firms that were not subject to CRA-stipulated rules and regulations. Therefore, for the story to work, the bulk of the subprime action had to happen in the GSEs, but as we shall see, it did not. Furthermore, in institutions subject to the CRA, not all loans fell under the CRA guidelines, so

---

25. For the best examples, consult Engel and McCoy 2011, Muolo and Padilla 2008, Fligstein and Goldstein 2012, Avery and Brevoort 2011, and Madrick and Partnoy 2011. See also Kevin Drum, "The Housing Bubble and the Big Lie," blog post, *Mother Jones*, December 24, 2011, motherjones.com/kevin-drum/2011/12/housing-bubble-and-big-lie.

the proportion of loans affected were quite small. Then, the timing seems a little off, since the CRA came into effect in 1977, but the housing boom dates from much later. It has become commonplace to point out that housing bubbles happened in many countries in the first decade of the millennium, but none of those other countries had any legislation similar to the CRA. And finally, Democrats and Republicans alike basked in the warmth of CRA-style hosannas to the "ownership society," at least until the whole shebang went south. Thus it is not clear that the CRA was much more than background static in the great pell-mell rush to push mortgages off onto all manner of persons ill-equipped to maintain and service them. Some politicians were avid cheerleaders for what had happened, but they did not actually create the elaborate set of mechanisms that constituted the housing bubble.

The primary riposte to the Fannie/Freddie meme is that Fannie and Freddie lost market share in the subprime market to private-sector firms from 2002 until late 2006, and the reason that happened was that it was the private label "originate and securitize" machine that was the main driver behind subprime mortgages and the housing boom in the last decade. Here is where the real pitched battles were fought between the neoliberal think tanks and their opponents. The evidence on the face of it seems pretty straightforward: existing data shows the exit from mortgage finance of savings and loans after 1975, the rise of securitizations by government-sponsored entities from 1972 onward, the loss of market share by Fannie and Freddie beginning in 2002, and the twofold rise of private mortgage-backed securities and finance companies in the early 1990s and the acceleration in 2002.[26] Most analysts by 2006 had been noticing that Fannie and Freddie had been losing market share because they had been avoiding the dicier "subprime" side of the mortgage market, partly because of their own government guidelines. Indeed, Bernanke (2007) before the crisis was arguing that the CRA had been ineffectual precisely because less than 30 percent of Fannie's and Freddie's portfolios consisted of mortgages that could be generously asserted were based on "affordable" or low-income properties. As Moody's reported in 2006, just as the bubble was about to burst:

> Freddie Mac has long played a central role (shared with Fannie Mae) in the secondary mortgage finance market. In recent years, both housing

---

26. See the figure in Drum, "The Housing Bubble and the Big Lie."

GSEs have been losing share within the overall market due to the shifting nature of consumer preferences towards adjustable-rate loans and other hybrid products. For the first half of 2006, Fannie Mae and Freddie Mac captured about 44% of total origination volume—up from a 41% share in 2005, but down from 59% in 2003. Moody's would be concerned if Freddie Mac's market share (*i.e.*, mortgage portfolio plus securities as a percentage of conforming and non-conforming origination), which ranged between 18% and 23% from 1999 through the first half of 2006, declined below 15%. To buttress its market share, Freddie Mac has increased its purchases of private label securities.[27]

The major contention of the think tank economists is that one had to drill down into the balance sheets of the GSEs and reclassify the external private-issued instruments they started buying around 2006 as effectively masked purchases of subprime at one remove (Thompson 2012). While that may or may not be true, it unduly stretches the definition of "responsibility" for the bubble in the first place and diverts attention from the original protagonists. The GSEs had been getting prodded by members of Congress to purchase more subprime; but mostly, the "advice" came too close to the pricking of the housing bubble (Engel and McCoy 2011, 40). This is the reason most outside analysts trace the housing bubble to the private sector and, in particular, specialized subprime originators like Countrywide and Ameriquest (Muolo and Padilla 2008) and the banking firms that repackaged them into baroque securities; it even corrupted profitable subsidiaries of "industrial firms" like GMAC and GE Capital; consequently, "the biggest factor contributing to the subprime boom was securitization" (Engel and McCoy 2011, 17). This trend dovetailed with another trend in the big banks, a transition from deriving much of their profit from loans to deriving it from fees for packaging mortgages (and other loans, such as credit card, auto loan, and student debt) into asset-backed securities (ABS), selling ABS and MBS, creating dummy structured investment vehicles (SIVs) to further reprocess MBS into CDOs,

---

27. Analysis of Freddie Mac by Moody's, December 2006, www.freddiemac.com/investors/pdffiles/fm2006_moodys.pdf. This evidence also calls into question the curious claims by Morgenson and Rosner (2011, 53) that in 1993 "the new Fannie and Freddie [Alternative Qualifying] program institutionalized the endorsement of untested underwriting criteria [for mortgages]." This and similar locutions attempt to bypass or evade the fact that Fannie and Freddie neither pioneered nor engineered the spread of subprime practices and that the timing of events is off for them to bear responsibility.

and so forth. One estimate suggests that income from fee-related activities at commercial banks as a percentage of total revenue increased from 24 percent in 1980 to 31 percent in 1990 to 48 percent in 2003 (Fligstein and Goldstein 2012). Combined with stunning increases in concentration in the mortgage origination market, such that the top twenty-five mortgage originators controlled 90 percent of the market in 2007, the consensus interpretation of events was that the mortgage boom was an adjunct to bigger changes in the private financial sector and not prompted by some outbreak of rabid mendacity among the population of home purchasers.

For the meme that "Fannie and Freddie Did It" to work, it would be necessary to refute and reject this emergent consensus narrative. One major arena in which this happened was the Congress-mandated Financial Crisis Inquiry Commission.

The function of the Financial Crisis Inquiry Commission was purportedly to do for our Great Crisis what Ferdinand Pecora's investigation did for the Great Depression (Perino 2010): provide trenchant research and a communal teaching experience concerning the causes of the crisis. On a public stage, our best and brightest would bring all the possibilities to the table, so that America might come to grips with its tragedy. Or at least that is the way it was sold to the public when it was included in the Fraud Enforcement and Recovery Act of 2009. But after a year and a half of hearings, many of which were made available online,[28] including questioning of over eight hundred witnesses and expenditure of $6 million on staff, the whole pretense of a definitive archive of explanations broke down even before the report was formally issued in January 2011. The four Republican members of the supposedly bipartisan ten-person panel issued a preemptive strike "report" in December 2010 that sought to torpedo the main event (even before the final version had come up for a vote). That sketchy counterstory was more or less included as one of two "dissenting reports" appended to the final published report (2011), the first under the names of Keith Hennessy, Douglas Holtz-Eakin, and Bill Thomas and the second under the name of Peter Wallison. Wallison's appendix made the case for the neoliberal "Fannie/Freddie did it" line summarized above.

What one would derive from reading the document was the concurrent posit of A and not-A as causes of the crisis. The six-person-endorsed

---

28. These disappeared suspiciously soon from the Web after the FCIC was wound up, but were then archived at fcic.law.stanford.edu/hearings.

body of the report pinned the crisis on "failure to effectively rein in excesses in the mortgage and financial markets" (US Federal Crisis Inquiry Commission 2011, xxxvi), which then got parsed as a laundry list of usual suspects: credit rating agencies, failures of regulators, OTC derivatives, crappy mortgages repackaged as sweets, Greenspan, executive compensation, Bernanke, shadow banking, and so on. However, the majority went out of their way to reject one cause: "We examined the role of the GSEs. . . . We conclude these two entities contributed to the crisis, but were not a primary cause. . . . The GSEs participated in the expansion of subprime and other risky mortgages, but they followed rather than led Wall Street" (xxvi). In other words, it went out of the way to insist everything contained in the Wallison appendix was false. The other minority appendix endorsed the Wallison line in passing, but seemed more concerned to absolve Wall Street of any culpability, proclaiming "derivatives did not in any meaningful way cause or contribute to the crisis" (414), and denying that "shadow banking" was even a coherent concept (427).[29] Consequently, it was exceedingly vague about what did cause the crisis, although it did flirt with the notion that it was all China's fault. The first Republican dissent did not even bother with much in the way of evidence.

It must be conceded that Wallison did preface his dissent with the right question: "Why [did] Congress bother to authorize [the FCIC] at all? Without waiting for the Commissioners' insights into the causes of the financial crisis, Congress passed and the President signed the Dodd-Frank Act" (443). Of course, the obvious answer was that the FCIC was set up to fail from the outset, but that might reflect badly on Wallison's willing participation. So instead he opted for an answer that shed some light on agnogenesis. He began by quoting Rahm Emmanuel saying "Never let a good crisis go to waste," and then suggested that the real purpose of the report was to gain some control over the "first draft of history." Wallison's behavior demonstrated that the neoliberal think tanks appreciated the importance of venturing beyond the mere short-term partisan bickering of the first dissent, or the sloppy endless laundry list of the majority report, to providing a simple pithy narrative to contrast with the general cacophony of noise concerning the crisis.

---

29. Wallison's dissent reprised this point: "Wall Street was not a significant participant in the subprime PMBS market between 2004 and 2007, or at any time before" (US Federal Crisis Inquiry Commission 2011, 504). This does border on Orwellian doublethink.

We do not propose to go into detail here as to why Wallison's own narrative indicting the GSEs is fatally flawed, although we believe it is.[30] The point here is rather to suggest that economists from both sides of the (narrowly conceived) political spectrum have conspired to divert attention from serious analysis of the crisis, each for their own respective agnotological purposes. The Bloomberg journalist Jonathan Weil best captured the brazen impudence of pretence behind the FCIC report:

> This, in journalistic parlance, is what we call a clip job. And that's the trouble with much of the commission's 545-page report. There's lots of breezy, magazine-style, narrative prose. But there's not much new information. You can tell the writers knew they were sprinkling MSG on a bunch of recycled material, too, by the way they described their sources. The text and accompanying notes often seem deliberately unclear about whether the commission had dug up its own facts, or was rehashing information already disclosed in court records, news articles or other congressional inquiries. . . .
>
> The FCIC's failure was predictable from the start. To examine the causes of the financial crisis, Congress created a bipartisan panel of 10 political appointees led by Democrat Phil Angelides, a former California state treasurer. What was needed was a nonpartisan investigation directed by seasoned prosecutors (like Pecora was) who know how to cross-examine witnesses and get answers. Whereas Pecora had no fixed deadline, Congress gave the crisis commission until December 2010 to complete its inquiry. Witnesses who didn't want to cooperate fully could simply milk the clock. The panel got a budget of less than $10 million to investigate all the causes of the financial crisis. Lehman's bankruptcy examiner got $42 million to produce a 2,200-page report on the failure of a single company. (Weil 2011)

Having watched some of the hearings online, the first author can attest that witnesses were not questioned rigorously, to say the least. Yves Smith of Nakedcapitalism.com reported the disgust of one of the FCIC staff, who complained, "I am still getting the stink out of my clothes." He understood that both the majority line that it was all the fault of wicked deregulation

---

30. See Min 2011. Min's work on various reasons to doubt Wallison is the basis for the complaints of Nocera (2011), Barry Ritholtz (www.ritholtz.com/blog/), and Paul Krugman. The short version is that Wallison and Pinto have played fast and loose with what counts as "subprime" in the GSE balance sheets.

and the Wallison line that "Fannie/Freddie did it" were equally unavailing. Both versions conspired to help perpetuate a myth that Wall Street financial firms were as much the victim of the crisis as everyone else and existed to keep the proceedings from tripping up the sausage machine that eventually became the Dodd-Frank act.[31] Supposedly neutral economists with impeccable credentials participated in promotion of this travesty. Anat Admanti of Stanford wrote, "Peter Wallison in his dissent attributes blame solely to the government housing policy of earlier administrations. While he is right to identify this as important, he misses other critical ingredients."[32] Jeffrey Miron of Harvard muddied the waters further by introducing the Rogoff-Reinhart neoliberal line: "In asking whether the recent financial crisis could have been avoided, the crucial fact is that crises of various flavors have occurred for centuries in countries around the world. Thus, any explanation based mainly on recent factors—subprime lending, derivatives trading, or financial deregulation—cannot be the whole story. A full account must identify factors that have been present widely, and for centuries."[33] How the Dutch tulip craze would help illuminate the structural deficiencies of a CDO-squared was left for someone else to figure out. We cannot find an example of an orthodox economist who came right out and said that the entire exercise was a cynical whitewash, although many bloggers came close.

The Democrat electoral debacle of November 2010 only exacerbated the tensions underlying the jousting agnotologies within the FCIC, as Representative Darryl Issa subsequently convened an investigation into the mismanagement of the inquiry to settle scores in spring 2011. His subpoenas then unintentionally delivered another lesson in agnogenesis: it seems Peter Wallison broke a number of confidentiality rules while serving on the FCIC, leaking secret Fed data to the AEI, while cochair Bill Thomas secretly prepped many of the representatives of the banks on the level of questions they might expect (US House Committee on Oversight 2011). The purpose of the FCIC had never been to find new things out, so

---

31. This comes from a posting by Yves Smith on Nakedcapitalism.com of January 26, 2011. At the time, Smith's posting could be found at www.americanprogress.org/issues/2011/07/wallison.html, but the page apparently has since disappeared.

32. "Address Excess Leverage," contribution to "Was the Financial Crisis Avoidable?," Room for Debate series, *New York Times*, www.nytimes.com/roomfordebate/2011/01/30/was-the-financial-crisis-avoidable/address-excessive-leverage (accessed November 6, 2012).

33. "More Than Just Greed," contribution to "Was the Financial Crisis Avoidable?," Room for Debate series, *New York Times*, www.nytimes.com/roomfordebate/2011/01/30/was-the-financial-crisis-avoidable/more-than-just-greed.

much as it was to make the preset think tank narrative look good in public. Journalists yawned—so what else is new on the Hill?—but few pulled back to reconsider what this meant about the ongoing miasma that surrounded discussions of the crisis. Here, years after the crisis hit, and millions of dollars thrown at the economics profession, people were still no closer to a richer and more plausible understanding of the crisis than in its immediate aftermath. Worse, this was the unapologetic bottom line of some of the economic orthodoxy as well! (See Lo 2012.) Where was the bracing lucidity born of years of training in the most difficult technicalities of theory, or the ballast of reams of numerical data at our fingertips? Where was the clarifying steel of econometric technique, or the glassy grand transparency of axiomatic method?

None of that seemed to have had any influence whatsoever. Is it any wonder that the most common impression among people who have not bothered to read up on the crisis is that it has been the fault of the government, and that Fannie and Freddie are somehow behind it all?

4. Conclusion

The two incidents analyzed in this essay provide perspective on the contemporary public role of the economics profession in the context of economic crisis. In both the Treasury-Fed and the FCIC cases economists had been called on to perform public roles; in neither case did their participation enlighten the public or develop hypotheses for scholarly vetting. Each effort produced garbled contradictory messages for the public: the government could/could not play an effective role in solving the crisis; Fannie and Freddie were/were not the cause of the crisis. And when the economists' contributions were considered in total, sorting matters out became nearly hopeless: market designers suggested at first that the crisis was primarily an *engineering* failure, which could be corrected by the government heeding the technical lessons of market design, whereas think tank economists insisted it was primarily a *government* failure, because of the inevitably reckless and feckless behavior of government regulators. These two options correspond to our earlier distinction between trusting the *economics profession* and trusting *The Market* to diagnose the crisis. But positions quickly got mixed up: the market designers who initially propounded the first story eventually adopted the language of think tank economists, while the think tank economists (such as Calomiris) who so successfully promoted the second story found occasion to favor the first.

The necessity for tergiversation derived from the inherent epistemic contradiction between trust of the experts and trust of the Great Information Processor known as The Market—you cannot do both consistently. The only way to paper the gap was to blow smoke toward the perplexed public.

Such appears to be the inevitable result for the orthodox economist participating in public discourse, at least during our neoliberal times. It is no longer possible for the heroic public intellectual to personally embody a shining beacon of rationality amid the rough and tumble of political discourse, at least in economics. Instead, orthodox economists tend to duck and weave between two incompatible positions, depending on which appears more convenient for the entity that provides their institutional identity.[34] The only way they can manage to accomplish this is by fostering greater ignorance amid the public, their purported primary audience. Indeed, the think tanks and corporations that employ economists explicitly seek to foster ignorance as part of their business plans: that is the postmodern phenomenon of *agnogenesis*. Economists, witting or no, have become the vanguard of the purveyors of ignorance in matters pecuniary, because they cannot face up to their own epistemic dilemma.

References

Armantier, Olivier, Charles Holt, and Charles Plott. 2011. "A Procurement Auction for Toxic Assets with Asymmetric Information." CalTech Social Science Working Paper 1330R.

Ausubel, Lawrence, and Peter Cramton. 2008a. "Auction Design Critical for Rescue Plan." *Economists' Voice* 5 (5).

———. 2008b. "Auctions for Injecting Bank Capital." Working Paper, University of Maryland. works.bepress.com/cramton/8.

———. 2008c. "A Troubled Asset Reverse Auction." Working Paper, University of Maryland. works.bepress.com/cramton/9/.

———. 2009. "No Substitute for the "P"-Word in Financial Rescue." *Economists' Voice* 6 (2).

Ausubel, Lawrence, Peter Cramton, Emel Filiz-Ozbay, Nathaniel Higgins, Erkut Ozbay, and Andrew Stocking. 2011. "Common-Value Auctions with Liquidity Needs: An Experimental Test of a Troubled Assets Reverse Auction." www.cramton.umd.edu/papers/finance/.

---

34. One might argue that portraying the economics *orthodoxy* (rather than a tiny, disreputable minority) as participating in agnogenesis places this narrative at odds with other cases of agnotology. But this misunderstands agnotology. For example, Robert Proctor (2012) has shown how the tobacco industry not merely countervailed an established scientific consensus but corrupted whole academic disciplines through its interventions.

Avery, Robert, and Kenneth Brevoort. 2011. "The Subprime Crisis: Is Government Housing Policy to Blame?" Federal Reserve Board of Governors, Finance and Economics Discussion Paper 36.

Bernanke, Ben. 2007. "GSE Portfolios, Systemic Risk, and Affordable Housing." Statement before the Independent Community Bankers of America Annual Convention, March. www.federalreserve.gov/newsevents/speech/Bernanke20070306a.htm.

"Bernanke's Comments on Asset Auction Process." 2008. Reuters, September 23. www.reuters.com/article/2008/09/23/financial-bailout-bernanke-auctions-idUSN 2338396920080923.

Brush, Silla, and Clea Benson. 2010. "Forged Comment Letters Sent to U.S. Regulators Writing Derivative Rules." *Bloomberg News*, November 30. www.bloomberg.com/news/2010-11-30/forged-comment-letters-sent-to-u-s-regulators-writing-derivatives-rules.html.

Calabria, Mark. 2011. "Fannie, Freddie, and the Subprime Mortgage Market." Cato Brief 120. www.cato.org/pub_display.php?pub_id=12846.

Calomiris, Charles, and Peter Wallison. 2008. "Blame Fannie Mae and Congress for the Credit Mess." *Wall Street Journal*, October 23.

Congleton, Roger. 2009. "On the Political Economy of the Financial Crisis and Bailout of 2008–9." *Public Choice* 140 (3–4): 287–317.

Cramton, Peter. 2008. "Auctioning the Digital Dividend." www.cramton.umd.edu/papers2005–2009/cramton-auctioning-the-digital-dividend.pdf.

———. 2010. "Market Design: Harnessing Market Methods to Improve Resource Allocation." *American Economic Association, Ten Years and Beyond.* papers.ssrn.com/sol3/papers.cfm?abstract_id=1888577.

Davies, William, and Linsey McGoey. 2012. "Rationalities of Ignorance: On Financial Crisis and the Ambivalence of Neoliberal Epistemology." *Economy and Society* 41 (1): 64–83.

Engel, Kathleen, and Patricia McCoy. 2011. *The Subprime Virus*. New York: Oxford University Press.

Ferguson, Charles. 2012. *Predator Nation*. New York: Crown.

Ferguson, Thomas, and Robert Johnson. 2009. "Too Big to Bail: The 'Paulson Put,' Presidential Politics, and the Global Financial Meltdown, Part II." *International Journal of Political Economy* 38 (2): 5–45.

Fligstein, Neil, and Adam Goldstein. 2012. "A Long Strange Trip: The State and Mortgage Securitization, 1968–2010." In *The Oxford Handbook of the Sociology of Finance*, edited by Karin Knorr Cetina and Alex Preda. Oxford: Oxford University Press.

Hayek, Friedrich. 1960. *The Constitution of Liberty*. Chicago: University of Chicago Press.

Kagel, John, and Dan Levin. 2001. "Behavior in Multi-Unit Demand Auctions: Experiments with Uniform Price and Dynamic Vickrey Auctions." *Econometrica* 69 (2): 413–54.

———. 2009. "Implementing Efficient Multi-Object Auction Institutions: An Experimental Study of the Performance of Boundedly Rational Agents." *Games and Economic Behavior* 66:221–37.

Klemperer, Paul. 2010. "The Product-Mix Auction: A New Auction Design for Differentiated Goods." *Journal of the European Economic Association* 8 (2–3): 526–36.

Krugman, Paul. 2008. "Fannie, Freddie and You." *New York Times*, July 14.

Lo, Andrew. 2012. "Reading about the Financial Crisis." *Journal of Economic Literature* 50 (1): 151–78.

Madrick, Jeff, and Frank Partnoy. 2011. "Did Fannie Cause the Disaster?" *New York Review of Books*, October 27.

McMillan, John. 2002. *Reinventing the Bazaar*. New York: Norton.

Michaels, David. 2008. *Doubt Is Their Product*. Oxford: Oxford University Press.

Min, David. 2011. "Why Wallison Is Wrong about the Genesis of the U.S. Housing Crisis: Responding to Wallison's Latest Defense of His Flawed Financial Crisis Inquiry Commission Dissent." Center for American Progress website, July 12. www.americanprogress.org/issues/housing/report/2011/07/12/10011/why-wallison-is-wrong-about-the-genesis-of-the-u-s-housing-crisis/.

Mirowski, Philip. 2002. *Machine Dreams*. New York: Cambridge University Press.

———. 2009. "Why There Is (as yet) No Such Thing as an Economics of Knowledge." In *Oxford Handbook of Philosophy of Economics*, edited by Harold Kincaid and Don Ross, 99–156. Oxford: Oxford University Press.

———. 2011. *ScienceMart*. Cambridge: Harvard University Press.

———. 2013. *Never Let a Serious Crisis Go to Waste*. London: Verso.

Mirowski, Philip, and Dieter Plehwe, eds. 2009. *The Road from Mont Pelerin*. Cambridge: Harvard University Press.

Morgenson, Gretchen, and Josh Rosner. 2011. *Reckless Endangerment*. New York: Times Books.

Muolo, Paul, and Matthew Padilla. 2008. *Chain of Blame*. New York: Wiley.

Nik-Khah, Edward. 2008. "A Tale of Two Auctions." *Journal of Institutional Economics* 4 (1): 73–97.

———. 2011. "George Stigler, the Graduate School of Business, and the Pillars of the Chicago School." In *Building Chicago Economics*, edited by Robert Van Horn, Philip Mirowski, and Tom Stapleford, 116–47. New York: Cambridge University Press.

Nocera, Joe. 2011. "The Big Lie." *New York Times*, December 23.

Oreskes, Naomi, and Erik Conway. 2010. *Merchants of Doubt*. New York: Bloomsbury.

Paulson, Henry. 2010. *On the Brink*. New York: Business Plus.

Paybarah, Azi. 2011. "Bloomberg: Plain and Simple, Congress Caused the Mortgage Crisis, Not the Banks." *Capital New York*, November 1.

Perino, Michael. 2010. *The Hellhound of Wall Street*. New York: Penguin.

Philips, Matthew. 2008. "Gaming the Financial System." *Newsweek*, November 18. www.thedailybeast.com/newsweek/2008/11/17/gaming-the-financial-system.html.

Pinto, Edward. 2009. "ACORN and the Housing Bubble." *Wall Street Journal*, November 12.

Posner, Richard. 2003. *Public Intellectuals: A Study of Decline*. Cambridge: Harvard University Press.

Proctor, Robert. 2012. *Golden Holocaust*. Berkeley: University of California Press.

Proctor, Robert, and Londa Scheibinger, eds. 2008. *Agnotology*. Stanford: Stanford University Press.

Rajan, Raghuram. 2010. *Fault Lines*. Princeton: Princeton University Press.

Ryan, Tim. 2008. "Lesson from Saving and Loan Rescue." *Financial Times*, September 24. www.ft.com/cms/s/0/8e19c058-8a35-11dd-a76a-0000779fd18c.html#axzz1oOrqY4OO.

Sismondo, Sergio. 2011. "Corporate Disguises in Medical Science: Dodging the Interest Repertoire." *Bulletin of Science, Technology and Society* 31 (6): 482–92.

Sorkin, Andrew. 2009. *Too Big to Fail*. New York: Viking.

———. 2011. "Vanishing Act: 'Advisers' Seek Distance from Report." *New York Times Dealbook*, February 14. dealbook.nytimes.com/2011/02/14/vanishing-act-advisers-seek-distance-from-a-report/.

Swagel, Phillip. 2009. "The Financial Crisis: An Inside View." *Brookings Papers on Economic Activity* (Spring): 1–63.

Thompson, Helen. 2012. "The Limits of Blaming Neoliberalism: Fannie Mae, Freddie Mac, and the Financial Crisis." *New Political Economy* 17 (4): 399–419.

Tkacik, Maureen. 2010. "Journals of the Crisis Year." *Baffler*, December, 84–95.

US Federal Crisis Inquiry Commission. 2011. *Final Report*. cybercemetery.unt.edu/archive/fcic/20110310173538/http://www.fcic.gov/report.

US House Committee on Oversight and Governmental Reform. 2011. *An Examination of Attacks against the Financial Crisis Inquiry Commission*. July 13. democrats.oversight.house.gov/images/stories/MINORITY/fcic%20report/FCIC%20Report%2007-13-11.pdf.

Wallison, Peter. 2008. "Cause and Effect: Government Policies and the Financial Crisis." *AEI Financial Services Outlook*, November.

———. 2009. "The True Origins of the Financial Crisis." *AEI on the Issues*, February 19.

———. 2010a. "Slaughter of the Innocents." *AEI Financial Services Outlook*. www.aei.org/files/2010/11/08/FSO-2010-10-11-g.pdf.

———. 2010b. "The True Story of the Financial Crisis." *American Spectator*, May.

Weil, Jonathan. 2011. "Wall Street's Collapse to Be Mystery Forever." *Bloomberg News*, January 27. www.bloomberg.com/news/2011-01-28/wall-street-s-collapse-to-be-mystery-forever-commentary-by-jonathan-weil.html.

White, Lawrence. 2008. "How Did We Get into This Financial Mess?" CATO Briefing Paper 110, November 18.

Contributors

Roger E. Backhouse is professor of history and philosophy of economics at the University of Birmingham and Erasmus University Rotterdam. He is coauthor, with Bradley W. Bateman, of *Capitalist Revolutionary: John Maynard Keynes* (2011) and, with Mauro Boianovsky, of *Transforming Modern Macroeconomics: Exploring Disequilibrium Microfoundations, 1956–2003* (2013). With Philippe Fontaine, he has edited *The History of the Social Sciences since 1945* (2010). He currently holds a Leverhulme Trust Major Research Fellowship to work on an intellectual biography of Paul Samuelson.

Bradley W. Bateman is president of Randolph College. He is the author of *Keynes's Uncertain Revolution* (1996). He is coauthor, with Roger E. Backhouse, of *Capitalist Revolutionary: John Maynard Keynes* (2011) and also coeditor with Backhouse of *The Cambridge Companion to Keynes* (2006). In addition to his work on Keynes, Bateman has written widely on the influence of religious ideas on American economic thought.

Peter Boettke is a university professor of economics and philosophy at George Mason University, the BB&T Professor for the Study of Capitalism, and director of the F. A. Hayek Program for Advanced Study in Philosophy, Politics, and Economics at the Mercatus Center at GMU.

Angus Burgin is assistant professor of history at Johns Hopkins University and author of *The Great Persuasion: Reinventing Free Markets since the Depression* (2012).

Robert W. Dimand is a professor of economics at Brock University, St. Catharines, Ontario, and an adjunct professor of economics at McMaster University, Hamilton, Ontario. He is the author of *The Origins of the Keynesian Revolution* (1988) and coauthor of volume 1 of *A History of Game Theory* (1996). He has edited or coedited a dozen books (most recently an International Economic Association conference volume, *Keynes's General Theory after Seventy Years* [2010; with Robert A. Mundell and Alessandro Vercelli]), and has published more than ninety journal articles, primarily on the history of macroeconomics, the early history of game theory, and the history of women in economics. He is president of the History of Economics Society (2012–13) and secretary-treasurer of the Canadian Economics Association.

Gil Eyal is professor of sociology at Columbia University. He is the author, most recently, of (with Brendan Hart, Neta Oren, Emine Onculer, and Natasha Rossi) *The Autism Matrix* (2010). His other books include *The Disenchantment of the Orient* (2006), *The Origins of Postcommunist Elites* (2003), and (with Ivan Szelenyi and Eleanor Townsley) *Making Capitalism without Capitalists* (1998).

Jean-Baptiste Fleury is associate professor at the University of Cergy-Pontoise and member of the THEMA research center. Since completing his PhD in 2009, his research interests have been in the evolution of the boundaries of economics after World War II. He recently explored this movement in the broad context of the teaching and popularization of economics in "The Evolving Notion of Relevance: A Historical Perspective to the 'Economics-Made-Fun Movement'" (2012).

Chris Godden is lecturer in the economic history of globalization at the University of Manchester. His research interests focus on media representations of the economy, the nonacademic writings of interwar British economists, and the academic development of economic history. He is working on studies of the Manchester economist George Daniels and the early twentieth-century economic historian George Unwin.

Craufurd Goodwin is James B. Duke Professor of Economics Emeritus at Duke University and was for many years editor of this journal. He is engaged in preparing a book-length study of Walter Lippmann as "public economist."

Susan Howson is a professor of economics and a fellow of Trinity College, University of Toronto. She is the author of *Lionel Robbins* (2011) and has published extensively on British economic policy in the twentieth century. She has also edited the *Collected Papers of James Meade* (1988) and (with Donald Moggridge) *The Wartime Diaries of Lionel Robbins and James Meade* (1990); she is now working on a biography of James Meade.

Moran Levy is a graduate student and a Paul F. Lazersfeld Fellow at the Department of Sociology at Columbia University. She received her MA degree in sociology from Tel-Aviv University as a student of the Adi Lautman Interdisciplinary

Program for Outstanding Students. Her master's thesis suggested a micro-sociological analysis of the emergence of an Israeli-Palestinian conflict in Mandatory Palestine. Her present research interests concern economic sociology and sociology of science and technology.

Alain Marciano is associate professor at the University of Montpellier 1. His work focuses on the history and methodology of recent economics and, more specifically, law and economics and public choice. He has published articles in *HOPE*, the *Journal of the History of Economic Thought*, the *International Review of Law and Economics*, and the *Journal of Economic Behavior and Organization*.

Tiago Mata is a senior research fellow at the Department of History and Philosophy of Science, University of Cambridge, where he heads a European Research Council–funded project titled "Economics in the Public Sphere." His research interests are on the sociology of economics, the post–World War II history of the social sciences and media history. His book-length history of 1960s radical economics is forthcoming with Cambridge University Press.

Rob Roy McGregor is professor of economics at the University of North Carolina at Charlotte. His research on the Federal Reserve has been published in leading economics journals. His book *Committee Decisions on Monetary Policy: Evidence from Historical Records of the Federal Open Market Committee*, coauthored with Henry Chappell and Todd Vermilyea, was published in 2005 by MIT Press.

Steven G. Medema is a professor of economics and director of the University Honors and Leadership Program at the University of Colorado, Denver. His research focuses on the history of twentieth-century economics, and he is the author of more than one hundred scholarly books and articles on the history of economics, law and economics, and public economics. His latest book, *The Hesitant Hand: Taming Self-Interest in the History of Economic Ideas* (2009), was awarded the 2010 Book Prize by the European Society for the History of Economic Thought.

Philip Mirowski is Carl Koch Professor of Economics and History and Philosophy of Science at the University of Notre Dame. His most recent book is *Never Let a Serious Crisis Go to Waste* (2013).

Edward Nik-Khah is an associate professor of economics at Roanoke College. During 2011–12 he was a research fellow at Duke University's Center for the History of Political Economy. Topics on which he has published include the political economy of market design, George Stigler's role as architect of the postwar Chicago School, and (with Robert Van Horn) the history of economics imperialism, focusing on the efforts of Stigler, Aaron Director, and Steven Levitt. Current research of his focuses on the development of neoliberal pharmaceutical science.

Liya Palagashvili is the Weaver Fellow at the F. A. Hayek Program for Advanced Study in Philosophy, Politics, and Economics at the Mercatus Center, and a PhD student in economics at George Mason University.

Warren Young is at Bar Ilan University, Israel. He was a consultant to the Archives Project, Federal Reserve Bank of Minneapolis. He has published and edited books and papers on the history of modern macroeconomics. Besides his collaboration with Rob Roy McGregor in this volume, he is working with McGregor on the role of Reserve Bank presidents, and their research staffs, in policy analysis in the Federal Reserve System.

Index

AALL. *See* American Association for Labor Legislation (AALL)
Acworth, William Mitchell, 60
Addams, Jane, 5
Admanti, Anat, 306
Affair of State: The Investigation, Impeachment, and Trial of President Clinton (Posner), 265–66
"After the War, What?" (Fisher), 27–28
Age of Uncertainty (TV documentary series), 14
  appendages to, 204–5
  approaches, 195–96
  corporate sponsorship, lack of, 209, 216
  as *Descent of Man*, 199
  first appearance on television, 197
  Friedman, Milton, on, 200
  intent of series, 195
  Malone, Adrian, and, 191–93
  opening scene, 200–201
  reviews of, 196
  sales of, 214
  subject matter as problem, 200
  viewers' response to, 201–3
Aging and Old Age (Posner), 263n10, 264
Agnotology, 282–84, 298
American Association for Labor Legislation (AALL), 26
American Medical Association, 26
American School of Economics, 154n34
Amis, Martin, 202, 203
The Anatomy of Criticism (Hazlitt), 154
Anderson, Benjamin, 140, 140n7, 143
Anderson, John, 123
Anti-Becker-Posner Blog, 270–71. *See also The Becker-Posner Blog*
Anti-intellectualism, 1–3

318 Index

Anti-intellectualism in American Life (Hofstadter), 1–2
Appreciation and Interest (Fisher), 27, 31
Armantier, Oliver, 285n8
Arrow, Kenneth, 245, 248
Auctions, 289
Austrian School of Economics, 144–46
Ausubel, Lawrence, 286, 291, 292–93

Baker, Newton, 100, 101
Banking Policy and the Price Level (Robertson), 87
Bardoux, Jacques, 78
Barro, Robert, 280, 281
Bastiat, Frédéric, 151, 162
Bauman, Zygmunt, 2, 3
Becker, Gary S., 255–61. *See also The Becker-Posner Blog*
and *Business Week*, 258–61, 268, 273
controversy and, 15
discrimination, studies on, 255
Economics of Life, 273
Friedman, Milton, and, 255, 257
and the Iraq War, 273n29
and the Mont Pèlerin Society, 257
Shepard, Stephen B., and, 258, 268n14
on social issues, 255–56
Stigler, George, and, 256, 257
Uncommon Sense, 272–73
The Becker-Posner Blog, 267–75. *See also Anti-Becker-Posner Blog*
approach taken, 271–72
and comments, 269–70, 274
creation of, 268–69
and Lessig, Lawrence, role of, 268–69
Beecher, Henry Ward, 200

Beige Books, Federal Reserve Banks, 168–69, 182–86
Bellamy, Edward, 96
Bell, Cliff, 108
Bell, Daniel, 10
Benda, Julien, 2, 3
Bernanke, Ben, 285–86, 301
Beveridge, William H., 43, 60, 117, 121
Birmingham Evening Mail, 197
Black Scholes model, 231, 235
Blogs, 267–68, 276. *See also The Becker-Posner Blog*
Bloomsbury Group, 82, 108
Bolshevism, 79
Booth, Charles, 5
Boston Globe, 199
Bowley, Arthur Lyon, 60
"Brain trust," 10, 146
"Break the Glass" memo, 285, 286, 288
Bretton Woods agreement, 149–50
British Fabian Society, 96, 98
British interwar economists, 38–62
early postwar views, 41–44
and industrial development, 44–46, 51–52
key figures, listing of, 60–62
and the new economy, emergence of, 44–46
protectionism and, 53–54
and psychological reactions to postwar difficulties, 46–49
public role of, 54–58
and "rationalization," 51–53
and unemployment statistics, 49–51
wartime views, 41–44
Brittain, Samuel, 12n13
Bryan, William Jennings, 27
Buckley, William F., 205
Bulow, Jeremy, 294

Calabria, Mark, 298
Calomiris, Charles, 291, 297
Cannan, Edwin, 60, 115, 158
Capitalism and Freedom
 (Friedman), 206, 208–9
Capitalism, Socialism, and
 Democracy (Schumpeter), 12
Carver, Thomas Nixon, 96
Cassel, Gustav, 80
Cato Institute, 298
Center for the Study of the Economy
 and the State, 257
Chapman, Sydney John, 42, 60
Chase, Stuart, 147n26
Chester, Norman, 124
Chitester, Robert, 208–10
Clay, Henry, 40, 43–44, 47, 53,
 57, 60
Clinton, Bill, 265–66
CMEPSP. *See* Commission on the
 Measurement of Economic
 Performance and Social
 Progress (CMEPSP)
Coats, A. W., 5
Cole, George Douglas Howard, 47,
 52, 53, 60
Commission on the Measurement of
 Economic Performance and
 Social Progress (CMEPSP),
 235, 245, 248–49
Committee of Economists, 116,
 118n2, 119
Committee on Higher Education,
 130–33
Common Sense of Political
 Economy (Wicksteed),
 137–38
Commons, John R., 6
Community Reinvestment Act
 (CRA), 300–301
The Constitution of Liberty (Hayek),
 283n4

Convertibility crisis, 125
The Convertibility of Sterling
 (Winder), 145
Cosmopolitan, 202
Cowen, Tyler, 271n25, 298
Cox, Christopher, 297
Cox, Harold, 40, 50, 60
CRA. *See* Community Reinvestment
 Act (CRA)
Cramton, Peter, 286, 291–94
Creative Commons, 268
Crew Chronicle, 197
Cripps, Stafford, 127
The Critics of Keynesian Economics
 (Hazlitt), 154, 155, 156
Crosland, Anthony, 132
"Cross of Gold" speech (Bryan), 27
Crucé, Émeric, 28
Curtis, Lionel, 121

Daily Telegraph, 197
Dalton, (Edward) Hugh John Neale,
 61, 115, 125
Daniels, George William, 40, 57, 61
DeLong, Brad, 271n25
Dervis, Kemal, 245
Dewey, John, 7
Dillard, Dudley, 156
Dollar, stabilizing the, 31–33
Dorfman, Joseph, 25n5
Douglas, Major, 112
Dreyfus affair, 221
Drift and Mastery (Lippmann), 6
Dworkin, Ronald, 266

Earth Institute (Columbia
 University), 245, 248, 249
Eastburn, David
 Beige Book input, 182–86
 FOMC input, 182–86
 Lasalle College Colloquium,
  lecture, 172

320　Index

Eastburn, David (*continued*)
  and the Philadelphia Federal
    Reserve Bank, 170–73
  Wisconsin, University of, lecture,
    171
Eastman, Max, 145
EAW. *See* Economic Aspects of
    Welfare (EAW)
Economic Advisory Council
    (Britain), 8–10, 84, 85
Economic Aspects of Welfare
    (EAW), 241
*Economic Consequences of the
    Peace* (Keynes), 69–70, 71n6
  Lippmann, Walter, and, 106
  popularity of, 72, 85–86
Economic crisis. *See* Great
    Recession of 2007–?
Economic indicators as public
    interventions, 220–49
  Economic Aspects of Welfare
    (EAW), 241
  Environmental Performance
    Index (EPI), 245, 247, 248,
    249
  GDP (gross domestic product),
    235–40
    alternatives to, 240–49
    generally, 220
    and the Great Depression, 236
    history of, 235–36
    proposed replacements or
      corrections, *244*
    World War II and, 238
  Genuine Progress Indicator (GPI),
    241, 245, 246, 247
  GNP (Gross National Product),
    240, 242
  Happy Planet Index (HPI), 244,
    245, 246, 247, 248, 249
  Human Development Index
    (HDI), 241, 242, 243, 244,
    246, 247

  Index of Sustainable Economic
    Welfare (ISEW), 241
  Japanese Net National Welfare
    (NNW), 241
  Physical Quality of Life Index
    (PQLI), 241
  public interventions
    agencies of intervention, 226,
      230
    and public impact of
      economists and expertise,
      229–34
    arenas of intervention, 227–29
    concept of, 221–29
    index numbers, generally, 230
    modes of intervention, 226–27,
      230
    targets of intervention, 227–29,
      232
    use of term, 220
*Economic Planning and International
    Order* (Robbins), 147
Economics Cassette Series, 256
Economics in One Lesson (Hazlitt),
    151, 152–53
The Economics of Life (Becker and
    Becker), 259n5
Edgeworth, F. Y., 27
Eliot, T. S., 81
Ely, Richard T., 6
Eminent Victorians (Strachey), 71n6
Employment Policy (Robbins), 122
Environmental Performance Index
    (EPI), 245, 247, 248, 249
EPI. *See* Environmental
    Performance Index (EPI)
*Essay on the Nature and
    Significance of Economic
    Science* (Robbins), 133
Expertise, cultures of, 1–17
  market, intellectual life as, 12–17
  popularization, 8–12
  social intelligence, 4–8

Fabians. *See* British Fabian Society
Failure of the "New Economics" (Hazlitt), 154, 155–56, 157
Fairchild, Fred R., 25n5
Fannie Mae (Federal National Mortgage Association), 297–303
FCIC. *See* Federal Crisis Inquiry Commission (FCIC)
Federal Crisis Inquiry Commission (FCIC), 298, 303–7
Federal Home Loan Mortgage Association. *See* Freddie Mac (Federal Home Loan Mortgage Association)
Federal National Mortgage Association. *See* Fannie Mae (Federal National Mortgage Association)
Federal Open Market Committee (FOMC). *See also* Minneapolis Federal Reserve Bank; Philadelphia Federal Reserve Bank; St. Louis Federal Reserve Bank
  dissent at, 187
  and Fed Bank presidents, 182–86
  generally, 167–69
Federal Reserve Act (1913), 24, 32, 33, 97
Federal Reserve Banks
  Beige Books, 182–86
  "Break the Glass" memo, 285–86, 288
  institutional background of, 167–69
  Minneapolis (*See* Minneapolis Federal Reserve Bank)
  Philadelphia (*See* Philadelphia Federal Reserve Bank)
  presidents of, 166–87 (*See also* Eastburn, David; Roos, Lawrence; Willes, Mark)
  as bureaucrats, 187
  pronouncements and, 169–70
  as public intellectual, 187
  St. Louis (*See* St. Louis Federal Reserve Bank)
Federal Reserve System, 167. *See also* Federal Reserve Banks
  background of, 167–69
  Board of Governors, 168
  as employer, 232
  Troubled Asset Relief Program (TARP), 284–96
Fischer, Louis, 141–42
Fisher, Irving
  "After the War, What?," 27–28
  Appreciation and Interest, 27, 31
  Equal Rights Amendment and, 20
  Hitchcock Lectures, 24
  How to Live, 20–21
  Index Number Institute, 8, 21
  on index numbers, 230
  League of Nations and, 20, 22, 25, 27–29
  League or War?, 24
  obituary, 21–22
  price level stability and, 24
  Prohibition and, 22–24, 29–31
  as public intellectual, 20–35
  The Purchasing Power of Money, 31
  quantity theory of money, 22
  reforms, attempted, 20
  Report on National Vitality: Its Wastes and Conservation, 26
  "Some Probable Economic Effects of the War," 28
  "Sound Money" campaign, 27
  and stabilizing the dollar, 31–33
  Stabilizing the Dollar, 24, 32
  turning point in life, 25–27

Fisk, Eugene Lyman, 20
Fitoussi, Jean-Paul, 235, 245, 246
Florence, Philip Sargant, 52
FOMC. *See* Federal Open Market Committee (FOMC)
Foster, William Trufant, 21
Foucault, Michel, 2, 3, 221, 224–25
The Foundations of Morality (Hazlitt), 158, 160, 161
Freakonomics, 15
Freddie Mac (Federal Home Loan Mortgage Association), 297–303
Free to Choose (TV documentary), 14, 193, 207–15
  financing of, 209, 216
  reviews, 213
Free trade doctrine, 57
Friedman, Milton, 14, 92, 158
  on *Age of Uncertainty* (TV documentary series), 200
  Becker, Gary S., and, 255, 257
  Capitalism and Freedom, 206, 208–9
  Free to Choose (TV documentary), 14, 193, 207–15
  Galbraith, John Kenneth, as opponent, 193, 206–7, 215
  Hazlitt, Henry, and, 150n29
  in *Newsweek*, 10–11
  Nobel Prize, 206, 207
  self-presentation, 213
  on unemployment, 170
Friedman, Rose, 210–11
From Bretton Woods to World Inflation: A Study of Causes and Consequences (Hazlitt), 150
From New Era to New Deal: Herbert Hoover, the Economists, and American Economic Policy (Barber), 24
Furner, Mary, 5

Galbraith, John Kenneth
  Age of Uncertainty (TV documentary series), 14, 191–207 (*See also Age of Uncertainty* (TV documentary series) *for detailed treatment*)
  criticisms of, 202–7
  on Fisher, Irving, 23
  Friedman, Milton, as opponent, 193, 206–7, 215
  on "history of economic thought," 198
  Onassis, Jacqueline Kennedy, and, 192
  self-presentation, 213
Gardner, Mrs. Jack, 94
GATT. *See* General Agreement on Tariffs and Trade (GATT)
GDP (gross domestic product), 235–40
  alternatives to, 240–49
  generally, 220
  and the Great Depression, 236
  history of, 235–36
  World War II and, 238
General Advisory Committee to the Atomic Energy Commission (AEC), 229
General Agreement on Tariffs and Trade (GATT), 123
General Theory of Employment, Interest, and Money (Keynes), 68, 71, 87–88, 154, 237–38
Genuine Progress Indicator (GPI), 241, 244, 245, 246, 247
Giffen, Robert, 44
Gill, Michael, 195
Glass, Carter, 33
GNP (Gross National Product), 240, 242
Goldwater, Barry, 204

The Good Society (Lippmann), 112
Government Sponsored Entities
  (GSEs). *See* Fannie Mae
  (Federal National Mortgage
  Association); Freddie Mac
  (Federal Home Loan
  Mortgage Association)
GPI. *See* Genuine Progress Indicator
  (GPI)
Gramsci, Antonio, 2, 3
Great Depression
  and GDP (gross domestic
    product), 236–37
  Hazlitt, Henry, as columnist
    during, 139, 141–42, 143n14,
    147, 149, 151
  Lippmann, Walter, as columnist
    during, 109–12
  and popular economic literature
    on, 39
  and stabilizing the dollar, 31
Great Recession of 2007–?
  agnotology, 282–84, 298
  auctions, 289
  Fannie Mae (Federal National
    Mortgage Association),
    297–303
  Federal Crisis Inquiry Commission
    (FCIC), 298, 303–7
  Federal Reserve Banks, 285–86
  Freddie Mac (Federal Home
    Loan Mortgage Association),
    297–303
  "The Market" and, 280–81,
    307–8
  Paulson Plan, 285n7, 286n10,
    287n14
  and Power Auctions and Market
    Design, 294
  private intellectuals and, 279–311
  Troubled Asset Relief Program
    (TARP), 284–96
Greenspan, Alan, 297

Gregory, Theodor Emanuel
  Gugenheim, 40, 61
GSEs. *See* Government Sponsored
  Entities (GSEs)

Haines-Stiles, Geoff, 196
Hamilton, Walton, 97, 107
Hansen, Alvin, 88
Happy Planet Index (HPI), 244,
  245, 246, 247, 248, 249
Haq, Mahbub ul, 241, 242
Haskell, Thomas, 5
Hatch, Orrin, 204
Hawtrey, Ralph, 23
Hayek, Friedrich A., 111, 119, 143,
  162, 205, 280
  The Constitution of Liberty,
    159n38, 283n4
  Nobel Prize lecture, 156n36
  The Road to Serfdom, 11
Hazlitt, Henry, 93, 137–63
  The Anatomy of Criticism, 154
  Anderson, Benjamin, and, 140, 143
  *From Bretton Woods to World
    Inflation: A Study of Causes
    and Consequences*, 150
  Business Tides column, 153
  Chase, Stuart, and, 147n26
  Cohen, Morris, and, 140
  *The Critics of Keynesian
    Economics*, 154, 155, 156
  Eastman, Max, and, 145
  economic ideas and, 143–54
  economic journalism of, 11,
    139–42
  Economics in One Lesson, 138,
    139, 151, 152–53
  ethics and, 157–61
  Failure of the "New Economics,
    154, 155, 157
  Fischer, Louis, and, 141–42
  Foundation for Economic
    Education, 150–51n30

Hazlitt, Henry (*continued*)
  The Foundations of Morality,
    158, 160, 161
  Friedman, Milton, and, 150n29
  Great Depression and, 139, 141–42,
    143n14, 147, 149, 151
  Hahn, Albert, and, 145
  on inflation, 153
  Institute for Economic Affairs, 145
  Mechanics and Metals National
    Bank of New York, 141
  Mencken, H. L., and, 142, 151n31
  Mont Pèlerin Society, 150n30,
    153n33
  at the *Nation*, 143, 158
  on the New Deal, 146, 148–49
  on the new economics, 154–57
  at *Newsweek*, 142, 145, 151, 153
  New York Evening Mail, column,
    141
  at the *New York Evening Post*, 141
  at the *New York Times*, 138,
    142–44, 148–51
  Robbins, Lionel, and, 144
  Samuelson, Paul, and, 142
  Sulzberger, Arthur, and, 149
  Thinking as a Science, 141, 154, 158
  Time Will Run Back, 138
  Viner, Jacob, on, 139
  at the *Wall Street Journal*, 137,
    140, 141
  Wright, David McCord, and, 146
HDI. *See* Human Development
  Index (HDI)
Health Insurance Acts, Britain, 49
Healy, Kieran, 270
Henderson, Hubert Douglas, 46, 61,
  119
  Keynes, John Maynard, and, 81, 84
Hendy, Philip, 128
Hennessy, Keith, 303
Hilton, John, 61
Hirst, Francis Wrigley, 61

History of Economic Analysis
  (Schumpeter), 162
Hobson, John Atkinson, 28, 40, 41,
  44, 53, 61, 119
Hobson, Oscar, 116, 118
Hofstadter, Richard, 3
  *Anti-intellectualism in American
    Life*, 1–2
Holtz-Eakin, Douglas, 298, 303
Hoover Institution, 207, 257
House, E. M., 101
How to Live (Fisher and Fisk),
  20–21, 22
"How to Mitigate the Next Slump"
  (Robbins), 120
How to Pay for the War (Keynes),
  17, 238
Human Development Index (HDI),
  241, 242, 243, 244, 246, 247
Human Development Report Team,
  241–42
Human Development Report, 242

IEA. *See* Institute of Economic
  Affairs (IEA)
Index Number Institute, 8, 21, 32
Index numbers, generally, 230
Index of Sustainable Economic
  Welfare (ISEW), 241
Indian Currency and Finance
  (Keynes), 84
Institute of Economic Affairs (IEA),
  12–13, 145, 206
"The Intellectual and the Market
  Place" (Stigler), 12, 13
Intellectual (term), defined, 2. *See
  also* Public intellectual
  (term)
Introduction to Economics (Seager),
  95
ISEW. *See* Index of Sustainable
  Economic Welfare (ISEW)
Issa, Darryl, 306

Jacoby, Russell, 2, 3
The Last Intellectuals, 222, 224
Japanese Net National Welfare (NNW), 241
Jay, Peter, 12n13
Johnson, Alvin, 107
Jones, John Harry, 40, 61
Jovanovich, William, 210

Kahane, Jacques, 118
Kahneman, Daniel, 245
Kant, Immanuel, 28
Kashkari, Neel, 285
Kelley, Florence, 5
Kennedy, John F., 10
Keybridge Associates, 283–84
Keynesianism. *See* Keynes, John Maynard
Keynes, John Maynard, 61, 68–90
    Bloomsbury Group and, 108
    Cassel, Gustav, on, 80
    Economic Consequences of the Peace, 69–70, 71n6
        Lippmann, Walter, and, 106
        popularity of, 72, 85–86
    GDP (gross domestic product) and, 237–39
    General Theory of Employment, Interest, and Money, 68, 71, 87–88, 154, 237–38
    goals of, 7
    How to Pay for the War, 17, 238
    Indian Currency and Finance, 84
    India Office, 84–85
    inside-outside distinction, 69
    liberalism of, 81–84
    Lippmann, Walter, and, 107–9
    Macmillan Committee, 85, 87
    Manchester Guardian Commercial, 70, 71–81, 89–90
    monetary theory, 84–89
    in *Nation and Athenaeum*, 81–84
    on postwar Britain, 42–43
    Réflections sur le franc, 70
    Robbins, Lionel, and, 116–18, 124
    A Short View of Russia, 70
    A Tract on Monetary Reform, 70, 85
Kichline, James, 183, 184
Kirkaldy, Adam, 62
Knight, Frank, 159–60
Krugman, Paul, 17, 92, 297–98
Kuznets, Simon, 236, 237–38

Laibson, David, 283
Landes, William H., 262
Laski, Harold, 107, 115
The Last Intellectuals (Jacoby), 222, 224
Layton, Walter, 82, 117
League of Nations, 20, 25, 27–29
League or War? (Fisher), 24
Lerner, Abba, 155n35
Lessig, Lawrence, 268–69
Lexecon Inc., 262, 273–74
Liberalism and Industry (Muir), 81
Liberty and the News (Lippmann), 6
The Life and Labour of the People of London (Booth), 5
Lippmann, Walter, 92–113
    British Fabian Society and, 96, 98
    early life, 94–98
    friendships of, 94, 107
    Godkin Lectures, 111
    The Good Society, 112
    Great Depression, as columnist during, 109–12
    Keynes, John Maynard, and, 107–9
    Method of Freedom, 111
    Mont Pèlerin Society, 112
    and the *New Republic*, 100, 102, 106
    The Phantom Public, 103, 105
    popular deliberation and, 6
    A Preface to Morals, 103, 105–6

Lippmann, Walter (*continued*)
   A Preface to Politics, 97–98
   on public intervention, 227
   Public Opinion, 103–5
   Robbins, Lionel, and, 111
   Russian problem and, 79
   scholarly reputation of, 102–9
   Today and Tomorrow (column), 93
London Economic Club, 118
London School of Economics (LSE), 5
LSE. *See* London School of Economics (LSE)

MacDonald, James Ramsay, 117
Macgregor, David Hutchinson, 55, 61, 119
Macmillan Committee, 85
Malone, Adrian (BBC producer), 191–92, 193, 200, 203
"The Market," economic crisis and, 280–81, 307–8
Marshall, Alfred, 68, 143
Martin, Albro, 205
Martin, Kingsley, 83
McIsaac, Archibald, 153
McKenna, Joseph, 155–56
Meade, James, 122
Measure of Economic Welfare (MEW), 235, 240
Melchior, Carl, 77–78
Mencken, H. L., 142, 151n31
Method of Freedom (Lippmann), 111
MEW. *See* Measure of Economic Welfare (MEW)
Milgrom, Paul, 294
Mill, John Stuart, 68, 95, 145n19
Minneapolis Federal Reserve Bank, 177–82. *See also* Federal Open Market Committee (FOMC)
Minogue, Kenneth, 205

Miron, Jeffrey, 306
Mises, Ludwig von, 144, 146, 155, 162
Mitchell, Wesley C., 6, 24, 97, 99, 107, 230, 236
Mont Pèlerin Society, 112, 150n30, 153n33, 257
Morgenson, Gretchen, 299, 300
Moser, Claus, 131
Muckraking, 99
Muir, Ramsey, 81, 82
   Liberalism and Industry, 81
Mumford, Lewis, 107, 141

Nashat, Guity, 258–59
   The Economics of Life, 259n5
National Bureau of Economic Research (NBER), 236, 240
National Gallery, 128, 132
National Science Foundation (NSF), 295–96
Nation and Athenaeum, 81–84
NBER. *See* National Bureau of Economic Research (NBER)
NEF. *See* New Economics Foundation (NEF)
New Deal, 146, 148–49
New Economics Foundation (NEF), 247–48, 249
   Centre for Well-Being, 245
New School for Social Research, 5
New Statesman, 83
New York Post, 209
New York Times, 17
   on the *Age of Uncertainty* (TV documentary series), 197
   on Fisher, Irving, 29
   Hazlitt, Henry, at, 138, 142–44, 148–51
New York World, 102
Nixon administration, 256
NNW. *See* Japanese Net National Welfare (NNW)

Nocera, Joe, 299
Nordhaus, William, 235
NSF. *See* National Science Foundation (NSF)

Olin Foundation, 209
Oppenheimer, Robert, 224–25, 228–29
The Other Economic Summit (TOES), 248
Overcoming Law (Posner), 265
Owen-Glass Bill, 33
Owen, Robert Latham, 23–24, 33

Partisan Review, 3
Paulson, Henry, 290
Pearson, F. A., 110
Pecora, Ferdinand, 303
Perlman, Selig, 6
The Phantom Public (Lippmann), 103, 105
Phelps, Edmund, 170
Philadelphia Federal Reserve Bank, 170–73. *See also* Federal Open Market Committee (FOMC)
Philadelphia Public Ledger, 24
Phillips curve, 170
Physical Quality of Life Index (PQLI), 241
Pigou, Arthur, 40
Pinto, Edward, 298, 299
Plant, Arnold, 88, 117
Popular economic literature
　British interwar economists and, 38–41
　Great Depression, 39
　New Deal, 39
Posner, Richard A., 262–67
　Affair of State: The Investigation, Impeachment, and Trial of President Clinton, 265–66
　Aging and Old Age, 263n10, 264

　Dworkin, Ronald, and, 266
　Oliver Wendell Holmes Lectures, 265
　Overcoming Law, 265
　Public Intellectuals: A Study of Decline, 15–16, 266
　Sex and Reason, 263
Power Auctions and Market Design, 294
PQLI. *See* Physical Quality of Life Index (PQLI)
A Preface to Morals (Lippmann), 103, 105–6
A Preface to Politics (Lippmann), 97–98
Principles of Political Economy (Mill), 95
Private intellectuals, 279–308
　and agnotology, 282–84, 298
　and the Troubled Asset Relief Program (TARP), 284–96
Prohibition, 29–31
Proposals for Consideration by an International Conference on Trade and Employment (Robbins), 123
Protectionism, British interwar economists and, 53–54
Public intellectual (term), 2–3. *See also* Private intellectuals; Public interventions
　Google, frequency of appearance of, 223
　redundancy of, 222
　use of, 220, 221–24, 233–34
Public Intellectuals: A Study of Decline (Posner), 15–16, 266
Public interventions
　agencies of intervention, 226
　analysis of public impact of economists and expertise, 229–34

Public interventions (*continued*)
  areas of intervention, 227–29
  culture of, 1–17
    market, intellectual life as, 12–17
    popularization, 8–12
    social intelligence, 4–8
  defined, 220
  economic indicators as, 220–49
  index numbers, generally, 230
  modes of intervention, 226–27
  targets of intervention, 227–29
Public Opinion (Lippmann), 103–5
Public role of economist, interwar Britain, 54–58
The Purchasing Power of Money (Fisher), 31

Radcliffe Committee on the Working of the Monetary System, 130
Radicalism, 79
Rajan, Raghuram, 298
"Rationalization," and British interwar economists, 51–53
Reader's Digest, 145
Reagan, Ronald, 204–5, 262
Recession of 2007–?. *See* Great Recession of 2007–?
Reckless Endangerment (Morgenson and Rosner), 299
Redefining Progress, 245, 249
Report on National Vitality: Its Wastes and Conservation (Fisher), 26
Reviewing Committee on the Export of Works of Art, 127
Ricardo, David, 57
The Road to Serfdom (Hayek), 11, 144–45
Robbins, Lionel, 114–34
  Committee on Higher education, report, 130–33
  Economic Planning and International Order, 120–21
  Employment Policy, 122
  Essay on the Nature and Significance of Economic Science, 133
  in Geneva, 120–21
  Hazlitt, Henry, and, 144, 147
  "How to Mitigate the Next Slump," 120
  Keynes, John Maynard, and, 116–18, 123, 124, 134
  at the London School of Economics (LSE), 114–16
  as professor, 116–22
  Proposals for Consideration by an International Conference on Trade and Employment, 123
  on public expenditure, 118–19
  Robbins Report (Committee on Higher Education), 130–33
  Stamp Memorial Lecture, 125
  World War II, during, 122–24, 134
Robbins Report (Committee on Higher Education), 130–33
Robertson, Dennis Holme, 40, 52, 61
  Banking Policy and the Price Level, 87
Roos, Lawrence
  American Bankers Association conference, 174
  Beige Book input, 182–86
  FOMC input, 182–86
  Institutional Investor Bond Conference, 176
  Memphis Rotary Club speech, 174
  New York Society of Security Analysts address, 175–77
  St. Louis Federal Reserve Bank, 173–77

St. Louis Rotary Club speech, 176–77
St. Louis Society of Financial Analysts speech, 176
Roosevelt, Eleanor, 148–49
Roosevelt, Franklin D.
  "brain trust," 10, 146
  Fisher, Irving, and, 21
Roosevelt, N., 29
Roosevelt, Theodore, 98
Rosenfield, Andrew, 262, 273–74
Rosner, Josh, 299, 300
Ross, Dorothy, 5
Rothbard, Murray, 23

Salter, Arthur, 117
Samuelson, Paul, 10, 14, 142, 256
Santayana, George, 95
Sargent Florence, Philip, 62
Sartre, Jean-Paul, 2, 3
Schaeffer, Evan, 269n20
Schumpeter, Joseph
  Capitalism, Socialism, and Democracy, 12
  History of Economic Analysis, 162
  on public role of economist, 56
Scoon, John, 145
Scott, C. P., 73, 75, 76, 77, 80
Scott, William Robert, 62
Seager, Henry R.
  Introduction to Economics, 95
Seligman, E. R. A., 31
Sen, Amartya, 235, 241, 242, 245, 246
Sex and Reason (Posner), 263
Shadwell, Arthur, 62
Shaftesbury, Lord, 23
Shepard, Stephen B., 258, 268n14
Shils, Edward, 12
Shirras, G. Findlay, 30
Simmel, Georg, 243
Smith, Adam, 141n9
Smith, Yves, 305–6
Snow, C. P., 9

Social ethics, 159–60
Social science, emergence in America, 5–6
Society for International Development (SID), 241, 242, 243
"Sociology of propaganda," 282
Soddy, Frederick, 21, 32, 112
"Sound Money" campaign, 27
Stabilizing the dollar, 31–33
Stabilizing the Dollar (Fisher), 24, 32
Stamp, Joseph Charles, 62
Stamp Memorial Lecture, 125
Stapleford, Thomas, 8
Steffens, Lincoln, 96
Stigler, George, 12–13, 256, 260–61
Stiglitz, Joseph, 235, 245, 246, 283
Stimson, Henry, 24
St. Louis Federal Reserve Bank, 173–77. *See also* Federal Open Market Committee (FOMC)
Stone, Richard, 122
Strachey, Lytton, 71n6, 108
Straight, Dorothy, 104
Sulzberger, Arthur, 149
Summers, Lawrence, 15
Swagel, Phillip, 285, 296

Taft, William Howard, 28
TARP. *See* Troubled Asset Relief Program (TARP)
Technocracy, 10
Thinking as a Science (Hazlitt), 141, 154, 158
Thomas, Bill, 303
Thorneycroft, Peter, 126
Time Will Run Back (Hazlitt), 138
Tobin, James, 235
TOES. *See* The Other Economic Summit (TOES)
A Tract on Monetary Reform (Keynes), 85

Treasury, TARP and. *See* Troubled Asset Relief Program (TARP)
Troubled Asset Relief Program (TARP), 284–96
Tugendhat, Georg, 118
Tugwell, Rexford, 147–48

UGC. *See* University Grants Committee (UGC)
UNDP. *See* United Nations Development Programme (UNDP)
Unemployment, 49–51
United Nations Development Programme (UNDP), 243
University Grants Committee (UGC), 132
UN Monetary and Financial Conference at Bretton Woods, 123

Vickery, James, 285n8
Viner, Jacob, 139
Volcker, Paul, 184

Wallas, Graham, 107
Wallison, Peter, 298, 299, 303, 304–5, 306
Wall Street. *See* Great Recession of 2007–?
Wall Street Journal, 212
  Hazlitt, Henry, at, 137, 140, 141
Warburton, Clark, 30–31
Warren, George F., 110
The Wealth of Nations (Smith), 141n9
Webb, Sidney, 5
Weil, Jonathan, 305
Westerfield, Ray, 21–22, 30, 34

Wherry, Frederick, 241–42
Wicksteed, Philip
  Common Sense of Political Economy, 137–38
Willes, Mark
  Beige Book input, 182–86
  "Effective Economic Policy: Some Key Requirements," 180–81
  Fogarty, James, interview with, 179
  FOMC input, 182–86
  Inflation Task Force of the House of Budget Committee, talk given, 181
  "The Inside Lags of Monetary Policy," 178
  Minneapolis Federal Reserve Bank, 177–82
  "A New Policymaker's View of Inflation," 179
  "Rational Expectation as a Counterrevolution," 181–82
  St. John's University talk, 181
Will, George, 298
Wilson, Woodrow, 28, 102
Wolman, Bill, 258
Woolf, Leonard, 81, 108
Woolf, Virginia, 108
World Bank, 232
World War I, social sciences and, 6–8
Wright, David McCord, 146

Yale Center for Environmental Law and Policy, 245, 248
Yeager, Leland, 160
Young, Allyn, 107

Zimmern, Alfred, 107
Zucker, Seymour, 258